The Leader Cult in Communist Dictatorships

The Leader Cult in Communist Dictatorships

Stalin and the Eastern Bloc

Edited by

Balázs Apor
Jan C. Behrends
Polly Jones
and
E. A. Rees

palgrave
macmillan

First published 2004 by
PALGRAVE MACMILLAN
Houndmills, Basingstoke, Hampshire RG21 6XS and
175 Fifth Avenue, New York, N.Y. 10010
Companies and representatives throughout the world

PALGRAVE MACMILLAN is the global academic imprint of the Palgrave Macmillan division of St. Martin's Press, LLC and of Palgrave Macmillan Ltd. Macmillan® is a registered trademark in the United States, United Kingdom and other countries. Palgrave is a registered trademark in the European Union and other countries.

ISBN 1–4039–3443–6
ISBN 978-1-4039-3443-7

This book is printed on paper suitable for recycling and made from fully managed and sustained forest sources.Logging, pulping and manufacturing processes are expected to conform to the environmental regulations of the country of origin.

A catalogue record for this book is available from the British Library.

Library of Congress Cataloging-in-Publication Data

The leader cult in communist dictatorships : Stalin and the Eastern Bloc / edited by Balázs Apor . . . [et al.].
p. cm
Includes bibliographical references and index.
ISBN 1–4039–3443–6
1. Soviet Union – Politics and government – 1917–1936. 2. Soviet Union – Politics and government – 1936–1953. 3. Dictatorship – Europe, Eastern – History – 20th century. 4. Europe, Eastern – Politics and government – 20th century. 5. Stalin, Joseph, 1879–1953. 6. Totalitarianism – History – 20th century. I. Apor, Balázs.

DK268.4.L4 2004
947.084′2′092–dc22 2004046700

Printed and bound in Great Britain by
CPI Antony Rowe, Chippenham and Eastbourne

Contents

Part III Beyond Moscow: The Cult's Peripheries

Part IV The Dilemmas of De-Stalinisation: Change and Continuity in Leader Cult Patterns in the Post-Stalin Period

Acknowledgements

This volume grew out of a conference, 'Stalin and the Lesser Gods: The Leader Cult in Communist Dictatorships in Comparative Perspective (1928–61)', which was held at the European University Institute, Florence, 15–16 May 2003. The conference was hosted and funded by the Institute.

Notes on the Contributors

Balázs Apor studied at the University of Debrecen, and is a researcher at the European University Institute, Florence, where he is working on a thesis on the cult of Mátyás Rákosi in communist Hungary in the period 1945–56.

Jan C. Behrends is Research Fellow at the Herder-Institut, Marburg, Germany. He specialises in the modern history of Germany, Poland and Russia, and in the comparative study of dictatorships. His publications include: (with Thomas Lindenberger and Patrice G. Poutrus, editors) *Fremde und Fremd-Sein in der DDR* (Berlin, 2003); (with Gábor T. Rittersporn and Malte Rolf, editors) *Sphären von Öffentlichkeit in Gesellschaften sowjetischen Typs* (*The Public Sphere in Soviet-Type Societies*) (Frankfurt on Main, 2003); (with Patrice G. Poutrus and Árpád von Klimó, editors) *Anti-Amerikanismus im Kalten Krieg: Deutschland in europäischen Vergleich* (Bonn, 2004).

Sarah Davies is Senior Lecturer in the Department of History at the University of Durham, England. She is the author of *Popular Opinion in Stalin's Russia* (Cambridge, 1997). She is currently working on a project entitled 'Stalin on Stalinism'.

Benno Ennker is Professor at the University of Tübingen. He has written extensively on the Lenin and Stalin leader cults, and his publications include: *Die Anfänge des Leninkults in der Sowjetunion* (Cologne, 1997).

Polly Jones is Lecturer in Russian at the School of Slavonic and East European Studies (SSEES–UCL). She completed her DPhil, comparing the processes of de-Stalinisation and de-Leninisation, at Oxford in 2002. She is the author of several articles on the Stalin cult and de-Stalinisation, and editor of *The Dilemmas of De-Stalinisation* (London: Routledge–Curzon, 2005).

Catriona Kelly is Professor at New College, Oxford. She is the author of *Comrade Pavlik: The Rise and Fall of a Soviet Boy Hero* (London, 2004). She has written extensively on Russian literature and culture and her most recent works include: *Refining Russia, Advice Literature, Polite Culture and Gender from Catherine to Yeltsin* (Oxford, 2001) and *Russian Literature* (Oxford, 2001).

Árpád von Klimó is Visiting Professor at the International University, Bremen, Germany. He received his PhD in 1995 from the Free University, Berlin, and his Habilitation in 2001. His publications include: *Tra Stato e Societa. Le elites amministrative in Italia e Prussia, 1860–1918* (Rome, 2002), and *Nation, Konfession, Geschichte. Zur nationalen Geschichtskultur Ungarns im europäischen Kontext, 1860–1948* (Munich, 2003).

Izabella Main received her PhD from Central European University, Budapest, in 2002 for a thesis on relations between the Catholic Church and the State in Poland from 1944 to 1989.

Alice Mocanescu is a researcher at the University of Durham, where she is working on a thesis on the cult of Nikolai Ceaşescu in Romania.

Jan Plamper received his PhD from the University of California, Berkeley, 2001, for his thesis on the Stalin cult in the visual arts. He is a Research Fellow at the University of Tübingen.

Artan Puto is a researcher at the European University Institute, Florence, Italy, and is working on a thesis dealing with the Albanian National Movement before the First World War.

E. A. Rees is Professor of Eastern European History at the European University Institute, Florence, Italy. He is the author of *Political Thought from Machiavelli to Stalin: Revolutionary Machiavellism* (Basingstoke, 2004). He is the editor of *The Nature of Stalin's Dictatorship: The Politburo, 1924–1953* (Basingstoke, 2003) and *Centre–Local Relations in the Stalinist State, 1928–1941* (Basingstoke, 2002).

Malte Rolf studied history, sociology and German literature at the universities of Tübingen and Berlin. He is finishing his PhD dissertation in 2004 with the title Das sowjetische Massenfest (1927–41). He is Assistant Lecturer at the Department of History, Humboldt-University, Berlin. He is the author of *Sovetskii massovyi prazdnik v Voronezhe i Tsentral'no-Chernozemnoi oblasti Rossii 1927–1932* (Voronezh, 2000).

Stanislav Sretenovic studied at the University of Belgrade, and the University of Nancy, France. He is a researcher at the European University Institute, Florence, and is working on a thesis dealing with Franco-Yugoslav relations, 1900–30.

Markus Wien is a researcher at the European University Institute, Florence and is working on a thesis dealing with German–Bulgarian economic relations in the 1930s.

Marcin Zaremba is Professor at the University of Warsaw and a member of the Polish Academy of Science. He is the author of *Komunizm, legitimizacja, nacjonalizm. Nacjonalistyczna legitimizacja władzy komunistycznej w Polsce* (Warsaw, 2001).

Introduction

1
Leader Cults: Varieties, Preconditions and Functions

E. A. Rees[1]

Max Weber famously outlined three different types of authority: traditional, rational-legal, and charismatic. The leadership systems of the twentieth century which generated their own leader cults (I. V. Stalin, Benito Mussolini, Adolf Hitler, Mao Zedong), might be seen as embodying what Weber characterised as the 'routinisation' of charismatic authority. Whilst Weber's typology offers a useful starting point for discussing leader cults it is also in some ways misleading.[2] The Communist, Nazi and Fascist regimes of the twentieth century sought to legitimise themselves through a combination of appeals to tradition, legal right and charisma. What is unique and striking about them is the way in which they sought to construct legitimacy, by investing ideas, events, institutions, particular offices and personalities with charisma. Part of this strategy involved the promotion of leader cults, aimed at creating a bond between leader and subject. In this book we examine the leader cults in communist ruled states of the USSR and of Eastern Europe, and seek to explore further the nature of the strategies of constructing legitimacy that these states engaged in.

The leader cult and the 'cult of the individual'

The communist regime under Stalin was highly authoritarian and developed an extraordinary cult of veneration around the figure of the leader.[3] At the 20th Congress of the Soviet Communist Party in February 1956 N. S. Khrushchev attacked Stalin's 'despotic' system of rule. He used the term *kult' lichnosti*, translated as the 'cult of the individual' or 'cult of personality', to explain the changes in the Soviet leadership system after 1934: the consolidation of Stalin's personal dictatorship, the ensuing criminal abuses of power, and the extraordinary adulation of Stalin, which turned him into an omniscient and infallible being.[4]

Khrushchev's term 'cult of the individual' placed stress on Stalin's psychology as an explanatory factor for what followed. But Khrushchev also related the rise of Stalin's despotic rule to specific changes in the structure of power in the USSR in the early 1930s. In his memoirs he even acknowledged that policy choices after 1928, such as forced collectivisation, might have contributed to this development. But Khrushchev refused to see Stalin's despotism as in any way related to the system of Bolshevik rule, to its structures, its practices and its psychology. Similarly he offered no real insight into the cultural and situational factors that provided the basis for such a system. In this work an attempt is made to explore the communist leader cult in all its complex manifestations and dimensions.[5]

A leader cult is an established system of veneration of a political leader, to which all members of the society are expected to subscribe, a system that is omnipresent and ubiquitous and one that is expected to persist indefinitely. It is thus a deliberately constructed and managed mechanism, which aims at the integration of the political system around the leader's persona. In Soviet Russia Dzhugashvilli assumed the persona Stalin.

The rise of modern leader cults is closely related to the aspirations and methods of twentieth-century revolutionary regimes. Gerhard Ritter long ago noted the demonic aspect of their politics: the reliance on violence, force and deception.[6] For the Bolsheviks, with their notion of class struggle and class war, politics was akin to warfare. The great leader cults of the twentieth century were associated with leaders who were variously depicted as demi-gods, supermen, gangsters, megolomaniacs and monsters. The regimes over which they presided witnessed unprecedented domestic convulsions, were drawn into the greatest wars of the twentieth century.

The cult of the leader needs to be placed in the context of the various strategies of legitimation of communist rule. The Soviet regime could not base its legitimacy on tradition, nor on rational-legal authority, but instead sought to persuade the population of its right to rule. In opposition to Weber we might propose three basic strategies of legitimation: (*a*) Symbolic or affective attachment, based on popular identification with the regime, its ideology, institutions, leaders and events in its history. (*b*) Ideological and programmatic support, based on perception of the realism and desirability of the regime's ideological goals and the way these goals were modified over time in accordance with changing circumstances (War Communism, the New Economic Policy the Command Economy, the War Economy, the Post-War Reconstruction, the Soviet Welfare Economy). (*c*) Performance attainment, based on the public's perception of the state's capacity to satisfy the basic needs of society and of its individual members, taking into account domestic and international constraints.

States beset by economic failure and by social conflict invariably respond by seeking to strengthen symbolic legitimation. Where there is low consensus on ideological and programmatic goals, regime's seek to reinforce symbolic attachment; appeal is made to the loyalty of their citizens, loyalty to the state, to the party, and to the leader. This is common particularly to ideological, mobilising regimes. This situation is also common in circumstances of war. Here, it might be argued, acute privation may give great strength to such symbolic attachment, where shared sacrifice is seen as offering some future good.

The three bases of legitimation outlined above are themselves fragile, in that they are dependent on the power of the state to secure some measure of acceptance. In the Soviet case these factors were tied to the emergence of the propaganda state.[7] How far regimes command popular assent, and how far they survive because of fear, deference, apathy or resignation is problematical. Obedience is secured by fear and perceptions of the strength and durability of the regime.

Cults: religious, royal and secular

The phenomenon of leader cults is extremely ancient, and can be traced back to classical times, and early human societies where political and religious authority were united. The deification of dead emperors and then of living emperors was used to legitimise personal power in ancient Greece and Rome, especially with the dynasty of Augustus.[8] Stalin, who read widely, was certainly familiar with these traditions.[9]

Twentieth century leader cults possess certain similarities with earlier religious and monarchical cults. The leader figures venerated in the twentieth century were attributed with quasi-miraculous powers. They were gifts of providence, with seemingly wondrous powers, as saviours of their nations with the power to 'heal' the land. They did not offer salvation in the afterlife, but were concerned with the life of mortals here and now on earth. They were free of the pomp and ceremony of royal rituals based on blood, lineage and descent, and their ties to other royal dynasties and to the hereditary aristocracy.

Like monarchy, the modern revolutionary leader cults of the twentieth century sought to fuse and to reinforce the charisma of the office and the charisma of its occupant, and sought to gain authority through association with other powerful and respected figures, including foreign dignitaries. All leader cults make a presumption, which never needs to be justified, to command the support and affection of its subjects. Like monarchical regimes the leader cult demanded carefully developed protocol to preserve the venerated figure's mystique. Like monarchs the leader dispenses state honours and awards for services rendered, serving to bind the subject to the leader and to the state. Modern constitutional monarchies, developed in an age of mass democracy, were intended to channel mass sentiment, which was seen as potentially irrational, away from the actual functioning of government.[10]

The study of religious movements tends to locate the emergence of cults in the early phases of new religious movements, when the sect of believers is still fairly exclusive, in which new converts are being drawn in. This is the period of the charismatic development, of the creative generation of new ideas and symbols; the initiation of new believers into the mysteries of the faith.[11] The communist leader cults should also be seen against the background of the great messianic and millenarian movements of the past, with their accompanying visions of apocalyptic transformation, of immense battles of great historic significance, which only in time yield the new harmonious order.[12]

The French Revolution promoted the notion of the religion of civic virtue, reason, patriotism and revolutionary resolve. Such civic religions cannot tolerate the claim of other competing religions, and are thus militantly atheistic. It is with the French Revolution and the Napoleonic period that we can date the rise of modern dictatorial systems and their leader cults. This new concern with the role of great, charismatic figures in history is seen in Hegel's concept of the 'world historical individual', in Marx and Engels' discussion on Bonapartism, and on 'revolution from above' as embodied by Otto von Bismarck, and in Nietzsche's notion of the superman. In Russia, Pisarev's idea of the 'benefactors of mankind' addresses the same theme and it is also found in Plekhanov's writings.[13]

Communist cults and the sacramentalisation of politics

From its inception the Soviet communist regime displayed a strong proclivity towards cultic practices, in which the role of the leader assumed a central position. On Lenin's death in 1924 a committee was set to oversee the 'immortalisation' of his memory. An institute was established to study his brain, a mausoleum was erected to house his remains, and his relics were preserved in church-like museums. The Soviet slogan: 'Lenin lived, Lenin lives, Lenin will live' embodied this aspiration towards immortalising the dead leader's memory. The transformation of Lenin into an icon was strongly opposed by his widow Nadezhda Krupskaya and by other senior political figures, but this was overruled. The critics of the project saw it variously as medieval, oriental or Asiatic, a practice akin to ancestor worship.

The Lenin Mausoleum combined elements of the Russian practice of venerating tsars and saints. It was designed as an awe-inspiring shrine and place of pilgrimage, situated at the very heart of the country's capital. The embalmed corpse symbolised the non-putrefaction of the body, the sign of holiness. Its inspiration may have lain in the monumental tombs constructed for Napoleon Bonaparte (Dome des Invalides) and Otto von Bismarck (Friedrichsruh).[14] The Lenin Mausoleum also invokes the image of the Egyptian pyramids, and was similarly intended to outlast the centuries.[15] This is one of the most extraordinary manifestations of the leader cults of the twentieth century. In Nazi Germany, Hitler and his architect, Hermann Giesler, also had their plans for a mausoleum in Linz.

As Berdyaev long ago argued, Soviet communism, as an ideological and cultural force, was deeply indebted to Russian Orthodoxy.[16] The Italian scholar Zincone compares totalitarian regimes to 'secular religions', and their parties, he argues, were akin to 'militant, confessional sects' such as the Jesuits and Dominicans.[17] They had their own shrines, festivals and pilgrimages. They had their own prophets, apostles, priests and disciples. They had their own holy scripts. They possessed their pantheon of revolutionary heroes. Their great festivals and parades replaced religious services and processions. The system of indoctrination was based on catechisms and homilies. The Red/Lenin corners replaced the place of the icon.

The manifestation of these cults appears almost trans-national and trans-historical, with the veneration of the leader as an omniscient, all-powerful being, as a benign and universal genius. The cult strives to confer a certain transcendent significance on the present moment of history, to which the past and future must all relate. Leader cults, like religious cults, attempt to create a point of reference for the whole belief system, centred on one man, the embodiment of the doctrine. The belief system aspires to universality; and exceptions to this rule are inherently subversive of the authority of the cult. Moreover, in its projection, the cult is ubiquitous, it is everywhere. This is why leader cults are seen as inherent in regimes that aspire towards 'totalitarian' control. The 'totalitarian' regimes of the twentieth century, with their powerful leader cults, their elitist organisations and doctrines, had as their avowed aim the integration of the masses into the political process as a community of believers.

Cults in open polities

Embryonic cults exist even in relatively open, democratic political systems. It is as though human society has a strong predisposition towards the creation of cults, reflected in the cults of film idols, pop stars and sporting idols. But political leader cults are qualitatively different because of the bearing they have on the way that power is exercised. Support for such cults has little to do with levels of education. In the twentieth century many of the outstanding intellectuals of the age proved very gullible in accepting the claims of such regimes.[18] All political systems have some cultic aspects, in terms of national symbolism, the veneration of the flag and anthem, the ceremonials associated with the assumption of office, national holidays, and the ceremonies commemorating their war dead.

The state, with the power to kill its own citizens and to wage war, has to be sanctified in some way, to legitimise itself; the pressure towards obedience and conformity is immense when its interests are invoked. Leader cults are part of the general process whereby the new power is symbolised and celebrated – in flags, hymns and anthems, medals, awards, prizes, stamps and coins, in the renaming of towns, streets and institutions. Leader cults are closely tied to the founding myths of new states, as in the Soviet case of the 'Great October Socialist Revolution' and the Civil War.

In open societies cults develop around particular offices as well as individuals. The presidency of the USA is perhaps the most striking example of this. The investment of the office of president, also the commander-in-chief, with charisma developed very strongly from the 1930s onwards, with the huge growth in the powers of the office, and the enormous expansion of the power of the federal government both domestically and internationally. The status of the office is reinforced by various symbols (The White House, The Seal, The State-of-the-Union address, Air Force One). The memorials to past great presidents – Washington, Jefferson, Lincoln, Roosevelt – on the Mall in Washington, can be seen as part of the cult of the office of president.

But one might also identify powerful cults in other mobilising regimes, such as the cult of Kemal Attaturk in Turkey, or the cult of Eva Peron in Argentina. In newly independent colonies from the 1950s onwards the leaders of the struggle for independence often became the objects of cults (Nkrumah, Kenyata, Kaunda, Nasser or Saddam Hussein).[19] The most developed leader cults are associated with what scholars have in the past identified as 'totalitarian' states.

Leader cults need to be distinguished from the glorification of political leaders in other more open political systems: where the 'public sphere' exists and retains its autonomy, where open, competitive structures function, the growth of such cults is limited. It is only the closure of the public sphere that allows the leader cult to incubate and become fully developed.[20] Leader cults flourish in closed political systems (closed both domestically and in their relations to the outside world), in regimes that foster a siege mentality. In comparison to the instrumental view of politics in the more stable democratic regimes, in revolutionary regimes politics was projected as a matter of vocation, a life's calling, and a cause to fight and die for. In these societies politics remained a matter of deep belief and conviction. But, as in all belief systems, faith may merge into dogma and superstition.

The rise of these leader cults can be taken as a barometer of certain development within a political system. Firstly, it is symptomatic of the extent to which political power has been personalised, and centred on one individual. Secondly, it provides testimony of how far political debate has been circumscribed and regulated. Thirdly, it offers some indication of how far control and censorship of the media has been established, and the extent to which the leader might be criticised, censured or mocked. Fourthly, it provides a measure of how far the authorities have control over the process of socialisation and education in the society.

The relations between leader and led need to be mediated, they need to be distanced from each other. The cult can only really develop where it has functionaries in charge of controlling this intermediation: editors, journalists, broadcasters, censors, educators and opinion shapers. The cult around Stalin was consciously promoted, to foster love and devotion to both the leader and the socialist motherland.[21] In this, language itself played a fundamental role, not just as a means of communication, but as a code, as a medium of defining issues, labelling groups and individuals.[22]

Hierarchies of the Stalin cult

The posthumous cult of Lenin was used to legitimise his successor. The Stalin cult was at first constructed, on the basis of Stalin's close association with Lenin.[23] By 1925 the major city of Tsaritsyn had been renamed Stalingrad, in honour of Stalin's civil war exploits. Stalin's deputies actively worked to promote his cult, as noted by the Russian historian Shitts, who describes how in 1929–30, in a period of difficulty for the Soviet regime, these leaders worked together to promote Stalin's cult, as a symbol of their unity.[24] For a systematic study of the evolution of the Stalin cult, readers are referred to the various biographies of Stalin.[25]

Stalin was quite conscious of the way that the Bolsheviks could invoke parallels with religious practice, as was reflected in his famous funeral oration to Lenin.[26] He used the Russian's veneration of the tsar (*tsar batyushka* – the little father) to bolster his own position, but viewed his own cult in a highly instrumental and sceptical manner (see Chapter 2).

The Stalin cult became the central basis for the legitimation of the Soviet regime. It was based on the notion of Marxism-Leninism as a rarefied science and the embodiment of truth, with the leader as someone possessed of almost superhuman powers – extraordinary intuition, foresight, exceptional powers to formulate solutions to problems, and an uncommon ability to inspire and mobilise those around him to achieve his ends. The Stalin era was a period of prolonged and acute economic adversity for the great majority of the Soviet people.

The projection of the Stalin cult was first made dramatically apparent in the celebration of his 50th birthday in December 1929. At this time Stalin was certainly more than *primus inter pares* within the ruling group. Stalin's personal dictatorship might be dated from the start of 1933, but elements of collective decision-making survived up until 1937 (see Chapter 5).[27] With the Great Terror of 1936–38 Stalin acquired the power of life and death over his colleagues, and was thereafter something qualitatively different to a simple dictator. Khrushchev characterised him in the last 15 years of his life as a 'despot'. But Stalin's rule was never simply a personal despotism, but rather an 'ideocratic despotism'.[28] In place of the Politburo the leader developed around him his own court, reminiscent of the court of an absolutist monarch.

Stalin's cult was buttressed by a series of cults around virtually all Politburo members. V. M. Molotov, head of government (Sovnarkom), L. M. Kaganovich, first secretary of the Moscow party organisation 1933–34, and thereafter head of the railway commissariat, and K. E. Voroshilov, minister of defence, had their own cults. N. I. Ezhov, as head of NKVD (the People's Commissariat for Internal Affairs) for a brief period in 1936–38, saw a flourishing of his cult, as did his successor in this post, L. P. Beria. S. M. Kirov and then A. A. Zhdanov, as first secretaries of Leningrad, had their own cults too. This pattern was extended to the party bosses in the major cities, and in the republics. Even the directors of major enterprises had their own cults, and had their portraits carried in triumph by their workers on public holidays.

The cults of the subordinate leaders, those in the inner ruling circle, were similar to those of the *vozhd'*. Towns, factories, collective farms, schools, streets and other places were named in their honour. Their writings and speeches were published. Their biographies constituted a distinct literary genre with its idealisation of the revolutionary life of service and the celebration of their subjects as gifted administrators, executives and problem solvers (*rukovoditeli* or *khozyaini*). Their birthdays were celebrated and on their deaths their apartments might be turned into museums.

In the USSR of the Lenin and Stalin era the image of politics in general was heroic and the party-state manufactured heroes on a mass scale. There were heroes of the revolutionary movement and the Civil War (Chapaev), the 'twenty-five thousanders' who were sent to assist in the collectivisation of agriculture, Komsomol and Pioneer heroes (Pavlik Morozov), mother heroines, Stakhanovite heroes of labour, the Chekists and Red Army men who were the guardians of the revolutions, the Panfilovtsy and the other heroes of the Great Patriotic War. A central motif in much of the regime's imagery is that of sacrifice, martyrdom, and the pathos of the fallen comrade, a rekindling of the idealism of the underground and Civil War era. The Stalinist artistic style was 'Socialist Realist' which aspired towards the epic, whilst the architectural style was monumental.

The rise of Stalin's cult coincided with the defeat of the last major opposition group, the proclamation of 'monolithic' unity and adherence to the 'general line'. It coincided with a new period of ideological offensive of the 'revolution from above' and of the Cultural Revolution. The underground and Civil War experience was reflected in an extraordinary militarisation of politics, in terms of language and imagery, in terms of administrative structures, with the aspiration of ordering society like an army (what Engels, in the nineteenth century, had mocked as 'barracks socialism'). The system of forced labour, the dragooning of the peasants into the collective farms was redolent of this militarisation. Stalin, who favoured military uniform, was the chief (*vozhd'*), who demanded obedience, duty and vigilance.

Cultic thought and practice

The cult was intended as cement to cover over such divisions, to reinforce a sense of purpose and unity. Unity was related to the truth of the Marxist-Leninist doctrine and adherence to this truth (*pravda*) was central to the party's sense of itself. Lenin in 'What is to be Done?' spelt out this Manichean view of the world: there were only two world-views – proletarian and bourgeois – and between them there was no middle position. The power to interpret the ideology was an absolute power that defined the parameters of political debate. The veneration of the leader, the interpreter of the doctrine, required its antithesis. Oppositionists charged with Trotskyism, Zinovievism, Bukharinism, were anathematised as apostates, heretics and schismatics.

The leader cult was only one aspect of cultic thought and practice that infused the life of the Communist Party. There was the cult of the founding fathers (Marx, Engels and Lenin), the cult of the Revolution, the cult of the proletariat and the cult of the party, the cult of the state itself – the USSR – each of which fostered its own myths. The cult of the party was especially powerful, requiring total obedience and obliging its members to reconstruct and re-educate themselves, to make themselves worthy members.[29] Not only the party but also other key institutions – the Red Army, the Cheka, the Komsomol, the Pioneers – each was the focus of the loyalties of particular constituencies. In the French Revolution it was the cult of the revolution, the nation (*patrie*) and the citizen. With the Nazi regime it was the cult of the race, the Volk and the Reich. The leader had to symbolise something greater than himself. The cult of the leader was always part of a much more densely structured argument to defend and justify the regime and its actions.

Initially the cult of Stalin stood in tension with the cult of Lenin, the cult of the party and the cult of the Revolution. The consolidation of Stalin's cult required a weakening of these other objects of veneration, or, at least, a reconfiguration of their relations to one another, and thus involved an important shift in the way the regime was legitimised. It reflected the reality that Stalin could command more public support than either the state or the party, and certainly more support than the regime's representatives and agents in the localities.

After the October Revolution the Russian political landscape was 'Sovietised' and stripped of the symbols of the old order. Social rituals and mass celebrations of the Revolution were woven into the daily lives of Soviet citizens; the calendar was organised around the commemoration of dates of great revolutionary significance; the dates of important Church rituals were commandeered by the regime.[30] It became an important aspect of the political culture of everyday life, fusing traditional attitudes to authority to the new symbolism of power.[31] The leader cult was part of the strategy whereby communist regimes invented their own traditions.[32]

The cult was projected through radio, film, music, the press and posters. The projection of the cult was part of a wider management of propaganda and cultural production, of which the mass production of *Staliniana* was one feature. It was modulated for different audiences, most obviously in the way it was adapted for children (see Chapter 6) and to take account of different regional, national and ethnic interests (see Chapters 3, 4, 7 and 8).

The reception of the cult

Such systems of veneration serve certain psychological needs of leaders and their followers.[33] For leaders, the adulation of followers is an intoxicant, it serves to ward away uncertainty and insecurity, it gives the individual a great sense of strength and power, and places him beyond the bounds of criticism. For the adherents of the cult, it invests their lives with a broader significance, a sense of wider purpose and achievement, and meets a longing for the fabulous, the mythopoeic, which transcends the mundane and the banal.

The cult changed in response to changing regime priorities; it changed also from one period to another, acquiring a different meaning and a different resonance with different social groups. Under the Stalin regime it is impossible to speak of any public opinion in the USSR, and to gauge popular sentiments is very difficult. The Soviet population in the 1920s and 1930s was in large measure alienated from the state. Stalin in the 1930s was not a popular figure. Even under his rule, Soviet citizens did not lose the capacity to distinguish between those aspects of the regime they supported and those they condemned.[34]

The base of the cult as it developed from the late 1920s was amongst the regime's officials, activists and sympathisers, those whom Martov referred to in 1917 as the 'pensioners of the State'.[35] The party activists (*aktiv*) provided the hardcore of support, as the regime's social agents, as agitators and propagandists, as volunteers during Civil War and collectivisation. Within the Red Army and the Cheka (and its successors), the two key bastions of communist power, which had their own cultic associations, care was taken to inculcate a particular sense of loyalty to the leader. Within the working class and intelligentsia there was a core of Stalinist supporters. The beneficiaries of Soviet power, particularly those who were advanced by the new opportunities for upward mobility, may have been the real base of the cult. The Bolsheviks were a young party in 1917, and in successive waves in 1928–31 and in 1936–38 they promoted a younger generation of cadres into leading posts.[36] And in this the youngest, who had been educated by the regime, could be turned against the more 'backward' older generations. From the late 1930s a major shift occurred in terms of the regime's base of support. The new Soviet intelligentsia, especially the beneficiaries of the purges, was defined as the main social base of the regime.

The cult also drew on Russian traditions, the tradition of authoritarian leadership, a deep étatist tradition with its own bureaucratic culture, and even a tradition of popular monarchism that had deep roots.[37] But it may also have drawn on the strong patriarchal peasant culture with its respect for the elder (*starosta*) with its strong collectivist ethic. The Stalinist regime, like the tsarist regime, sought to link itself with the popular classes as a counterweight to the middle ranks and the nobility.

But the cult drew on other traditional values that were in tension with the regime's revolutionary protestations. For the elite it could be seen as a guarantee of their power. For the disadvantaged the Stalin cult offered the hope of redress. As the regime passed from its revolutionary phase to its phase of consolidation, from the late 1930s onwards, the cult came to symbolise the new social order that had been created. Whereas Nicholas I had stood for 'Autocracy, Orthodoxy and Nationalism', Stalin might have been seen to stand for 'Autocracy, Marxism-Leninism-Stalinism, and Soviet Patriotism'. This Soviet Patriotism was allied to militarisation of the regime and of popular consciousness.

There are, of course, limits to how far states can control society, or indoctrinate citizens. Totalitarian theory exaggerated the powers of states in this regard. Given the function of cognitive dissonance such indoctrination is always problematic, but the aspiration to such control was a central defining feature of these regimes. The constant projection of the leader cult over decades must have had a deep impact. Repressive regimes, even where terror is not employed, foster anxiety, helplessness, conformity and a desire to evade personal responsibility.[38] The Stalin regime's strength and its capacity for social mobilisation created even amongst its critics a desire to be reconciled with it, a belief that this was perhaps the wave of the future, which they were unable to recognise.[39]

The legitimisation of the regime was not based simply on empty propaganda, but also on real achievements. All great achievements could be identified with the *vozhd'*. The great projects of the state – the five year plans, the huge new towns, the new factories, the giant showcase achievements such as the Moscow Metro – were intended to win public support. They were intended to offset the darker, more repressive side of its rule. Similarly the exploits of modern heroes – the Soviet flying aces, explorers, Stakhanovite workers, artists and scientists, military heroes – were also associated with the leader.

The cult reflected and bolstered cultural and intellectual traditions that offered a simplified view of the world where contradictions were overcome. It offered psychological and emotional reassurance, a focus of stability and unity, in a world of uncertainties. It aimed at something other than simple acquiescence to communist rule. It aimed at an emotional bonding of the community of believers, it sought to instil enthusiastic commitment, the faith of true believers in the leader and the regime. Marxism-Leninism, notwithstanding its claim to embody a scientific world-view, was, like all ideologies, primarily a question of belief. The believers would be vindicated by the ultimate deity – history. In the words of Fidel Castro 'History will absolve me'.

Cults and political culture

We can thus relate the rise of the cult to specific features of the political cultures of states. Tsarist Russia and Stalin's USSR rationalised their systems of authoritarian rule by reference to an ideology/belief system – the authority of scientific Marxism-Leninism versus the divine right of kings. But it was also rationalised on pragmatic grounds. Against the background of Russian tradition and recent Russian history – military defeats in 1904–05, 1917, revolution, civil war, foreign intervention and the threat of internal fragmentation – it was easy for Stalin and his deputies in the 1920s to make the argument for unity and for the strong state. The guarantee against the abuse of power lay in the hands of Stalin, the purity of his motives and his firm principles.

The cult was about strengthening the people's symbolic attachment to the regime and its leader. With the 'Great Retreat' of the 1930s and the rediscovery of Russian national traditions, Stalin could be placed in the tradition of great Russian state-builders like Ivan the Terrible and Peter the Great.[40] Stalin used the enemy syndrome and conspiracy mania to elevate his cult and to enforce discipline within the regime and inside the wider society, using the threat of internal and external enemies to boost the population's identification with the regime. In 1937–38 the newly promoted elite were showered with awards – Orders of Lenin, Red Banners of Labour – to reinforce this attachment.[41]

The leader was associated only with the regime's successes and triumphs. Catastrophic policy failures, with collectivisation in 1930, the famine of 1932/3, and the German invasion in 1941, could never be acknowledged. The cult allowed Stalin to unburden himself of policy failures – as he did famously with his article 'Dizzy with Success' in 1930 during collectivisation, and during the famine crisis of 1932/3, both of which were blamed on local officials, and again in 1939 when he blamed the excesses of the purges on Ezhov. Part of the cult was to reinforce the notion of the leader's unimpeachable motives, like those of the good tsar. This had an impact. The widespread opinion during the terror of 1936–38 was that the former dissidents had somehow been 'meddling' in matters of state and thus got only what they deserved.[42]

Given the regime's pedagogical obsession, society remained a permanent classroom. Society was forced into a state of infantile regression, fostering a naïve and sentimentalised notion of leadership. But there is also something theatrical and contrived about such cults. Much of the politics of the Stalin era was a form of public drama, with heroic themes and also tragic undertones, most clearly expressed in the scripted show trials of the 1930s.[43] The carnivalesque great May Day and October Revolution parades also had their solemn side, where the leader acknowledged the cheers of the crowd and conferred his own benediction on the faithful.

The cult sought to bind the individual and the leader together in complex ways. The individual was bound to the leader by a code of honour, a sense of allegiance and duty, symbolised by the collective oaths sworn to the leader at initiation ceremonies by Pioneers, Komsomol members and by members of the armed forces, although parallels may be found here with youth organisations and the armed forces of other, non-totalitarian states. The celebration of the leader's birthday was an opportunity for the presentation of gifts and for an outpouring of thanks and expressions of gratitude.

The image of Stalin

In the case of Stalin the cult projected various images: (*a*) the apprentice revolutionary and Lenin's pupil and heir; (*b*) the defender of the state; (*c*) the prophet, apostle and teacher; (*d*) the builder of the new world; (*e*) the inspirer of his people, whose bounteous good fortune was to live under his rule. Stalin, like the tsars before him, was projected as the physical and spiritual embodiment of the state; standing above all contending groups and individuals, representing society's unity in its diversity. He was the nurturer if not the source of everything creative and constructive. His modesty and asceticism was highlighted, as was his attentiveness to the views and opinions of ordinary workers and party members.[44]

The cult around Stalin was not static but evolved as the regime itself changed. It emerged in the late 1920s as the embodiment of the 'revolution from above'. In the period 1934–35 there was an attempt to provide Stalin with a more humane image, reflected in photographs of his meetings with ordinary workers, peasants and children, or dressed in national costume. In the 1930s the theme of 'Stalin: Leader, Teacher and Friend' is one that recurs in the art of the period.

With the Great Terror the cult of Stalin attained its apotheosis. In 1937 Stalin and other leaders denounced the excessive adulation surrounding subordinate and provincial leaders.[45] Stalin was depicted as the implacable defender of the state against its enemies, both domestic and foreign. It was symbolised by the Stalin Constitution of 1936; the canonical account of the Revolution and Stalin's role in it as presented in *The Short Course History of the Communist Party of the Soviet Union* of 1938, the publication of his official biography in 1939, and the 60th birthday celebrations in 1939. But Stalin was aware of the danger of the cult leading to excess and absurdity. He quashed Ezhov's suggestion that Moscow be renamed Stalinodar in 1937, and in 1938 he dismissed the idea of producing a biography of himself for the instruction of children. Within his inner circle Stalin would at least feign disapproval of excessive flattery. In this way, by modulating the cult, Stalin could reinforce his own position.

With the 'Great Patriotic War' Stalin emerged as the *generalissimo*, the great war leader, and the symbol of an indomitable will to resist the invader. During the war he identified himself, especially after Stalingrad, with the Red Army's successes. His status as architect of the great victory was celebrated in film, art and literature.[46] The leader cult at this time saw a clear fusion of Soviet patriotic themes with traditional Great Russian Imperial themes.[47] The war, eclipsing the October Revolution, became the great event that legitimised the Soviet regime until its ultimate demise.[48] Stalin's stature as war leader was greatly enhanced, the militarisation of the regime and of popular consciousness was reinforced. The command stratum of society was replenished with new cadres and the regime's public support was greatly enlarged, especially amongst the veterans of the war. After the war Stalin was genuinely popular with with large swathes of Soviet society.[49] This reflected the strength of the symbolic attachment forged between the people and the leader, the state's success in gaining popular consent for its goals, and its demonstrated capacity to secure military victory.

After 1945 we have Stalin as a world statesman. His 70th birthday celebrations in 1949 projected him as the head of the International Communist movement, together with the leaders of the East European states, and with Mao Zedong, leader of the newly triumphant Chinese Communist Party. The celebrations coincided with the most intense phase of the Cold War, the Berlin crisis (the blockade ended in May), and the preliminary stages of the Korean War. It was associated with ideological retrenchment, and the intensification of political controls in the USSR and Eastern Europe, symbolised by the expulsion of Tito from the Comintern and by the show trials of communist dissidents in Czechoslovakia, Hungary, Bulgaria and Albania. It coincided with the Soviet successful testing of the atom bomb, confirming the country's status as a global superpower.

Cults under Communism, Fascism and Nazism

Ian Kershaw rightly argues that whereas the Führer cult was intrinsic to the Nazi system and cannot be understood without an appreciation of its central role, the cult of the *vozhd'* in the Soviet system was an accretion onto a system of collegial rule of the Politburo. The importance of local initiatives in sustaining the Nazi regime, Kershaw's notion of 'working towards the Führer', and Hans Mommsen's concept of 'progressive radicalisation' offer some parallels with the Stalin leadership, but these need to be handled with great care.[50] In both regimes the cult was part of a complex signalling system. It established the relative order of leaders in the ruling hierarchy; of who owed obeisance to whom.

However, the leader cult in Nazi Germany differed fundamentally from that in the USSR. Stalin's authority within the Soviet Communist Party and the international communist movement derived from his standing as rightful successor to Marx, Engels and Lenin. Hitler and Stalin were very different leaders. Compared to Hitler's mesmeric, demonic oratory, Stalin's speeches were slowly delivered, based on the relentless presentation of figures and argument to make his case. Stalin's appeal was primarily to the intellect. The Soviet regime had nothing of the ritualisation of the leader cult; the serried ranks of the Nuremberg rallies, the torchlit processions, and the parades of goose-stepping stormtroopers. The Nazi leadership in its projection was more archaic, with its appeal to the irrational, to the mystic and the pagan. There was nothing equivalent to the Führer worship of the Nazi regime in Stalin's USSR.

The cult of Stalin, like that of Hitler, was a cult curiously empty of content. Individuals, within strict limits, could project what they wished on these leaders. Hitler's appeal played on different themes: anti-communism, anti-modernism, anti-Semitism, being opposed to Versailles and as advocate of a *volkisch* pseudo-tradition of the ultra-nationalist right. Stalin's repertoire of roles was more restricted, reflecting the more deep-seated revolutionary transformation imposed on the society. But Stalin's image evolved from revolutionary organiser, tribune, disciple of Lenin, to victorious war leader, great statesman and head of the world communist movement. But the impersonality of the Stalin cult derived from its central function as the embodiment of the Soviet state and of the international communist movement.

The communist, Nazi and Fascist regimes had their own specific characteristics. Italy only loosely approximated to a totalitarian state and the cult of Mussolini was that of a populist demagogue; in the case of Hitler we have a true 'charismatic' figure, whose stature within the Nazi Party and in the German state was built in large measure on a genuine appeal to mass opinion and through the development of modern means of communication and propaganda; the Stalin regime was more primordial, more dependent on coercion for its survival, more thorough-going in its revolutionary ambitions to transform society, and was one where the cult in its initial phase was narrowly based and in large measure manufactured.

In the case of the Soviet Communist, Nazi and Fascist regimes the triumph of authoritarian, highly ideologised political regimes was in part a product of internal crisis. The leader cults were part of an attempt both to create a new official political culture that overcame the deep divisions within the state, and to construct a new sense of nationhood, a new identity. In each case there was an attempt to construct new allegiances, new cultural values that surmounted those inherited from the past. In this the state was untrammelled by past convention, traditions or established moral codes.

Exporting the cult

The Soviet military occupation of Eastern Europe was accompanied by the symbolic appropriation of these territories, through the erection of war memorials commemorating the Soviet dead, which were established immediately after the end of the fighting in 1945. These included the war monument at Berlin-Tiergarten, situated next to the Reichstag, displaying a triumphant soldier and two T-34 tanks. The large Berlin-Treptow cemetery was marked with a statute representing the motherland (*rodina-mat'*) and tombstones bearing quotations from Stalin, one of the largest surviving monuments to the Stalin cult anywhere in Europe. In Poland the Warsaw–Praga monument, on the right bank of the Vistula, displays two Soviet soldiers and a Pole, symbolising the 'brotherhood in arms' of the Slavic people, and another major monument was set up in Cracow. In Budapest a major war memorial was established on Szabadság tér, replacing the Sacred Flagstaff, one of the most important monument of the pre-war Horthy regime. Also in Budapest the Liberation Monument erected on top of Gellért hill, was completed in 1947, in the design of which K. E. Voroshilov commissioned the Soviet artist Alexander Gerasimov.[51] Similar monuments were set up in Czechoslovakia and other liberated countries.

These war memorials were part of the elaboration of the 'cult' of the Great Patriotic War as the apotheosis of Soviet triumph over Nazism. In the occupied states they performed a specific function, not simply to commemorate the Soviet dead, but as a reminder to these states of the sacrifices made in their 'liberation' by the USSR, as well as playing on the question of war guilt and collaboration with the Nazi. In this the USSR sought to capture the moral high-ground, where opposition to the occupying Soviet forces could be construed not only as ingratitude but of implicit support for the discredited regimes of the past. The legitimacy of the new regimes in these countries was partly founded on the sacrifices made by the USSR. For this reason iconoclastic attacks on Soviet war and other memorials was treated as sacrilege, as something especially shocking and reprehensible.

The East European people's democracies from 1948 onwards underwent a deep process of Sovietisation, which included the tansplanting of the Stalin cult to these states. The leaders of the communist parties in these states were obliged to develop cults of their own. Wladisław Gomułka, the leader of the Polish party after Khrushchev's denunciation of Stalin in 1956, spoke of how the more scrupulous of those leaders had viewed this with distaste, but had been obliged to comply with Moscow's dictates.[52] Even non-ruling communist parties managed to create within their own enclosed structures their own leader cults, as with Maurice Thorez and Palmiro Togliatti.

The cult of Stalin was very different to that of the leaders in the satellite states under his control. In these states Moscow's control operated through a counterbalancing of individual leaders, where no one individual could become too indispensable. In Eastern Europe most states followed the same pattern, a period from 1945–47 when each followed its own national path, then from 1948, and the onset of the Cold War, the move towards full Sovietisation, which saw the most intense development of leader cults (see Chapters 9, 10, 11 and 12). After 1956 these cults lapsed in most of the Eastern European states. In China Mao claimed a status at least equal to Stalin, and his cult gained a new impetus with the Cultural Revolution of 1966. Leader cults flourished in North Korea and North Vietnam. Some of the Eastern European countries, notably Romania and Albania, were influenced by the leader cults in China and North Korea.

The significant variation as regards the development of leader cults in the USSR and the Eastern European countries after 1945 reflects these different circumstances. The strong cults around Nicolae Ceaşescu, Josip Brozs Tito, Enver Hoxha, and the posthumous cult of Georgi Dimitrov, stand in contrast to the weaker cults around Mátyás Rákosi, Walter Ulbricht, Boleslaw Bierut, Klement Gottwald and Wladyslaw Gomulka. In some cases – Tito, Hoxha, and later Ceauşescu – the leader cults became a demonstration of national independence.

The internationalisation of the communist leader cult was nowhere more manifest than in the practice of embalming its leaders. In this Moscow set the example and provided the expertise. The small team of embalmers employed by the laboratory of the Lenin Mausoleum were responsible for embalming not only the bodies of Lenin and Stalin, but also Georgi Dimitrov, leader of the Bulgarian Communist Party; Horloogiyn Choybalsan, the Stalinist dictator of Mongolia; Klement Gottwald, the leader of the Czech Communist Party; Ho Chi Minh, the President of North Vietnam; Agostino Neto, the leader of the People's Republic of Angola; Linden Forbes Burnham, the President of the Republic of Guyana; and Kim Il Sung, the leader of North Korea.[53]

Dismantling the cult

Given the nature of these leader-centred regimes, the death of the leader created particular anxiety, and posed problems of legitimation. Stalin's death in March 1953 witnessed scenes of mass public grieving.[54] His funeral became a major part of the rites of the party-state. His body was placed in the mausoleum alongside that of Lenin. However, with his death, steps were soon taken to cut back the most excessive manifestations of the cult.[55] The publication of Stalin's *Collected Works* halted with volume 13 in 1955, having only got up to 1934. Similarly the cults of the Eastern European communist leaders were moderated. Khrushchev's denunciation of the Stalin cult at the 20th Party Congress in February 1956 dealt a major blow to the whole belief system. The 22nd Party Congress in October 1961 ordered the removal of Stalin's body from the mausoleum. Some inconclusive attempts to revive the cult were made at the time of the 90th anniversary of Stalin's birth in 1969.[56]

The destruction of Stalin monuments in the USSR was followed also in the countries of the Eastern Bloc. Only after 1949 had monuments to Stalin been erected in Central and Eastern Europe in any number. In Warsaw a monument to Stalin was planned to be installed in front of the Palace of Culture, but disagreement over design held up its realisation, although a statute to F. E. Dzerzhinsky, founder of the Soviet secret police, was erected. The largest monuments to Stalin were erected in Prague and Budapest. The Stalin monument in Budapest functioned as the main focus of communist party demonstrations and mass festivals. It was the first symbol to be demolished in the revolution of 1956. The Prague monument was also destroyed in 1956. That year the Czechoslovak Communist Party took the decision to cremate Gottwald's remains, on the grounds that embalming was contrary to their traditions. The monument to Stalin in East Berlin, on Stalinallee (the former Frankfurter Allee) survived until 1961.

As well as being sustained by their regimes, leader cults also had some base of public support; and when the Soviet regime sought to dismantle the Stalin cult in 1956 strong elements of public support survived (see Chapter 13) and in the satellite state local leaders sought to contain the damage to their own positions (see Chapter 14). But de-Stalinisation, in dismantling the basis of personal dictatorship, and restoring some semblance of collective leadership, in part involved a restoration of other cultic objects – the restoration of Lenin's cult, the reappraisal of Marxism-Leninism, the restoration of the cult of the Revolution, and the new emphasis on the USSR and the people. The cults surrounding the post-Stalin leaders, Khrushchev and L. I. Brezhnev, were not even a pale imitation of that cult, but something qualitatively different. In the USSR and Eastern Europe the image of the post-Stalin leaders remained closely managed (see Chapter 15). In Yugoslavia and Albania the cults seem to have disintegrated relatively quickly once the support systems surrounding them were removed.

The function of the leader cult

The communist regimes of the USSR, Yugoslavia, Albania, China, North Korea, North Vietnam and Cuba shared some common characteristics. All developed out of relatively small, highly ideologised, militant, vanguard, revolutionary movements. They were all tempered by the experience of the underground, revolution, civil war, partisan warfare or national liberation struggle. The leaders of these movements were deeply shaped by this initial experience. They commanded an authority within their respective movements, which in most cases lasted several decades. Figures such as Lenin, Stalin, Tito, Hoxha, Mao, Ho Chi Minh, Kim Il Sung and Castro were outstanding historical actors, invested with the aura of successful military leaders and state builders, around whom it was easy to weave myths and legends.

These vanguard movements, having conquered power, transformed themselves into governing regimes. The activists of the underground and the commissars and commanders of the civil war periods dominated the new governing structures of the party-state. These regimes relied to a large extent on coercion to consolidate their power. Each of these regimes evolved through periods of revolutionary advance, interspersed with periods of retrenchment and consolidation. The transformation of these vanguard movements into governing regimes was, in almost all cases, beset by serious internal conflicts: factional conflicts, ideological conflicts, struggles between contending institutions, conflicts between different national groups, conflicts between different generations (the underground generation versus the post-revolutionary generation of activists and cadres).[57]

The communist leader cult served three very different, but related functions. Firstly, its role was to legitimise the power of the small ruling group around the leaders. Secondly, it was intended as a mechanism to manage and defuse the potentially explosive conflicts within the governing stratum itself. Thirdly, it aimed to manage relations between the ruling group, the governing stratum, and the wider society. In this, as we see under Stalin, and under Mao in China, mass mobilisation of society might be used against elements of the governing stratum in periods of revolutionary convulsion.

The cult was crucial in managing relations between the different levels of the power structure. The dangers of the governing stratum transformation itself into an entrenched, self-perpetuating caste posed a challenge to the ruling group itself, and carried important implications as regards the organisation and management of the wider society. The leader cult might be used either to obstruct such a consolidation, or to lend legitimacy to it.

Soviet-type societies, with their graded systems of rank and privilege (*nomenklatura*), reinforced obedience to authority. Where this might be upset was when the leader invited the rank and file to criticise officialdom. The Stalin who in 1935 said that 'cadres decide everything' was also the Stalin who in 1937 could invoke the 'little people' against the bureaucrats. The cult thus has to be seen in its dynamic role of regulating social relations over time; as both the cult of the governing stratum and of popular anti-bureaucratic initiatives; as a cult that combined both socialist and nationalist features.

This sociological approach to the leader cult is confirmed when we look at the disintegration of cults. With the death of Tito and Hoxha the ruling group sought to revive the cult of the posthumous leader as a way of unifying the governing stratum, and of consolidating its control over society. The dissolution of these cults, partly under the pressure of economic failure, made it impossible for the ruling group to maintain the unity of the governing stratum, or to maintain social cohesion. In these circumstances, a new basis for legitimising political authority had to be found; in the case of the federal regions of Yugoslavia in an appeal to nationalism. A similar logic underlined the disintegration of the USSR in 1991.

The communist states of Eastern Europe – Poland, Hungary, Romania, Bulgaria, Czechoslovakia and the German Democratic Republic – were surrogate regimes which sought to emulate the Soviet model.

Conclusion

The communist regimes of the twentieth century represented a historically unique attempt to mass manufacture charisma of institutions, ideas and personalities, and to impose cultic veneration on their populations. Whilst the Stalin cult drew on past tradition and precedents, the strategy of creating a leader cult was deliberate and calculated. In this sense historical traditions have to be understood in the way in which they are transmitted, and renewed from one period to another. The cult cannot be explained simply by reference to tradition. Traditions were taken up, reused and reinterpreted in response to very specific needs from one epoch to another. At the same time traditions of deference, respect for authority, and conformity, may have deep cultural roots. The dialectic of the cult meant that whilst the leader captivated the masses, the masses perceived him as belonging to them.

The experience of the Soviet communist regime suggests that symbolic attachment was very important in the Stalin era. In the 1920s and 1930s, against a background of mass privation, there was a low level of consensus regarding the ideological and programmatic objectives of the regime. The war and post-war reconstruction changed things in important regards – it created a greater willingness on the part of the population to accept privations, as part of the price of victory and for the restoration of the economy, and strengthened symbolic attachment to the regime. The great enemy of the leader cult and the system of state legitimation in the USSR was time – the death of the generation of leaders, of cadres, of the public, for whom the heroic and utopian appeal of the revolutionary regime had been a reality.

The post-Stalin period in the USSR and Eastern Europe saw similar attempts by these regimes to improve material welfare, and improve social and cultural conditions for the mass of the population. With this went a shift away from over-reliance on symbolic attachment to an emphasis of ideological-programmatic appeal, and performance attainment. The crisis of the communist regimes from 1987 onwards stemmed from an exhaustion of symbolic attachment; a loss of faith in ideological-programmatic appeal; and the abject failure in performance attainment. Together this constituted a comprehensive crisis of legitimation for these regimes. Not only did the cult of the leader decline, so too did other cultic symbols – that of the party, the USSR. The posthumous cult of Lenin retained a strong following, and even that of Stalin held onto a core of ardent believers, reflecting in large measure nostalgia for a lost golden age.

Notes

1. I am indebted to my co-editors – Balázs Apor, Jan C. Behrends and Polly Jones – for many helpful comments and suggestions.
2. *From Max Weber: Essays in Sociology*, translated and edited with an Introduction by H. H. Gerth and C. Wright Mills (London, 1991 reprint), pp. 245–64. In contrast to Weber's conception of legitimacy, we might posit the advice proffered by Machiavelli to the Prince regarding the various stratagems he should deploy in order to win 'honour'. See Niccolò Machiavelli, *The Prince* (Harmondsworth, 1986). For a fuller discussion of 'machiavellism' and Bolshevism see E. A. Rees, *Political Thought from Machiavelli to Stalin: Revolutionary Machiavellism* (Basingstoke, 2004).
3. Luciano Cavalli, *Charisma, Dictatorship and Plebiscitary Democracy* (Florence, 1984).
4. N. S. Khrushchev, *The 'Secret' Speech*, introduced by Zhores A. Medvedev and Roy A. Medvedev (Nottingham, 1976).
5. For a discussion of Khrushchev's view of Stalinism see E. A. Rees (ed.) *The Nature of Stalin's Dictatorship: The Politburo, 1924–1953* (Basingstoke, 2003), pp. 229–32.
6. Gerhard Ritter, *The Corrupting Influence of Power*, trans. F. W. Pick (London, 1952).
7. Peter Kenez, *The Birth of the Propaganda State: Soviet Methods of Mass Mobilization, 1917–1929* (Cambridge, 1985).
8. Jane F. Gardner (ed.) *Leadership and the Cult of Personality*, trans. from Greek and Latin (London, 1974).
9. O. Volobuev and S. Kuleshov, 'Istoriya ne terpit polypravdy', *Sotsialisticheskaya industriya*, no. 146, 25 June 1988, p. 3.
10. David Cannadine, 'The Context, Performance and Meaning of Ritual: The British Monarchy and the "Invention of Tradition", *c.* 1820–1977' in Eric Hobsbawm and Terence Ranger (eds) *The Invention of Tradition* (Cambridge, 1983), ch. 4.
11. Peter Brown, *The Cult of the Saints: Its Rise and Function in Latin Christianity* (Chicago, 1981).
12. J. L. Talmon, *Political Messianism: The Romantic Phase* (New York, 1961); René Fülöp Miller, *The Mind and Face of Bolshevism*, trans. from the German by F. S. Flint and D. F. Tait (London, 1927).
13. Erik van Ree, *The Political Thought of Joseph Stalin: A Study in Twentieth-Century Revolutionary Patriotism* (London and New York, 2002), ch. 12. The author argues that the leader cult is rooted in nineteenth-century social democratic practices, and highlights Plekhanov's discussion on the role of the individual in history.
14. From the vast literature on the cults of Napoleon and Bismarck see Jean Tulard, *Napoleon: The Myth of the Saviour*, trans. Teresa Waugh (London, 1985); M. P. Driskel, *As Befits a Legend: Building a Tomb for Napoleon, 1840–1861* (Kent, Ohio, 1993); Richard E. Frankel, *Bismarck's Shadow* (Oxford, 2004).
15. Olga Velikanova, *Making of an Idol: On Uses of Lenin* (Göttingen, 1996); Olga Velikanova, *Obraz Lenina v massovom vospriyatii sovetskikh lyudei po arkhivnym materialam* (Lewiston, NY, 2001); N. Tumarkin, *Lenin Lives! The Lenin Cult in Soviet Russia* (Cambridge, Mass., 1997). On the mausoleum see N. N. Stoyanov, *Arkhitektura Mavvzoleya Lenina* (Moscow, 1950).
16. N. Berdyaev, *The Origins of Russian Communism* (London, 1937).
17. Vittorio Zincone, *Lo Stato totalitario* (Rome, 1999).

18. Mark Lilla, *The Reckless Mind: Intellectuals in Politics* (New York, 2001).
19. The cult of Saddam Hussein appears to have borrowed features from both the Hitler and the Stalin cult: Con Coughlin, *Saddam: The Secret Life* (London, 2002), pp. 170–2.
20. A. J. Polan, *Lenin and the End of Politics* (London, 1984). See Roy Medvedev, *Let History Judge* (Oxford, 1989), ch. 11 'The Conditions Facilitating Stalin's Usurpation of Power'.
21. Sarah Davies, *Popular Opinion in Stalin's Russia* (Cambridge, 1997), p. 150.
22. J. Arch Getty and Oleg V. Naumov, *The Road to Terror: Stalin and the Self-Destruction of the Bolsheviks, 1932–1939* (New Haven, Conn., and London, 1999) and Nathan Lites, *The Operational Code of the Politburo* (New York, 1951).
23. Graeme Gill, 'The Soviet Leader Cult: Reflections on the Structure of Leadership in the Soviet Union', *The British Journal of Political Science*, 10: 2 (April 1980). For other works by Graeme Gill see the Bibliography.
24. I. I. Shitts, *Dnevnik 'Velikogo Pereloma' (mart 1928–avgyst 1931)* (Paris, 1991). Interestingly Shitts refers to the Soviet leader cult as being inspired by the cult of Kemal Attaturk in Turkey, and refers to it as 'Kemalism'.
25. See especially Robert McNeal, *Stalin, Man and Ruler* (New York, 1988); Robert C. Tucker, *Stalin in Power: The Revolution from Above, 1928–1941* (New York and London, 1990); Robert C. Tucker, 'The Rise of Stalin's Personality Cult', *American Historical Review*, 84 (1979), pp. 347–66.
26. Isaac Deutscher, *Stalin* (Oxford, 1967), p. 270; Nina Tumarkin, 'Religion, Bolshevism and the Origins of the Lenin Cult', *Russian Review*, 40: 1 (1981), pp. 35–46; Katerina Clark, *The Soviet Novel: History as Ritual* (first edition Chicago, 1981).
27. Rees (ed.), *The Nature of Stalin's Dictatorship*, chs 1 and 7.
28. I borrow this phrase from Carl A. Linden, *The Soviet Party State: The Politics of Ideocratic Despotism* (New York, 1983).
29. This was summed up by Trotsky in his famous phrase 'I know that I cannot be right against the party' at the 13th Party Congress. Or in Pyatakov's famous statement of his need to submit himself to the party's will. Leonard Schapiro, *The Communist Party of the Soviet Union* (London, 1978), p. 385, cites N. Valentinov, 'Sut' bolshevizma v izobrazhenii Iu. Piatakova', *Novyi zhurnal* (New York), no. 52 (1958), pp. 140–61.
30. Karen Petrone, *Life Has Become More Joyous, Comrades: Celebrations in the Time of Stalin* (Bloomington, Ind., 2000); Christel Lane, *The Rites of Rulers: Ritual in Industrial Society – The Soviet Case* (Cambridge, 1981); Jeffrey Brooks, *Thank You Comrade Stalin! Soviet Public Culture from the Revolution to Cold War* (Princeton, NJ, 2000).
31. Stephen White, *Political Culture and Soviet Politics* (Basingstoke, 1979); Margaret Mead, *Soviet Attitudes Towards Authority: An Interdisciplinary Approach to Soviet Character* (London, 1955).
32. Eric Hobsbawm and Terence Ranger (eds) *The Invention of Tradition* (Cambridge, 1983). This book curiously omits any study of the invention of tradition under communist governments.
33. On the psychological needs that powerful leaders fill see Eric Fromm, *Fear of Freedom* (London, 1942).
34. Alex Inkeles and Raymond A. Bauer, *The Soviet Citizen: Daily Life in a Totalitarian Society* (Cambridge, Mass., 1959).
35. Jane Burbank, *Intelligentsia and Revolution: Russian Views of Bolshevism, 1917–1922* (New York and London, 1986), p. 20.
36. Sheila Fitzpatrick, 'Stalin and the Making of a New Elite, 1928–1939', *Slavic Review*, 38: 3 (1979), pp. 377–402.

37. M. Cherniavsky, *Tsar and People: Studies in Russian Myths* (New Haven, Conn., 1961); Maureen Perrie, *Pretenders and Popular Monarchism in Early Modern Russia* (Cambridge, 1995).
38. See Jadwiga Koralewiz, Ireneusz Bialecki and Margaret Wade (eds) *Crisis and Transition: Polish Society in the 1980s* (London, 1987).
39. N. Mandelstam, *Hope Against Hope* (Harmondsworth, 1971), pp. 149–50. Nadezhda Mandelstam recalls how at moments her husband, the poet Osip Mandelstam, was beset by doubts as to his own previously intransigent opposition to the Soviet regime.
40. N. S. Timasheff, *The Great Retreat: The Growth and Decline of Communism in Russia* (New York, 1946); E. A. Rees, 'Stalin and Russian Nationalism' in Geoffrey Hosking and Robert Service (eds) *Russian Nationalism, Past and Present* (London, 1997); Maureen Perrie, *The Cult of Ivan the Terrible in Stalin's Russia* (Basingstoke, 2001); Nicholas V. Riasanovsky, *The Image of Peter the Great in Russian History and Thought* (New York and Oxford, 1985).
41. Rees (ed.) *The Nature of Stalin's Dictatorship*, pp. 225–6.
42. Evgenia S. Ginsburg, *Into the Whirlwind* (Harmondsworth, 1968).
43. J. Arch Getty, 'Samokritika Rituals in the Stalinist Central Committee, 1933–1938', *Studies in Comparative Communism*, 17: 2 (summer 1984), pp. 111–21.
44. Véronique Garros *et al.* (eds) *Intimacy and Terror* (New York, 1995), p. 205.
45. Oleg Khlevnyuk, 'The First Generation of Stalinist "Party Generals"' in E. A. Rees (ed.) *Centre–Local Relations in the Stalinist State, 1928–1941* (Basingstoke, 2002), pp. 58–9.
46. John Barber, 'The Image of Stalin in Soviet Propaganda and Public Opinion during World War 2' in John Garrard and Carol Garrard (eds) *World War 2 and the Soviet People* (New York, 1993), pp. 38–49.
47. This is vividly captured in the picture of Stalin offering his toast to the 'Great Russian people' in the picture by Mikhail Khmelko, *To the Great Russian People.* The scene is of sumptuous reception set in the Great Hall of the Kremlin with its ornate golden decoration and huge chandeliers, with Stalin and other leaders (dressed in frock coats) and surrounded by bemedalled military commanders. See *Soviet Socialist Realist Art, 1930s-1960s*, Catalogue from the Exhibition at the The Museum of Modern Art (Oxford, 1992).
48. Nina Tumarkin, *The Living and The Dead: The Rise and Fall of The Cult of World War II in Russia* (New York, 1994).
49. E. Zubkova, *Russia After the War: Hopes, Illusions and Disappointments, 1945–57* (Armonk, NY, 1998).
50. Ian Kershaw, '"Working Towards the Fuhrer": Reflections on the Nature of the Hitler Dictatorship' in Ian Kershaw and Moshe Lewin (eds) *Stalinism and Nazism: Dictatorships in Comparison* (Cambridge, 1997), pp. 88–106; Hans Mommsen, 'Cumulative Radicalisation and Progressive Self-Destruction as Structural Determinants of the Nazi Dictatorship' in Kershaw and Lewin, *Stalinism and Nazism*, pp. 75–87.
51. Reuben Fowkes, 'The Role of Monumental Sculpture in the Construction of Socialist Space in Stalinist Hungary' in David Cowley and Susan E. Reid (eds) *Sites of Everyday Life in the Eastern Bloc* (Oxford, New York, 2002).
52. Zbigniew K. Brzezinski, *The Soviet Bloc: Unity and Conflict* (Cambridge, Mass., 1967).
53. Ilya Zbarsky and Samuel Hutchinson, *Lenin's Embalmers* (London, 1997), ch. 12.
54. Vladimir Bukovsky, *To Build a Castle* (London, 1978), pp. 81–3. Bukovsky recounts how in 1952 with the unveiling of the Doctor's Plot he suffered a recurrent night-

mare of Stalin being killed and he being helpless to stop it. He recalls the death of Stalin: 'Stalin's death shook our life to its foundations. Lessons in school virtually came to a halt, the teachers wept openly'.

55. R. Service, 'The Road to the Twentieth Party Congress', *Soviet Studies*, no. 2 (1981).
56. Victor Zaslavsky, *The Neo-Stalinist State: Class, Ethnity and Consensus in Soviet Society* (Brighton, 1982).
57. E. A. Rees, 'Stalinism: The Primacy of Politics' in John Channon (ed.) *Politics, Society and Stalinism in the USSR* (London, 1998).

Part I

The Making of the Cult: Methods and Individuals

2

Stalin and the Making of the Leader Cult in the 1930s

Sarah Davies

While the cult of the leader has been a distinctive feature of communist regimes since the time of Lenin, Stalin's cult was a particularly striking example of the phenomenon.[1] A recent study regards it as the defining theme of public culture in the Stalin era, symbolising the 'moral economy' of the USSR.[2] Not surprisingly it has attracted considerable attention from scholars who have analysed its political, cultural and social dimensions.[3] This chapter uses recently accessible sources to shed light on Stalin's own analysis of the phenomenon and to consider how he shaped the making of the cult.[4]

It is frequently assumed that unlike Lenin, who allegedly disliked the veneration he received, Stalin enjoyed and actively helped to manufacture his own cult.[5] Stalin's encouragement of the rewriting of history to magnify his own role, his authorisation of cinematic and other cultural representations of his image, his lavish public birthday celebrations, his acceptance of epithets such as 'genius' and 'father of the peoples', all appear to confirm his fundamental endorsement of the phenomenon. Traditionally many historians have interpreted the cult primarily as a means by which Stalin enhanced his authority during and after the power struggle within the party. Others, notably Robert Tucker, have argued that it fulfilled an important psychological as well as political need for Stalin: 'Abundant evidence indicates that Stalin needed a cult as a prop for his psyche as well as for his power. He craved the hero worship that Lenin found repugnant.'[6]

However, alternative perspectives offered by some of those closest to the dictator indicate that Stalin's attitude may have been more complicated. Molotov highlights his feelings of ambivalence, recalling that 'Stalin struggled with his cult and then came to rather like it'.[7] Yuri Zhdanov, the son of A. A. Zhdanov, who was briefly married to Stalin's daughter Svetalana, claims that his father-in-law, 'a modest person', was rather intolerant of the adulation. While on holiday with him after the war, Zhdanov remembers that during breakfast, when somebody brought over a copy of *Pravda* containing a report from an international congress, Stalin asked 'What are they writing there? Is it again, "Long live the great leader of the peoples of the world, comrade Stalin"?' He 'screwed up the newspaper and threw it in the bushes. This was his real attitude to the cult of personality.' Artem Sergeev implies that Stalin felt a certain detachment from his own propaganda image – when his son *Vasilii* asserted 'But I'm a Stalin too', Stalin shouted 'No you're not . . . You're not Stalin and I'm not Stalin. Stalin is Soviet power. Stalin is what he is in the newspapers and portraits, not you, no not even me.'[8]

Such evidence based on recollections is impossible to verify. It is unlikely that we will ever know what Stalin's 'real attitude' to the cult was. We can, however, reconstruct his public approach to the phenomenon on the basis of available documentary material.[9] The first section of this chapter examines his speeches, writings and documented conversations, identifying recurring motifs in his analysis of the leader cult before a range of different audiences, including family groups, his inner circle, foreign journalists and writers, and large meetings of party workers. The second section investigates Stalin's role as regulator of his image. The main focus of the chapter is the 1930s, the period when the cult developed into its fully-fledged form, and when Stalin was most inclined to comment on it.

Stalin's analysis of the leader cult

Although Stalin's analysis of the cult is relatively limited, several clear themes do emerge from the sources. His overall interpretation of the significance of the great leader in history remained consistent with the Marxist orthodoxy, exemplified in Georgi Plekhanov's work on the individual in history, that great individuals are only important in so far as they reflect wider social forces. This fundamental principle led him to condemn the notion of 'cult of personality' – the glorification of the leader *as a person*, as opposed to promotion of the leader as representative of the cause. While Stalin was doubtless aware of the various political advantages of the cult, he did not refer to these, except indirectly, in the context of appeal to the 'backward' masses. On other occasions he expressed only criticism of the cult, particularly in reference to its cynical exploitation by 'careerists' within the party, and to its harmful effects on the education of the new intelligentsia.

In speeches of the 1930s, Stalin repeatedly de-emphasised the role of leaders (*vozhdi*) accentuating instead the key historical importance of broader social forces. Thus he affirmed in February 1933 to the First Congress of collective farm shockworkers (*kolkhozniki-udarniki*) that the time had long passed when *vozhdi* were considered the only creators of history. The history of states was now decided primarily by millions of workers.[10] Similarly, in his address to Red Army graduates in May 1935, Stalin objected to the notion that all Soviet achievements should be attributed to the *vozhdi*, and proceeded to discuss the significance of cadres.[11] In a speech to leading workers and Stakhanovites of the metallurgical and mining industries on 29 October 1937 he noted that it was usual to make toasts to leaders, continuing 'That, of course, is not bad. But apart from the big leaders there are also the middling and small leaders'. He then stressed how important it was for leaders to have the trust of the people, noting that 'Leaders come and go, but the people remains.'

Stalin certainly did not deny the difference that great individuals, such as Lenin, could make, notably in his conversation with Emil Ludwig in 1931. Objecting to Ludwig's comparison between Peter the Great and himself, he went on to compare Lenin and Peter, describing the latter as a drop in the sea (*more*) in relation to Lenin who was the whole ocean (*okean*). When Ludwig suggested that he was contradicting the materialist understanding of history by acknowledging the role of outstanding individuals, Stalin retorted that Marx did not deny the role of individuals, he simply argued that individuals can only operate within a given set of conditions. The great individuals are those who understand these conditions and how to change them.[12]

For Stalin, Lenin represented the ultimate great individual who correctly understood the correlation of historical forces, and he was unstinting in his praise of Lenin's contribution. There are numerous examples of this. One, which is also interesting for the light it sheds on his approach to the leader cult in general, is his speech at a reception for participants of a festival of Tadzhik culture on 22 April 1941 (the anniversary of Lenin's birth). After remarking that people have a bad and unbolshevik habit of praising leaders while they are alive and forgetting them once they are dead, Stalin went on to speak about Lenin 'who raised us, taught us, sometimes criticised us, sometimes praised us, who made us men'. It was Lenin who taught them to work as Bolsheviks should: 'We are his shadow, his fledglings (*ptentsy*) and pupils'. Stalin continued that it would be false modesty on his part to say that the current leaders had achieved nothing, but that all the same, these successes were thanks to Lenin.[13]

Although the language Stalin used in reference to Lenin on this and other similar occasions is cult-like, it should still be interpreted in the context of Stalin's Marxism – that Lenin's greatness was due to his understanding of the historical situation.

These general ideas concerning the relationship between the great individual and broader social forces were elaborated on in a revealing speech which is worth considering in some detail for the light it sheds on Stalin's presentation of his own role in Soviet history.[14] Following the parade to celebrate the 20th anniversary of the revolution in 1937, Politburo members and some others including the Comintern head, G. Dimitrov, met in Voroshilov's flat. This was a relaxed and intimate setting in which Stalin probably felt able to expatiate without the normal restraints. During dinner, the toastmaster, A. I. Mikoyan, apparently made 30 toasts! Then Voroshilov gave the floor to Stalin, who toasted Lenin, after which Dimitrov recalled the greatness of Lenin, said how lucky it was that Stalin had followed him, and toasted the latter. Stalin responded that Dimitrov was wrong from a Marxist point of view, and, echoing his statement of a week earlier (see above), said 'individuals always appear if the things which give rise to them are not rotten. Individuals come and go, the people remains forever, and if the cause is not rotten, then the individual will appear.'[15]

He then went on to show how the struggle with the various opposition groups in the party should be interpreted in this light. In his view, the opposition failed because it did not take account of the will of the 'average (*serednyatskaya*) masses', the backbone of the party, but tried instead to achieve a majority of votes in the Central Committee. Unlike most official histories of this period, Stalin downplayed his own significance after Lenin's death. He admitted that the prominent figures in the party had been Trotsky, Bukharin, Rykov, Tomskii, Zinoviev and Krupskaya. Stalin himself was well known, but not on the scale of Trotsky. Although in charge of organisational work in the Central Committee, 'what was I compared with Il'ich? A poor specimen (*zamukhryshka*).' Molotov, Kalinin, Kaganovich, Voroshilov were all unknowns. So how was it that all these unknowns were able to overcome the more prominent members of the party? According to Stalin it was because the party wanted it. Admitting that he was a poor speaker compared with them, he claimed that the opposition did not take into account the feelings of the party masses who value actions above speeches.

Using the metaphor of the army to stand for the whole country, he explained, no doubt with the recent army purges in mind, that if the army has good officers, even if the generals are poor, the officers will overthrow the generals.

> The people put forward those who will lead them to victory, individuals in history come and go, the people remains and is never mistaken. If there hadn't been that backbone in the party, that basic of basics, those figures could have won, it's not the individual [*lichnost'*] that matters. It's very difficult to say who made me. Did you make me, or me you? You say that I am an outstanding person, it's not true. A noble fear of not failing the trust the masses and people have placed in you in the struggle with those figures – that's what was decisive, the fear of failure, and we emerged as leaders. Molotov, Voroshilov, Kalinin, Kaganovich, Mikoyan, Chubar' and others worked intensively.'

After this, Stalin made a toast to the average man (*serednyak*). Dimitrov replied that it was now clear to him that without the backbone nothing would have succeeded, but that this backbone would not have formed in such quantity, and especially quality, in such a short time if Stalin had not encouraged it. Stalin continued that in 1927 720,000 party members voted for the Central Committee – 'us *zamukhryshki*', while 4–6,000 voted for Trotsky and 20,000 abstained. He maintained that party officers are created only when they are properly led. In Russia they developed from 1900 thanks to favourable conditions in the country. The brilliant Lenin led them *in concrete economic and political circumstances* (author's emphasis). Communist parties in other countries were weak because they lacked the officers. Stalin concluded by repeating the idea about the need for leaders to fear failure if they were to retain popular trust. In an intriguing commentary on S. M. Kirov's murder, he added 'We needed Kirov's sacrifice to understand that. Kirov with his own blood opened the eyes of us idiots (excuse the expression).'[16]

In Stalin's internal self-presentation, then, his triumph over the opposition was due primarily not to superior personal qualities or to successful political intriguing, but rather to the fact that he had correctly interpreted and represented the interests of key social groups. This conception of the role of the individual in history underpinned his analysis of the whole phenomenon of 'cult of personality'. In line with Bolshevik thinking, Stalin accepted the significance of the great leader within concrete historical conditions, but criticised the notion of 'cult of personality', in which the personal qualities, the charisma of the leader-hero became the primary focus of loyalty rather at the expense of the cause he or she represented. On several occasions he denounced this practice as 'unbolshevik', 'S.R. (Socialist Revolutionary)', '*intelligent*' or '*meshchanskii*' (philistine).

In a letter of August 1930 Stalin criticised one party member, I. Shatunovskii, for expressing his devotion (*predannost'*) to Stalin, suggesting that he abandon this 'unbolshevik' principle of devotion to individuals and direct his devotion rather towards the working class, its party, its state. This should not be confused with devotion to individuals which Stalin described as 'empty and unnecessary *intelligent* rattle (*pobryakushka*)'.[17] A similar sentiment emerges from his disparaging analysis of an image and headline in *Komsomol'skaya pravda*. The picture showed a group of happy, well-dressed, young Soviet people celebrating International Youth Day in 1937, while the caption read 'On 6 September, 23rd International Youth Day, millions of Soviet young men and women demonstrated their love for the motherland, devotion to the party and *vozhd'* of the people comrade Stalin'. These phrases were underlined by Stalin, who also wrote above it '*meshchane*' (philistines).[18] Although it is impossible to be sure what Stalin meant by this, it can be inferred that he objected to what he perceived to be the representation of young people as devoted to the *vozhd'* (and motherland), rather than the cause of the party, in a newspaper which was supposed to be directed towards young communists.

On several occasions Stalin spoke out explicitly against the formation of a cult around himself. In July 1933 he expressed opposition to a forthcoming exhibition on his life organised by the Society of Old Bolsheviks on the grounds that 'such undertakings lead to the strengthening of the "cult of personality" which is harmful and incompatible with the spirit of our party'.[19] As is well known, in February 1938 he categorically opposed the publication of Smirnova's *Tales of Stalin's Childhood* by the Komsomol publishing house Detizdat. Stalin referred to the book's potential to inculcate the 'cult of personality, *vozhdi*, infallible heroes'. This theory of masses and heroes was an 'S.R. theory' and was unacceptable to Bolsheviks. He advised them to burn the book.[20]

This letter to Detizdat suggested that the author had been misled by among others, *podkhalimy* (sycophants). Although Stalin derived evident political advantages from his cult, it was potentially a double-edged sword, capable of obstructing the serious goals of party and state. He realised, for example, that it could be exploited quite cynically by sycophantic careerists within the party. Naturally suspicious, he probably also assumed that behind every flatterer there lurked a potential traitor, feelings which would have been exacerbated by the experience of 1936–38. He was doubtless also aware that local leaders were modelling their mini-cults on his own. From 1937 these mini-cults came under regular attack by the central leadership.[21] Stalin's objections to a variety of cult behaviours, particularly in the late 1930s, should be viewed in this context.[22]

Dimitrov records Stalin's displeasure with a section of the draft Comintern appeal for May Day 1939 which read 'Long live our Stalin! Stalin means peace! Stalin means Communism! Stalin is our victory!' He accused its chief editor, the Comintern secretary D. Manuilskii, whom he suspected of having had Trotskyite leanings and of being generally unreliable, of 'toadying'.[23] He turned on E. M. Yaroslavskii in 1940, complaining about the 'excessive and sickening flattery' of leaders, in reference to an article by Moskalev in the journal *Istorik-Marksist*: 'I. V. Stalin at the head of Baku Bolsheviks and workers in 1907–08' (January 1940), which was also summarised in *Pravda* by E. Gorodetskii on 4 February. On 10 February he wrote to the editors, authors and Politburo members, accusing the authors of inaccuracies, such as the fact that he had never been editor of the oil workers' newspaper *Gudok*, and that Voroshilov's role in Baku had never been so prominent ('Comrade Voroshilov was only in Baku for a few months, and then left Baku without leaving visible traces behind him' – this was, probably not coincidentally, a time when Voroshilov's reputation was being undermined following the disasters of the Winter War with Finland.)[24] Yaroslavskii responded to Stalin on 27 April, providing a number of sources for the claims, mainly Stalin-era publications. Stalin wrote back to him on 29 April disputing these 'facts', and arguing that historians should not rely on so-called memoirs. He maintained that neither he nor Voroshilov needed false services ascribed to them since they had enough real ones:

> Clearly this is necessary for the careerist authors of 'memoirs' and the authors of some suspicious articles 'about *vozhdi*' who want to promote

> themselves by way of excessive and sickening flattery of the leaders of party and government. Do we have the right to cultivate in our people these feelings of servility and grovelling? Clearly not. Indeed it is our duty to exterminate these shameful and servile feelings in our people . . . Sycophancy is incompatible with scientific history.[25]

Stalin also publicly criticised one of the most characteristic cult practices: the lengthy ovations accorded to him at party meetings. He expressed irritation especially when these occurred at meetings of leading party workers, whom he felt were clapping rather than taking party matters seriously. At a gathering of the directors of meat and milk *sovkhozy* in October 1932, he asked 'why are you applauding – you should be ashamed'.[26] After A. A. Zhdanov had introduced him at a meeting of workers in the defence industry in June 1934, there were the usual stormy applause and ovations, to which Stalin responded 'it always happens like this with us – when they want to turn a serious matter into a joke, they start to applaud'. He continued:

> You are very kindly disposed towards your *vozhdi* – however damned they may be – and welcome them with applause. With us rays of joy and kindness never leave our faces. But we have capitalist encirclement, so we're surrounded by enemies, who are more civilised and more cultured than us.[27]

Addressing the 1934 November plenum he said 'comrades here in the Central Committee we're not accustomed to applauding. It's not a meeting or a conference'[28] and at a discussion with propagandists of the new *Kratkii kurs* (*Short Course of the History of the VKP(b)*):

> Comrades – this isn't a meeting here. Why are you spending so much time applauding? I didn't expect that qualified people would applaud. It's not right . . . We don't need praise, but help, help in the form of corrections, in the form of comments, in the form of instructions, arising from your experience as propagandists. That's what's needed, not praise and applause.[29]

As well as these concerns about the malign influence of the cult on party members, Stalin also expressed some anxiety that it could undermine efforts to educate the new intelligentsia, i.e. leading cadres in the party and state, many of whom had been promoted following the purges. From 1937 onwards he became increasingly preoccupied with these, and especially their inadequate education and training. The *Kratkii kurs*, the most important educational work of the decade, was intended for them. As he declared in his speech of September 1938, this work was not designed for ordinary workers at factories, or for ordinary officials (*sluzhashchie*) at enterprises, but for those cadres whom Lenin termed professional revolutionaries, for leading cadres: the leaders of the armed forces, industry, agriculture, health, teachers, students. Stalin felt that these groups had been neglected hitherto thanks to a spirit of anti-intellectualism, a *makhaevshchina* which had prevailed within the party.[30]

Although the *Kratkii kurs* has often been regarded the quintessential expression of the Stalin cult,[31] it was actually less focused on the role of the *vozhd'* and his colleagues than it would have been without Stalin's editing of P. N. Pospelov and Yaroslavskii's initial draft. Yaroslavskii had included in the draft a detailed account of Stalin's pre-revolutionary career, and those of other leading Bolsheviks (Yakov Sverdlov, Molotov, etc.), which contained the usual hagiographical references, for example to Stalin's bravery in exile. Stalin removed this entire section, as well as some other references to his role. The Soviet historian N. Maslov argued at the height of the anti-Stalin campaign of the *perestroika* years that this 'modesty' by Stalin was not motivated by any concern to diminish the cult, but rather by the desire to remove anything that might come over as too unrealistic or likely to attract mockery. This is not implausible; however the intervention is also consistent with Stalin's commitment to Marxism-Leninism, and with his stated aim of raising the theoretical level of the new intelligentsia, which he felt was their weakest spot.[32]

In his September speech Stalin noted that hitherto most textbooks had been written according to a model of 'educating people through characters (*na litsakh*), eulogising these characters'. Stalin suggested that this was the wrong way to educate cadres. Cadres should be educated on the basis of ideas, theory, theory in his definition being the laws of historical development:

> If there is that knowledge, then there will be cadres too, but if people don't have that knowledge – there won't be cadres, just an empty space. And what will individuals give? I don't want to oppose individuals to ideas, although, of course we have to speak about individuals, but only so far as it's necessary. The essence is not in individuals, but in ideas, in the theoretical tendency.[33]

Stalin made similar points in his speech to the Politburo two weeks later:

> History focused on individuals gives nothing for the education of our cadres, or gives very little, history should be focused on ideas . . . That's why there is little in the *Kratkii kurs* on individuals, that's why all the material is arranged according to the key points in the development of the ideas of Marxism-Leninism. This educates people more, it leads to less

> interest in particular individuals and *vozhdi*, it's more beneficial for the forging of a real Marxist-Leninist consciousness.[34]

For Stalin, then, an excessive focus on individuals could only detract from the correct theoretical understanding of history necessary for the educated strata. The study of individuals and biography were more suitable for the masses, a point which he made quite explicitly at the end of 1946 to the team responsible for the new Stalin biography, alleging that the masses, the simple people, could not begin the study of Marxism-Leninism on the basis of Lenin and Stalin's collected works – they needed biography. He suggested that a new Lenin biography should be prepared as 'this is a proven way of helping the simple people begin their study of Marxism'.[35]

David Brandenberger has argued in a recent study of the construction of Stalin's official biography that Stalin regarded the cult, along with Russocentrism and populism, as necessary for mobilising a poorly educated population.[36] It is indeed the case that from the mid-1930s, much Stalin-centred propaganda was designed to have mass appeal – most obviously the 'folklore for Stalin'.[37] There is also some evidence of Stalin justifying the cult as strategically useful propaganda for culturally 'backward' sections of the Soviet population. To close relatives he maintained that it was a necessary, if temporary, evil, to be tolerated for the sake of the 'masses' who were accustomed to worshipping the tsar. In her diary, Maria Svanidze describes an impromptu visit by Stalin, members of his family and entourage to the newly opened Moscow Metro on 22 April 1935. Stalin was greeted by a crowd of delighted members of the public, and according to Svanidze, appeared genuinely moved by their spontaneous enthusiasm. Svanidze continued 'He once said about the ovations made to him that people need a tsar, i.e., someone whom they can worship and in whose name they can live and work.' Later on 9 May, when they discussed the Metro excursion again, and the popular enthusiasm it had generated, Stalin again mentioned the 'fetishism' of the popular psyche and the desire to have a tsar.[38]

He drew similar conclusions in his conversation with Leon Feuchtwanger in January 1937. The conversation was summarised by Feuchtwanger in his book, *Moscow 1937*, but a more detailed perspective emerges from the archival record of the conversation.[39] When Feuchtwanger told Stalin how he found some manifestations of the cult tasteless and excessive, Stalin agreed, but said that he only answered one or two of the hundreds of greetings he received and did not allow most to be printed, especially the most excessive. He claimed that he did not seek to justify the practice, but to explain it: evidently the workers and peasant masses were simply delighted to be freed from exploitation, and they attributed this to one individual: 'of course that's wrong, what can one person do – they see in me a unifying concept, and create foolish raptures around me.'[40]

Feuchtwanger then asked a very legitimate question: why could he not stop the most excessive forms of rapture? Stalin responded that he had tried several times but that it was pointless as people assumed he was just doing so out of false modesty. For example, he had been criticised for preventing celebrations of his 55th birthday (see p. 39). According to Stalin, the veneration of the leader was the result of cultural backwardness and would pass with time. It was difficult to prevent people expressing their joy, and to take strict measures against workers and peasants.[41] Feuchtwanger responded that what concerned him was not so much the feelings of workers and peasants, but the erection of busts and so on. Echoing some of his comments (above) about the abuse of the cult, Stalin answered that bureaucrats were afraid that if they did not put up a bust of Stalin, they would be criticised by their superiors. Putting up a bust was a form of careerism 'a specific form of the 'self-defence' of bureaucrats: so that they are left alone, they put up a bust'.[42]

In Stalin's discourse, then, the cult of personality was an unbolshevik aberration which was open to abuse by opportunists and potentially detrimental to the education of the new intelligentsia. It continued to exist primarily because of its appeal to the culturally backward masses. What impact, if any, did such an approach have upon the making of the cult?

Stalin as regulator of his image

When Feuchtwanger raised the question of tasteless busts of the leader, Stalin commented rather disingenuously 'There's no time to get involved in that kind of thing, we have other matters and concerns'.[43] Although he obviously did not want to or could not monitor every aspect of it, it is clear that he did, nevertheless, devote a remarkable amount of attention to regulating his image in the 1930s. He appears usually to have had the final say on what could or could not be published about his life and work (in central Soviet publications at least). For example, when A. Belyakov wrote an article for publication in *Molodaya gvardiya* in 1938, which contained references to Stalin, L. Z. Mekhlis informed the editors that without Stalin's sanction it could not be published.[44] Those who did not follow the proper procedures could be reprimanded: the editors of *Pravda* and *Izvestiya* were criticised by the Politburo in 1934 for announcing the 10th anniversary of Stalin's *Foundations of Leninism* without the prior knowledge and agreement of the Central Committee and Stalin.[45] In August 1935 L. P. Beria was criticised for republishing some of Stalin's articles from 1905–10 without his sanction, following which the Politburo took a decision to publish his authorised collected works.[46] Stalin also found time to act as editor-in-chief of many texts containing references to himself – not only the well-known case of his own biography, but also party slogans, newspaper reports, film scripts and so on.

His interventions often reveal a concern to tone down, or to be seen to be toning down, some of the excesses of the cult. S. Sukharev argues that this was certainly the case in the period 1932–34, when, in his view, a battle was under way between two political courses: moderate and extreme. He believes that in this period Stalin was obliged to restrict the cult, to present an image of collective leadership.[47] There are many examples of this. While a draft report for *Pravda* described a reception of a delegation of *kolkhozniki* of Odessa province in November 1933 as a reception by Stalin, Stalin himself added the names of Kalinin, Molotov and Kaganovich.[48] He also criticised the writer A. Afinogenov for highlighting the *'vozhd'* rather than the collective leadership of the Central Committee in his play *Lozh'*.[49] When the Marx-Engels-Lenin Institute (IMEL) produced a history of 30 years of the party in 1933, he removed some references to himself.[50] In the same year he also objected to the proposed exhibition on his life (see above),[51] and advised the Ukrainian party not to publish a brochure on Stalin for the 15th anniversary of the Komsomol.[52] In 1934 he excised some mentions of himself from an IMEL work on Lenin.[53] He also edited Stetskii's draft slogans for May 1934, removing the 'Stalin' from the slogan 'Under the banner of the Bolshevik Party and its Leninist CC – forward to new victories! Long live the great, victorious banner of Marx, Engels, Lenin, Stalin'.[54] He decreed that the proposed Stalin Institute in Tiflis be turned instead into a branch of IMEL,[55] and explicitly forbade any public celebrations of his 55th birthday.[56]

Sukharev claims that after the murder of Kirov at the end of 1934, Stalin's restraint disappeared, and a frenzy of glorification began, exemplified by the publication of Beria's cultic work *On the History of the Bolshevik Organisations in the Transcaucasus* (1935). It is undeniable that the cult did reach new heights from the mid-1930s. Yet at the same time Stalin did not completely abandon his attempts to tone down some of its most excessive manifestations. In this respect there is perhaps more continuity in Stalin's approach throughout the 1930s than has been suggested by Sukharev.

The slogans produced for May Day and the October anniversary, and edited by Stalin, are a good barometer of the state of the cult. As we have seen, in 1934 Stalin deleted his name from the phrase 'banner of Marx-Engels-Lenin-Stalin'. By October 1939, the climate had changed, and it remained in the final slogan 'Long live the great, victorious banner of Marx-Engels-Lenin-Stalin! Long live Leninism!' and the phrase *'delo Lenina-Stalina'*. He did, however, eliminate his name from phrases such as *'Stalinskaya konstitutsiya'* and *'Stalinskii blok.'*[57] He was clearly acutely sensitive to the potential nuances of the Stalin 'label', and appears to have pursued different strategies depending on whether slogans were oriented towards a domestic or an international audience. Dimitrov records how Stalin insisted that his name be removed from 'under the banner of Marx-Engels-Lenin-Stalin' in the draft Comintern appeal for May Day in 1939, although it had been included in the Central Committee slogans. He explained:

> It is not a question of *prestige*, but a question of *principle*. Slogans are our own 'national business,' and in this case we slipped up; there was no call to write them like that! But this is *an international appeal*: here we have to put things more precisely![58]

Stalin was of course being disingenuous when he claimed they had 'slipped up' by including his name – he must have approved its inclusion in the national slogans, judging it to be strategically necessary for the domestic audience.

Stalin continued to pay close attention to the editing of reports of Kremlin receptions for publication in *Pravda*. He would sometimes (but not always) cut out or tone down the references to the endless clapping which accompanied these quintessentially cultic occasions. He also tried to reduce the language of adulation, or to distribute it more equally with other colleagues. He edited the report on the Kremlin reception for participants of the 1 May 1937 parade, altering the phrase 'Country of the great Stalin constitution' to 'USSR'. He eliminated the sentences 'great was the joy of the people who had the happiness of seeing their own Stalin and their Government', and 'Comrade Voroshilov speaks of Stalin as the greatest man of our times who is loved without limits by our Red Army and entire Soviet people.' He also crossed out 'The participants of the May 1 parade expressed the thoughts and feelings of the entire Red Army, wholeheartedly dedicated to and loving without limits their friend and teacher, *vozhd'* of the people Stalin.'[59] Likewise he edited from the report of the reception of leading workers and Stakhanovites of metallurgical and mining industry in October 1937 the cries of 'Long live beloved com. Stalin' and added 'ovations', and cries of '*Ura*' after the words of Voroshilov and Kaganovich. At this reception Kaganovich had made a lengthy and elaborate toast to him. Kaganovich, who, as one of the leading contributors to the cult, clearly made a habit of such toasts,[60] on this occasion used the metaphor of 'steel founder' (*stalevar*) to describe Stalin, who had been responsible for destroying the:

> harmful admixtures and dross from the metal of the accursed trotskyite-bukharinite wreckers and spies, the hirelings of Japanese and German fascism, and has smelted steel of a higher and unprecedented category – the wonderful united cadres of the builders of socialism, stakhanovites and shock workers . . . The great steel founder of our socialist construction leads our socialist furnace without accidents and slow-downs . . .

and so on in that vein.[61] Stalin eliminated this panegyric entirely.

Stalin also intervened to regulate the naming of places after himself. The practice of renaming places after leaders predated Stalin's hegemony, and initially he seems to have been content to let it continue. In August 1929 he told his secretary A. N. Poskrebyshev that he had no objections to Sakharstroi taking his name, and that Poskrebyshev should respond to all future such requests with agreement.[62] However by the mid-1930s the stream of requests for renamings had become a torrent. Kirov's murder had been followed by endless requests to name places after him, and this developed into a wider movement for renamings after other *vozhdi*. By 1936 Stalin was already trying to restrict the practice. In 1936 the Director of Kharkhov electromechanical factory attempted to legalise via the Central Executive Committee (TsIK) the 'im Stalina' which the factory had held (informally – presumably through a local decision) for eight years. As the process had been dragging on and on, he asked for help from the Poltiburo to speed it up. While some members of the Politburo approved the renaming, others proposed a discussion of the issue. However Stalin declared emphatically that he was not in favour, writing 'I am against. I advise that it should take the name of Kalinin, Molotov, Voroshilov, Kosior, Postyshev or another of the leading comrades.' Nevertheless, despite Stalin's objections, on 25 March the Politburo went on to approve the attaching of Stalin's name to the factory.[63]

Further concerns were expressed by Stalin in May. On 5 February 1936 I. A. Akulov had sent the Politburo requests received by the Central Executive Committee for renamings: a Vitebsk sewing factory, Znamya industrializatsii, after Stalin; Simferopol *zernosovkhoz*, after Kalinin; Tubdetsanatoriya of the Central Asian railway, after Kaganovich; and Makhaev coke-chemical factory no.4, after Postyshev. Stalin responded: 'As regards the naming after Stalin, I'm totally against. As for the others, I do not object.' Molotov resolved that the question of reducing the torrent of renamings should be discussed at the Politburo. On 20 May 1936, Stalin raised an item 'On renaming towns etc.' as a result of which the Politburo agreed to ban from 1 June 1936 the renaming of towns, small towns, district centres and railway stations.[64]

As well as continuing to regulate the use of the Stalin image, throughout the 1930s Stalin continued to distinguish between an unhealthy focus on Stalin the individual, and the more acceptable Stalin as personification of the cause, the *delo Lenina-Stalina*. While the *delo Lenina-Stalina* could be promoted within certain limits, Stalin discouraged preoccupation with private aspects of his life, such as his childhood and family.[65] This became a constant battle as the public was then, as now, curious about the private lives of celebrities. Those whose job it was to promote Stalin amongst young people were especially anxious for details of his childhood and youth, which he was equally anxious not to divulge, or at least only in limited and strictly controlled quantities, such as the *Molodaya gvardiya* volume of memoirs which appeared to coincide with the leader's 60th birthday celebrations in 1939.[66]

We have already noted Stalin's intervention in the case of Detizdat's plans to publish Tales of Stalin's Childhood.[67] In April 1939 *Komsomol'skaya pravda* tried to publish flattering memoirs of Stalin's youth by G. Elisabedashvili, a fellow-student at his school in Gori. Although these had been approved by the Tbilisi branch of IMEL, Stalin was opposed, saying that 'apart from everything else, the author has shamelessly lied'.[68] Not surprisingly, the Georgians were particularly active suppliers of cult material concerning Stalin's childhood and youth, not least because the cult was a potentially useful way of boosting the republic's status and that of Beria.[69] However, Stalin did not always encourage their efforts.[70] In September 1940 he refused to authorise the publication in Russian by Goslitizdat of Gamsakhurdiya's *Detstvo vozhdya*, even though it had already been published in Tbilisi.[71] Likewise *Komsomol'skaya pravda* was prevented from publishing memoirs by former students at Stalin's Gori school and Tbilisi seminary which *Zarya vostoka* had printed in August 1936.[72] A strategic distinction appears to have been made between what was acceptable for the Georgians and what was suitable for consumption by the Soviet public as a whole.

Stalin allowed only occasional public glimpses of his family. His visit to his mother in Tbilisi in October 1935 was a rare example of the genre, but even this he treated with ambivalence. He was obviously not entirely opposed to some press coverage of the incident, for when Poskrebyshev sent him a correspondent's report of the visit for confirmation, which described his mother's joy at seeing her son, and went into some detail about the contents of her room, Stalin replied simply that it was not his job to confirm or deny what was in the report.[73] However, a week later, obviously incensed by the press's excessive coverage, he told Politburo members to stop 'the vulgar rubbish' that was appearing in the central and local press – alleged interviews with his mother and 'all sorts of publicistic rubbish, even portraits'.[74] He was also cautious regarding public portrayals of his children. He used his daughter Svetlana when it suited him, but in 1938 refused to give *Komsomol'skaya pravda* permission to publish a memoir of a young participant of the Georgian delegation to the Kremlin in March 1936 which revealed quite intimate details of how she had played with Svetlana.[75]

Excessive concentration on Stalin's everyday life was also frowned upon – the public did not need to be overly concerned about the places he had stayed while in exile, for example. A 1934 *Pravda* article on Turukhansk which included a picture of the house where Stalin lived along with its interior merited Stalin's resolution 'Rubbish (*Che-pu-kha*)'.[76] In 1935 *Molodaya gvardiya* published an account by El'-Registan of the writer's travels through the USSR. As part of his journey El'-Registan had visited places where Stalin had lived in exile: however, the journal was denied permission to publish these.[77] In 1939 the Soviet news agency TASS requested permission to release to the press a telegram from the town of Vologda, 'Dommuzei I. V. Stalina', on the house where he had stayed in 1911 and which had been restored and was attracting lots of visitors. Stalin turned this down.[78]

Stalin's approach to the leader cult was in many ways complex and contradictory. He obviously did not discourage many cult initiatives, nor could the cult have assumed such proportions without his sanction. Yet at the same time he continued to limit some of its excesses and to promote a discourse critical of the 'cult of personality'. Of course this was in itself an essential part of the making of the cult. Without this element of 'modesty', and its Leninist precedent, it would have lost much of its effectiveness as a means of boosting his personal authority.

This does not mean, however, that we should completely disregard other possible motives for Stalin's concern to limit the cult, or dismiss his pronouncements as mere rhetoric. It is now clear that Stalin took Marxism seriously, and that the cult could not be comfortably accommodated within this intellectual framework.[79] It is also likely that Stalin was genuinely concerned about the potentially detrimental effects of the cult on the party and the new intelligentsia, while acknowledging its advantages as a strategic weapon for mobilising particular sections of society. A mixture of motives seem to have been at work. To attempt to establish which of these were most significant would be to enter the realm of speculation.

Perhaps in the end this is less important than the impact Stalin's approach had upon the evolution of both his own cult, and, to some degree, of the East European cults modelled on it. Stalin's influence ensured that the cult stayed with certain limits. In accordance with Bolshevik ideology and practice, the leader was always promoted as a representative of the *party* and its cause. His image was a largely impersonal one, with the private, human, individual traits reduced to a minimum.[80]

Finally it is also significant as well as ironic that his critical public discourse was used to facilitate the transition to de-Stalinisation. After all, it was Stalin's letter to Detizdat which was published in *Voprosy istorii* in 1953, immediately after his death, as part of the campaign against the cult of personality in its wider sense.[81] Three years later Khrushchev chose to ignore this aspect of Stalin's complex legacy.

Notes

1. I am indebted to the Arts and Humanities Research Board for funding this research, and to the participants of the workshop 'Stalin and the Lesser Gods' for making me rethink my initial ideas.
2. J. Brooks, *Thank You, Comrade Stalin! Soviet Public Culture from Revolution to Cold War* (Princeton, NJ, 2000).
3. These include G. Gill, 'Political Myth and Stalin's Quest for Authority in the Party' in T. Rigby, A. Brown and P. Reddaway (eds) *Authority, Power and Policy in the USSR* (London, 1980), pp. 98–117; G. Gill, 'The Soviet Leader Cult: Reflections on the Structure of Leadership in the Soviet Union', *British Journal of Political Science*, 10,

2 (1980), pp. 167–86; Kh. Kobo (ed.) *Osmyslit' kul't Stalina* (Moscow, 1989); J. Heizer, 'The Cult of Stalin, 1929–1939', University of Kentucky PhD diss., 1977; B. Kiteme, 'The Cult of Stalin: National Power and the Soviet Party State', Columbia University PhD diss., 1989; J. Plamper, 'The Stalin Cult in the Visual Arts, 1929–1953', University of California, Berkeley, PhD diss., 2001.

4. See Erik van Ree, *The Political Thought of Joseph Stalin* (London, 2002) and L. Maksimenkov in 'Kul't. Zametki o slovakh-simvolakh v sovetskom politicheskom kul'ture', *Svobodnaya Mysl'*, 11 (1993), pp. 26–43.
5. R. Medvedev, *Let History Judge* (Oxford, 1989), pp. 313–19. N. Tumarkin suggests that Lenin's attitude to the cult may have been more ambivalent: in her *Lenin Lives: The Lenin Cult in Soviet Russia* (Cambridge, Mass., 1997), pp. 103–7. A problem with the conventional view of Lenin's attitude is that it is based on far from impartial memoir sources.
6. R. Tucker *Stalin in Power* (New York, 1990), p. 3; 'The Rise of Stalin's Personality Cult', *American Historical Review*, 1979, 84/2.
7. F. Chuev, *Sto sorok besed s Molotovym* (Moscow, 1991), p. 261.
8. S. Sebag Montefiore, *Stalin: The Court of the Red Tsar* (London, 2003), p. 4.
9. Many of the sources discussed are from RGASPI's fond 558, the Stalin fond. This contains only a selective group of documents pertaining to Stalin's life and activity. For one, perhaps overly sceptical, discussion of the possible limitations of the fond, see Z. and R. Medvedev *The Unknown Stalin* (London, 2003), pp. 57–94.
10. I. V. Stalin, *Sochinenyia* (Moscow, 1952–55, and Stanford, 1967), vol. 13, p. 255.
11. Stalin, *Sochinenyia*, vol. 3/14 (edited by R. H. McNeil) (Stanford, 1967), p. 56.
12. Stalin, *Sochineniya*, vol. 13, pp. 105–6.
13. RGASPI (Rossiiskii Gosudarstvennyi Arkhiv Sotsial'no-Politicheskii Istorii) 558/11/1125/13–14. This was the corrected version of the speech. The earlier versions are slightly different, although the sense is roughly the same.
14. Robert Tucker paraphrases the speech quite faithfully in his *Stalin in Power*, pp. 482–6 and asserts (not entirely plausibly) that the speech reveals Stalin modelling himself on Ivan Groznyi. Dimitrov's record of the speech is reproduced in I. Banac (ed.) *The Diary of Georgi Dimitrov, 1933–1949* (New Haven, 2003), pp. 65–7.
15. RGASPI, 558/11/1122/161.
16. RGASPI, 558/11/1122/162–5.
17. Stalin, *Sochineniya*, vol. 13, p. 19.
18. RGASPI, 558/11/203/147–147ob.
19. RGASPI, 558/1/4572/1.
20. RGASPI, 558/11/1121/24. Published in *Voprosy istorii*, 11 (1953).
21. S. Davies, *Popular Opinion in Stalin's Russia* (Cambridge, 1997), pp. 169–70; S. Fitzpatrick, *Everyday Stalinism* (New York, 1999), pp. 30–1.
22. Stalin's own cult seems to have diminished somewhat in the immediate pre-war period. Davies, *Popular Opinion in Stalin's Russia*, p. 152.
23. Banac (ed.) *The Diary of Georgi Dimitrov 1933–1949*, p. 105.
24. RGASPI, 558/11/1509/82–4.
25. RGASPI, 558/11/842/35–44.
26. RGASPI, 558/11/1116/42.
27. RGASPI, 558/11/1118/1–2.
28. RGASPI, 558/11/1118/42.
29. RGASPI, 558/11/1122/1.
30. RGASPI, 558/11/1122/10–18.

31. It was highlighted, for example, in Khrushchev's Secret Speech.
32. N. N. Maslov, '"Kratkii kurs istorii VKP(b)" – entsiklopediya kul'ta lichnosti Stalina', *Voprosy istorii KPSS*, 11 (1990), p. 57; M. V. Zelenov, 'I. V. Stalin v rabote nad "Kratkim kursom istorii VKP(b)"', *Voprosy istorii*, 11–12 (2002).
33. RGASPI, 558/11/1122/3–4.
34. *Voprosy istorii*, 4 (2003), p. 19.
35. RGASPI, 629/1/54/23–26, published in L. Maksimenkov 'Kul't. Zametki o slovakh-simvolakh v sovetskom politicheskom kullture', p. 35.
36. D. Brandenberger, 'Constructing the Cult: A Case Study of Stalin's Official Biography' (unpublished ms).
37. F. Miller, *Folklore for Stalin: Russian Folklore and Pseudofolklore of the Stalin Era* (Armonk, NY, 1990).
38. Diary of Maria Anisimovna Svanidze, *Istochnik*, 1 (1993), 18–20.
39. L. Feuchtwanger, *Moscow 1937* (London, 1937).
40. RGASPI, 558/11/1120/8–9.
41. RGASPI, 558/11/1120/9.
42. RGASPI, 558/11/1120/10.
43. RGASPI, 558/11/1120/11.
44. RGASPI, 558/11/1496/83.
45. RGASPI, 17/163/1019/83.
46. RGASPI, 558/11/88/21–3.
47. S. V. Sukharev, 'Litsedeistvo na poprishche istorii', *Voprosy istorii KPSS*, 3 (1990), pp. 102–18. Recently, Arch Getty has rejected the idea of a struggle between two courses in this period, attributing the simultaneous pursuit of hard- and soft-line policies to leadership indecision and *ad hoc* responses. J. Arch Getty and O. Naumov, *The Road to Terror* (New Haven, 1999), p. 102.
48. RGASPI, 558/11/1117/49–50.
49. RGASPI, 558/1/5088/118–118ob.
50. RGASPI, 558/1/3087.
51. RGASPI, 558/1/4572/1.
52. RGASPI, 558/11/1493/147.
53. RGASPI, 558/1/3118.
54. RGASPI, 17/163/1020/56–63.
55. RGASPI, 17/163/1020/12.
56. RGASPI, 17/163/1048/26.
57. RGASPI, 17/163/1238/199–204.
58. Banac (ed.) *Diary of Georgi Dimitrov*, p. 105.
59. RGASPI, 558/11/1479/54–5.
60. See also his toast at the reception of railway workers when he described Stalin as the 'first engine-driver of the Soviet Union', *Pravda*, 2 August 1935. For more evidence of Kaganovich as a major contributor to the Stalin cult, see R. W. Davies *et al.* (eds) *The Stalin–Kaganovich Correspondence 1931–1936* (New Haven, Conn., 2003).
61. RGASPI, 558/11/1086/37–44.
62. RGASPI, 558/11/786/106.
63. RGASPI, 17/163/1101/137–8.
64. RGASPI, 17/163/1105/58–9.
65. This was in line with Bolshevik tradition. See J. Brooks, 'Revolutionary Lives: Public Identities in *Pravda* during the 1920s' in S. White (ed.) *New Directions in Soviet History* (Cambridge, 1991), pp. 27–40.

66. *Molodaya gvardiya*, 1939, no. 12. See the chapter by Catriona Kelly in this volume for examples of how Stalin was presented to young people.
67. RGASPI, 558/11/1121/24.
68. RGASPI, 558/11/1499/39–54.
69. On N. Lakoba's role in promoting the cult in Georgia, see M. Kun, *Stalin: An Unknown Portrait* (Budapest, 2003), pp. 47–51.
70. Both Miklós Kun and Evgenii Gromov refer to a similar example from 1950, when Stalin refused to allow the publication in Russian of P. Kapanadze's *Recollections of the Childhood and Youth of the Leader*, on the basis that they contained fabricated and inaccurate information. The memoirs had previously been published in Georgian. See Kun, *Stalin: An Unknown Portrait*, p. 7 and E. Gromov, *Stalin. Vlast' i iskusstvo* (Moscow, 1998), p. 23.
71. RGASPI, 558/11/787/2.
72. RGASPI, 558/11/1495/113–16.
73. RGASPI, 558/11/92/22–3.
74. RGASPI, 558/11/92/81. A report had appeared in *Pravda* on 27 October.
75. RGASPI, 558/11/1499/4–6.
76. RGASPI, 558/11/1494/6–10.
77. El'-Registan, 'Neobychainoe puteshestvie', *Molodaya gvardiya*, 10–12 (1935); RGASPI, 558/11/1494/21–5.
78. RGASPI, 558/11/207/22–3.
79. Van Ree makes a convincing case for Stalin's Marxist convictions in *The Political Thought of Joseph Stalin*.
80. On the impersonal nature of Mátyás Rákosi's cult, see the chapter in this volume by Balázs Apor.
81. See Maksimenkov, 'Kul't. Zametki o slovakh-simvolakh v sovetskom politicheskom kul'ture', p. 42, for more on this point.

3

'A Very Modest Man': Béla Illés, or How to Make a Career through the Leader Cult

Árpád von Klimó

Among all nineteenth-century political ideologies, socialism was the one to focus most on 'classes', 'masses' and other abstract historical and social entities and developments. Yet it also became the ideology of a political movement that produced a great number of 'personality cults'. It can be hypothesised that it was the high level of abstraction of the socialist system of ideas that fostered the emergence of the cults of certain individuals. Narratives of heroic revolutionaries or martyrs that suffered for mankind could impersonate the 'structures' that promised to overcome the sufferings of humanity. The cults of communist leaders should therefore be understood as secularised forms of religious rituals. Here we define 'cult of personality' as a sum of symbolic actions and texts which express and ritualise the particular meanings ascribed to a particular person in order to incorporate an imagined community.

In Hungary, in the period of 1948–53, the propaganda machine of the communist party used all available mass media to disseminate the leader cult of Mátyás Rákosi throughout all layers of society, from the party, army, mass organisations, universities, schools, towns and villages. One man played a central role in this process from the very beginning. He was deeply involved in the propagation of the 'historical role' of the Red Army that liberated Hungary, the idealisation of the Soviet Union and sovietised Russian culture and the promotion of the cults of Rákosi and Stalin. This person was Béla Illés (1895–1974), a writer who played an active, though minor, role in the Hungarian communist movement, and who experienced the Bolshevik and Stalinist transformation of Russian society during his exile in Moscow between 1924 and 1944. Through analysing his career during the Second World War, in post-war and in Stalinist Hungary, we analyse how his ideological and political goals and strategies merged with his personal ambitions and career opportunities. We can understand the functioning, the successes and disasters of Stalinist leader cults better, if we look more closely at the individuals that participated in their creation and propagation. Here we focus on Illés' activities as a member of the Hungarian–Soviet Society of Culture, and of different editorial boards of literary journals, and as a writer who wrote (and sold) a great number of propagandistic books during the Stalinist years in Hungary. In this context we analyse the role of his personal network that promoted his career.

Paradoxically enough, even Stalinist literary critics never took Illés' work seriously or regarded it as an important contribution to Hungarian literature. For this reason this chapter is primarily based on the oeuvre of Illés and on official sources and texts. Since the location and fate of Illés' personal documents are both obscure, primary sources from party and state archives are only occasionally used.

The narrative construction of the cult of Rákosi: passages from a novel

> 'A Soviet airplane!' shouted some hundred Hungarians. 'One of us, ours!' shouted five or six honvéds [soldiers].[1] A package fell out of the plane. As it fell, it broke up into thousands and thousands of pieces. Thousands and thousands of white pigeons were gliding over the heads of the prisoners of war. The pigeons began to descend, swinging and coming nearer and nearer to the Hungarians. 'Leaflets!' 'A message!' In fact – the Soviet Armed Forces Command sent a message to the honvéds. Mátyás Rákosi's words headed the message of this Soviet message: 'Every prisoner-of-war must now take position, must decide. Either, to support the enemies of the people, the system that is corrupting the land and makes him suffer, too, or, to stir up his brothers, the Hungarians at home, and help them to fight for the way he found during his own sufferings, the way that leads away from the misery to the salvation of the fatherland . . .' The airplane had disappeared long since, when they read the message. Nevertheless they asked the airplane to take with it their answer to the message. First a few and then hundreds and thousands of people shouted after the airplane that had disappeared into the light: 'We know the way! We understood you! Bring us weapons!' 'Weapons! Weapons!'[2]

> 'A very modest man is Rákosi' repeated S. 'Whoever meets him for the first time, talks to him for the first time, wonders at the fact that this man, about whom he heard so much, is so modest. Rákosi asked us about our families, whether we had enough food or if we liked the Russian *Makhorka* [tobacco]. He looked around in our camp, looked into the books we got from the library. He told the storeroom administrator to give István Nagy new boots, and he told the doctor to put some iodine or other medicine on Péter Kiss's shaving cuts. Rákosi is a modest man like me, thinks every Hungarian soldier, and he speaks, acts, talks about what hurts him, what he fears, what he hopes, what he likes to have. Rákosi

> is listening carefully, he only speaks once in a while. He asks something, agrees or disagrees. And when the poor Hungarian, who didn't dare to open his mouth at home pours out his heart and says what he never dared to tell anyone before, he thinks that Rákosi is a modest man like himself . . . And then, suddenly, he feels, and he wonders, that he himself is not the same man he used to be. He is not so frail, not so helpless, and not so dull any more. When he confided to Rákosi his misery and his desires, the feeling of being new-born again came over him. He begins to believe that from now on everything will be different, and he begins to understand that everything must change, and that he must not be quiet but shout, not wait but act . . . When S. remembered meeting Rákosi, they would ask him: 'And when will we meet Rákosi? And when can we talk with Mátyás Rákosi?', then S. would answer: 'He also works for you.'[3]

Béla Illés' 684-page long novel, entitled *Honfoglalás*, was awarded the Kossuth Prize in 1955, the highest prize of the Hungarian People's Republic at the time. The title *Honfoglalás* means the 'conquest and settling of the fatherland'. The concept was frequently used in Hungarian political language to refer to the first conquest and settling of the Danube basin in the ninth century by the Hungarian tribes. The word, however, is also often used to describe a radical, wide ranging political and social change, and it thus became a metaphor to describe a new national beginning. In the novel, it refers to the land-reform of 1945 that led to the dispossession of the former land-owning classes, the aristocracy and the clergy. The concept also bears a religious connotation, drawing a parallel between the return of the Israelites to their promised land and the Hungarian conquest of the Danube basin. The concept was frequently used with this subtext during the Millennarian festival of 1896, when the Hungarian kingdom celebrated the 1000th anniversary of its existence. According to Illés, the historical 'liberation' of the Hungarian people – in fact the conquest of the country by Soviet troops in 1944–45 – was to be considered a historical event similar in significance to the conquest of the fatherland more than a thousand years earlier. Thus, he interpreted the consequences of World War II and the Potsdam treaty within a wider national historical context. The Soviet occupation ought therefore to be understood as the logical and unavoidable consequence of centuries of Hungarian history, seen as a series of wars of independence against recurrent German and Western assaults.[4]

The monumental epic tells three parallel stories. The first story narrates the adventures of a group of Hungarian soldiers held captive by the Soviets after the battle at the river Don, in 1943. In the prisoners' camp, a Hungarian-born Soviet officer, Major B., tells them the 'truth' about the war: they have been betrayed by their corrupt officers and the Hungarian aristocracy who collaborated with the Nazis to suppress the Hungarian people. Some of the soldiers decide to become partisans and fight side by side with

Soviet troops liberating their homeland – a heroic undertaking that is defined in the novel as the beginning of a new *honfoglalás*. In the second story, Illés tells his own adventures as a Soviet propaganda officer. He turns out to be the 'beloved' bald-headed Major B. mentioned in the first story. A third subplot of the novel focuses on Hungarian officers, greedy, corrupt and cynical aristocrats, only interested in their personal well-being, and ready to sell their fatherland to the brutal and cruel Germans or to the Anglo-American allies.

For the narrative construction of the leader cult, Illés had to represent the 'Hungarian people' as modest and simple characters with a child-like innocence. The Hungarian prisoners-of-war were in a difficult situation. They were starving, and illness and death were common. But in their deepest misery, salvation – in the guise of Soviet tanks – was near. These innocent souls were purged of their sins by their communist advisors and Soviet teachers. They entered a new world hierarchically structured around a centre, where the ultimate truth was protected by the party. Illés' novel followed the example of the typical plot construction of Socialist Realist novels, as outlined by Katerina Clark.[5] The prisoners-of-war, with the guidance of a mentor figure, go through an initiation process, a 'rite of passage', during which they learn about the higher-order knowledge of Marxism-Leninism. In the end they all become integrated into a new collective entity, the 'great family' of Stalinism. This typical structure of the Stalinist educational novel of the 1930s was now transferred to Hungary. At the beginning of Illés' story, the modest Hungarian soldiers could not speak or move because they were not used to being able to speak or move without being beaten by their aristocratic masters. The Hungarian people, consisting of peasants, workers and 'progressive' intellectuals, were still in the grip of reactionary forces. Unlike their ancestors, they were given the historical opportunity to liberate themselves – with the help of the Red Army – through becoming true communists.

Illés narrated the process of transformation from being innocent and ignorant, to becoming true members of the Hungarian nation as a form of conversion. The Word representing the Holy Ghost (pigeon) came from out of the mouth of Mátyás Rákosi. Just like Hitler in Leni Riefenstahl's film *Triumph des Willens* (*Triumph of the Will*), the leader enters the scene from 'heaven', in an airplane.[6] In the beginning only few could understand the Word and thereby realise that the Soviet airplane was 'their' airplane, too (the Soviet Union being the fatherland of all proletarians), but then hundreds and thousands understood it and started dancing in a kind of holy madness, shouting to the airplane that had long disappeared. In the second passage, cited from Illés' book, when Major B. tells the prisoners-of-war about his experience of meeting Rákosi, they sense a certain aura emanating from the distant leader. When the Major spoke of Him, everyone 'held his breath'. The 'wise and beloved Hungarian leader' Rákosi was a 'modest man', a man of the people: he was the people and the people were him.[7] Illés dissolved the difference between the imagined community of the Hungarian nation and its leader: the leader and the led were one and the same. Rákosi was portrayed as a 'good, holy king' who comes down to his people, listens to them, cares for them, and heals their wounds. This 'king' has two bodies too: 'even if he is not here, he is still here'.[8] Illés used religious and nationalist subtexts and metaphors together with a simplified Stalinist class-'analysis' in his popular construction of the 'new' conquest and settling of Hungary led by its wise and beloved leader. He was fulfilling his duty as a faithful 'party-soldier' fighting, with pen in hand.

The relationship of Illés and Rákosi: constructed biographies, parallel careers

Following the Socialist Realist master narrative, Illés wrote highly artificial and fabricated novels, but at the same time he drew on his own life experiences. It was widely known that the 'bald-headed' Major Géza Bálint in the novel was himself. How did he represent himself? He painted the picture of his *alter ego* as lazy, in a richly humorous depiction. Major Bálint is a man who devoted his life to the communist party, but who is also 'mad', as one of his Soviet superiors puts it. The Major is characterised as very emotional, full of ideas and fantasies. He is both an artist and a fighter for the communist cause who devotes his creative energy to the party and to the 'true Hungarian nation'; to the abstract unities that were, according to the logic of the leader cult, embodied by Mátyás Rákosi. The relationship of the 'crazy' propaganda officer and the great and wise leader is also illustrated by another scene in the novel. After Bálint/Illés gives a speech about Rákosi in a church, and a soldier asks whether they will have a chance to meet the leader, Bálint answers:

> 'I can't say,' said Bálint. 'But I hope, I believe, yes, I know, that you will experience personally the work of his hand.' In the church of Dawidowka the silence – as after the rumble of guns at the front – could be heard.[9]

Again, the mention of Rákosi's name creates a kind of silence, a holy atmosphere, which makes the nature of the relationship of leader and writer clear: Rákosi is Christ and Illés is his prophet.

As is known from Rákosi's memoirs and Illés' letters written to him after 1945, the Hungarian dictator and the writer enjoyed a good relationship before the Second World War. For instance, Illés is a frequently recurring figure in Rákosi's memoirs, when the author reflects about his agitation activity during the war at the front, and in the camps of Hungarian prisoners-of-war. Rákosi writes very positively about Illés and even recalls several anecdotes involving the writer too.[10] At the same time, the description of

Rákosi's relationship with Illés in the memoirs has a strong paternalistic overtone. The author emphasises that when he first met the 'young' Illés in Moscow in the early 1920s he 'helped him wherever he could'. Similarly, when writing about his arrival to Moscow in 1940, Rákosi emphasises the strong support and inspiration which he provided to the 'desperate' writer.[11]

Rákosi and Illés shared many similar experiences in life. The communist politician was only three years older than the writer; both were born into Jewish families from the Hungarian periphery and moved to Budapest shortly after the turn of the century. Before they fought as volunteers in the First World War, they gained higher education: Illés as student of the Budapest Faculty of Law, Rákosi at the College for Foreign Trade. Illés, who wrote the official biography of Rákosi in 1952, tried to paint the leader's social background as a little more 'proletarian' and 'working class', emphasising the 'misery' of the family and the commitment of the 'hard working father'.[12] Illés also omitted to mention the Jewish background of both Rákosi and himself. He only reflected on this issue publicly in the early 1960s. According to his autobiographical account, his father once warned him that 'to become a Hungarian is more than just a Jewish business. The real man stays true to the flag, to his oath, even if they beat him on his head with the flagpole.'[13] The father's warning is strikingly similar to the sufferings endured by the ideal communist hero in Socialist Realist novels. In order to achieve conversion, he has to suffer, or even sacrifice himself, for the higher truth embodied by the abstract symbol of the imagined community (nation, class, party, humanity, etc.). Illés represented his own conversion according to this Stalinist pattern, itself influenced by earlier narratives of the conversion of saints and national heroes. In his autobiography, and also in his biographical text on Rákosi, Illés also emphasised both his and Rákosi's early nationalist 'vocations'. Already in their early childhood they were portrayed as enthusiasts of national liberation cults, such as the one around Ferenc Rákóczi, the eighteenth-century freedom fighter, and around the heroes of the 1848 revolution.[14]

Both Illés and Rákosi were active participants in the Hungarian Soviet Republic of 1919. Their contributions, however, were exaggerated retrospectively, according to the general pattern of official party functionaries' biographies. After 1919, their paths began to diverge. Rákosi was imprisoned by the Horthy regime in 1925, and he was only released from prison in 1940. After leaving for the Soviet Union he became the top functionary of the Hungarian party organisation in Moscow. Illés lived in exile in Vienna and in his native region around Kassa (Košice) which became a part of Czechoslovakia after 1920. In 1923 he moved to the Soviet Union, and suddenly, he became a 'friend' of the Bolshevik literary establishment: Furmanov, Fadeev, Alexei Tolstoy, Gorky, Sholokhov, Ostrovskii and Leonov. Photographs in his official biography indicate that he tried his best to be portrayed with as many famous communist writers and sympathizers as possible: Quasimodo, G. B. Shaw, Anna Seghers, Karin Michaelis, Johannes R. Becher. Alone, he wanted to be portrayed as a Soviet soldier, even long before he joined the Red Army. After the Second World War Illés would often wear a Soviet uniform, particularly after his promotion to colonel of the Red Army in 1949. Later, after 1956, Illés loved to be portrayed as the pipe-smoking 'Uncle Béla', a popular anecdote-teller, who cultivated 'ancient' and 'authentic' Hungarian folklore. During this last stage of his career, Illés often mentioned his ambitions to become the twentieth-century communist version of such popular nineteenth-century Hungarian novelists as Kálmán Mikszáth and Mór Jókai.

At the time of the publication of his first novel in 1916, Illés had already written hundreds of articles in German and Hungarian in several émigré newspapers and magazines. His literary skills and his good connections paved the way for a party career that always remained dependent upon the actual needs of culture politics and propaganda. Unlike Rákosi, Illés never held an executive position in the party administration, despite the fact that his activities as an artist were strongly tied to changing ideological positions. From this perspective his literary career can be divided into three sub-periods: before Stalinism, during Stalinism, and after Stalinism. Illés had already become a political writer with his second novel, *Spartacus élete* (*The Life of Spartacus*), published in 1919. In 1929, his first epos, *Ég a Tisza* (*Burning Theiss*), appeared in the Soviet Union. The book contained a foreword by Béla Kun, which had to be left out in later editions, only to be included again after 1956.[15] This book treated the 'heroic' struggles of the Communist Party of Hungary in the 'revolution' of 1919.[16] The plot gave a certain interpretation of historical events from the perspective of the Communist Party, but it was still far less schematic than the works that appeared in the 1930s and 1940s. By the time of publication, Illés had already become a successful party functionary in the field of literature. In 1927 he was elected – with the assistance of Furmanov – as one of the secretaries of the Soviet Writers' Union and a secretary of the Revolutionary Proletarian Writers' Association (RAPP) in Moscow. When Stalin dissolved the association in 1932 and Socialist Realism became the only acceptable way of writing, Illés became one of the executives of this new policy.[17] At the First Soviet Writers' Congress where the centralised, controlled, and collectivised version of literary life in Stalin's empire was officially introduced, Illés also gave a speech. Until 1940, he contributed actively in the attempts to transform literature into a tool of Stalinist propaganda. Although he survived the purges of the 1930s, he fell out of grace. In 1940, he lost his party membership for some time. After the German attack on the Soviet Union joined the army as a private. After the battle of Moscow his officer's title was restored and his party membership was renewed as well.

After all the sacrifices he had to endure for the sake of communism, Illés had good reason to hope for a rapid career in the 'new', post-war Hungary.

Conditions for this were good. He was a relatively well-known Soviet and Hungarian communist writer, an officer of the Soviet Army, the editor-in-chief of the Hungarian newspaper of the Red Army (*Új Szó* – New Word), and he also had good connections with Rákosi and other party leaders and also with some important functionaries of the Soviet Union and the Red Army.

Béla Illés and the Sovietisation of Hungarian literature (1948–53)

Illés was far from friendly with József Révai, the chief ideologue of the party since 1935, and was not respected by Hungary's leading communist intellectual György Lukács either. Despite the individual opinion of the two most important figures of Hungarian post-war literary politics, he was still necessary to the party, as a popular – and also loyal – writer who could contribute to the task of Stalinising Hungarian culture. Besides his voluminous epic work, he wrote countless articles, essays and anecdotes, in which he idealised and humanised the Soviet system, its heroes and leaders, and the Stalinist version of 'Russian' culture. Through his largely invented or stylised 'memories' and reminiscences, he tried to paint warm and sympathetic portraits of Gorky, Furmanov, Alexei Tolstoy, and other famous communists. Illés was *the* master of Socialist Realism in Hungary, whereas most of the other Hungarian writers had to learn this kind of 'skill'.

The Sovietisation of the Hungarian literary scene was not only a pedagogical process, but also a political, administrative and economic one. The main institutions and functionaries involved were the Central Board for Culture of the Hungarian Workers' Party (MDP) led by József Révai, the Ministry of Public Education (headed by Révai too), and the Ministry of Culture. On the basis of the Soviet model, a Hungarian Writers', Union (*Írószövetség*) was founded in 1948; it was in fact a combination of trade union and control organ. Writers who did not become members of the Writers' Union were unlikely to be published. Although the president of the organisation was József Darvas, Illés also had a seat in the executive committee. After the so-called coalition period (1945–48), and as a result of the establishment of the dictatorship of the Hungarian Workers' Party in 1948/9, literary journals and reviews were centralised. Most of the journals were banned, and a new literary journal, the *Irodalmi Újság* was launched in November 1950. Similarly to its Soviet model, the *Literaturnaya Gazeta*, it became the official paper of the Writers' Union. Being the most experienced Hungarian Socialist Realist writer, Illés became the first editor-in-chief of the journal. In 1951 at the First Congress of Hungarian Writers, Révai outlined the principles of Socialist Realism and condemned all deviations from the only tolerable way of writing in the new state. The definition of Socialist Realism, however, remained relatively vague.[18] According to Révai, literary works had to be based on *partisanship* (a criterion determined by the party according to current tactical necessities); had to have a socialist content (glorification of the heroes of industrialisation and collectivisation or the heroic struggles of progressive forces of the past against reactionary enemies); and it had also to be popular (by this, most functionaries understood a kind of nationalist and/or folklorist painting).

Stalinist literary policy in Hungary consisted of a combination of administrative, institutional, and repressive measures (against potential or actual deviants) and certain privileges (dished out to the followers of Socialist Realism). As Socialist Realism remained largely undefined, a great number of writers found it difficult to write in accordance with the vague and often contradictory demands of the new system. This might partly explain the high percentage of Soviet texts imported during this time. The number of translations from Russian into Hungarian, in total and as a percentage of all translations into Hungarian, increased during Stalinism and decreased in the Kádár years.[19] Whilst the number of translations from Russian works and the number of their copies amounted to more than half of all translations into Hungarian between 1945 and 1959, the proportion of Russian translations and the number of copies of translated Russian books dropped in the next 15 years drastically to a sixth and a fifth, respectively. During the Stalinist period (1949–61) Soviet classics of Socialist Realism were printed in larger numbers than Hungarian books.[20]

Illés as a Hungarian Soviet writer was not only one of the main promoters of the Sovietisation of Hungarian literature, alongside with Révai, Lukács and others, but he also profited substantially from it. A writer in a capitalist system interested in maximising the sales of his own books could only dream of the position Illés held at the time. He could influence both supply and demand.

As one of the founders of the Society for Hungarian-Soviet Culture in 1945 and a member of its presidium, he wielded a strong influence on the decisions of the association. The society ordered many of his texts, for example, *The Soviet Army: the Armed Force of Freedom and Peace* (1950), to be published in large print-runs. The weekly magazine of the organisation, *Jövendő* (*Future*), also published enthusiastic reviews of Illés' books.[21] The same holds true for most of the newspapers and journals that appeared in the Rákosi era. In a ranking found in the documents of the Central Department of Literature/Publishing Houses of the Ministry of Popular Education, Illés was classed second amongst all authors of books for young people.[22]

Illés, being a Soviet officer, and a high-ranking Muscovite, was beyond criticism. His position was also protected by his network of connections with other functionaries and leaders of the party, especially by his good relationship with Rákosi. Although Rákosi was not particularly well known as a patron of members of the literary intelligentsia – this was Révai's prerogative –, he certainly intervened in Illés' favour on occasion. When Illés appealed to Rákosi – even for the merest trifles – the leader would not hesitate to help him. For instance, because of Rákosi's influence, one of the few large apartments in Budapest was bestowed upon the writer, as he had requested. The dictator also paid attention to the visits of Illés' son, Vladimir, from Moscow to Budapest, and he even took care of the repair of the heating in the writer's home.[23] In exchange, Illés became one of the most active promoters of the cult of the Hungarian party leader. Besides the novel cited above, he was trusted to write the official biography of the dictator, and he also contributed to the literary anthology published for the occasion of Rákosi's 60th birthday in 1952.[24] In the anthology volume Illés had the privilege of representing the link between Lenin and Rákosi in literary form.[25] In his short story about the first meeting of Lenin and Rákosi in 1920, after the fall of the Hungarian Soviet Republic, the relationship of the Soviet leader and Rákosi is described as a traditional mentor–disciple relationship, where 'the mighty eagle taught the young eagle how to fly.'[26]

The Rákosi–Illés relationship can be described as a patron–client relationship of the Stalinist type.[27] Illés was a keen supporter of the Sovietisation of Hungarian cultural life and an important constructor of the Rákosi cult. In return, due to the personal intervention of Rákosi, he was granted scarce goods, such as housing, and other privileges. The fact that he and his patron even had certain 'affective ties' (a kind of a friendship) also contributed to the remarkable profit which the writer gained from his relationship with the Hungarian party leader.

Illés' status as a privileged writer was further strengthened by the fact that he also had a good relationship with another important member of the political elite, Mihály Farkas.[28] Farkas and Illés were old friends. Farkas began his party career in the party unit of Kassa (Košice) in 1920, when Illés was working there as a propaganda activist. After the appointment of Farkas as Minister of Defence in September 1948, Illés was promoted to the rank of colonel of the Hungarian army.[29] Farkas, who was a Muscovite too, and together with Rákosi and Ernő Gerő a member of the ruling *troika*, attempted to restructure the Hungarian armed forces along the lines of the Soviet model and tried to integrate Hungary into the Soviet military system. In aiming for this goal, he was supported by the Soviet advisers and most of the Muscovites, including Illés.[30] In return, many of Illés' novels and short stories were published because of the demands of the Hungarian People's Army. The documents of the Ministry of Popular Education show the striking numbers of copies and print-runs of Illés' books and brochures ordered by the Ministry of Defence, between 1949 and 1952.[31]

Due to his influential 'patrons' in the highest political circles, Illés became one of the best-selling Hungarian writers during the Rákosi years. The publishing house Révai printed his book, *Songs of Weapons and Heroes*, in 1950 and circulated it in 10,000 copies, a number that was only surpassed by Tolstoy's *War and Peace*, which sold 13,000 copies. In this year, only 20 per cent of all editions surpassed 10,000 copies.[32] The print-run of his epic about the Hungarian Revolution of 1919, which was first published in Russian in 1941 and in German in 1945, exceeded one million copies. Illés also profited from the fact that his works were regarded as politically safe as Soviet literature, which meant that nobody would dare to censor it. Illés was particularly brazen during his management of the publishers Athenaeum (founded 1842), and, before 1945, Hungary's biggest publishing house. During his tenure as manager at Athenaeum, no less than three collections of his short stories were printed by the house. The unique position of Béla Illés as Hungary's 'most popular writer' lasted, however, only for few years: his reign did not survive the collapse of Rákosi's dictatorship.[33] Whereas 14 new titles of Illés were published between 1949 and 1953, only three new titles saw the light after 1953 (1955, 1956, 1958). It seems clear that Illés profited remarkably from his relationship with Rákosi and Farkas, who favoured him as kings favour their courtiers.

Changing literary politics in Hungary (1953–61) and the decay of Illés' career

When Rákosi's position was severely shaken after Stalin's death in 1953, the lucky star of Illés began to sink, too. In the Writers' Union, the issue of the 'mistakes' made during his presidency began to be raised. For example, Lajos Kassák, a veteran of the avant-garde in Central Europe, who was stigmatized as being a 'leftist' in 1948, said bitterly during a discussion:

> With regard to the work of comrade Illés I have to say that he is still like a stranger in Hungary, because he didn't live here for 25 years. But if you didn't live here and don't know the literary problems of this country, if you don't know how things have to be handled in Hungary, why have you been elected president?[34]

Illés had to step down, but he still remained a member of the presidium. After the events of October 1956, especially in the mirror of the writers' revolt, he was also needed by the new power elite, as one of the few remaining faithful party members. A few years later, however, he was no longer indispensable, and as one of the chief representatives of Stalinist literary policy, he became an unpleasant burden on the new party leadership. In a meeting of the Politburo on 1 April 1959, János Kádár said of Illés:

> We have to treat very seriously the fact and punish those who are telling lies or fooling the party and the government. Béla Illés has no right to do so, he wrote in a certain short story, that he sits in his cold room with his coat on. But the party had his heating repaired long ago.[35]

The accusation might seem awkward, but Kádár simply questioned Illés' privileged status, making it clear that the party can give, but, at the same time, the party can also take away. At the same meeting, Kádár also talked about the great 'damage' which the Muscovite writers had caused to Hungarian literature by their use of paternalist relationships: 'For 14 years in the Soviet Union, works of Hungarian literature were only published if certain friends of the writers could influence the publishers.'[36]

It seems clear that the new leader wanted the party to exercise exclusive control over the export of literary products to the Soviet Union and hoped that this would put an end to the abuses of patron relationships by the Muscovite authors. As a result of the shift in the literary policy of the new party leadership, Illés gradually disappeared from the public and political sphere after 1961 – though a long illness also contributed to his withdrawal. The new political and literary environment, which had caused Illés' dismissal, argued that the context of the cult of Rákosi and the Soviet Union, had allowed certain writers to sell literary works that would otherwise have been impossible to sell.

Melinda Kalmár, in her book on the ideology of the early Kádár regime, argues that literature lost its leading role in the cultural policy of the communist dictatorship after the revolution of 1956.[37] Her argument was based on the analysis of discussions at Politburo meetings, in the beginning of 1957, where members of the new leadership criticised many of the 'wrongdoings' – literary politics included – of the Rákosi era. Kádár's criticism, for example, emphasised the lack of 'modernity' of the cultural policy and propaganda of the Stalinist leadership in Hungary. According to Kádár, Révai, the chief ideologue of the Rákosi years, who was also responsible for education, humanities and literature, did not sufficiently exploit the possibilities of the modern mass media, and, at the same time, he was not sufficiently concerned with 'the concrete Hungarian situation'.[38] (Kassák had brought the same accusation against Illés in 1953.) Kádár was right to point out that Révai, like Lukács, belonged to a traditional intellectual elite that understood 'culture' in conventional terms, as the product of literati and artists. Like the German communist writer and German Democratic Republic culture minister Johannes R. Becher, Révai was also convinced that literature could change the mind of the masses and educate the people. This aesthetic apprehension of ideology that characterised Stalinism – reified as 'Socialist Realism' – was described by Kalmár as 'didactic and cultic'. When the failings of Stalinist literary policy became visible and the party began to disintegrate ideologically – a process already under way before Stalin's death – the Writers' Union gradually turned into a public forum for discussions, and later, in 1956, into an alternative public sphere. This process was a response to the centralisation of culture, which Kádár had also claimed to be dangerous. In contrast to the practices of literary politics in the Rákosi era, he would rely more heavily on indirect and informal – but also more efficient – means of controlling published opinions. He also showed more interest than his predecessors in the press, radio and television, as useful tools to create mass loyalty to the political system. This clearly indicates that, despite the crucial role the press, radio and other forms of mass communication (theatre, film, manifestations, demonstrations, etc.) played in promoting the cult of Rákosi and other communist leaders, literature always remained the privileged object of control by party officials. To prevent a disaster similar to that caused by Stalinist literary policy – in which Illés had been one of the main actors – the Kádár-era pushed literature into the background. A certain plurality of opinions was even allowed – signified by the casual publication of 'critical' texts – but these opinions, nevertheless, were orchestrated in such a way as not to harm Kádár's modernized dictatorship.

Conclusions

Recalling the passages of Illés' epic concerning the narrative of Soviet–Hungarian 'liberation' and 'settlement', in the context of the scarce information we have regarding the career of the writer in the Soviet Union and in Stalinist Hungary, we might be puzzled by the fact that the differences between fictional and factual texts are not always as visible as expected. Illés was skilled in the art of stylising his own life, blurring the borders of his biography, his fictional texts and his political activity. In this respect, he was, in fact, *the* master of Socialist Realism in the field of art and in reality.[39] If we understand Stalinism as an attempt to create a new civilisation, a 'New Man', a new relationship between ideology, politics, art, and everyday life, we may understand more clearly the actual functions of leader cults in Soviet-type societies. We may also be able to find an answer to the strange, 'archaic', forms of much Stalinist propaganda.

The extensive, total and boundless claims the Communist Party and the Soviet government under Stalin demanded from individuals and social groups generated a great void, since these claims were not founded on a reality as total and stimulating, as the party had promised. This void endangered the legitimacy of the system, as Kádár astutely recognised after 1956. Therefore, the gap between the ideal world still to come and the socio-political reality of the present had to be bridged by the creation and proliferation of usable myths, promoted by 'ideological fighters', like Illés. Among these myths we find philosophical and historical narratives of the liberation of mankind, nationalist and sometimes even ethnic ideas, promises of political salvation, fairy tales of invincible heroes (or sometimes heroines), superhuman sufferings and triumphs of Stalinist *Übermenschen*, in short: the fantastic *Gesamtkunstwerk* of the wise and infallible party, its God-like leaders and their prophets.[40] But the extensive appeal to charismatic and traditional ideas of legitimacy was not only the consequence of the emptiness created by the totalising claims of Stalinist culture. It was also enforced by the Stalinist mental imprisonment or self-imprisonment. Stalinist discourse did not only influence the thoughts and deeds of the Stalinist functionaries and even their victims, Stalinist language also functioned as a communicative prison that limited the scope of what could be thought and said. Inside this prison, borders between functionally differentiated systems, institutions and disciplines like the book market, art, literature, historiography, politics, ideology, began to dissolve, because everything was subordinated to the service of the great idea, as defined by the wise and infallible leader. The nullification of modern differentiation and the blurring of functional borders paved the way for other 'archaic' social and cultural phenomena, such as corruption, clientelism, and patronage. Illés – like many other writers of the era – made extensive use of the great amount of social capital accumulated during his long career in the Communist Party since 1919.

A system closed in on itself to such an extent would sooner or later collide with its environment. The Stalin years were marked by a brutal 'civil war', which party and the state fought against the majority of society which could not be integrated into the system. Long before 1956, violence and terror characterised everyday life in Hungary – Illés could interpret this only as an expression of war between Good and Evil, between his imagined 'future' and 'past'.

Notes

1. 'Honvéd' means home-guard. Hungarian soldiers are called 'honvéd' since the revolutionary army of 1849 was founded. Illés uses this term also to highlight the 'national' character of his heroes.
2. Béla Illés, *Honfoglalás* (Budapest, 1955), p. 377. All translations are my own.
3. Ibid., pp. 369–70.
4. The partisan group representing the heroes of the Hungarian nation in the book is therefore named 'Rákóczi', referring to the Hungarian prince who fought in the eighteenth century against the Habsburgs and who – more importantly – was occasionally allied to the Russian tsar.
5. Katerina Clark, *The Soviet Novel: History as Ritual* (3rd edition Bloomington, 2000), pp. 159–77.
6. It is interesting to note that in Mikhail Chiaureli's film, *The Fall of Berlin* (1949), Stalin also enters the last scene in a silver airplane.
7. 'He knows what the poor people suffer from, he knows it very well. He feels what hurts us – oh, how he feels it!' Béla Illés, *Honfoglalás,* p. 211.
8. Ibid., p. 148.
9. Béla Illés, *Honfoglalás*, p. 72.
10. Mátyás Rákosi, *Visszaemlékezések 1940–1956*, ed. István Feitl, Márta Gellériné Lázár and Levente Sipos (Budapest, 1997), pp. 80–1, 88, 101.
11. Ibid., pp. 80–1.
12. *Mátyás Rákosi – Sein Leben in Bildern* (Budapest, 1952); Béla Illés, *Für die Freiheit des ungarischen Volkes. Aus dem Leben des Genossen Mátyás Rákosi* (Zürich, 1952). For a more critical biography from a late state-socialist perspective see János Nemes, 'Rákosi Mátyás', *Társadalmi Szemle,* 38/1 (1983), pp. 73–85.
13. Quoted in András Diószegi, *Illés Béla alkotásai és vallomásai tükrében* (Budapest, 1966), p. 25.

14. Illés claimed that reading the works of Gorky as a child had had a profound impact on him. Béla Illés, 'Selbstbiographie', *Hamburger Volkszeitung*, 24 October 1922.
15. On the fate of the Hungarian communist Béla Kun see William J. Chase, *Enemies Within the Gates? The Comintern and the Stalinist Repression, 1934–1939* (New Haven, 2001), pp. 293–25.
16. Béla Illés, *Brennende Theiss*, Foreword by Béla Kun, (Berlin, 1959).
17. Gábor András Szántó, 'Sztálin és a szocialista realizmus' in László Illés and József Farkas (eds) *Mítosz és utópia. Irodalom- és eszmetörténeti tanulmányok* (Budapest, 1995), pp. 304–17.
18. Lóránt Czigány, 'Lépéskényszer. Az irodalom államosítása Magyarországon', 1946–51 [1980], in id., *Nézz vissza haraggal! Államosított irodalom Magyarországon, 1948–88* (Budapest, 1990), pp. 55–9.
19. Figures taken from Alajosné Varga, *A magyar könyvkiadás 30 éve. 1945–1974* (Budapest, 1975), pp. 119–24.
20. Miklós Molnár, 'Az 'Irodalmi Újság' története', unpublished essay for the Columbia University Project on Hungary, 1957, p. 8. Special thanks to Federigo Argentieri for providing me this document.
21. An example: *Jövendő*, 12 June 1947.
22. Magyar Országos Levéltár (National Archives of Hungary-MOL) XIX-I-3-a-22d. Letter dated 9 October 1950.
23. András Kő and Lambert J. Nagy (eds) *Levelek Rákosihoz* (Budapest, 2002), pp. 138–40.
24. On the biography see Balázs Apor's contribution in this volume. Béla Illés, 'Történelmi lecke', in Pál Réz and István Vas (eds) *Magyar Írók Rákosi Mátyásról* (Budapest, 1952), pp. 80–92.
25. Rákosi personally informed Illés about the meeting in January 1952. MOL-M-KS, 276. f. 65/332. ő.e.
26. Illés, 'Történelmi lecke' p. 89. Molnár's memory seems to have failed him when he wrote in 1957 that Rákosi needed a close link with Lenin to be constructed *after* 1953, in order to overshadow his now infamous title 'Stalin's best Hungarian disciple'. Molnár, 'Az 'Irodalmi Újság' története', p. 26.
27. For patronage relations in the Soviet Union see Sheila Fitzpatrick, 'Intelligentsia and Power: Client–Patron Relationships in Stalin's Russia' in Manfred Hildermeier (ed.) *Stalinismus vor dem Zweiten Weltkrieg: Neue Wege der Forschung* (Munich, 1998), pp. 35–53.
28. Farkas belonged to the leading group of the Hungarian Party in Moscow since 1943. Katalin Petrák, *Magyarok a Szovjetunióban 1922–1945* (Budapest, 2000), p. 352.
29. Hadtörténelmi Levéltár (Military History Archives, Budapest), Honvédelmi Minisztérium (Ministry of Defence) 1949. eln. 16465sz.
30. *A béketábor magyar hadserege*, ed. Hadtörténelmi Levéltár (Budapest, 2001).
31. MOL XIX-I-3-a-23. Népművelési Minisztérium, Kiadók (1949–53).
32. Varga, *A magyar könyvkiadás 30 éve*, p. 55.
33. Friedhilde Krause, 'Nachwort' in Béla Illés, *Das Attentat* (Leipzig 1962), p. 175.
34. PIL (Politikatörténeti Intézet Levéltára), Révai papers, 793f./3 ő.e.
35. *Zárt, bizalmas, számozott. Tájékoztatáspolitika és cenzúra 1956–63* (Budapest 1999), pp. 116, 133.
36. Ibid., p. 133.
37. Melinda Kalmár, *Ennivaló és hozomány. A kora kádárizmus ideológiája* (Budapest, 1998).

38. Ibid., p. 48.
39. On the blurring of fictional and factual biographies in High Stalinism see Clark, *The Soviet Novel*, pp. 91–159.
40. The term was coined by Boris Groys, *Gesamtkunstwerk Stalin. Die gespaltene Kultur in der Sowjetunion* (Munich, 1988). For the Nietzschean influence, via Gorky, on the concepts of Socialist Realism, see Hans Günther, *Der sozialistische Übermensch. M. Gor'kij und der sowjetische Heldenmythos* (Stuttgart, 1993).

4

Leader in the Making: The Role of Biographies in Constructing the Cult of Mátyás Rákosi

Balázs Apor

Biographical representations in Stalin's time

One of the most typical manifestations of the cults of communist leaders was the extensive proliferation of their biographies. The life stories of I. V. Stalin, Mao Zedong, Mátyás Rákosi, Georgi Dimitrov, Maurice Thorez, and the rest, were published in great numbers and were used for a multitude of propaganda purposes. The lives of leaders were studied by schoolchildren, at courses and seminars in 'party schools' and throughout all levels of education. The life stories of communist leaders also became a central point of reference: journalists referred to them in their articles, speakers at mass demonstrations mentioned the 'exemplary deeds' of the party leader and academics – historians, philosophers, and so on – emphasised the particular leader's contribution to the ideological development of the party and the historical changes in the nation's existence. Biographies could be published in many distinct forms. Besides 'official biographies', which were normally published as a separate book or booklet, biographical material could also appear in the form of pamphlets, brochures or leaflets. Biographical information also became frequently incorporated into different material such as history books, general course descriptions and syllabi. Other media, apart from written texts, were also used to present the leaders' lives to the public. Motion pictures (for example, newsreels or real films) were efficient ways of conveying biographical elements – although not in Rákosi's case –, novels could be used to depict the feats of the leader, and even sound recordings (interviews) were employed to portray the events of a specific person's life.

Biographical writing had a long tradition in Soviet Russia even before Stalinist times. The usefulness of biographies in promoting particular leaders was already acknowledged by Russian political parties at the time of the revolution in 1917. Within the framework of the 'cult of the freedom fighter', Soviet parties published pamphlets, poems, songs and short biographical sketches to commemorate their own revolutionary heroes and party leaders, and, thereby to consolidate their status on the unstable Russian political scene.[1] Although, the early years of Bolshevik rule, with its focus on the masses as the driving force of history, downplayed the role of the individual, the revolution's central place in Bolshevik mythology soon led to the publication of several (auto)biographical anthologies of veterans and heroes of 1917.[2] The beginning of the 'heroic age' in the late 1920s was manifest also in the celebration of the lives of the builders of socialism (i.e. heroes of labour) through the circulation and popularisation of biographical writings. The major ideological shift of the mid-thirties towards Russian national myths and symbols provided a further boost to the utilisation of biographies.[3] The emergence of 'national Bolshevism', significantly reshuffled the pantheon of Soviet heroes, rehabilitated pre-revolutionary Russian historical figures (Ivan the Terrible, Peter the Great, Kutuzov, etc.) and resulted in the dissemination of their biographies on a large scale, especially during the war.[4]

As Katerina Clark has argued, the roots of Stalinist biographical representations can be found in nineteenth-century radical fiction, and, to a lesser extent, in medieval hagiographic writings about Orthodox saints.[5] As she points out, the structure of the plot of literary works that functioned as a model for Socialist Realist writers of the 1930s generally followed the pattern of a human biography.[6] The biographical perspective remained the core unifying theme of the Socialist Realist master plot as it crystallised in the early 1930s. A typical novel in High Stalinism was, in fact, a ritualised representation of the Marxist-Leninist interpretation of history, portrayed in biographical terms. The development of a typical hero's character in the Soviet novel of the 1930s – as the protagonist gradually acquired 'consciousness' – epitomised the Bolshevik perception of historical progress.[7] As Socialist Realism and Soviet political discourse merged in the years of High Stalinism, the biographical perspective became an essential building block of the Bolshevik historical narrative. Generally, the flow of events in historical works of the 1930s was centred around 'great events' and the lives of 'great men', as opposed to the abstract social categories of Marxism in the 1920s.[8] Furthermore, historical biography became a popular genre. The majority of works that were published in the late 1930s were in fact biographies, either of Russian historical figures (Brusilov, Peter the Great, Aleksandr Nevskii, Kutuzov, Suvorov, etc.), or of top-ranking communist leaders (Stalin, Kirov, Voroshilov, or Ordzhonikidze).[9]

Although the circulation and propagation of heroes' biographies had become a routine practice of communist propaganda in the Soviet Union and in the Eastern Bloc, the compilation and publication of 'official biographies' of Stalin and the 'lesser gods' was far from an easy task. As the biographies of Stalin, Rákosi, and even Lenin show, these projects took a rather long time and normally involved the participation of numerous high-ranking party officials in the research and editing process, and even the intervention of the party leader himself; nevertheless – in spite of the huge amount of efforts invested – some biographies were still rejected.[10] As in the cases of socialist heroes and Russian national figures, the biographies of Stalin and the 'mini-Stalins', or local party leaders, were also characterised by the fusion of (party) history and the life story of the leader. In effect, these official biographies became the personalised representations of the history of national – sometimes international – working-class movements that provided a personalised account of the local party's struggles and sacrifices. At the same time biographies also enlisted the official values and ideological tenets professed by the regime and provided an example, in an idealised form, of the behavioural patterns that it hoped to instil in the public. The official biographies of local leaders could thus be regarded as cross-sections of local party history and introductory texts to communist lore in general. But the biographies of communist leaders could also be considered as cross-sections of their own cults. The biography was a summary or outline that contained the whole range of myths about the particular leader in a simplified, condensed form. At the same time it could also function as a guide to, or map of, the cult, from which one could gain mastery of the symbols and the language of the leader cult. The official biography also fulfilled a significant legitimising function as it strove to explain why and how the leader in question became the only possible alternative capable of shepherding the country towards a better future. As the boundaries between personal life story and party history, and the leader's personality and the collective identity of the party in general, were blurred, the official biography was also meant to strengthen the legitimising basis of the regime and its governing party.

The complex character and multifunctionality of biographies were acknowledged and consciously exploited by Stalin. Numerous times in the mid-1930s he personally intervened in the matter of history-writing, advocating the role of 'great men' in advancing historical progress, and he also influenced the rehabilitation of pre-revolutionary 'tsarist' historical figures.[11] Stalin also significantly contributed to the editing process of a number of historical works – *The Short Course* chief amongst them – and some biographies (e.g. Suvorov).[12] The dictator's complex view of the importance of biographies, however, became explicit when he revised the manuscript of the second edition of his own biography in 1946. At a meeting he convened for all authors involved in the process, he claimed that 'the toiling masses and simple people cannot begin the study of Marxism-Leninism with Lenin's and Stalin's writ[ings]. They should start with the biography. The biography is a very serious issue – it has enor[mous] mean[ing] for the Marx[ist] enlight[enment] of the simple people.'[13]

The importance of the biographical perception of history in Stalinist thinking, coupled with the fact that Stalin deemed biographies crucial in mass mobilisation campaigns and in the construction of his own cult, and that Khrushchev, in his 'Secret Speech', also referred to Stalin's short biography as a significant manifestation of 'the cult of personality',[14] make a strong case for the study of biographies in the process of constructing the cult of communist leaders in the Soviet Union and the peripheries of the Soviet empire.[15]

The construction and dissemination of Rákosi's biographies

The very first biography of Mátyás Rákosi was published well before he could influence Hungarian policy-making in any significant way. The earliest book about his life, written by György Szamueli, was issued in 1935 in Moscow, with a foreword by Béla Kun.[16] Due to the Great Purges, however, Szamueli's book suffered the same fate as many other publications of the time. As the book contained numerous references to leading figures of the Comintern (Kun, for example) arrested in the years of 1936–37, it had to be re-edited, and was re-released in 1937 with a different foreword.[17] Even the name of the author had to be changed and Szamueli's identity became hidden, under the pseudonym, E. Téglás.[18] In addition to the two different editions, the first biography of Rákosi was published at the time when Soviet public discourse was teeming with heroes, and the genre of biography was the dominant form used to give them publicity. The immediate context that directly fostered the publication of a Rákosi biography was his second trial (in 1934–35) before a Budapest court, an event that generated an intense international response and thus can be compared in significance to the trial of Dimitrov in Leipzig a few years earlier.[19] Realising the high propaganda potential of the trial(s), an extensive international campaign, ostensibly for the release of Rákosi was launched from the Soviet Union; however, it also provided an excellent opportunity to further popularise communist ideals. The publication of the biography of the 'illuminating beam of light', as Henri Barbusse once called Rákosi, was an essential part of this process.[20]

One of the remarkable characteristics of Szamueli-Téglás book, as compared to the later biographies of Rákosi, was that it did not yet portray a 'father' figure of the Stalinist 'great family'.[21] Although Rákosi gradually acquired certain mentor-like characteristics in the book, and during his trials he became a 'banner' for the working class to rally around, his portrayal remains closer to that of an 'ordinary' communist hero of the time, in this case the 'hero of the Comintern'. Partly as a result of this, and partly due to the frequent references to working-class movement figures purged after 1937, the biography by Szamueli was never published again after 1945, and was not used for propaganda purposes in post-war Hungary.

Although no genuine, officially approved biography of Rákosi was available throughout the coalition years (1945–48), apart from a short interview with the communist leader on the radio recorded on 4 October 1945, the dissemination of biographical outlines of Communist Party leaders in the form of pamphlets or leaflets, or as articles in communist newspapers and/or political journals, was a standard practice of communist propaganda in these years.[22] These publications, were however, distributed primarily during intense *agitprop* periods, especially during the election campaigns of 1945, 1947 and 1949, on the initiative of central party organs.[23] For instance, proposals by the Hungarian Communist Party's (MKP) Propaganda-Agitation Department advocating the publication of biographical pamphlets of political leaders were first implemented during the 1945 election campaign. The proposal suggested the dissemination of election leaflets popularising 12 communist high ranking candidates. The leaflets would contain a picture and a short biography of the leader in question and his address to the specific constituency in which the material was distributed.[24]

There was a considerable increase in the emphasis upon the propagation of leader figures during the next election campaign in 1947. As the MKP expected a major breakthrough at the elections, it was the central decision-making body of the party, the Politburo, that decided on the most important propaganda issues. At its meeting on 31 July, besides dealing with a number of related agitation matters (e.g. the endorsement of Rákosi's speech to launch the campaign), the Politburo defined the specific propaganda tasks to be carried out by the newspapers under MKP control. It entrusted the official newspaper of the party, *Szabad Nép* (*Free People*), with the task of publishing a series of articles popularising communist leaders. According to the Politburo's guidelines, these articles would include a picture of the leader in question, a short biography and a brief description of his or her current political activity.[25] The first article to be published on the columns of the *Szabad Nép* in this series introduced Rákosi to the readers of the newspaper. In the next few days and weeks, similar articles were published on other leading figures of the MKP, including Mihály Farkas, József Révai, Erik Molnár, János Kádár, and so on. The Politburo meeting that assigned to the *Szabad Nép* the task of popularising the MKP's leaders during the election campaign also assigned a similar task to the *Magyar Nap* (*Hungarian Sun*). This weekly was ordered to publish a series of biographical writings on communist political leaders under the title: 'The lives of the MKP's leaders'.[26] Despite the instructions issued by the Politburo, the actual biographical element in the articles nevertheless remained overshadowed by the lengthy commendatory descriptions of the particular leader in question. However, the portrayal of the leaders on the pages of the *Szabad Nép* and *Magyar Nap* provides an example of the striking similarity between representations of prominent individuals in communist political discourse of the time. In all cases, the article's main focus was on the leaders' approachability, their commitment to work, and their qualities as leading politicians; images conveyed by the various authors through the use of a markedly uniform vocabulary.[27]

Just as in 1947, the publication of short biographical pieces on communist leaders also became an essential element of the electoral campaign of 1949. As these were the first elections after the communist take-over, intended to confer formal legal legitimacy on the new regime, the promotion of the party and its leaders was given priority in communist agitation. Before the campaign started, the Agitation Department of the newly formed Hungarian Workers' Party (MDP) suggested the publication of propaganda leaflets popularising the top leaders of the Party.[28] The Department proposed the distribution of 4-page-long materials containing pictures and the biography of each politician, and provided guidelines for the structure of the biographical essays. The proposal also suggested that the biographical leaflet of Rákosi should be longer and more colourful than the leaflets popularising other leaders.

Apart from utilising biographical writings for agitational purposes during periods of intense mobilisation, communist propaganda also made use of Rákosi's biographies in party education. For instance, one proposal of the Secretariat of the MDP, in November 1948, authorised the Association of Hungarian Freedom Fighters to give lectures on the lives of Rákosi, Lenin and Stalin as part of its two-month-long evening course.[29] As the instruction of the life of the leader was considered a rather serious matter, in 1950 the Agitation and Propaganda Department (APO) published numerous sets of guidelines on the proper way of teaching Rákosi's life at courses and seminars run by the school for party education. At the same time, the same department worked out a number of distinct syllabi for various party-affiliated institutions. In early 1951, for example, the department proposed the teaching of the biographies of Lenin, Stalin and Rákosi at the one-year journalism course in two blocs of 3 lessons, under the rubric 'Party and Party Building'.[30]

The year of the communist take-over in Hungary (1948), also saw the beginning of inclusion of biographical material about the leader in history textbooks for school children. The first edition of such a textbook was published in 1948, for 14-year-old primary school pupils, and was followed up by similar publications for 9–10, 10–11-year-old youngsters and 17–18-year-old secondary school students in successive years.[31] Predictably, the amount of information about the leader in textbooks depended on the target audience. Biographical information about Rákosi, however, never constituted a separate chapter in any of the history books; the leader's life remained embedded within the greater thematic structures of Hungarian history.[32] The way in which Rákosi was presented to the children was also adjusted to the age of the pupils. The textbook for 9–10-year-old children, for example, contained moral stories from the leader's childhood, trying to portray him as the most talented and committed pupil in school,[33] whereas the history books for older children focused more on his qualities as conductor of the

Hungarian working-class movement, and his exemplary behaviour during his trials.

Apart from presenting the model life of the Hungarian party leader, textbooks for children became the vehicles of the leader cult in many other ways. The textbook written for secondary school children, for example, included eight volumes of Rákosi's collected speeches in the recommended reading section, as well as three other publications on him. References to Rákosi or quotations by him also featured extensively in textbooks for younger children. Apart from the leader's frequently quoted statements on the political and economic state of the country, his remarks or evaluations on the nation's past were also regularly incorporated in the texts.[34] The 'revealing' comments by the leader about the reasons for the defeat in the 1849 War of Independence, and his assessment of the historical significance of the peasant leader, György Dózsa, in 1514, for instance, were usually included in the teaching materials.[35]

The relative success and endurance of school textbooks for children is fairly remarkable: the primary school history book, for example, was awarded the silver Kossuth prize as early as 1949, and it also survived the first wave of de-Stalinisation in 1953–54, with the material on Rákosi remaining untouched. The ambiguity and restrictedness of the 'New Course' in Hungary was also marked by the fact that none of the other textbooks had to be modified significantly. The Rákosi cult was only purged from history textbooks after 1956, when most teaching materials of the Rákosi era were abandoned by the Kádár regime, and completely new history books were written for educating young people.

In the years 1945–47, the biographies of leaders were primarily used for immediate agitation purposes, usually within the framework of a broader campaign (e.g. elections). As soon as there was no potential political opposition left on the Hungarian political stage, after 1948, communist propaganda underwent a remarkable metamorphosis that triggered a crucial change in the use and function of leader biographies. Besides retaining its mobilisation aspect, the primary function of propaganda became to supplement the regime's indoctrination efforts. With the aim of integrating society under the banner of socialism, the biographical representation of the Hungarian working-class movement (i.e. the life of Mátyás Rákosi) was exploited to inculcate the basic ideological tenets of the regime and the behavioural patterns it expected from its citizens.

The official biography

In January 1948 the Propaganda Department suggested the publication of a series of biographical brochures on the best-known Hungarian and international communist leaders and martyrs such as Rákosi, Dimitrov, J. B. Tito etc.[36] The proposal, however, was never implemented and the plan was shelved for three more years.

Apart from suggestions prepared by central party organs, certain individual attempts to write the biography of the leader were also made. Just as in the Soviet Union, several members of the intelligentsia, devoted to the cause – mostly writers (Sándor Gergely, Gyula Háy, Sándor Rideg etc.) seeking the favours of the highest potential patron – offered their services to write the beloved leader's biography or an aspect of his life. Nevertheless, their proposals, too, were rejected or were simply left unrealised.[37]

The initiative of publishing Rákosi's official biography was finally accepted at the meeting of the Secretariat, on 29 August 1951, when the most important decision-making body of the MDP decided to organise the celebration of the Hungarian party leader's 60th birthday.[38] The proposal was put forward by József Révai, who, among other issues related to the birthday celebrations, suggested the publication of Rákosi's biography and the organisation of an exhibition on the dictator's life on the premises of the Institute for the History of the Working Class Movement. (At the same meeting the idea of making a film based on Rákosi's life was rejected.)[39] The Secretariat also set up a committee, headed by Révai, that became responsible for the organisation of the birthday celebrations of the Hungarian dictator. The task of preparing the writing and the publication of Rákosi's biography was assigned to László Réti, director of the Institute for the History of the Working Class Movement and Ferenc Karinthy, a well-known writer. A few weeks later, the APO suggested the establishment of an editorial board for writing, editing and supervising the manuscript of Rákosi's biography.[40] The committee consisted of 12 people, each responsible for editing different chapters of the draft. The importance attached to the production of the biography of Rákosi was clearly indicated by the fact that almost the entire apex of the party was involved in the editorial board: two members of the 'troika' (Ernő Gerő, Mihály Farkas), the ideological dictator, Révai, the head of the Agitation and Propaganda Department, Márton Horváth, and Rákosi's brother, Zoltán Bíró. The actual manuscript was written by László Réti and checked by the APO. It was undoubtedly seen by Rákosi himself but his precise contribution to the production process of the material is unknown. According to János Nemes, who also took part in organising the birthday celebrations, a brochure based upon the Réti text was translated into several languages, and the Ministry of Foreign Affairs sent the translations to a few Hungarian embassies abroad.[41] Surprisingly, Réti's biography was never published – neither in the brochure version nor the full text – and the publication process was suddenly halted. According to a letter by Horváth to Gerő, the editorial board finally decided not to disseminate Réti's text, as it needed to be 'substantially reworked'.[42] Although the relatively late stage in which the production of the biography was cancelled might be indicative of Rákosi's personal intervention, the role of the party leader in stopping the process remains unclear. Nevertheless, the withdrawal of Réti's work was regarded by the birthday committee as a temporal decision. Horváth's letter to Gerő dated 6 June 1952, which was also sent to Révai, Farkas and Zoltán Vas, seems to indicate that the editorial board actually planned to revise Réti's text and publish it later as the official biography.

Although the exact reasonning behind the aborted publication of the Réti manuscript is uncertain, certain theories can be tentatively advanced regarding its abandonment. Like the biography of Stalin, Réti's text about Rákosi was saturated with enormous falsifications and exaggerations of the leader's role in influencing the course of events. In Réti's case, however, it seems that the extent of historical distortions went far beyond the acceptable limits, and the possibility of provoking ridicule of the leader became an imminent threat. The description of the young Rákosi, for instance, eating a whole package of food at British customs because the officials would not let him bring it through is more an indication of greed then alleged poverty, whilst the portrayal of 'the handsome young Hungarian lad with sleek black hair', who 'made the girls' hearts beat whenever he danced the 'csárdás', makes Rákosi resemble a dandy more than a devoted communist and future leader.[43] The description of an impoverished Rákosi with his toes poking out of his shoes and the claim that he was the first to teach the lyrics of the 'Internationale' to Hungarian demonstrators (in March 1912), further emphasise the comic potential of the image of the leader in Réti's biography. Apart from the relative frequency of such absurd statements, the structure of the manuscript remained rather uneven, overburdened with lengthy quotations from Rákosi and Stalin, and with extensive elaboration of the historical context. At the same time the style of Réti's work remained tediously turgid and effusive, bearing a close resemblance to Stalin's official biography in this regard.[44] No matter how tempting it might be, Réti's abandoned biography can hardly be used as a representative example of what constituted an excess in the construction of the Rákosi cult. Apart from the numerous ridiculous statements, quoted above, the style, the structure, and even the editing process of Réti's biography was very similar to Stalin's official biography, and with some extra effort it could easily have been adjusted to the standard of the Soviet leader's life story. The fact that the biography was rejected in the end therefore does not clearly indicate the limits of the leader cult; it implies that the moderation of the Rákosi cult tended to be rather spontaneous and that its perimeters were constantly shifting.[45]

As the publication of the biography by Réti was finally aborted, and the date of the birthday 9 March, was looming large, Béla Illés, a loyal and trustworthy writer, became the emergency solution, entrusted with the task of composing Rákosi's biography.[46] It seems that Illés had to do the job under immense time pressure. He met Rákosi on 15 January 1952 (at 9 p.m.) for a discussion about the leader's life, and as early as a month later the biography was being distributed as the primary material for teaching the life of the leader at party courses.[47] (He made extensive use of Réti's materials, however.) As soon as Illés had finished writing the manuscript, it was rapidly translated into a number of languages, and was finally published as the official biography of Rákosi in February 1952, with the title *Népünk szabadságáért* (*For Our People's Freedom*). In order to authorise Illés' text as the sole interpretation of Rákosi's life, the Orgburo (*Szervező Bizottság* – SZB) of the MDP accepted Horváth's proposal to put an end to the proliferation of any biographical material not checked by the APO. The resolution of the SZB of 11 February 1952 announced that only the official biography of Rákosi could be used for propaganda or educational purposes. At the same time, the decree also prohibited the publication and distribution of any separate material on Rákosi.[48]

As soon as Illés' booklet was ready, the MDP launched an extensive agitation campaign, within the framework of the broader birthday propaganda campaign, to popularise the life of Rákosi, making full use of the new biography. An outline of the manuscript was translated into several languages (English, German, French, Russian, Romanian, etc.) and newspapers and journals were ordered to publish complimentary reviews and abstracts of the work.[49] Apart from the official biography, the celebration of Rákosi's life at the time of his birthday also became the subject of various other publications. An anthology of photos from the leader's life was compiled, complementing Illés' booklet,[50] and an exhibition in the Institute for the History of the Working Class Movement, entitled *Rákosi Mátyás harcos élete* (*The Stalwart Life of Mátyás Rákosi*), also attempted to represent the arduous periods of Rákosi's rugged past.

A few weeks before the party leader's birthday, short evening courses were organised by the party exclusively for instruction on Rákosi's life – primarily on the basis of the new biography.[51] Moreover, special seminars and lessons, dedicated to the Hungarian party leader's life, took place at all levels of education during the month of Rákosi's birthday. (The APO even designated which sections of Illés' biography should be read aloud.)[52] As an official biography was available, most of the biographical outlines and teaching materials were updated in accordance with Illés work.[53] In October 1952, for example, the APO worked out new thematic plans for the courses at the Stalin Academy for Political Officers to teach Rákosi's life, primarily on the basis of the official biography.[54] Although the material on the party leader's life in school textbooks remained more or less intact after the publication of Illés' book – it was often quoted though –, a number of guidelines based on the text were published illustrating the way in which the biography of the leader should be taught in party seminars and in school classrooms.

Besides prescribing the method of teaching Rákosi's biography, the communist propaganda also tried to regulate how the life of the leader should be perceived. The press published numerous accounts in which students spoke of the inspiration provided by Rákosi's example. For example, an instructor of propagandist seminars talked about the greatest challenge of his life and the unforgettable, enlightening effect of the seminar he tutored.[55] Similarly, schoolchildren emphasised the special, festive-like, atmosphere in the classroom when Rákosi's biography was taught: 'It is impossible to talk about the life of Rákosi in a dirty, untidy room, it is impossible to give a boring, dull lecture on the topic.'[56] During the birthday agitation campaign, the instruction on the party leader's life and the distribution of his biographies were carefully controlled and the public response to the biography cautiously monitored by the APO. According to a report prepared by the party organ, and sent to Rákosi, the biography by Illés became extremely popular among the party members and quickly sold out.[57] The document emphasised that in the two weeks preceding Rákosi's birthday at least half a million had studied the life of the Hungarian dictator in evening classes and another half a million had participated in public meetings or 'reading circles' on the same theme. The report also noted the unexpected success of Rákosi's life story among the peasantry. According to the account, the lectures and presentations on the life of Rákosi were followed by a significant increase in the numbers of applications to evening courses among peasants, and the growth in the number of pledges in collective farms. It was also emphasised that manifestations of hostility towards the biography were rare: 'in this field the enemy has no foothold'.[58] Whether the lack of negative attitudes concerning the biography is an indication of its success, or whether it merely reflects ignorance, needs to be studied further. Nevertheless, the report illustrates the extraordinary effort invested in the construction of the biography by the Communist Party, and the expectation that it would be positively received.

The biographical narrative

According to Rákosi's biographical narrative, as crystallised in Illés' booklet, the leader came from a poor working class family, with a long 'revolutionary' tradition, that constantly had to struggle for its daily bread. Due to his poverty-stricken background, Rákosi started to show an interest in the plight of the deprived as a child, and was already watching workers' demonstrations at an early age. He became committed to the cause of the working-class movement while still a teenager, and participated in the protest marches of 1906 in Szeged, at the age of 14. Having completed his secondary school education, he immediately joined the Social Democratic Party, and as the Secretary of the radical Galilei-Circle in Budapest, he 'prepared himself for the hard and dedicated life of the revolutionary fighter'.[59] As a result of years of scholarship in London and Hamburg and the prisoner-of-war camp in Russia during the First World War Rákosi became a devoted Bolshevik, and, in November 1918, was 'one of the founders' of the Communist Party (no other founders were normally mentioned).

One of the core elements of Rákosi's biographical narrative was his activity during the Hungarian Soviet Republic of 1919, especially the heroic feat of defending the mining town, Salgótarján; a victory exclusively accredited to him. The battle, in which the invading Czech troops were stopped and were driven back by miner-militias and the Hungarian Red Army, was often paralleled with Stalin's defence of Tsaritsyn in the Russian Civil War. The narrative of the event was also frequently utilised to emphasise his heroic virtues, his 'enormous organisational talents', his dynamism, and his intransigent attitude towards the enemy, all of which ensured he emerged triumphant from the conflicts he had to face.

Although the myth of Salgótarján remained an essential building block of the Rákosi-cult, the nucleus of all biographical depictions of the leader was undoubtedly the description of his trials in 1925–26 and in 1934–35.[60] These trials in front of the 'fascist Blood Council' and the 15 years he spent in prison elevated Rákosi above ordinary members of the Comintern, making him the most esteemed figure of the Hungarian working-class movement, and later the undisputable leader of the Communist Party.[61] The accounts of the trials in Rákosi's biographies focused predominantly on the behaviour of the accused in front of the court. The life stories of the leader emphasise that Rákosi presented an example of 'grim courage', 'communist fortitude', 'unbreakable willpower', 'Marxist-Leninist discernment', 'superior knowledge', 'insights of a genius' and 'great tactical skills'.[62]

The account of the trials also provided a great opportunity for the authors to highlight Rákosi's prophetic abilities and his timeless wisdom. When Rákosi claimed that land would only be distributed in Hungary by the communists, the judge exclaimed: 'Rákosi do not be a prophet!'[63] As communist propaganda attributed the distribution of land in 1945 exclusively to Rákosi and the Communist Party, despite the fact that it actually resulted from the common effort of the political parties at the time, it became possible to claim that what the communist leader had once foretold finally came true.

All in all, the trials were presented as a great historic victory of the Hungarian working-class movement, where the accused, Rákosi, became the accuser and the counter-revolutionary, 'reactionary' Horthy regime, and 'predacious imperialism' in general, was placed in the dock. Due to his extraordinary virtues and the exemplary communist behaviour he showed at the trials, Rákosi, at least according to the biographies, proved that he possessed the abilities of an ideal revolutionary fighter and thus became *the* leader of the Hungarian workers.[64]

The narrative of the trials and Rákosi's activity in the Comintern in the early 1920s also provided the Rákosi cult a modest global perspective. All biographies of the leader underlined the 'great respect' Rákosi enjoyed as a Secretary of the Executive Committee, and also emphasised his successful missions abroad, which advanced the strengthening and ideological cleansing of several European communist parties (Italian, German, French).[65]

Rákosi's alleged worldwide significance was further enhanced during the trials, illustrated by Illés in the following way:

> From the shores of the Arctic Ocean to the palm-groves of the south, the Polish border to the Yellow Sea, thousands of towns, a hundred million people of a hundred thousand villages shouted in a hundred languages, with one heart: – Set Rákosi free![66]

The embellished representations of Rákosi's alleged struggles, sacrifices and sufferings, especially in 1919 and during the trials, were all meant to demonstrate the leader's entitlement to his post. The illustration of Rákosi's intellectual development, that is, the way he acquired his 'superior knowledge', was the second pillar of the justification of Rákosi's leadership and the image of him as the 'teacher' of the nation. In the biographies of the communist leader, education played a central role throughout his whole life. No matter how difficult the circumstances were, Rákosi always studied hard and was always the best pupil of each institution he attended. Besides being shown as a pupil, Rákosi was also portrayed as a teacher who ceaselessly shared his knowledge with his less-educated comrades and companions. He had already helped his less-talented schoolmates while attending the secondary school in Szeged, he organised study groups in the prisoner of war camps and later, in prison, he taught the principles of Marxism to his communist inmates. Nevertheless, his qualities as the teacher of the Hungarian people became more apparent at the time of his trials, when he turned the convict's bench into a pulpit from which he preached the ideas and goals of the communist movement, and pointed out the route towards a better future for the entire Hungarian nation.

Apart from focusing on his merits as a teacher, the biographical narratives aimed to endow Rákosi with additional legitimacy by forging a link – both physical and spiritual – between the 'leader of the Hungarian people' and prominent figures of the international working-class movement and Hungarian history. Illés, in his book, strove to indicate Rákosi's affinity with the Hungarian eighteenth-century freedom fighter, Ferenc Rákóczi, through stressing that in Sopron the Rákosi family moved to the courtyard of the Hotel Fehér Ló (White Horse), the hotel in which Rákóczi once lived.[67] Illés also highlighted the fact that in London Rákosi regularly visited the British Library, 'the great library in which once Marx worked'.[68] Nevertheless, the most significant link was established with Lenin, the major source of legitimacy within the communist movement. Illés, who also portrayed the first meeting of the young Rákosi and Lenin in 1920 in a separate short story, likened the encounter to that between a master and his apprentice.[69] Despite emphasising Lenin's qualities as a mentor, Illés tried to suggest an equal relationship between the two politicians: Lenin sat next to Rákosi, and instead of listening to the Hungarian communist's report about the events of 1919, they had a 'friendly' talk. In the end Lenin was pleased by the performance of his pupil: 'The mighty eagle taught the young eagle to fly and was satisfied with his apprentice.'[70]

In general, the biographical narrative applied two major techniques to underline Rákosi's position as the party leader. The biographical accounts either exaggerated and/or falsified Rákosi's qualities and his impact on the course of history, or they diminished – or simply erased – the significance of other historical actors (e.g. Béla Kun), who could overshadow the leader's image as the main conductor of Hungarian history. Interestingly enough, Rákosi himself also made a significant contribution to the proliferation of legends and myths about his life. In an interview he gave on the radio in 1945, for example, he was already laying the grounds for exaggerations of his influence on the flow of historical events.[71] One of the most remarkable of the stories he told the reporter was about his journey on the train from Siberia – where he was kept as a prisoner-of-war – to St Petersburg, with a delegation travelling to the Fourth Congress of the Soviets to Moscow, to decide upon the peace treaty of Brest-Litovsk. According to Rákosi's account, the majority of the delegation had intended to vote against the peace treaty but as a result of his personal influence, most of them had changed their minds and became keen supporters of peace. More remarkable was Rákosi's input on the construction of the 'Lenin-link'. In the notes taken of the conversation between Rákosi and Illés in January 1952, the Hungarian leader's relationship with the spiritual father of the communist movement is the dominant theme.[72] Apart from a detailed account of their first meeting, Rákosi described Lenin as his main patron in the Comintern in the early 1920s. Rákosi, in his autobiographical remarks to Illés, also exaggerated his personal impact on the international working-class movement, and portrayed himself as one of the most prominent leaders of the Comintern in the early 1920s.

> I was the first of the Hungarian communists with whom it was possible to talk to in a meaningful way. I was the first real communist about whom one could tell that he read Marx and Lenin, was adept at military affairs, had travelled a lot, and knew languages. I was highly esteemed.[73]

Conclusions

The biographical narrative, and in particular the official biography, of Rákosi bears close resemblance to a prototypical Socialist Realist novel.[74] The humble background from which the leader came, the early commitment to the cause and the emphasis laid on the ordeals, sacrifices and martyrdom of the protagonist were all fundamental building blocks of the Socialist Realist master plot. Rákosi's biography is a typical manifestation of the life story of a father figure in the Stalinist 'great family', whose entire life, from his early childhood on, and his extraordinary qualities as a mentor, were meant to endorse his entitlement to guide the people on the route to socialism.[75] Like the prototypical Socialist Realist hero, the life of Rákosi was also fully embedded in the history of the working-class movement. Indeed the biography was the personalised history of the Hungarian Communist Party. As the biographies were supposed to represent an idealised life totally dedicated to the idea of communism, no aspects of Rákosi's life were described apart from his activity in the communist movement. There were no details of private life (family background, love, marriage, etc.) included in the life story of the leader, and his individual characteristics also remained in the background. Moreover, the virtues attributed to Rákosi were the basic exemplary values of an idealtypical revolutionary hero. His standard epithets ('serious', 'stern', 'intent', 'calm', etc.) were, in fact, the set of epithets predominantly used to depict father figures in Socialist Realist novels.[76] The lack of reference to Rákosi's personal features and the extreme idealisation of his qualities made the biographies of the leader somewhat impersonal. He lost his individual characteristics and became the embodiment of officially professed values. In his biographies, Rákosi personified all ideals, principles and aspirations of the communist state. He became a complex symbol with a collective face; the epitome of officially celebrated, ideal values. Rákosi's 'cult of personality', as manifested in his biographies, was not a worship based on the leader's individual merits, but rather the glorification of the highly abstract, impersonal values of the communist movement.

The creation of a fairly deindividualised and extremely idealised biography of the leader was primarily motivated by the need to present an exemplary behavioural pattern for the society to emulate.[77] Through the dissemination and teaching of Rákosi's life story, communist propaganda attempted to inculcate a basic set of ideal communist values in society, in accordance with the general strategy to reshape social identity, and create the socialist 'new man'. The production and distribution of Rákosi's biographies, therefore, did not only contribute to the construction of the 'cult of impersonality' of the leader, but also to the grandiose endeavour to implement communism in Hungary.

Notes

1. Orlando Figes and Boris Kolonitskii, *Interpreting the Russian Revolution: The Language and Symbols of 1917* (New Haven and London, 1999), p. 75.
2. Claude Pennetier and Bernard Pudal, 'Stalinisme, culte ouvrier et culte des dirigeants' in Dreyfus Michel *et al.*, *Le siècle des communismes* (Paris, 2001), p. 372.
3. On the ideological change in Soviet propaganda see David Brandenberger, *National Bolshevism: Stalinist Mass Culture and the Formation of Modern Russian National Identity, 1931–1956*, (Cambridge, Mass. and London, 2002).
4. Ibid., p. 145.
5. Katerina Clark, *The Soviet Novel: History as Ritual* (3rd edition Bloomington, 2000).

6. Ibid., p. 45.
7. Ibid., pp. 15–16.
8. Brandenberger, *National Bolshevism*, pp. 52–3.
9. Ibid., p. 145, and Clark, *The Soviet Novel*, p. 124.
10. On Stalin's official biography see David Brandenberger, 'Constructing the Cult: A Case Study of Stalin's Official Biography', paper given at the 29th Conference of the Study Group on the Russian Revolution, 'Stalin: Power, Policy and Political Values', Hatfield College, University of Durham (UK), 3–5 January 2003.
11. This was as part of the critique of the Pokrovskii school of historiography. For Stalin's role in shaping history-writing see Maureen Perrie, *The Cult of Ivan the Terrible in Stalin's Russia* (Basingstoke, 2001); Robert C. Tucker, *Stalin in Power: The Revolution from Above, 1928–1941* (New York and London, 1992), pp. 530–50; see also Brandenberger, *National Bolshevism*. On Stalin's role in the construction of his own cult see Sarah Davies' chapter in the present volume (Chapter 2).
12. Brandenberger, *National Bolshevism*, p. 148.
13. As cited in Brandenberger, 'Constructing the Cult', p. 15. See also Erik van Ree, *The Political Thought of Joseph Stalin. A Study in Twentieth-century Revolutionary Patriotism* (London and New York, 2002), pp. 162–5.
14. N. S. Khrushchev, *The 'Secret' Speech*, Introduced by Zhores A. Medvedev and Roy A. Medvedev (Nottingham, 1976). See also Brandenberger, 'Constructing the Cult', pp. 1–3, and van Ree, *The Political Thought of Joseph Stalin*, pp. 309–10.
15. As Erik van Ree remarked: 'the cult rested importantly on hagiographies' in id. *The Political Thought of Joseph Stalin*, p. 162. David Brandenberger also noticed that 'biography lies very close to the heart of the personality cult': Brandenberger, 'Constructing the Cult', p. 3.
16. Georg Samueli, *Rakoshi, Matias* (Moscow, 1935).
17. Árpád Pünkösti, *Rákosi a hatalomért, 1945–1948* (Budapest, 1992), p. 12. On the effect of the purges on the Comintern see William J. Chase, *Enemies Within the Gates? The Comintern and the Stalinist Repression, 1934–1939* (New Haven, 2001).
18. E. Téglás, *Rákosi Mátyás* (Moscow, 1937). The author himself fell victim to the Great Purges. Chase, *Enemies Within the Gates?*, p. 496.
19. Rákosi was first put to trial in Hungary in 1925 and was sentenced for 8 and a half years of imprisonment. In 1934, instead of releasing him, the Hungarian authorities brought Rákosi to court again (for his activity in the 1919 Hungarian Soviet Republic), and he was sentenced to life imprisonment.
20. *Rákosi elvtárs élete. Szakszervezeti Ismeretterjesztő előadások* (Budapest, 1952), p. 11.
21. Clark, *The Soviet Novel*, pp. 114–36.
22. For the printed version of the interview see *Egy nagy harcos életéből. Rádióbeszélgetés Rákosi Mátyással 1945. október 4-én* (Budapest, 1945).
23. Short biographies of political leaders were used for propaganda purposes by most of the contemporary Hungarian political parties, as well.
24. PIL (Politikatörténeti Intézet Levéltára), 274. f. 21/5. ő.e.
25. PIL, 274. f. 3/99. ő.e., Records of meeting of the Politburo, 31 July 1947.
26. PIL, 274. f. 3/99. ő.e. In the case of Ernő Gerő, the Politburo even designated what characteristic features of him should be emphasised in the article: the fact that he adopted a child.
27. 'Mátyás Rákosi is a prominent political asset of the whole nation not just the Communist Party', 'József Révai is the asset of the whole nation, not just the Communist Party', *Szabad Nép*, 10 and 24 August 1947. János Kádár: 'If you meet him once you will like him straightaway'; Mihály Farkas: 'You talk to him for five

minutes and you feel as if he had been a good friend of yours for ages', *Szabad Nép*, 23 and 20 August 1947.

28. MOL (Magyar Országos Levéltár), 276. f. 108/9. ő.e. The Hungarian Communists' Party and the Hungarian Social Democratic Party united in June 1948.
29. MOL, 276. f. 54/39. Meeting of the Secretariat, 8 November 1948.
30. MOL, 276. f. 89/10. ő.e.
31. For primary school students: László Zsigmond, Klára Fejér and Béla Karácsonyi, *Történelem. Az általános iskolák VIII. osztálya számára*, 5th edn, (Budapest, 1952). For secondary school pupils: Lajos Lukács, *A magyar nép története III. rész (1849-től napjainkig)* (Budapest, 1951). The material for technical schools: Endre Kovács, Gyula Simon and Béla Bellér, *Történelem. A Szakiskolák IV. osztálya számára*, (Budapest, 1954).
32. In a primary school textbook, published in 1952, the biographical information on Rákosi appeared in three different chapters: *Történelem. Az általános iskolák VIII. osztálya számára*. (Budapest, 1952).
33. Similar fictitious moral stories from Lenin's and Stalin's childhood were also included in the same book. Éva Kovács, 'Vezérekről, példaképekről gyermekeknek', *História*, 9: 5–6 (1987), pp. 42.
34. Ibid., p. 43.
35. E.g. Béla Karácsonyi, *A magyar nép története. I. rész 1526-ig* (Budapest, 1954), p. 105; Péter Hanák (ed.) *Történelem. A középiskolák II. osztálya számára* (Budapest, 1949), pp. 168–9.
36. PIL, 274. f. 21/1. ő.e.
37. MOL 276. f. 65/332. ő.e.
38. The actual date of Rákosi's birthday was 9 March 1952.
39. MOL, 276. f. 54/158. ő.e.
40. MOL, 276. fond 89/163. ő.e.
41. János Nemes, *Rákosi Mátyás születésnapja* (Budapest, 1988), p. 29.
42. Márton Horváth's letter to Gerő (6 June 1952), MOL 276 f. 65/389. ő.e.
43. Réti's manuscript can be found at: MOL 276 f. 65/389. ő.e.
44. Brandenberger, 'Constructing the Cult,' p. 18. For the Hungarian translation of Stalin's biography see *J. V. Sztálin. Rövid életrajz* (Budapest, 1949).
45. This seems to coincide with David Brandenberger's argument about the *ad hoc* nature and inconsistency of the organisation of the Stalin cult. Brandenberger, 'Constructing the Cult', p. 3.
46. Árpád Pünkösti, *Rákosi a csúcson* (Budapest, 1996), pp. 424–38. On the position of Illés in the Hungarian literary scene after 1945, and his relationship with Rákosi see Chapter 3.
47. For the notes about the meeting see MOL 276. f. 65/332. ő.e. see also PIL, 720. f. 1. ő.e.
48. MOL, 276. f. 55/193. ő.e.
49. MOL, 276. f. 89/193. ő.e. For the English language brochure based on Illés' text see *Mátyás Rákosi: On the Occasion of his Sixtieth Birthday* (London, 1952). A 'review' of Illés' book: Károly Kiss, 'Rákosi elvtárs életéről', *Szabad Nép*, 24 February 1952.
50. *Rákosi Mátyás élete képekben* (Budapest, 1952). This book was translated to a number of foreign languages as well.
51. MOL, 276. f. 89/10. ő.e.
52. Pünkősti, *Rákosi a csúcson*, p. 427.
53. Some examples: *Rákosi elvtárs élete*, and *Rákosi elvtárs harca*, Vols 1–3 (Sztálinváros, 1952).

54. In four lessons altogether. MOL, 276. f. 89/123. ő.e.
55. 'Hogyan készültem a Rákosi elvtárs harcos életéről szóló szemináriumra?', *Szabad Nép*, 2 March 1952.
56. *Szabad Ifjúság*, 16 November 1952.
57. MOL, 276. f. 89/10. ő.e.
58. Ibid.
59. Béla Illés, *Népünk szabadságáért* (Budapest, 1952), p. 5.
60. Rákosi faced five different courts altogether in 15 years.
61. *A Rákosi-per* (Budapest, 1950), pp. 3–11.
62. Illés, *Népünk szabadságáért*, pp. 31–43.
63. *A Rákosi-per*, p. 129.
64. For critical approaches to Rákosi's far less heroic life see Pünkösti, *Rákosi a hatalomért*; id., *Rákosi a csúcson*; see also István Feitl, Levente Sipos, 'Előszó' in Mátyás Rákosi, *Visszaemlékezések 1892–1925* (Budapest, 2002), pp. VII–XXXVIII; Tibor Hajdú, 'Kérdőjelek R.M. hiányzó portréjához', *Élet és Irodalom*, 11 February 1983; János Nemes, 'Rákosi Mátyás' in Ilona Sánta (ed.) *Politikuspályák* (Budapest, 1984), pp. 51–70.
65. Illés, *Népünk szabadságáért*, p. 26.
66. Ibid., p. 33.
67. Ibid., p. 4.
68. Ibid., p. 7.
69. Béla Illés, 'Történelmi lecke' in Pál Réz and István Vas (eds) *Magyar Írók Rákosi Mátyásról* (Budapest, 1952), pp. 80–92.
70. Ibid., p. 89.
71. *Egy nagy harcos életéből. Rádióbeszélgetés Rákosi Mátyással 1945. október 4-én* (Budapest, 1945).
72. MOL 276. f. 65/332. ő.e.
73. PIL 720. f. 1. ő.e.
74. As outlined in Clark, *The Soviet Novel*.
75. Rákosi's biography, just like Stalin's, is distinct from a *Bildungsroman* in the sense that there is no real conversion of the leader: Rákosi is endowed with timeless qualities.
76. Clark, *The Soviet Novel*, p. 301.
77. On de-individualised heroes representing 'Bolshevik virtues' see Clark, *The Soviet Novel*, pp. 46–7 and p. 70.

Part II
The Functions of the Leader Cult

5
The Stalin Cult, Bolshevik Rule and Kremlin Interaction in the 1930s

Benno Ennker

This chapter examines the history of the Stalin cult within the political history of Bolshevik rule and the establishment of Stalin's personal dictatorship in the 1930s.[1] It analyses the group dynamics which developed within Stalin's ruling circle at the beginning of that crucial decade. This should be placed in relation to the process by which the leader constructed his authority within the highest echelons of the party. Stalin's top lieutenants reacted to this process by launching the image of the new leader into the Soviet public sphere. By 1933 the absolute power of the dictator had been solidified, and the leader cult had become an important pillar of the political system.

The evolution of the Stalin cult

In the second half of the 1920s many voices within the Bolshevik Party called for a 'firm hand' or a 'leader'. Faced with sustained internal opposition, expectations within the leadership increasingly focused on Stalin.[2] During these years Stalin emerged from relative obscurity to become the foremost protagonist of ideological radicalisation and social mobilisation, from the war hysteria of 1927, the campaign to requisition grain in Siberia in January 1928, the Shakhty affair, to subsequent arrests of top officials in heavy industry. In 1929 this radicalisation of Bolshevik policies turned into a 'cultural revolution' as the first Five Year Plan was pushed through in its most extreme form. All these decisions led to a 'charismatic situation' which, in the language of the time, was dubbed the 'intensification of class struggle' and the 'attack of socialism on all fronts'.[3] The perception of severe internal crises and external threat contributed to a civil war mentality within the Central Committee and an increasing willingness to appoint Stalin undisputed leader, or *vozhd'*.[4] Various individual initiatives were launched before December 1929 to proclaim him 'leader' and to introduce a harsher dictatorship.[5] But neither at the centre nor at the peripheries can we detect the signs of cultic veneration of Stalin before his 50th birthday celebrations in December 1929.[6]

On 20 December 1929, one day before Stalin's 50th birthday, preparations to celebrate the occasion were made in the Politburo. At the instigation of the leadership the birthday celebration took the form of a public campaign to proclaim Stalin the new leader – a position nominally vacant since Lenin's death in 1924. This found a well-orchestrated echo in the form of some 1000 salutations and congratulations addressed to Stalin from 'workers' – a carefully crafted manifestation of the *vox populi.*[7] The new leader was called the 'best pupil, heir and successor of Lenin', and this epithet was immediately canonised in a manifesto of the Central Committee as well as in various panegyrics by Stalin's lieutenants.[8] The Central Committee resolution was drafted by Lazar' Kaganovich and revised by other members during the meeting. The leadership collective took part in the creation of their master's cult.[9] They were responsible for publicly proclaiming him *vozhd'*. For Stalin's closest associates, only a few weeks after their definitive victory over the so-called 'right opposition' around N. I. Bukharin, this act served to confirm their group identity, through the person of Stalin.[10] In these crucial days for the regime, marked by the beginning of forced collectivisation and, as Stalin deemed it, the 'liquidation of the kulaks as a class', the leading political group hoped to gain extra legitimacy by appointing a leader for the upcoming civil war.[11]

But did this first wave of panegyrics already constitute a fully developed leader cult? This was clearly not the case, as can be seen in the public rhetoric of leading Bolsheviks during the years 1930 and 1931.[12] Stalin did not yet have enough power to instigate a fully developed leader cult. In the spring of 1930, his authority amongst local party activists suffered severely, when he felt it necessary to declare a retreat from forcible collectivisation.[13] The insecurity about Stalin's authority provoked fears amongst Stalin's group, that Bukharin and his followers might regain influence.[14] At the same time members of the 'Old Guard' of former party leaders, who retained some influence, were critical of the new cultic veneration of Stalin.[15] The *vozhd'* himself felt obliged to make ostentatious attempts to distance himself from any form of leader cult in public, and to present himself as a modest *primus inter pares*.[16]

From 1929 onwards, Stalin established full personal control over the Soviet media.[17] After the preparations for Stalin's 50th birthday, Glavlit, the Soviet censorship authority, published exact regulations to control the publication of Stalin's images in the press.[18] This media monopoly then shaped Stalin's self-image. In order to enforce his authority in 1932, Stalin concentrated on controlling internal party discourse.[19] After he sent a letter to the journal *Proletarskaya Revolyutsiya*, Stalin's power in ideological matters increased substantially.[20] This gave rise to fierce competition among Bolshevik theoreticians to produce Stalin legends. During 1931–32 three leading party intellectuals, Maxim Gor'ky, Emilyan Yaroslavskii and Mikhail Kol'tsov, mooted the idea of a book on Stalin, but their efforts failed.[21] Only in 1939 was an official biography published and this was rewritten in 1947.[22]

At the Central Committee plenum in January 1933, Stalin gave a triumphal speech about the alleged 'successes' of the First Five Year Plan.[23] This was a signal to relaunch and expand his leader cult. The *vozhd'* was now called the unique 'inspirer of all successes during the construction of socialism' for the masses.[24] The entire propaganda machinery focused on him. L. M. Kaganovich, S. M. Kirov, G. K. Ordzhonikidze, and K. E. Voroshilov initiated this new campaign.[25] Within a few days, the leader's adulation took the form of collective letters that appeared in the press.[26] These manifestos were signed by industrial or collective farm shock-workers (*udarniki*) and would from now on fill the pages of newspapers for the whole of Stalin's rule. Initially launched by the party leadership, the Stalin cult then produced a new 'mass basis'. Its populist forms were intended to portray a direct link between the leader and people.

Stalin's personal dictatorship was erected in parallel to the rise of his cult. This process of establishing personal rule while building the cult may be observed in two political spheres: in the interpersonal dynamics at the Kremlin court, of Stalin's inner circle (*okruzhenie Stalina*), a milieu of rivalry and competition among the leading collaborators, 'fighting for Stalin's soul';[27] and in all branches of society, such as the collective letters of workers and peasants addressed to Stalin, or official receptions in the Kremlin.[28] The cultural strategy of 'popularising' the cult resulted in the discursive construction of a specific relationship between 'the people and the leader'. The cult's content increasingly resembled patterns of archaic folklore, creating the traditional heroic and patriarchal legends of the Stalin cult.[29]

With the celebrations of Stalin's 60th birthday in 1939, the process of iconising his persona was complete. For six weeks tremendous numbers of congratulations were published daily, indicating a broad social mobilisation within Soviet society.[30] All representatives of Soviet officialdom paid tribute to Stalin. In the course of this, the *vozhd'* was endowed with outstanding attributes. He was called the 'Lenin of today', in reference to the Bolshevik tradition, but also 'genius' and 'father'. One could observe various forms of 'deification' and 'love of the people'. Above all, emphasis was placed on the populist dimensions of the cult.

A Stalinist equilibrium: the quest for absolute power and 'bureaucratic interests'

As can be seen from the evolution of the cult, the first wave of cultic panegyrics for Stalin as 'the leader' was largely episodic. Its continuity as a stable ritual was not secured before Stalin's authority had reached those absolute dimensions that characterised his personal dictatorship.

In the second half of 1930, the group dynamics within the innermost circle of the leadership received a new impetus. The shift was caused by the upheavals to which Stalin's lieutenants were exposed as they confronted the challenges of running the Soviet state apparatus. Under Stalin's aegis, his associates could not content themselves with merely exercising 'indirect power' from the distant commanding heights of the Politburo. For this reason Stalin began manoeuvring to reorganise the entire apparatus of government, then still under the command of A. I. Rykov, considered to be a member of Bukharin's 'Right Opposition'. In Stalin's view, this apparatus formed a 'counterbalance to the Central Committee', which he wanted to disband, considering it to be a 'bureaucratic apparatus of consultants and secretaries'.[31] As Stalin wrote to V. M. Molotov in September 1930, he aimed at nothing less than 'solving the question of leadership once and for all'. In his view, the organs of the party and the state should be 'closely interwoven and inseparable from each other'. This whole effort was characterised by Stalin as part of 'our struggle against the bureaucratism which is consuming us'.[32]

Stalin sent his suggestions to Molotov on 22 September, from Sochi, and instructed him to discuss them 'with our closest friends' and pass their objections on to him. However, by focusing on the question of who should take over from Rykov as head of the government, he launched a test of his own status: although proposing Molotov as Rykov's successor, Stalin focused attention on himself with the words: 'With this we'll have complete unity between Soviet and Party leaders, and this will unquestionably double our strength.'[33] Reading this latter argument, Stalin's associates were forced to consider whether Stalin himself should take over the leadership of the Soviet government. The leader had triggered a debate about his leadership.

In October 1930, with Stalin still on vacation, there was a vigorous exchange of views amongst the Politburo members on the question of the leadership of Sovnarkom. Molotov made it clear that he was opposed to Stalin's becoming head of government. Although avoiding any comments on Stalin's personal suitability for this position, he stated that the position of head of government might interfere with the duties of the party leader.[34] A letter by Kaganovich pointed in the opposite direction. It was full of expressions of admiration and praise for Stalin. Kaganovich referred to 'the party members' and the 'masses', who allegedly desired Stalin to be nominated head of government. 'Particularly in the last few years the leading role of the Party and of the Central Committee has reached unparalleled heights thanks to you,' he declared. 'The most important basic economic and political activities were and are determined by you, irrespective of the position you hold, and that is how things should remain.'[35] In his statement Kaganovich concentrated entirely on Stalin's leadership qualities. Voroshilov called upon Stalin to 'openly take over the entire leadership . . . This leadership already lies in your hands anyway', but pointed out that, without the merging of both offices, this would not be fully effective. For this reason Stalin should 'take over the leadership of the country properly, in the manner you are capable of,' as the only one 'possessing the talent of a strategist'.[36] Anastas Mikoyan also took up the latter argument when he expressed his preference for a 'unified leadership such as that which existed under Il'ich'. Only if Stalin were to become head of government could there be a 'uniform and consistent leadership, the authority of the Sovnarkom (the Council of People's Commissars) would prevail among the masses and there would be a strong leadership to build up the economy.'[37] Among Stalin's henchmen, Ordzhonikidze was the most outspoken in his preference for Molotov as head of government. He seemingly ignored the question of the general secretary's candidature for the post. Instead he quoted Stalin's own statement, given earlier, that he had not found the 'full . . . merging of party leadership and Soviet leadership to be effective'.[38]

The comments passed on to Stalin in the course of the 'leadership discussion' conveyed to him the considerable differences of opinion within the Politburo. Moreover, in the summer, serious differences arose with Mikoyan and between Ordzhonikidze, head of the Commissariat of Workers' and Peasants' Inspectorate, and Kuibyshev, head of the Supreme Council of the National Economy (Vesenkha).[39] At that time, Stalin's inner circle resembled less a disciplined group of communists than a Mafia family infighting after the defeat of a rival gang. Stalin now managed to bring this group together through a combination of high-level reshuffles, as in the cases of Ordzhonikidze and Kuibyshev, and the exertion of drastic external pressure. By making an example of one of them, Mikhail Kalinin, he demonstrated that he was able to link any of them with the 'counterrevolution'.[40] Stalin's lieutenants were given a clear indication of what they could expect if they were found to be lacking obedience.

The year 1930 finally ended with the full take-over of the government by Stalin's group. The *vozhd'* himself had decided to remain outside the government. In the course of the internal discussions his associates had assigned to him – with varying degrees of emphasis – the highest authority. What this meant was not yet clear, for Stalin's proposals for institutional reforms did not remain undisputed, and his henchmen could only be made to agree under drastic external pressure, often verging on blackmail. The Central Committee plenum, which was supposed to pass a resolution on the restructuring of the government, had to postpone its meeting several times indicating the frictions and difficulties encountered on the way to the final decision.[41]

With the appointment of Molotov as chairman of Sovnarkom in December 1930, Bolshevik rule entered a new phase. Factionalism remained taboo. The treatment of Bukharin's group showed Stalin's henchmen that all forms of sanction, including marginalisation and criminalisation, would be employed in order to enforce an absolute ban on factions. In addition, his associates were now forced to distance themselves from stigmatised people.[42] In Stalin's view it remained necessary to sustain an atmosphere of unconditional acceptance of any of his decisions. Furthermore he could generate permanent competition among his lieutenants and give himself enough space to manoeuvre. It was this sense of competition within Stalin's inner circle that kept the regime's engine running. And it was from this environment that the leader cult was launched into the wider Soviet public. To attain this state of affairs no explicit Stalin cult within the Politburo was necessary. What was needed was a relationship of absolute authority that would not contradict the public panegyrics to the leader given in his associates' speeches. Still, Stalin's distrust of 'lip service' and 'double-dealers' remained.

The focusing of all power on Stalin's persona gives the impression that under his regime a 'total and absolute rule' was established, in which politics in the sense of fighting for power and influence was abolished. A closer look reveals, however, that within the circle of Stalin's closest associates sharp conflict developed. Inevitably the tasks of government were organised bureaucratically, based on a division of labour. This, and the pressure of the industrialisation programme, meant that political energies were absorbed, and channelled into goals and duties defined by the ministries. The bureaucratic division of labour within the state executive inevitably affected social relationships within the party leadership. With the merging of government and Politburo membership, the threat posed by 'bureaucratic interests' extended into the group of Stalin's closest adherents.

According to the Bolshevik world-view, 'bureaucracy' had always been considered a foreign and hostile notion. Any modern bureaucracy works according to its own clearly defined rules and laws, is characterised by a division of labour and professionalism, which prevents it from directly obeying revolutionary orders. Stalin largely owed his political career to portraying himself as a force in the Bolshevik struggle against 'bureaucracy'. The 'anti-bureaucratic scenario', promoted by Stalin since the end of the 1920s, had become firmly entrenched.[43]

A prime example is provided by the case of Sergo Ordzhonikidze. As head of the People's Commissariat for Heavy Industry, he was a strong defender of departmental interests and a kind of guardian of his own cadres.[44] As such Ordzhonikidze frequently clashed with Molotov, head of Sovnarkom, and with V. V. Kuibyshev and V. I. Mezhlauk, successive heads of Gosplan, especially over questions of investment for heavy industry. Stalin was not directly involved in the work of government or in managing the economy; this task was delegated to Sovnarkom, Gosplan and the People's Commissariat of Heavy Industry. Where conflicts arose that could not be resolved at the level of government or in the Politburo, Stalin acted as a final arbiter.[45] Thus he was able to remain aloof from routine institutional work which inevitably involved struggles concerning legitimate departmental interests. This provided an additional opportunity to create an unbridgeable distance between his authority and that of his colleagues in the Politburo.[46]

Stalin's special status could also represent a source of power for individual lieutenants, who tried to make use of this social capital for their own purposes. This holds true for those with a generally weak position like Kaganovich, who rose at the beginning of the 1930s to become 'second secretary', and who owed his entire political career to Stalin. Kaganovich began to give eulogies in praise of Stalin, much to the annoyance of Ordzhonikidze and Mikoyan.[47]

Already in December 1929, Kaganovich had formulated the resolution ascribing to Stalin the role of the 'best pupil, heir and successor of Lenin' and proclaiming him the new 'leader'. Within the internal leadership discourse, he also promoted Stalin's absolute authority. Kaganovich provoked an internal competition in thus praising the *vozhd'*. He had introduced the public cult discourse into the private dealings in the Kremlin's corridors of power.

At the beginning of the 1930s a 'certain independence of individual members of the Politburo in the administration of their departments' did still exist, as O. V. Khlevnyuk has pointed out. In some cases they were in touch with 'certain "groups" of the highest and the middle nomenclature including regional leaders'. Thus for this period one could speak of an unstable 'Stalinist equilibrium'. On the one hand every member of the Politburo submitted unconditionally to the authority of the supreme judge and 'master'. On the other, Stalin had to take account of the existence of 'tribal estates' (*vochina*) and networks around him. From that perspective the Politburo members did have a certain leeway, within which they could effectively stand up for the interests of their departments, their subordinates and their regional clientele. In a new move, Stalin began to stigmatise these independent realms as 'bureaucratic interests'.

The regime of mistrust and the Stalin cult

How did the interactions within Stalin's inner circle contribute to the Stalin cult? According to Voroshilov the inner circle included, besides himself, Molotov, Kaganovich, Mikoyan, Kuibyshev and Ordzhonikidze[48] – that is, both members of the Politburo and candidates, but by no means all those in Stalin's following. After the removal of Rykov and S. I. Syrtsov from the Politburo in December 1930, the government was made up exclusively of those loyal to him.[49] The General Secretary was now able to select confidants as he pleased, to confer with them on various issues. Whereas the forms of consultation became more informal, personal relationships among the top political leaders were characterised by greater formality. Stalin was accustomed to being addressed in familiar terms by several Bolshevik leaders.[50] However, he did not choose his confidants in the top party leadership on the basis of such familiarity. In contrast to the camaraderie of the 1920s, the relationships within the ruling group in the 1930s became more distant and hierarchical. Although Kaganovich was his deputy party leader and 'confidant' in the sense that he was the constant recipient of Stalin's proposals, instructions and thoughts, the relationship between the two remained that of 'master' and 'servant', and the latter could entertain no thought of adopting the familiar form of address.[51]

Starting from the first year of the new government, clashes of interest among the departments had an effect on the Politburo. Throughout all the consequent conflicts Stalin remained in complete control by playing one administrator off against another. Most importantly, he played the role of the devoted teacher of his followers.[52] He had sufficient opportunities for this during 1931. A large number of his comrades exhibited a mixture of weariness in office and refractoriness, both of which grew out of the necessity of representing the economic interests of their departments. During this period the threat of resignation was a favourite means of exerting pressure without risking political conflict.[53] The men in Stalin's leadership were ill equipped to deal with the daunting task of planning and running the economy of the Soviet Union. Looking back on this period, Molotov himself revealed that he and his colleagues had felt overwhelmed by the tasks.[54] Stalin was aware of these deficiencies and often let it be known through harsh criticism; he often had his immediate deputies do the scolding.[55] These disputes, however, were often followed by additional measures to reorganise the People's Commissariats.[56] One important means that Stalin employed to overcome the shortcomings of his administrators was his cadre policy.

In September and October 1931, while on holiday, Stalin launched sharp attacks against important nominations of deputy ministers. The 'fundamental threat to the national economy' posed by deficiencies in the transportation system could not simply be overcome by Central Committee decrees, he told Kaganovich: such decrees would only be 'put on the back burner' by the 'bureaucrats' in charge. What the nation needed were 'new people who believe in our cause and who can successfully replace the bureaucrats – people one can find everywhere in our party if one only looks.'[57] Dedication and 'belief in our cause' were the vague criteria of the cadre policy that Stalin preached to his men and that – as they knew – he applied to them personally. In a letter to Kaganovich, Stalin rejected the candidacies of I. V. Kosior and R. I. Eikhe as deputies for the People's Commissariat of Means of Communication – Transport (NKPS): 'We don't need personages, we need competent candidates'.[58] For Stalin, competence meant not so much a professional qualification, but primarily unconditional allegiance. In these two cases the men were members of the Central Committee and regional secretaries in the Ukraine and Western Siberia, and were among his followers in the provinces. This regional power base was precisely what made Stalin suspicious of them.

Stalin's ability to have his way in every conflict derived from the fact that his administrators exhibited the very loyalty that he sought in his cadre policy. There were, however, differences in degree among them. In the case of Kaganovich, for example, it was especially pronounced, as Molotov remarked in retrospect: 'In our group he was the two hundred percent Stalinist.'[59] No other leading Bolshevik was so unstintingly loyal. In the correspondence that Stalin initiated among his inner circle in 1930, Kaganovich was conspicuous for his emphatic acceptance of Stalin's absolute authority. From 1931 to 1936, during the months when the leader was on holiday and Kaganovich represented him in Moscow, his reports regularly concluded with such phrases as 'Please give me instructions'. In one of the first letters in August 1931 Kaganovich wrote: 'I actually didn't want to tire you, especially in the first days of your holiday, but it must be so – more often than normal, for it's hard for us to rule without you.'[60] His most pointed expression of subordination to Stalin was given in a letter from August 1932: 'You have not only the official political right but also the moral right of a comrade (*tovarishchesko-moral'noe pravo*) to make whatever use you please of what you have made of me as a politician, that is, as your pupil.'[61] The patriarchal structures of the leader cult had clearly penetrated the internal communications between Bolshevik leaders.

The most important doctrine that Stalin inculcated in his administrators was the notion that politics was reducible to 'organisation'. From roughly the time when he took office as general secretary, he embraced this concept and later spelled it out at the 17th Party Congress in 1934: Only 'incorrigible bureaucrats and paper-pushers' could believe in the power of unanimous statements and resolutions. Once the right course of action had been decided on, success depended solely 'on the right choice of people, on the control of how decisions of the executive organs are carried out'.[62] This principle of 'organizational work', and thus the general secretary's idea of polity, represented his method of balancing trust and distrust. Stalin's doctrine for his followers furthermore stipulated absolute subordination to the Politburo and ultimately to his personal will. Those who instead pursued the interests of their own departments received stiff reprimands, as was often the case with Ordzhonikidze. The latter had to be reminded that members of the Politburo were not supposed to 'trick one another', as for example in one of Stalin's warnings: 'The Bolsheviks should not take this path, assuming, of course, they don't intend to transform our Bolshevik Party into a conglomeration of competing departments.'[63] Only a few days before, Stalin had warned the Politburo, in a letter to Kaganovich, saying: 'Comrade Ord[zhonikidze] is continuing to conduct himself badly. He does not realise that his behaviour (with his jabs at comrades Molotov and Kuibyshev) objectively serves to undermine our leading group (*nasha rukovodiashchaia gruppa*), which was formed historically in a struggle against opportunism of all kinds, and that this behaviour threatens to destroy it. Why doesn't he see that he'll have *no* support from our side if he takes *this path*?'[64]

Stalin had long regarded the government authorities as hostile to him. This affected his attitude towards the Rykov government in 1930. His suspicion that the 'bureaucracy' might infect some of his closest associates extended even to Kuibyshev.[65] In any case, after taking over the government in 1931, he was again haunted by the 'antibureaucratic scenario'. Despite the arrest of key economic experts in the government and the demolition of the apparatus connected to Rykov, the danger cropped up at the centre of Stalin's Politburo. 'Bureaucratic interests' among the top Soviet authorities had survived and were now penetrating the Politburo.[66] The letters reveal that Stalin already possessed a high degree of authority among the members of the Politburo. Conflicts and differences of opinion did exist in the Politburo, but they concerned departmental positions and interests. As head of government, Molotov had a tense relationship with Ordzhonikidze, then chairman of the Supreme Economic Council and later of the People's Commissariat for Heavy Industry.[67] Kaganovich, who was good friends with Ordzhonikidze, also came into conflict with Molotov on questions of departmental responsibility, especially after being named People's Commissar of Transport.

Terms such as departmentalism (*vedemstvennost'*) and departmental interest (*vedomstvennye interesy*) had been terms of abuse in Bolshevik language from the beginning. To a certain extent the rules of the game under Stalin permitted the defence of 'bureaucratic interests'. But after 1933, Stalin vehemently opposed such interests.

The social power relationships in the innermost circle of the Kremlin took shape, and the asymmetry of power between Stalin and his associates was continually reinforced. In this phase, however, the asymmetry was mitigated by the pretence of a 'collective leadership' (Stalin as 'comrade' and 'first among equals'). In view of the real conflicts of interest in the top decision-making bodies of the Bolshevik rulers, Stalin at times attempted to play a productive role, acting as a broker on some occasions and exploiting the conflicts for his own gain on others. At all times, however, he was the judge looking down from above. In this circle Stalin's authority was clearly acknowledged and never contested.

The absolute taboo on factional struggle remained – while conflicts of interest still inevitably existed. It forced Stalin's lieutenants to stress that, by struggling for the interests of their departments, they did not want to engage in power conflicts and did not 'undermine our leading group', as Stalin had put it. It was he who embodied this group. What happened at the beginning of 1933 was therefore not accidental: after the especially harsh conflicts over the allocation of capital assets in preparation for the second Five Year Plan, Stalin's report was echoed by a new and comprehensive campaign, launched by his most intimate lieutenants, to promote his leader cult.[68]

'Working towards the Führer' Bolshevik-style

Increasingly, 'devotion' became a practical criterion in cadre policy, necessary to win Stalin's trust. In addition, Stalin himself continued to be guided in his words and deeds by the 'antibureaucratic scenario'. Stalin's policy toward conflicts in his inner circle could be described as balancing trust and mistrust against one another, thus maintaining a kind of equilibrium. From 1933 onwards, this equilibrium began to weaken, while at the same time the asymmetry in power relationships became even more pronounced. Political decisions were delegated increasingly to the Secretariat of the Central Committee, run by Kaganovich on Stalin's behalf. There were informal gatherings of chosen Politburo members 'in Stalin's office'. More and more, the Politburo as a collective organ surrendered its power to the leader. Stalin insisted on being seen as the embodiment of the party dictatorship.

After all opposition had been crushed, conditions for the exercise of power changed considerably. In the early 1930s Stalin was still an 'older' brother or 'best friend' (Kaganovich) for his closest followers in the top echelons of the party-state: a man with whom one could still have the occasional dispute. In the second half of the decade, such labels were no longer used of him.[69] Profound changes occurred in the language used to refer to Stalin. With reference to a letter of Stalin and A. A. Zhdanov demanding the Politburo's removal of G. G. Yagoda as chairman of the NKVD (People's Commissariat for Internal Affairs) and the promotion of Nikolai Ezhov, Kaganovich wrote to Ordzhonikidze in 1936: 'The momentous, wise decision of our father (*nashego roditel'ya*) has matured and has met with immense approval from the party and state.'[70] This may not have been representative for the style of all other members of the Politburo. Voroshilov in his letters to Stalin kept the comradely 'Dear Koba' and used the familiar form of address.[71] Although one cannot find evidence for an explicit leader cult within the Politburo, Kaganovich's cultic language constrained the other members to observe certain norms, namely the view that Stalin was infallible. The Bolsheviks came close to having a leader cult *within* the leadership.

Top leaders had to engage in constant struggle for the allocation of funds to their departments, meaning that existing rules, laws and national interests often fell by the wayside.[72] In addition, human capital, in the form of qualified administrative experts, had to be protected from repeated disruption and repression by the organs of the party and NKVD.[73] To a certain extent this resulted in the development of patrimonial relationships, within which corresponding political networks developed and extended into the top political echelons.[74] Until 1934 a particularly dense network of informal regional relationships existed for Ordzhonikidze, Kirov and Kuibyshev.[75]

This gave Stalin grounds for recurrent appeals for an all-out struggle against 'bureaucratism' and the 'heroes of the departmental spirit'. At the same time, conflicts, which he himself sometimes instigated between departments and organisations, gave him the opportunity to solidify further his position as supreme arbiter.[76]

These informal networks became more and more precarious during the party purge. From 1936 onwards, the former power configuration in centre–periphery relations broke down. The Stalinist leadership 'strove to turn the purge into an anti-bureaucratic revolution'.[77] The regional elites were purged as Stalin's strategy against what he perceived as entrenched institutional interests and potential centrifugal forces. Whilst attacking republican and regional leader authorities who often had their own leader cults,[78] the Stalin cult offered the main symbol of the state's centralisation and the unity of the 'Soviet people'.[79] Stalin came to symbolise the 'moral-political unity of Soviet society'.[80]

As a ruler Stalin managed to become independent of the collective leadership of the Politburo and the Central Committee. Indeed, the Politburo convened less and less often; it became customary to reduce the amount of work that had to be done at its sessions by settling problems in advance with Stalin and issuing 'special directives'.[81] A contrast to the period 1931 to 1933 and a sign that Stalin had effectively established himself as absolute ruler was the fact that by 1934 the director of his private secretariat and the special division in the Central Committee, A. N. Poskrebyshev, wrote most of the Politburo decisions; the approval of the Politburo members was usually obtained simply by passing them round. Collective decision-making had virtually ceased. The Politburo 'had been transformed from a collective organ into a formal appendage of the decision-making mechanism, oriented to the autocratic rule of the leader'.[82]

As the Politburo prepared in 1930 to launch the Stalinist take-over of the state, under conditions of a 'self-imposed state of siege',[83] this siege mentality was forced even in the mid-1930s. Its logic required hermetic seclusion from 'hostile' interests. It was an integral part of Stalin's educational programme to remind his followers regularly of this principle. This 'self-imposed siege' transformed the Politburo and the apparatus of the Central Committee into a forum submissive to Stalin's will. How did this evolve? What can we conclude from the fact that the Stalinist regime functioned even when its master was absent and did not interfere?[84] It is possible to speak of the enormous spiritual power that Stalin exerted over his Politburo. His correspondence with other Politburo members reveals the success of his efforts to educate them. From this perspective, we can identify what Ian Kershaw in the context of Nazi Germany has called 'working towards the Führer'.[85] In the Soviet case Stalin managed to achieve such a thorough socialisation of his cronies that they reached decisions in the same way as if he had been present. He furthermore developed an entire registry of indirect forms of disciplining them, exerting perfect control over social relations in his environment. Thus for his cronies, Stalin's 'will' became the point of orientation and the mechanism of discipline that governed them. Under these conditions, Stalin's power over the party leadership worked through a Stalin cult which, in his intimate ruling circle, was not publicly expressed, so much as internalised.

This process of adaptation to Stalin's will spread through the party and Soviet society. Stalin's principle of mistrust was elevated to the status of a basic Bolshevik law. In a secret circular letter sent to the provincial secretaries on 29 July 1936, written by Ezhov and edited by Stalin, it was stated: 'The essential mark of every Bolshevik in the current situation should be the ability to recognise and identify enemies of the party, no matter how well they are able to disguise themselves.'[86] 'Bolshevik vigilance' was at the core of Stalin's mistrust. In applying the principle, the enemy was defined so broadly that all fell under suspicion.[87] People in responsible positions who were denounced as being 'untrustworthy' were excluded from the party, arrested, exiled or often shot.[88] The only strategy within the horrible chaos of terror was apparently to attempt to fulfil Stalin's will and thereby to gain his trust. Working towards the *vozhd'* for these people was a social practice of the Stalin cult, publicly demonstrating that they had internalised its values. This is what Zhdanov meant in his speech on 21 January 1938, at the peak of the Great Terror, when he said he wanted 'to be like Stalin',[89] Certainly this was not a call to imitate Stalin, but to internalise the notion of 'working towards the Führer'.

In the Great Terror, Stalin generalised his 'strategies of mistrust'. In 1937 and 1938 recurrent terror campaigns were directed against all institutions and spheres in the Soviet state that had not been brought into line: the central and provincial government bureaucracies, the Red Army and the structures of the regional secretaries of the of the Bolshevik Party.[90] At that time, it would have been a fatal mistake for any Politburo member to defend their People's Commissariats.[91] These developments thoroughly destroyed the Politburo members' illusion that they enjoyed a secure status as members of 'Stalin's circle'.[92] From the summer of 1938, following the arrest of V. V. Chubar', first deputy chairman of the Council of People's Commissars and a member of the Politburo, no one in the inner circle could feel safe any longer.

Some conclusions

The Stalin cult was not just the 'beautiful façade' of Stalin's real power. The cult and the evolution of Bolshevik rule during the 1930s were intimately related. The Kremlin circle of Stalin's close lieutenants was the source of initiatives to launch the cult. This usually did not happen as a result of conscious decisions. Rather, this process resulted from competitive interactions within Stalin's inner circle, which had resulted in Stalin's acquisition of absolute authority and spiritual power over his followers. The consequent necessity for them to court for his favours led to the social practices of the Stalin·cult. As a comprehensive realisation of the principle of 'working toward the Führer', the cult was an essential element of Stalin's personal dictatorship.

Notes

1. I am grateful to the Volkswagen Foundation for funding the research for this article as part of the project 'Herrschaft als soziale Praxis in der Geschichte der Sowjetunion unter Lenin und Stalin, 1917–1953'. Some parts of this contribution will be published in: Klaus Heller and Jan Plamper (eds) *Personality Cults in Stalinism (Personenkulte im Stalinismus)* (Göttingen, 2004).
2. A. V. Kvashonkin *et al.* (eds) *Bol'shevistskoe rukovodstvo: Perepiska 1912–1927. Sbornik dokumentov* (Moscow 1996), pp. 309–12; A. Ya. Livshin and I. B. Orlov (eds) *Pis'ma vo vlast'. 1917–1927. Zayavleniya, zhaloby, donosy, pis'ma v gosudarstvennye struktury i bol'shevistskim vozhdyam* (Moscow, 1998), pp. 436–7.
3. The term 'charismatic situation' is derived from Rainer Lepsius, 'Das Modell der charismatischen Herrschaft und seine Anwendbarkeit auf den "Führerstaat" Adolf Hitlers' in *Demokratie in Deutschland* (Göttingen, 1993), pp. 100–2; I. V. Stalin, *Sochineniya*, vol. 11 (Moscow, 1952), pp. 222–38.
4. B. Ennker, 'Führerdiktatur – Sozialdynamik und Ideologie. Stalinistische Herrschaft in vergleichender Perspektive' in Matthias Vetter (ed.) *Terroristische Diktaturen im 20. Jahrhundert: Struktur elemente der nationalsozialistischen und stalinistichen Herrschaft* (Oplachen, 1996), pp. 92–4.
5. See the letters by Soviet citizens to Stalin and the Central Committee in 1927 in RGASPI (Rossiiskii Gosudarstvennyi Arkhiv Sotsial'no-Politicheskii Istorii) 17/85/514 12, 16, 45, 93, 125, 218; RGASPI, 17/85/85 22.
6. For conferences of the Moscow Party organisation, 1927–29, see TsAODM (Tsentral'nyi Arkhiv Obshchestvennykh Dvizhenii Moskvy), 3/8/16. 1–5; 3/9/79. 1–130; 3/10/15 1–9. Report (*svodka*) of 5 November 1929 on resolutions of the party organisations preparing the Central Committee plenum, Informatsionnyi Otdel TsK (RGASPI, 17/32/186, 229–40).
7. RGASPI, 17/85/531–5.
8. *Stalin: Sbornik statei k pyatidesiatiletiyu so dnya rozhdeniya* (Moscow-Leningrad, 1930).
9. RGASPI, 17/3/769 5, 22–4; 81/3/74. 210–28.
10. Benno Ennker, 'Politische Herrschaft und Stalinkult 1929–1939' in Stefan Plaggenborg (ed.) *Stalinismus: Neue Forschungen und Konzepte* (Berlin, 1998), pp. 165–8.
11. M. Lewin, *Russian Peasants and Soviet Power: A Study of Collectivisation* (Evenston, Ill, 1968), pp. 452–3.
12. Molotov speaking to journalists, 21 January 1930 (RGASPI, 82/2/972 1–11); Kaganovich at the Komsomol Congress, 16 January 1931 (RGASPI, 81/3/352 1–134). Some panegyric formulas in brackets in a resolution draft rather suggest that the author was quite uncertain.
13. Sheila Fitzpatrick, *Stalin's Peasants: Resistance and Survival in the Russian Village after Collectivization* (New York, 1994), pp. 287–90; Lynn Viola, *Peasant Rebels under Stalin: Collectivization and the Culture of Peasant Resistance* (New York, 1996),

pp. 171–2. For Stalin's image in letters by peasants and rural party activists and for canvasses of opinion see GARF (Gosudarstvennyi Arkhiv Rossiiskoi Federatsii), R-1235/141/582, 583, 586; 393/2/1874. 12–16; 393/2/1875. 68–86, 175–202; RGAE (Rossiiskii Gosudarstvennyi Arkhiv Ekonomiki), 7486/37/100 141–138ob. See Nikolai Ivnitskii *et al.* (eds) *Tragediya sovetskoi derevni: Kollektivizatsiya i raskulachivanie. Dokumenty i materialy. 1927–1939*, vol. 2 (Nov. 1929–Dec. 1930) (Moscow, 2000), pp. 388–93; Nicolas Werth and Gaël Moullec (eds) *Rapports secrets soviétiques: la société russe dans les documents confidentiels, 1921–1991* (Paris, 1994), pp. 132–6.

14. Robert Tucker, *Stalin in Power* (New York and London, 1990), pp. 204–22.
15. Aleksandr G. Solov'ev, 'Tetradi krasnogo professora (1912–1941gg.)' in *Neizvestnaya Rossiya. XX vek*, vol. 4 (Moscow, 1993), pp. 140–228.
16. Tucker, *Stalin in Power*, p. 146ff.; R. Conquest, *Stalin. Der totale Wille zur Macht* (Berlin, 1991), p. 238; Dmitrii Volkogonov, *Triumf i tragediya. Politicheskii portret I. V. Stalina* (Moscow, 1989), vol. 2, pp. 58–9.
17. Jeffrey Brooks, *Thank You, Comrade Stalin! Soviet Public Culture from Revolution to Cold War* (Princeton, NJ, 2000), pp. 59–60.
18. Aarlen V. Blyum, *Za kulisami 'ministerstva pravdy'. Tainaya istoriya sovetskoi tsenzury, 1917–1929* (St Petersburg, 1994), p. 128.
19. There are hardly any publications for that year. But for the time between October and November 1932 his unpublished speeches at internal party meetings comprise nearly 200 pages in the archives. See *Opis' lichnogo fonda Stalina*, RGASPI, 558/11/165.
20. L. G. Babichenko, 'Pis'mo Stalina v "Proletarskuyu revolyutsiyu" i ego posledstviya', *Voprosy istorii*, no. 6 (1990), pp. 32–51; Vladimir A. Dunaevskii, 'O pis'me Stalina v redaktsiiu "Proletarskaya revolyutsiya" i ego vozdeistvii na nauku i sud'by lyudeii', *Istoriya i stalinizm* compiled by A. N. Mertsalov (Moscow, 1991), pp. 284–97.
21. David Brandenberger, 'Sostavlenie i publikatsiya ofitsial'noi biografii vozhdya – katekhizisa stalinizma', *Voprosy istorii*, no. 12 (1997), pp. 141–50.
22. *Iosif Vissarionovich Stalin: Kratkaya biografiya* (Moscow, 1939). For early critics cf. RGASPI, 558/4/648. 2–21. Stalin issued directions to historians on revising the biography and wrote some parts of it himself: RGASPI, 629/1/54. 2–26; 558/11/1281 1–106. Second edition: *Iosif Vissarionovich Stalin. Kratkaya biografiya*, compiled by G. T. Aleksandrov, B. R. Galaktionov, V. S. Kruzhkov, M. V. Mitin, V. D. Mochalov and P. N. Pospelov (Moscow, 1947).
23. Stalin, *Sochineniya*, vol. 13, pp. 161–215.
24. 'Doklad tov. Stalina', *Pravda*, 14 January 1933, p. 2. Also see reports on the 'reactions of the masses' to Stalin's speech in *Pravda*, 12 January 1933, p. 3; 14 January 1933, p. 2; 17 January 1933, p. 3.
25. See Voroshilov's 20 January 1933 report on results of the Central Committee session, RGASPI, 74/2/20. 1, 39–40; Ordzhonikidze's 26 July 1933 speech in Magnitogosk, RGASPI, 558/1/427 1; 'Vpered k novym pobedam', *Pravda*, 19 January 1933, p. 1; 'Bol'sheviki Leniningrada – tov. Stalinu', *Pravda*, 19 January 1933, p. 1; L. M. Kaganovich, 'Ob itogakh ob' edinennogo plenuma TSK i TsKK VKP(b)', *Pravda*, 20 January 1933, pp. 2–3; 'Moskovskie Bol'sheviki – tov. Stalinu', *Pravda*, 19 January 1933, p. 1. Kaganovich now proclaimed the invincibility of the party, not because it was founded by Lenin, 'but because now at the top of the Party there is his greatest comrade-in-arms, comrade Stalin.' 'Po povodu smerti Lenina', 'Po zavetam Lenina', *Pravda*, 21 January 1933, p. 1.

26. See, for example, correspondence about publishing the letters as a brochure, 2 February 1933 (RGASPI, 558/11/748. 40–50); or, collective letters of 17 May and 26 August 1933 (RGASPI, 558/11/748. 61–7).
27. Yurii G. Fel'shtinskii, *Razgovory s Bukharinym* (New York, 1991), p. 127.
28. See, for example, receptions on 10 November 1935 (RGASPI, 558/1/3180 1–9), on 4–7 November 1935 (RGASPI, 588/1/3166. 1–4), and a reception for Stakhanovite leaders on 29 October 1937 (RGASPI, 588/1/3215 1–18).
29. *Tvorchestvo narodov SSSR* (Moscow, 1938); *Lenin i Stalin v poezii narodov SSSR* (Moscow, 1938); Frank J. Miller, *Folklore for Stalin: Russian Folklore and Pseudo-folklore of the Stalin Era* (New York, 1990).
30. See a 16-page bibliography for formulating congratulatory greetings, *Chto schitat' o zhizni i deyatel'nosti I. V. Stalina* (Leningrad, 1939).
31. Lars T. Lih *et al.* (eds) *Stalin's Letters to Molotov* (New Haven, Conn., 1995), pp. 214, 217.
32. Ibid., pp. 217–19.
33. Ibid., pp. 217–18; Oleg V. Khlevnyuk, *Politbyuro: Mekhanizmy politicheskoi vlasti v 1930-e gody* (Moscow, 1996), pp. 40–3.
34. RGASPI, 558/11/769 55–62.
35. RGASPI, 558/11/738 110–1.
36. Voroshilov to Stalin, 8 October 1930. RGASPI, 74/2/37. 9–12.
37. Mikoyan to Stalin (not dated) beginning October 1930. RGASPI, 558/11/765. 68a.
38. Ordzhonikidze to Stalin, 9 October 1930. RGASPI, 558/11/778. 43.
39. A. I. Mikoyan, *Tak bylo: Razmyshleniya o minuvshem* (Moscow, 1999), p. 292; Stalin to Molotov, 24 August 1930, Kvashonkin *et al.*, *Stalinskoe Politbyuro*, p. 119; Sheila Fitzpatrick, 'Ordzhonikidze's Takeover of Vesenkha: a Study of Soviet Bureaucratic Politics', *Soviet Studies*, 37: 2 (April 1985), pp. 153–72.
40. Stalin to Molotov, 6 August 1930, *Stalin's Letters*, pp. 200–1; Stalin to Molotov, no earlier than 23 August 1930, ibid., pp. 203–4. Stalin to Molotov, 2 September 1930, ibid., pp. 210–11; Khlevnyuk, *Politbyuro*, pp. 36–7.
41. On this whole process Khlevnyuk, *Politbyuro*, pp. 49–52; Derek Watson, *Molotov and the Soviet Government Sovnarkom, 1930–41* (Basingstoke, 1996), pp. 27–45.
42. J. A. Getty, *Origins of the Great Purge: The Soviet Communist Party Reconsidered, 1933–1938* (Cambridge, 1985), pp. 92–136. A different view can be found in Khlevnyuk, *Politbyuro*.
43. Lars T. Lih, 'Introduction', in *Stalin's Letters*, esp. pp. 10–17, 34, 42, 48, 52–61.
44. Oleg V. Khlevnyuk, *Stalin i Ordzhonikidze: Konflikty v Politbyuro v 30-e gody* (Moscow, 1993), p. 31. Fitzpatrick, 'Ordzhonikidze's Takeover'.
45. Feliks Chuev, *Tak govoril Kaganovich* (Moscow, 1992), p. 61; Mikoyan, *Tak bylo*, p. 520.
46. On theoretical interpretations of authority building: Wolfgang Sofsky and Rainer Paris, *Figurationen sozialer Macht: Autorität, Stellvertretung, Koalition* (Opladen, 1991), pp. 32, 92.
47. Mikoyan, *Tak bylo*, p. 318.
48. RGASPI, 74/2/37 9–12.
49. Syrtsov, who was ousted as candidate member of the Politburo, spoke at his interrogation a few weeks later of a group led by Stalin that met regularly but from which other Politburo members, namely Kuibyshev, Rudzutak and Kalinin, were excluded. Khlevnyuk, *Politbyuro*, p. 46f. He was apparently in error regarding Kuibyshev. Looking back at the entire Stalin period, Molotov stated that there had 'always been a leading group in the Politburo' and that it excluded Kalinin,

Rudzutak, Kosior and Andreev. F. I. Chuev, *Sto sorok besed s Molotovym; Iz dnevnika F. Chueva* (Moscow, 1991), p. 424.

50. Among those with whom he had such a relationship were Molotov, Ordzhonikidze, Kalinin, Voroshilov, Kirov and Mikoyan, besides 'oppositionists' such as Bukharin and Kamenev. Mikoyan, *Tak bylo*, pp. 318, 351–2.
51. R. Medvedev, *Oni okruzhali Stalina* (Moscow, 1999), pp. 89–166. See 'Lazar' Kaganovich: Kar'era stalinskogo komissara' in O. V. Khlevnyuk, R. W. Davies, L. P. Kosheleva, E. A. Rees, L. A. Rogovaya (eds) *Stalin i Kaganovich Perepiska. 1931–1936gg.* (Moscow, 2001), pp. 23–9.
52. Khlevnyuk, *Politbyuro*, p. 96.
53. This is the interpretation of Khlevnyuk, ibid., 82ff.
54. F. Chuev, *Molotov Remembers: Inside Kremlin Politics – Conversations with Felix Chuev*, ed. A. Resis. (Chicago, 1993), p. 181. In the Russian edition, which is structured differently, I could not find this statement.
55. He had previously used this approach in August 1930, when he used Molotov against Mikoyan: Stalin to Molotov, 24 Aug. 1930 in Lih *et al.* (eds) *Stalin's Letters*, pp. 204–6. Molotov was also sent to dissuade Kuibyshev from stepping down as Gosplan chairman: Molotov to Kuibyshev, 14 Aug. 1931 in Kvashonkin *et al.*, *Stalinskoe Politbyuro*, p. 121. Khlevnyuk, *Politbyuro*, pp. 82–3. While on vacation in August 1931, Stalin used his deputy Kaganovich to transmit his criticism of Kuibyshev to the Politburo: Kuibyshev's 'behavior makes a bad impression all around. He seems to be running from his work.' See *Stalin i Kaganovich Perepiska*, pp. 50–1. The resignation was withdrawn. In like manner, Mikoyan's request to resign was rejected by the Politburo on 15 Oct. 1931. See Kvashonkin *et al.*, *Stalinskoe politbyuro*, p. 123.
56. Watson, *Molotov and the Soviet Government.*
57. *Stalin i Kaganovich Perepiska*, pp. 109–10.
58. *Stalin i Kaganovich Perepiska*, p. 126.
59. Chuev, *Sto sorok besed*, p. 319.
60. *Stalin i Kaganovich Perepiska*, p. 38ff.
61. Ibid., p. 284.
62. Stalin, *Sochineniya*, vol. 13, pp. 262–79.
63. *Stalin i Kaganovich*, p. 711.
64. *Stalin i Kaganovich*, p. 51. Underlining in the original.
65. Kuibyshev, chairman of the Supreme Council of the National Economy (Vesenkha), became the target of fierce criticism from Ordzhonikidze, commissar for the Workers and Peasants' Inspectorate (NKRKI) at the 16th Party Congress. This came as a surprise but was most certainly arranged with Stalin. As a result Kuibyshev lost his post to Ordzhonikidze: Fitzpatrick, 'Ordzhonikidze's Takeover'.
66. Khlevnyuk, *Politbyuro*, pp. 79–94.
67. Kuibyshev and Kaganovich, 10 Aug. 1931, in *Stalin i Kaganovich*, p. 710; Kaganovich to Stalin, 12 Aug. 1931, ibid., pp. 41–2; Stalin to Kaganovich, 17 Aug. 1931, ibid. pp. 50–1; Stalin to Kaganovich, 19 Aug. 1931, ibid., pp. 51–3; Stalin to Orzhonikidze, 9 Sept. 1931, ibid., p. 711.
68. Ibid., pp. 79–89.
69. Ibid., p. 94.
70. Khlevnyuk, *Stalin i Ordzhonikidze*, pp. 76–7.
71. Voroshilov to Stalin, 25 June 1936, and 9 July 1936, in *Sovetskoe rukovodstvo. Perepiska, 1928–1941*, Sostaviteli A. V. Kvashonkin, L. P. Kosheleva, L. A. Rogovaya and O. V. Khlevnyuk (Moscow, 1999), pp. 331–4.

72. Ibid., pp. 123–5.
73. Ibid., p. 94.
74. G. M. Easter, *Reconstructing the State: Personal Networks and Elite Identity in Soviet Russia* (Cambridge, 2000), pp. 89–105; James Harris, *The Great Urals: Regionalism and the Evolution of the Soviet System* (Ithaca, NY, 1999), pp. 70–104.
75. Easter, *Reconstructing*, pp. 80–95.
76. Ibid., p. 95f.
77. O. Khlevnyuk: 'The First Generation of Stalinist Party Generals' in E. A. Rees (ed.) *Centre–Local Relations in the Stalinist State, 1928–1941* (Basingstoke, 2002), p. 56.
78. Ibid., p. 59.
79. B. C. Kiteme, 'The Cult of Stalin: National Power and the Soviet Party State', PhD diss., Columbia University, 1989, pp. 119–56.
80. V. Molotov, 'Stalin kak prodolzhatel' dela Lenina' in *Stalin. K shestesyatiletiyu so dnya rozhdeniya* (Moscow, 1940), pp. 18–31. B. Burkov, *Moral'no-politicheskoe edinstvo sovetskogo obshestva* (Moscow, 1951).
81. Khlevnyuk, *Politbyuro*, p. 97.
82. Ibid., pp. 117–18.
83. On October 20 the Politburo took a decision against the so-called conspiracy of the 'Industrial Party' with measures to protect Stalin personally as well as the Central Committee's apparatus, tranferring it to the Kremlin, after all 'untrustworthy' elements were removed from its buildings. RGASPI, 17/162/9 54. Hughes refers to the 'self-imposed state of siege' in this context: J. Hughes, 'Patrimonialism and the Stalinist System: The Case of S. I. Syrtsov', *Europa-Asia Studies*, 48: 4 (1996), pp. 551–68, 562.
84. Arch Getty, examining how the Politburo functioned during Stalin's long vacations in 1931–36, argues that he did not take a very active role either in promoting initiatives or through policy intervention. Getty mistakenly downplays Stalin's power in his relationship with his henchmen: J. Arch Getty, 'Stalin as Prime Minister: Power and the Politburo' in Sarah Davies and James Harris (eds) *Stalin: A New History* (Ithaca, NY, 2004).
85. I. Kershaw, *Hitler (1. Vol.) 1889–1936* (Stuttgart, 1998), pp. 665–749. On the leader cult of Hitler also see I. Kershaw, *Der Hitler-Mythos: Führerkult und Volksmeinung* (Stuttgart, 1999).
86. *Izvestiya TsK KPSS*, no. 8 (1989), pp. 91–2.
87. In November 1937 Stalin defined 'enemy' in the broadest sense: 'Whoever through deeds or thoughts – yes, thoughts, too – attacks the unity of the socialist state will be liquidated by us without mercy.' Cited by Erik van Ree, *The Political Thought of Joseph Stalin: A Study in Twentieth-Century Revolutionary Patriotism* (London, 2002), p. 134. In this Beria followed Stalin to the letter: 'An enemy of the people is not just someone who does damage, but also someone who doubts the party line. There still are many such persons among us, and we must liquidate them'. Cited by Dmitri Volkogonov, *Stalin: Triumph and Tragedy* (edited and translated by Harold Shukman (London, 1991), p. 279.
88. The Central Committee plenum of June 1937 proposed that all members of the Central Committee 'who cannot be trusted' be expelled: O. Khlevnyuk, 'Party and NKVD: Power Relationships in the Years of the Great Terror' in B. McLoughlin and K. McDermott (eds) *Stalin's Terror: High Politics and Mass Repression in the Soviet Union* (Basingstoke, 2002), p. 25. L. Z. Mekhlis, chief of the Central Committee press department, proposed to the Politburo in November 1937 the discharge of S. B. Ingulov, chief of the Soviet censorship (Glavlit), as

being 'not politically trustworthy': see *Istoriya sovetskoi politicheskoi tsenzury. Dokumenty i kommentarii* (Moscow, 1997), pp. 72–5.

89. To be precise, Zhdanov's call was formulated as 'To be like Lenin and nowadays like Stalin': RGASPI, 77/1/673 1–35. This speech was published on 28 Jan. 1938 in *Pravda*. Stalin, in an address to a meeting for the election of the Supreme Soviet on 11 December 1937, proposed that the deputies of the Supreme Soviet should be 'like Lenin'. Stalin, *Sochineniya*, vol. 1 (14), ed. Robert McNeal (Stanford, cal., 1967), pp. 262–3.
90. Tucker, *Stalin in Power*, pp. 427–30. Easter, *Reconstructing the State*, pp. 149–60.
91. For the fates of and the pressure on Molotov, Kaganovich, Ordzhonikidze and Voroshilov: Yu. N. Zhukov, *Tainy Kremylya. Stalin, Molotov, Beriya, Malenkov* (Moscow, 2000), pp. 63–4. Even Molotov and Kaganovich were not exempt from intimidation, with pressure applied through the arrest of close family members. Watson, *Molotov*, p. 173; Khlevnyuk, *Politbyuro*, pp. 241–2, 245–6; Khlevnyuk, *Stalin i Ordzhonikidze*, pp. 83–129. At the February-March plenum of the Central Committee in 1937, Ezhov attacked the People's Commissars' practice of defending their people against the NKVD. See *Voprosy istorii*, 2 (1992), pp. 19, 21. During the same session Molotov attacked Voroshilov for declaring that there were 'at present only a few enemies of the people' in the Red Army: *Voprosy istorii*, 8 (1994) pp. 5, 24–5.
92. Kvashonkin *et al.*, *Stalinskoe politbyuro*, p. 55; Khlevnyuk, *Politbyuro*, p. 238.

6
Grandpa Lenin and Uncle Stalin: Soviet Leader Cult for Little Children

Catriona Kelly

A major innovation of the twentieth century, across many different types of political system – constitutional monarchies, republics with elected multiparty democracies, and one-party, 'totalitarian', states – was the emergence of genres of political propaganda aimed explicitly at children.[1] Children had a firm place in Soviet political propaganda from the start. 'Ruler and child' icons proliferated; model biographies were ubiquitous. Children learnt by heart songs and poems praising Lenin and Stalin; they were taught to ornament their essays with Lenin and Stalin quotations. They read, and commented upon, selected texts by the leaders, and paid eulogistic tribute to them in lessons. Exposure to such material was obviously crucial in shaping attitudes to the regime, both at the time when children were learning about the leaders and later on. Yet despite the centrality of the leader cult for children to the operation of the regime, and to the mentality of its growing citizens, it has received remarkably little attention in historiography. Existing treatments are largely iconological in character – that is, they deal with the content of representations rather than with how these were used and what impact they made upon children.[2] Accordingly, this chapter, though paying some attention to icon types, will be more closely concerned with other issues: first, children's specific experience of ruler cult *practices*: the rituals employing ruler icons that they experienced, the artworks and letters that they dedicated to leaders; and second, the extent to which the ruler cult was able to inspire belief and trust in the leaders among children, both in their youth and when they came to maturity.

Soviet ruler cult for children: a brief history

From, at the latest, the founding of the 'children's communist movement' (later the 'Pioneers') in May 1922, a ruler cult pervaded the official literature and art directed at children. However – as with adults – Lenin's death brought about a qualitative distinction in terms of the amount of coverage accorded. In February 1924, for example, the very first issue of *Pioner* magazine carried as its front-page item 'The Leader's Death' (*Smert' vozhdya*), a sermon addressed to 'All children's groups and proletarian children in the Union of Soviet Socialist Republics', and meant to be read aloud and discussed in 'all Pioneer troops and sections (*zven'ya*), in all schools, orphanages, and among all peasant and pioneer children'. The children were reminded of Lenin's love for children, with whom he had however met 'only rarely, during the few moments of his life that his great work left free'. Lenin had committed himself to 'bettering the life of proletarian children'. His life was, moreover, an example to all children, who were to learn from it 'not to lose control of themselves' (*ne zateryat'sya*) in a crisis such as this, and 'to study, fight and live as Il'ich fought and lived'.[3]

Other texts were concerned precisely with 'how Il'ich fought and lived'. In January and February 1924, the Leningrad children's magazine *Vorobei* began putting out 'Lenin as child' propaganda for its young readers, illustrated with photographs of Lenin as a student at the *gimnaziya* (classical secondary school) and so on.[4] The legendary early biography of the leader – his outstanding school performance and extraordinary ideological fervour – had already crystallised at this early stage, and remained canonical until the end of Soviet power, as did the practice of underlining to children the relevance of Lenin's lives for them. From 1924, the Octobrists, the junior wing of the Pioneers, wore an image of curly-headed Volodya Ulyanov as a badge, rather than the flaming bonfire shown on the Pioneer badge proper, and it was customary for young Pioneers to hold ceremonial meetings under statues of a slightly older Vladimir Ulyanov, this time usually aged around 12.[5]

Already by 1924, then, a division had become clear that was to persist in later representations of the Soviet leader: between the father-figure who watched over and cared for children, and the exemplary life-pattern for children's own emulation. But the two identities of the leader were at some level inseparable. In the words of Trotsky, addressing 'the Soviet proletarian and peasant child' in the inaugural issue of *Pioner*, the point was to 'be worthy of your teacher (*vospitatel'*) and leader' – a convenient formulation that at once brought ruler and children together, and kept them apart.[6] In honour of Lenin's death, the Pioneers had become 'Young Leninists' (*yunye lenintsy*), a word signifying both an acolyte of the ruler's memory and a disciple of his teaching. And child-focused propaganda also, of course, dwelt on the adult Lenin, not just as political leader but as role model (*'Proshchai, uchitel', ty nash kumir/Zavety tvoi ne zabudet ves' mir'* – 'Farewell, great teacher, our idol you are/Your precepts live on both here and afar').[7] Perhaps the most famous such representation of Lenin for children occurs in M. M. Zoshchenko's cycle of stories about the leader, first published in 1940, where Lenin is a non-smoker, a devotee of fresh air, a fitness fanatic, and determinedly committed to egalitarianism and self-sacrifice into the bargain.[8] But the stereotype itself is considerably older, going back to official biographies of the mid-1920s, which propagandised to younger readers the central Soviet notion of *zakal*, or 'steeliness', the efficient, hard-working mind in the muscular and well-tempered body. Zoya Lilina's *Little Lenin*, for instance, emphasised that Lenin had found time for sport – thrashing the local village lads in the popular game of *babki* – as well as for study and absorption in the recent political history of his native land. The narrator, an imaginary Pioneer leader, told his Octobrist listeners, that Lenin had been quite a little rascal (*shalun*) when he was small. However, such elements were corralled off into early childhood.[9]

The division between Lenin the paragon of virtue and Lenin the approachable human being evident here could be seen also in propaganda representing Lenin as the ruler and figurehead of state authority. During the 1920s, representations of Lenin tended to be sternly tutelary in character. Often, no children at all appeared with the leader, and when they did, there was no close physical contact. In 'Lenin with Children', a painting by Pavel Kuznetsov done shortly after the leader's death, for example, Lenin sat at one side, while on the other stood a line of children gazing at him respectfully; the effect was of detached admiration and not of affection and closeness.[10]

It hardly seems surprising to come across a complaint from one Soviet educationalist, V. N. Shul'gin, that incompetent teachers had turned Lenin 'into a fierce old grandfather, some kind of ascetic old saint and humbug, a bogey to *frighten* children with'.[11] Yet the very fact that Shul'gin could offer such remarkably frank criticism was, of course, an indication of ambiguity in the understanding of Lenin at this period. A tutelary figure he certainly was, but, until the educational reforms of 1932 reinstituted the leading role of teachers and school directors, tutelage did not necessarily have to be associated with authoritarianism. Accordingly, propaganda for children about Lenin showed him as approachable, in direct contact with children, in the same way that he was supposed to be accessible to ordinary people.[12]

The designs for monuments to Lenin that children were encouraged to make during the mid-1920s shared this emphasis on approachability. They might show the leader as oversized, but they also showed him as downbeat and unpretentious: dressed in his famous cloth cap and, in one striking and quite powerful image produced by a group of 14-year-olds, helping a group of workers to rotate the world on its axis with the help of a conveyor belt.[13]

Equally, presents offered by groups of children – Pioneers, say, or orphans – usually consisted of low-key items – decorated files for Lenin's work-notes were particularly popular. In a way, presents of this kind turned the leader into a kind of honorary schoolchild, with the children visualising his daily life in ways relating to their own.[14]

The sense of a 'special relationship' between Lenin and children could be driven only so far, however. There were few sources demonstrating what

Lenin's relationship with children had actually been like. Indeed, rumours that Lenin had disliked and avoided children openly circulated in the 1920s.[15] Nadezhda Krupskaya, a moving spirit behind the 'Lenin for children' cult, did her best to try and scotch such disloyal whispers. Yes, she assured the readers of *Delegatka* magazine in 1931, 'It is all true. Vladimir Il'ich did love children. In the presence of children his face lit up, his eyes filled with laughter, he enjoyed listening to their chatter and playing noisy games and generally having to do with them (*vozit'sya*).' Lenin, she reiterated, had treated children in an uncondescending and unpatronising way, and had detested the bourgeois habit of using them as playthings.[16]

While Lenin had penned numerous speeches and articles in which he addressed the place of teenagers and young people in Soviet society, there was a scarcity of key writings on children and their place in society.[17] Equally, the early 1920s did not see the publication in large numbers of photographs of Lenin, his eyes lit up with laughter, enjoying the company of children.[18] Bolshevik mistrust of family intimacy and domestic sentimentality was certainly one reason for this: images of this kind would have seemed too 'petit-bourgeois' for comfort. Indeed, in 1933, *Pioneer Leader* journal published an explicit attack on such visions of Lenin, criticising pictures that showed the leader laughing with peasant boys or fawning on kittens. 'Do they really make Lenin look like the leader of the international proletariat, the most bitter enemy of the capitalists?' the writer demanded.[19]

The need to fill the vacuum left by the disappearance of religious images and photographs of the royal family from educational institutions, hospitals, orphanages and clubs had made imperative the creation of an alternative ruler symbolism from the moment the February Revolution took place. After the Civil War, however, the process took on still greater intensity, with school textbooks, the decoration of schools, and the trappings of the Communist children's movement all playing their part in conveying the magnificence of Lenin. In August 1923, for example, the Women Workers' Section of the *Krasnaya Presnya* district committee of the Communist Party presented a newly formed local Pioneer troop with a photograph of the leader.[20] But the watershed for the children's version of the Lenin cult, as with the adult version, was the death of Lenin himself in January 1924. In February 1924, the Secretariat of the Central Committee of the Komsomol had produced an exemplary plan for a 'Lenin corner' to be set up in schools and Pioneer clubs: such a 'corner' was supposed to contain, among other things, a portrait, a biography written by the children themselves, a photo-spread of Lenin's life, extracts from his speeches, details of his final illness, memoirs by acquaintances, and information about what Lenin had done for children.[21]

In the second half of the 1920s, as Soviet leaders jockeyed for position in the wake of Lenin's death, figures such as Trotsky and Stalin lent ostentatious support to the Pioneer movement; and Trotsky also contributed to the construction of the myth of Lenin as child-lover. But they did not have themselves photographed with children, and did little to promote children's issues in a practical way. Exceptional, in this context, was Dzerzhinsky's contribution to the child welfare movement (he was a champion of institutional care for the thousands of homeless children – *besprizornye*). *Pravda* on 20 July 1936 to mark the ten-year anniversary of Dzerzhinsky's death included passages where the former head of the Cheka had poured out his affection for children – 'I could never love a woman in the way that I love them!'[22]

During the first 15 years of Bolshevik rule, then, the emphasis was less on indulging children and on treating them affectionately, than upon projecting a willingness to co-operate with them and to respond flexibly to their needs. Quite logically, petitions from Pioneers themselves were usually phrased with frankness and self-confidence. According to a ritual established in the 1920s, Pioneer groups would select members of the Central Committee as patrons of the troop, and then write asking the person concerned for a biography, a portrait, and some good advice on the best conduct of affairs in the troop.[23] By the mid-1920s the act of adopting some prominent politician as a role model had become a fixed part of the indoctrination of children, and there was a considerable degree of egalitarianism in the tone of address when those leaders were contacted by their young disciples.

In the late 1920s, however, came monumental changes to the nature of ruler iconography. Portraits of Stalin became increasingly visible, and by 1931, Lenin's dominance in pictorial terms was starting to be eroded, with the dead leader increasingly often appearing alongside the living one, or consigned to a secondary group along with Marx and Engels.[24] So far as children were concerned, a watershed year was 1934, when pictures of Stalin began to appear far more prominently in the Pioneer press. *Pioner* magazine, for instance, carried a joint portrait of Lenin and Stalin in its issue commemorating Lenin's death; three issues later, the ruler addressed readers directly, under a large portrait and the headline, 'Comrade Stalin Speaks'.[25] *Pionerskaya pravda* had images of the leader in all three of the first issues of the year, and in the sixth issue carried an article, 'We Talked to Comrade Stalin' in which Pioneers recounted a meeting with the leader.[26] And then, in July 1935, came the pioneering example of the genre of 'ruler with adoring small child', in the form of an illustrated *Pravda* story, 'I gave a bouquet to Stalin!' Here, 'pioneer Nina Zdrogova' excitedly recounted how she had been thanked for her tribute with a kiss and 'We're going to be friends, you and I,' as well as chocolates and a bag that turned out to contain cherries ('I checked later').[27] Almost a year later, on 29 June 1936, *Pravda* printed what was instantly to become a famous and ubiquitous image, showing Stalin with a small girl from the Buryat-Mongol Republic, Gelya Markizova.

It is a widely held misapprehension that the Stalin cult never, or very rarely, evoked the leader as a child. In fact, such coverage was quite prominent in devotional spreads about him for a junior audience. An early example came in the form of an article contemporary with the brouhaha round the promulgation of the 1936 Soviet constitution, in which Stalin's alleged schoolmate, M. Titvinidze, recalled how the outstanding gifts of the young 'Soso' had already been evident in the classroom.[28] Similar items also appeared in the 60th-birthday coverage put out by *Pionerskaya pravda*, which included two separate articles dealing with different phases of Stalin's youth.[29] For this occasion also, official presents given by children to the leader included an embroidered picture, 'Stalin's Childhood', presented to him by a group of Pioneers from Perm' province.[30] Coverage of this kind, both in journalism and in face-to-face activism, was also part of the 1949 jubilee celebrations.[31] A list of model topics for 'conversations round the bonfire', or informal political discussions at Pioneer camps, put out in 1952 was headed by 'The Childhood and School Years of V. I. Lenin and I. V. Stalin' (others included 'Thank you great Stalin for a happy childhood', 'The red tie', 'The great constructions of Communism', 'The Stalinist plan for the transformation of nature', and 'Friendship and comradeliness').[32] One might note also David Gabitashvili's 1953 icon, 'The Thirst for Knowledge', which shows a schoolboy Stalin poring over a book.[33] In fact, the thrust of discussion should run the other way round: pretty well the only respect in which Stalin *was* portrayed as a model for ordinary mortals was when he was a small child.[34] While the 'child Stalin as role model' had some weight within ruler cult propaganda for children, child-centred material was without question dominated by another manifestation of the leader, the 'Stalin as patron and protector' role.

The 'child and ruler' icon of Stalin was, then, the crucial genre, and one that had significantly altered since Lenin's time. Unlike Lenin, Stalin actively liked children, was happy to be photographed with them, and seems to have had a genuine rapport with them. At the same time, an air of the otherworldly, of unreality, hung over all encounters with 'dear Comrade Stalin' – who, in some texts for children, was represented as actually having magic powers.[35] They always took place on some ceremonial occasion, and were usually accompanied by a ritual exchange – as in the case of Nina Zdrogova's flowers versus chocolate and cherries, or Gelya Markizova's bouquet versus kiss. And they were heavily overlaid with symbolism, with the children whom Stalin met representing the Soviet Union in its unity and diversity: very often, the children came from a 'subordinate' culture within the union. Through exploitation of traditional gender stereotypes, a power asymmetry was created: the *narod* was not only junior in terms of age, but also feminine and hence passive (and, by being associated explicitly with the 'Orient', the child-as-nation 'Europeanised' the status of a leader who might otherwise himself have been seen by his Russian subjects as an 'Oriental'). Interpretations of this kind should not be regarded as fanciful: they were explicit in the literature of the time as well. The Tadzhik poet Vapi, in a translated piece published in *Vozhatyi* in 1936, glossed the meeting of Stalin and Mamlakat Nakhangova thus:

> Stalin's joy is clear to the world:
> Memleket [sic] is cheerful and young,
> Memleket is full of heroism,
> Memleket means – the nation.[36]

As Jeffrey Brooks has shown, the trope of gratitude from the nation to the party leadership, and most particularly to the Soviet Union's 'beloved leader', Joseph Vissarionovich himself, was ubiquitous in propaganda: 'Stalin and others employed rituals of theater to draw citizens into public displays of support.'[37] The 'thanking' ritual was an absolutely central part of propaganda for children too. The phrase, 'Thank You Dear Comrade Stalin for a Happy Childhood!', which appeared for the first time in 1936, was emblazoned over the doorways of nurseries, orphanages and schools, pinned up on walls, printed on book and magazine covers, and chanted by children at festivals.[38] 'Thanking' ceremonies took place throughout the country in schools and in nursery schools on important occasions, such as the openings of party congresses, the anniversary of the October Revolution, and the leader's own birthday. Children cheered the leader to the echo; they shouted 'Thank You Dear Stalin for a Happy Childhood'.

The second way in which the cult had meaning for adults was that the relationship between leader and children was supposed to inspire appropriate emotions in adult viewers. The anticipated adult reactions included a sentimental conviction that the ruler concerned must be a kind, humane individual since he was obviously so devoted to children. But there was another important meaning – adults were supposed to *emulate* the child's unquestioning devotion. In the 1920s, child activists had been models, in their fervent commitment, for adult endeavours, and politically engaged children – above all Pioneers – had been urged to lead their parents and other 'backward' adults out of darkness into light.[39] As one woman brought up in the late 1930s recalled, the ritual of thanking Stalin was akin to thanking God for one's daily bread; and, in a comparable misappropriation of evangelical tradition, adults were brought to believe that they must become 'as a little child' if they were to enter into the Stalinist paradise.[40] The leading literary journal *Krasnaya nov'* marked Stalin's 60th birthday with a spread of poems by children (alongside work by leading Soviet writers and a selection of Stalinist folklore), whose compiler, Sergei Bogomazov, emphasised, 'Children's feelings for Stalin are the feelings of the entire country'.[41]

Creating and filling a vacancy: ruler cults after the death of Stalin

In the post-war years, the Stalin cult for children, like that for adults, was to remain all-pervasive. Now praised as the 'Generalissimus', Stalin was shown wearing military uniform as he accepted the vast bouquets from children, but otherwise the iconic canon remained just as it had been in 1936–39, the days of the cult's first climax.[42] Nursery school teachers still dwelt on the omnipotence of the leader, making a prominent statue the high point of a 'getting to know your city' expedition, and introducing the leader into as many areas of their teaching about 'Soviet patriotism' as they could contrive. When children learned about other countries in the Soviet empire, their teachers dwelled on Georgia, the birthplace of Stalin; when they were preparing children for the transition to 'big' school, they told them about Stalin's concern for the school-building programme; and when the Pioneer movement was discussed, children would be told how much Stalin loved the pioneers.[43] The most significant shift was a decline in texts showing direct contact with the leader (accounts of 'How I Met Stalin' or of fantasy trips to the Kremlin) in favour of texts that showed contact with him in some remote or mediated form. In A. Nekrasov's 'Two Victories', published for the birthday celebrations in 1949, for instance, a brave boy explorer who went on an expedition to the Far East was rewarded not by meeting Stalin, but by receiving a telegram from him.[44] Equally, at this point children's poems about the leader were extremely official and abstract: a piece published in *Pioner*'s December 1949 issue, for example, evoked the ruler as national leader:

> Flag winds with flag
> Like the petals of spring flowers!
> Stalin watches and smiles:
> That's what the power of the nation is like![45]

At this period, too, children's own poems, if anything, occupied a smaller place than they had in previous celebrations of the ruler's life: for example, the *Pionerskaya pravda* 1949 jubilee edition published one child's poem (*'On – prostoi, lyubimyi vsemi nami/I mudrei ego na svete net'* – He is simple, loved by all of us, And wiser than he, there is no one on this earth), but devoted more space to a spread of anthology favourites by adult poets such as Surkov, Isakovsky and Mikhalkov.[46]

Children were particularly prominently included in reportage about the mourners at Stalin's funeral. The photo-coverage in *Pravda* on 9 March 1953 included a special section, 'Children Bid Farewell to the Leader', showing the usual beribboned small girls paying their respects to the corpse. In a similar vein, the magazine *School and Family* (*Sem'ya i shkola*) carried a photo-spread in its April issue, under the title 'Children in the Days of National Mourning', where a group of children – who once again, according to established propaganda convention, were almost all girls – remembered their reactions when they heard of the leader's death. Emotional states were predictable – 'I wept terribly', 'Tears choked my throat', 'My mother and I read Mikhail Sholokhov's "Farewell, Father" and wept' – and so was the determination to derive some didactic benefit from the tragedy. Grief should inspire survivors to do more schoolwork: 'Stalin was happy when he saw pupils getting good marks. Stalin was sad when they got bad ones,' remarked one eight-year-old. A nine-year-old who had lost her own father lamented a death that felt like losing her father all over again. 'I dreamed of meeting comrade Stalin and talking to him. But now I'll only see him in the mausoleum . . . I'll try to write nicely and more tidily, with no mistakes'.[47] A month later, a second article asserted that children had loved Stalin more than anything else in the world. 'One cannot compare this even with the feeling they have for their father or their mother'. If a child drew a figure that towered over houses and trees, it would turn out to be Stalin. If a child was ill-treated at home, it would appeal to Stalin. Children entering a war orphanage thought that they were coming to stay with Stalin. And children constantly wrote poems to Stalin.[48]

For a year or so, propaganda management continued to preserve the imagery and rituals that had obtained in Stalin's lifetime. The first anniversary of Stalin's death, in March 1954, was commemorated respectfully in children's magazines, and in family newspapers, such as *Sem'ya i shkola*. An official manual for nursery school teachers that appeared in 1954 made teaching 'love of the Soviet motherland, for the Soviet people, for the great leaders Lenin and Stalin' an official part of the syllabus.[49] In the same year, however, an important change was made to the Pioneer oath: members of the organisation now promised 'in the presence of their comrades' to 'be true to the testaments of Lenin' – the post-1942 reference to the 'Great Stalin' was dropped.[50] And once de-Stalinisation began in earnest, after Khrushchev's 'Secret Speech' in 1956, it was felt quickly in the world of education. For example, the September 1956 issue of *Soviet Pedagogy* carried an editorial insisting that it was essential to 'overcome the consequences of the cult of personality in pedagogy'. Alongside comments on the desirability of purging textbooks for trainee teachers, there were observations on the need to clean up school textbooks, especially in order to curb the 'harm' that the cult had wrought in promoting a contradictory and irrational list of historical heroes: Peter I, Ivan the Terrible, Aleksandr Nevsky, Suvorov, Kutuzov, Shamil, and so on.[51] Though nothing was said explicitly about revising textbooks in order to expunge references to Stalin, educational administrators rapidly recognised the need to withdraw 'cultic' material of this kind from circulation.[52]

As de-Stalinisation took hold, posters, statues and murals of Stalin in all child-centred sites began to disappear. By 1962, there were clear signs of a burgeoning 'Khrushchev cult' to replace the celebration of 'Uncle Stalin'. Sergei Mikhalkov, one of the most assiduous contributors to Stalinist children's literature, readily dedicated his skills to this new genre, showing, in 'Be Prepared!', the new leader enthusiastically greeting the astronaut German Titov after his return from space.[53]

After the new leader's fall from grace in 1964, however, 'cults of personality' directed at the living were treated more cautiously. In compensation, there was now an all-out expansion of the Lenin cult, which, in Nina Tumarkin's words, 'placed special emphasis on the propaganda of Lenin for children'.[54] This involved not only proliferation of the traditional 'young Lenin as model' imagery,[55] but also development of the 'ruler as patron and protector' side of the cult, with Lenin now being promoted to the 'avuncular' status formerly occupied by Stalin.[56] And in 1970, the photo-coverage in *Ogonek* included an allegedly genuine snapshot of Lenin walking in the park at Gorki and holding hands with his small nephew, Viktor.[57] While the Lenin cult was still something to be taken very seriously, the 'stern' side of what was expected from children was to some extent displaced on to role-model martyrs such as Pavlik Morozov or Zoya Kosmodem'yanskaya, who were in turn also acquiring an increasingly static, routinised role in the culture.[58]

'The dreams of happy children': the reception of the Lenin and Stalin cult

A vital characteristic of leader cult propaganda was that the audience reaction was already anticipated within it. As we have seen, children's literature taught children how to respond to Stalin icons; and the compilations of children's poems about Lenin and Stalin were prescriptive as well as descriptive, teaching children about how they should respond to the leader and how they should write about him. A collectively written poem by a group of 11-year-olds from a Moscow school was entirely orthodox in terms of its phrasing, except for a single adverb: the reference to the children 'greedily' scanning Lenin's 'deceased countenance' was comically incongruous, suggesting as it did bloodthirsty curiosity, rather than grief:

> To the tramp of a thousand feet,
> By the scarlet-and-black mourning
> Of the columns,
> Our school took its leave of Il'ich.
> We gazed greedily at his deceased countenance
> And were silent

As though afraid to disturb the silence
Of the sadness.[59]

But any humorous effect here was certainly unintentional. Both this piece and all the other poems, stories and memoirs included in the anthology alongside it underline that grief was sincere and profound: 'I couldn't believe that such a great man had died. I couldn't explain the feeling; I didn't want to weep; no, I just couldn't believe that such a great man had died. When Lenin was alive, I hadn't felt anything nearly so strong.'[60] Another child's fantasy ('I dreamt a fairy had arrived, waved her wand, and Lenin rose from his coffin, safe and sound') unpleasing as it would have been to hardline Commissariat of Enlightenment (Narkompros) critics of fairy tales, certainly expressed unquestioning devotion to Lenin's persona.[61] We might cite also the case of a group of intelligentsia children in Baku who spontaneously organised a memorial meeting in the store-room of their communal flat. 'They used a leopard-skin patterned blanket to cover a trunk, put a Lenin portrait on top, put a lit candle on either side and made speeches.'[62] Apart from the leopard-spotted blanket, the set-up was impeccably orthodox.

Recollections and oral history suggest that devotion to Stalin was just as widespread. Galina Ivanova (later to become a famous singer under her married name Vishnevskaya) recalled that she and her contemporaries, young schoolchildren in the late 1930s, felt something akin to religious awe:

> The slogan ['Thank You Stalin for a Happy Childhood'] would be used to finish children's performances at every kind of gathering during the next many years. We would hear it at every film showing, at every play, from every radio set in the huge Soviet Union. We believed in Stalin not as we believed in God – for we knew nothing at all about God – but as an ideal embodiment of Humanity. We had been so thoroughly brainwashed that we were convinced – without Stalin we would perish. 'Stalin is Lenin today!'[63]

Vishnevskaya was, in a sense, the classic 'Stalinist subject': she was in the 'young schoolchild' age-group, and from a family in the 'conscious working class';[64] she was also female. Of all these characteristics, age was the most important. As a small boy, Evgeny Evtushenko recalled being lifted up by his father to see Stalin standing on the tribune:

> I waved my little red flag and I was sure Stalin could see me too. And I passionately envied my contemporaries who were lucky enough to give Stalin bunches of flowers and to get patted on the head by him, as he smiled his famous smile through his famous moustaches.[65]

Andrei Sergeev, in similar vein, remembered sitting in 1939 (he was then aged 6) and

> copying pictures of Pushkin as a little boy and of Marshal Voroshilov into my Pushkin centenary exercise-book. Voroshilov was the best leader of all. Only Stalin was better than him. Stalin was the nicest, kindest, most reassuring person in the world – and an essential part of my childhood. THANK YOU STALIN FOR A HAPPY CHILDHOOD – this made me imagine a winter sunset with houses along a broad path, going up a gently rising slope, and people walking along, and children dragging their toboggans.[66]

Even the children of 'enemies of the people' were capable of absorbing the universal enthusiasm: in 1989, Margarita Semenova recalled with horror singing songs in the children's choir praising the 'leader of nations', and ecstatically dancing the *lezghinka*.[67]

Among younger children, then, there was fairly general admiration and love for the leader. Among older children, there is some evidence from memoirs that adolescent females were more likely to continue subscribing to emotions of awe and loyalty. Larisa Vasil'eva, who wrote fulsome poems of mourning upon Stalin's death, and insisted on attending the leader's funeral in her mother's best astrakhan coat (which ended up in tatters when she narrowly escaped the fatal crush), was considerably older than Vishnevskaya (16 in 1953), and from an infinitely more privileged background (the daughter of a famous tank designer), but equally unquestioning in her attitude to the cult.[68] The daughter of highly placed officials in the Ministry of Trade, who attended a prestigious all-girls' school, records that during the festivities for Stalin's 70th birthday in 1949, she and her classmates confected a special tribute, a portrait of the leader carefully hand-embroidered on silk.[69]

By contrast, some male memoirists who experienced leader cults in adolescence recall feeling indifferent or cynical about them. Anatoly Rybakov, for instance, remembered a subversive poem about Stalin that circulated when he was in his teens:

> Dobryi vecher, dyadya Stalin,
> Ochen' grub ty, neloyalen,
> Leninskoe zaveshchanie
> Spryatal v bokovom karmane.
>
> [Good evening, uncle Stalin,
> You're very rude and treacherous.
> You hid Lenin's testament
> In your side pocket.][70]

Some years afterwards, Naum Korzhavin (according to his later recollection) was overcome by hideous disappointment when the Pioneer oath was changed to include a promise of loyalty to the party leaders. An oath of fidelity to 'the cause of Lenin and Stalin' really meant no more, he felt, than 'promising to be faithful to those in authority'.[71]

But not all young women were filled with piety: for instance, among the girls from the Moscow school where the silk embroidery of Stalin was made was one cynic who scandalised others by observing that the lilac silk they had used was reminiscent of the material that was then often used for pairs of women's knickers.[72] Conversely, not all young men were cynical; there were also male 'believers'. For instance, the literary critic Lev Anninskii was to recall in the late 1980s that when his class of 15-year-old Muscovites was set the essay topic, 'Stalin Has Raised Us' to mark the leader's 70th birthday, he, as an act of ostentatious supererogation, wrote his tribute in verse.[73] And some propaganda was evidently aimed precisely at boys, suggesting that a hero with a genuine popular following was a devotee of the leader. Soviet crack pilots had a huge reputation among children, particularly boys, in their own right; stories about such pilots' devotion to Stalin would be likely to have a positive effect on young male audiences.[74] Stalinist children were brought up at an era when the reinforcement of gender stereotypes was considered important, but gender was perhaps more likely to affect the *way* in which children venerated Stalin than *whether* they venerated him.

A further point about the cult should also be borne in mind. What the cases of Vishnevskaya, Anninskii and Vasil'eva, taken together, seem to illustrate is the particular effectiveness of leader cults among outstanding children – who may have subconsciously understood identification with the leader as a component in their own success. Such individuals could be seen as miniature versions of the *vydvizhentsy*, the high achievers from humble backgrounds that many scholars have seen as the key group of Stalin supporters.[75]

However, as Soviet sources recognised, children had a considerably lesser degree of intellectual and temperamental reliability than the *vydvizhentsy*. Perceived as more malleable than adults, they were also regarded as more subject to chance influences, both from adult authority figures and from other children, and were held to have a far less direct sense of their own self-interest or of personal principle.[76] While these ideas should not be pushed too far – children were, as we shall see, capable of recognising a message and rejecting it – they do have some foundation. And if children were subject to influence, the influences that they encountered might be very diverse. There is no doubt that the attitude of kindergarten supervisors and teachers, not to speak of Pioneer leaders, had a major role in disseminating reverence for the leaders.

In the Soviet Union, where, by the mid-1930s, teachers had experienced nearly twenty years of entirely state-controlled education, it would have seemed suicidally risky to make even the most delicate suggestion that leader cult had ridiculous or exaggerated elements. In the Third Reich, the schools were less constrained than in Stalin's USSR, nevertheless memoirs recall that the teaching body at many schools had become cowed to a significant degree by the late 1930s.[77]

But if pedagogical staff could not undermine leader cult directly, they could do so indirectly – by instilling in their charges alternative educational and philosophical ideals, or, conversely, promoting the cults so ineptly that their pupils ended up without an effective grasp of even the central facts. Rural schools often remained so under-resourced in terms both of equipment and of personnel that 'communist education' was a dead letter.[78] In the recollections of a woman brought up in Chelyabinsk province during the 1940s, who completed four years of primary education, 'We studied Stalin, there were books, for instance there were poems, they taught that, we did have it. Not much though, but some. But they read us no lectures.'[79] And in city schools, 'communist education' often remained a parallel and autonomous track of educational experience, confined to Pioneer meetings and formal school gatherings, with teachers in the school subject that was supposed to be most intimately connected with 'communist education', Russian literature, sometimes providing a specially vivid sense of an alternative set of values.[80]

Even where teachers were obedient to orthodoxy, and successful in communicating it, their work could be undermined by the scepticism of parents. When one Moscow Jewish girl met the start of the anti-cosmopolitan campaign in 1948 by telling her father, 'For the first time in my life, I am ashamed of being Jewish,' he shot back, 'For the first time in my life, I am ashamed of being your father.'[81] Valentina Bogdan, a factory engineer who had serious doubts about the Stalinist system despite her success within it, was horrified when her daughter came back from nursery school announcing, 'Auntie Tania [the nursery teacher] said that the person we must love more than anybody else is Comrade Stalin!' She steered her way out of the dilemma by saying carefully that there were different kinds of love and that love for the family was quite different from love for a leader, such as Stalin, who was loved when his behaviour merited that he should be.[82] The emphasis on what might be called situation-dependent loyalty was absolutely typical of the Russian intelligentsia at this period. Some children seem to have absorbed the lesson about the school/home split without needing to be taught it; still others remember never having 'believed in' Stalin to begin with,[83] just as some children given a religious upbringing recall that they never believed in God.

The function of peer pressure was equally double-sided. On the one hand, the administrative structure of the Stalinist school – with 'class monitors' providing a further line of surveillance beyond 'class teachers', and with the class and the Pioneer troop equated, so that the discipline of the latter reinforced the discipline of the former – was meant to harness peer pressure to official ends.[84] Yet peer pressure cut in more than one direction: the rules of the playground neatly inverted those of the classroom. In the classroom, children obediently parroted V. V. Mayakovsky's 'Ode to a Soviet Passport'; in the playground, they exultantly recited obscene parodies of the same poem.[85] Throughout the late 1930s and 1940s, the authorities racked their heads over episodes where children scrawled swastikas on their exercise books, set up anti-Soviet secret societies, and even, on occasion, defaced portraits of the leaders during recess.[86] And there were also children who quite innocently subverted the cult rituals, as with the story of a girl who turned in a regulation school essay in the late 1940s about her favourite subject, dogs, and did not forget (to her classmates' hilarity) to add the sentence, 'Comrade Stalin is the best friend of all dogs.'[87] Soviet schools were volatile places, the haunts of subversion and uneasy compromise as well as of obedience, deference and belief.[88]

De-Stalinisation often had at least as great a shock effect upon people in their late teens and twenties as it did upon the middle-aged and elderly. In the words of a young man of about 19, speaking at a public debate held at a technical college in Stalingrad in November 1956:

> Since childhood we have been raised to love Stalin, we 'drank him in with our mother's milk', as the saying goes. If Stalin made mistakes like this, how can people have thought of him in the way they used to? I didn't have those facts to hand and I can't get my head round things.[89]

The events of 1956 were to make the central qualities associated with childhood in the Stalinist myth – innocence, trust and unquestioning reverence – seem the symptoms of mass psychosis rather than of appropriate citizenship.[90] Accordingly, alongside a partial rehabilitation of the entirely different 1920s Soviet model of the child – as a force for creative innovation – the post-Stalin era saw increasing impatience with the identification between 'childhood' and 'happiness', and indeed with the fetishisation of 'childhood' in any sense.[91]

An important part of Stalin's appeal had been that it was possible to dream about meeting him, about being singled out for attention, about being understood for the first time when other adults did not understand. He was romantically remote; Lenin, on the other hand, was admirable but also dead, and in a culture which prohibited belief in the after-life, that meant he was not accessible at all. The inevitable result was that he did not inspire awe. 'They took us to the Mausoleum when I was at school, and we spent the whole trip back discussing what he was stuffed with – was it sand or what?' so one Muscovite woman born in the late 1950s recalled.[92] The existence of parodies and jokes would not in itself have been a sign of Lenin's lack of potency as a symbolic figure for children; increasingly, though, he *only* figured for them in parodies and jokes such as the following comic riddle:

> Chto za staryi bol'shevik
> Zabralsya k nam na bronevik?
> Kepku on napravo nosit,
> Bukvu 'r' ne proiznosit.
> Chelovek on neprostoi,
> Dogadaisya – kto takoi?
>
> What's this old Bolshevik
> Who's climbed up on our armoured car?
> He wears his cap tipped to the right,
> He can't say the letter 'r'.
> He's not just any old man off the street.
> So guess, who could it be?[93]

One could in any case question how successful indoctrination in love for Soviet rulers ever was, in the long term, once children – that naively devoted but also unstable group of admirers – had turned into adults. Interviewing work in St Petersburg and elsewhere has suggested a very low level of retention of information about the Lenin and Stalin cults: most informants are unable to recall in any detail what they were taught about the leaders, though some impact was made on many children by important national events, such as funerals.[94] But 'default belief' could be disrupted by the fact that the Soviet system so frequently failed to live up to the cultic images it had created. A child who wrote to 'our dear leader, teacher and friend of the whole Soviet nation' from a village in Ivanovo province in 1937 to plead for help with her own 'far from cheerful life' (she and her brother were too hungry, weak and poorly dressed to attend school) was likely to remain a loyal subject only if her needs were fulfilled.[95] The adulation expected from Soviet citizens during the 1930s and 1940s, with its central motif of gratitude for the 'care' expended upon them by leader and party could be the source not only of loyalty but also of disillusion and blame.[96] Thus the legend of omnipotent Stalin generated a sense of remoteness from the powerful, and lack of connection between people and party, as well as warm affinity. The pervasive cynicism towards the Party leadership that set in during the post-Stalinist and post-Soviet eras should accordingly be seen not just as a transition to a new kind of political culture, but as an inversion of the understanding of omnipotent rulers versus dependant masses that had been central to the ruler cult.

Notes

1. Acknowledgement is made to the British Academy, the Leverhulme Trust (Grant F/08736/A), the Ilchester Fund of the University of Oxford, and New College,

Oxford, for sponsorship of the larger project on which this chapter draws, 'Childhood in Russia, 1890–1991: A Cultural and Social History'. Reference to interviews carried out as part of the work sponsored by the Leverhulme Trust is made as follows: the code 'Ox/Lev SPb-02' etc. refers to interviews conducted by Aleksandra Piir in St Petersburg (in-depth interviewing, using a 68-point questionnaire, is proceeding from October 2002 to March 2004 among about 30 informants across a range of generations who grew up in working-class families); the code 'CKQ-Ox-03' refers to interviews carried out in Oxford by Catriona Kelly using the same questionnaire (these informants come from a range of different Russian cities and from official/intelligentsia backgrounds); and 'CKQ-SPb-03' and 'CKQ-E-03' refer to interviews carried out by Catriona Kelly in St Petersburg, June 2003, and Ekaterinburg, September 2003 (among informants born in the late 1920s and early 1930s, from a range of different social backgrounds). My thanks to the institutions involved, and also to Ms Piir, and my collaborator Professor Albert Baiburin, Faculty of Ethnology, European University, St Petersburg, for their help. For more details on the interviewing process, see K. Kelli (C. Kelly), '"Shkol'nyi val's": povsednevnaya zhizn' post-stalinskoi sovetskoi shkoly', *Etnologiya* (St Petersburg), no. 1 (2004).

2. N. Tumarkin, *Lenin Lives! The Lenin Cult in Soviet Russia* (Cambridge, Mass. 1997), pp. 227–32, carries a brief discussion of Lenin imagery for children, based on a handful of mid-1920s sources only. My own essay, 'Riding the Magic Carpet: The Stalin Cult for Little Children', forthcoming in *Slavic and East European Journal*, 2004, concentrates on the content of texts rather than their uses.
3. Inside cover of *Pioner*, 1 (1924).
4. See nos. 1 and 2 for that year: see also 'Lenin i yunye lenintsy' for the first anniversary, no. 1 (1925).
5. As depicted, for instance, in 'U nas zhil Lenin', *Ogonek*, 3 (1970), p. 7, a photograph illustrating a Lenin centenary item about the Kuibyshev Lenin museum, and showing local schoolchildren being received into the Pioneers..
6. Trotsky, unnumbered flysheet in *Pioner*, 1 (1924).
7. Poem by a group 3 collective in N. Sats (ed.) *Deti o Lenine* (Moscow, 1925), p. 14. This very interesting anthology consists of poems and pictures by children, mostly aged about 12–14, from the L. B. Kamenev First Experimental School in Moscow.
8. These stories were included in the elementary school reader *Rodnaya rech'* until late 1946, when, as a sequel to the public denigration of Zoshchenko initiated by Andrei Zhdanov, Vladimir Bonch-Bruevich wrote to Zhdanov denouncing Zoshchenko's *otsebyatina* (wilful self-assertion) in portraying Lenin. They were then hastily cut from the book. See Rossiiskii Gosudarstvennyi Arkhiv Sotsial'no-Politicheskii Istorii (RGASPI), f. 17 op. 125 ed. khr. 457.
9. Z. Lilina, *Lenin malen'kii. Dlya detei mladshego vozrasta*, 3rd edn (Moscow and Leningrad, 1930), pp. 4, 7, 13.
10. This picture, later destroyed by Kuznetsov, was reproduced in *Sovetskoe iskusstvo*, 1 (1925).
11. V. N. Shul'gin, *Obshchestvennaya rabota shkoly i programmy GUS'a* (Moscow, 1925), pp. 8–9.
12. For meetings with the leader, see 'Lenin i deti', *Pioner*, 1 (1924).
13. Sats (ed.) *Deti o Lenine*, p. 31.
14. A. I. Volkova, *Podarki V. I. Leninu i N. K. Krupskoi* (Moscow, 1970): see e.g. the birthday present (file decorated with bright applique of the hammer and sickle)

sent to Lenin by denizens of the V. I. Lenin Children's Home in Vyatka, April 1923, p. 6.

15. Tumarkin, *Lenin Lives*, p. 129, quoting P. N. Lepeshinsky, 'Po sosedstvu s V. I.' in D. Lebed' (ed.) *Lenin* (Khar'kov, 1923), p. 76.
16. N. Krupskaya, *Pedagogicheskie sochineniya v 10 tomakh* (Moscow, 1957–62), vol. 6, pp. 219–21.
17. The fourth edition of Lenin's *Sochineniya*, for instance, can muster only a handful of references: vol. 19 (Moscow, 1948), pp. 182–5 (children's work in the peasant household); vol. 29 (Moscow, 1950) p. 303 (prospects for children in the socialist society of the future). Trotsky on several occasions did speak on this theme: 'A revolution does not deserve its name if it does not take the greatest care possible of the children – the future race for whose benefit the revolution has been made.' ('The Struggle for Cultured Speech' (1923), in L. D. Trotsky, *Problems of Everyday Life*, trans. anon. (New York, 1973), p. 53.)
18. A rare exception was V. D. Bonch-Bruevich, 'Lenin v gostyakh u detei', *Pioner*, 2 (1929), pp. 2–3, which described a school visit on 24 December 1919 by Lenin and Krupskaya at which Lenin became 'the best friend of children'. It was illustrated by a picture of Lenin and Krupskaya with some small boys. It was in the Stalin era that pictures of Lenin with children proliferated: see e.g. *Detskii kalendar' na 1946 god* (Moscow, 1945), image for first half of January, which shows Lenin and a small girl.
19. L. Bochin, 'U kostra', *Vozhatyi*, 15–16 (1933), p. 12.
20. Tsentral'nyi Arkhiv Obshchestvennykh Dvizhenii Moskvy (TsAODM), f. 69 op. 1 d. 172 l. 46.
21. See 'Kopii postanovlenii Sekretariata TsK VKLSM po shkol'noi i pionerskoi rabote za 1919–1925 gody' (typescript in TsKhDMO reading room), l. 52.
22. S. Dzerzhinskaya, 'F. E. Dzerzhinsky i deti (otryvki iz pisem Feliksa)', *Pravda*, 20 July 1936, p. 3.
23. A typical such letter was sent in February 1925 by a troop in Mozyr' to Stalin: RGASPI, Otdel khraneniya dokumentov molodezhnykh organizatsii. 1/22/458 15.
24. Tumarkin, *Lenin Lives!*, pp. 248–50.
25. *Pionerskaya pravda*, no. 1 (1934), no. 4 (1934).
26. *Pionerskaya pravda*, no. 1 (1934), p. 1; no. 2 (1934), p. 1; no. 3 (1934), p. 1; no. 6 (1934), p. 2, etc.
27. 'Ya peredala buket Stalinu! Rasskaz pionerki Niny Zdrogovoi', *Pravda*, 1 July 1935, p. 2.
28. M. Titvinidze, 'Kak uchilsya tovarishch Stalin', *Pionerskaya pravda*, no. 119 (1936), p. 3.
29. *Pionerskaya pravda*, 18 December 1939, p. 3, and 20 December 1939, p. 3. Cf. a similar item by L. Stepnaya, 'V shkole', *Druzhnye rebyata*, 12 (1939), pp. 12–13, and in *Pioner*, 12 (1939), pp. 3–4, etc.
30. *Pionerskaya pravda*, 24 December 1939, p. 3.
31. I. Petrov, 'Shkol'nye gody Iosifa Vissarionovicha Stalina', *Vozhatyi*, 12 (1949), pp. 4–5, or the item in the same issue by L. Semenova, a Pioneer leader in school no. 1, Vladimir, describing the ceremonial meetings for the jubilee, the content of which included material about Stalin's school years. ('Sbory, posvyashchennye I. V. Stalinu', p. 11).
32. N. S. Panova, 'Iz opyta raboty pionerskogo lagerya', *Sovetskaya pedagogika*, 6 (1952), pp. 11–22.

33. Reproduced in M. Cullerne Bown, *Socialist Realist Painting* (New Haven, Conn., 1998), p. 235.
34. For the godlike adult Stalin, see e.g. the peroration to Aleksandrov, Galaktionov, Kruzhkov, Mitin, Mochalov and Pospelov, 'Stalin', *Bol'shaya sovetskaya entsiklopediya* (2nd edition, Moscow, 1949–58, 53 volume), 52, p. 619.
35. See further in Kelly, 'Riding the Magic Carpet'. One might note, for instance, the popularity of the *riddle* form in texts for and by children about Stalin: see e.g. Ivan Eroshin, 'Stalin', *Kolkhoznye rebyata*, 12 (1936), p. 3.
36. *Vozhatyi*, 1 (1936), p. 2.
37. Jeffrey Brooks, *Thank You, Comrade Stalin!* (Princeton, NJ, 2000), p. xvi.
38. See the cover of *Druzhnye rebyata* for October 1936. For a later example, see e.g. the photograph of the Trekhgorka Factory's summer dacha in E. I. Papkovskaya (ed.) *Knizhka o malen'kikh trekhgortsakh* (Moscow, 1948), p. 37. See also the carnival scenario – *Detskii karnaval. Letnii prazdnik dlya detei srednego vozrasta* (Moscow, 1939), pp. 16–17.
39. C. Kelly, '*Byt* and Identity', forthcoming in S. Franklin and E. Widdis (eds.) *All the Russias* Cambridge, 2004); id., 'Shaping the 'Future Race': Regulating the Daily Life of Children in Early Soviet Russia', in vol. edited by Eric Naiman (Christina Kiaer(as) *Everyday Life in Revolutionary Russia* (Indiana, 2005).
40. Larisa Vasil'eva, *Deti Kremlya* (Moscow, 1997), p. 85.
41. S. Bogomazov, 'Deti o Staline', *Krasnaya nov'*, 12 (1939), p. 254.
42. See the photograph published to mark Stalin's seventieth birthday in *Ogonek*, 52 (1949).
43. On using a Stalin statue as a lever for indoctrination, see K. N. Grekova, 'Nash rodnoi gorod Magnitogorsk' in E. I. Volkova (ed.) *Vospitateli detskikh sadov o svoei rabote* (Moscow, 1948) p. 118; for Stalin and patriotic education, see Radina, 'Oznakomlenie detei', in A. P. Usova (ed.) *Voprosy obucheniya v detskom sadu* (Moscow, 1952), p. 102 (Georgia), p. 94 (schools), p. 96 (Pioneers).
44. A. Nekrasov, 'Dve pobedy', *Pioner*, 12 (1949), 4. On this side of the cult, see further Kelly, 'Riding the Magic Carpet'.
45. Ira Dmokhovskaya (class 6, school 329, Moscow), 'Prazdnik', *Pioner*, 12 (1949), p. 28.
46. *Pionerskaya pravda*, 9 December 1949, p. 3, p. 4.
47. A. D. Sergeeva, 'Deti v dni narodnoi skorbi', *Sem'ya i shkola*, 4 (1953), pp. 6–9.
48. G. Kononenko, 'Deti i Stalin', *Sem'ya i shkola*, 5 (1953), pp. 5–7.
49. *Rukovodstvo dlya vospitatelya detskogo sada* (Moscow, 1954), p. 6.
50. 'Perechen' postanovlenii Byuro Tsentral'nogo Komiteta VLKSM 1948–1954', typescript held on open access in the reading room of RGASPI-OKhDMO, l. 186.
51. 'Preodolet' posledstviya kul'ta lichnosti v pedagogike', *Sovetskaya pedagogika*, 9 (1956), p. 6.
52. See Polly Jones, *Strategies of De-Mythologisation in Post-Stalinism and Post-Communism: A Comparison of De-Stalinisation and De-Leninisation* (unpublished DPhil thesis, University of Oxford, 2002) esp. chapters 3 and 4, for more information on de-Stalinising school textbooks.
53. 'Chto kasaetsya Khrushcheva/On dovolen ot dushi': S. Mikhalkov, 'Bud' gotov!', *Sobranie sochinenii*, 1, (Moscow, 1963) pp. 320–9.
54. Tumarkin, *Lenin Lives!*, p. 260.
55. A. I. Ulyanova, *Detstvo i otrochestvo V. I. Lenina* (1955). In the post-Stalin era, too, it was customary to hold admissions to the Pioneers in Lenin museums and other such Lenin-commemorative places.

56. I recall seeing this image, for instance, on a visit to a Pioneer camp in the Gulf of Finland in summer 1979.
57. *Ogonek*, 16 (1970), p. 9.
58. On Pavlik Morozov, see C. Kelly, *Comrade Pavlik: The Rise and Fall of a Soviet Boy Hero* (London, 2004).
59. Poem credited to an anonymous group 3 (3-ya gruppa) collective, Sats (ed.) *Deti o Lenine*, p. 8. My emphasis.
60. Anonymous 14-year-old girl (group 6), in Sats (ed.) *Deti o Lenine*, p. 8.
61. Anonymous eight-year-old girl (group 1), in Sats (ed.) *Deti o Lenine*, p. 12.
62. Lidiya Ivanova, *Vospominaniya: Kniga ob otse* (Paris, 1990), p. 112.
63. G. Vishnevskaya, *Galina: istoriya zhizni* (Paris, 1984), p. 35.
64. For another example of a historical subject from this background who recalled feeling extreme loyalty to Stalin, see CKQ-E-03 PF2A, p. 2, 19 September 2003 (female informant, b. Sverdlovsk, 1928: the daughter of a party official and a skilled tailor). This woman recalled that belief in Stalin even survived the arrest of her father, then secretary of the city communist party in Petropavlovsk-Kamchatka, in 1937: 'it was someone's mistake all right, but not Stalin's' (ibid.).
65. E. Evtushenko, *Volchii pasport* (Moscow, 1998), p. 58.
66. A. Sergeev, *Al'bom dlya marok*, in *Omnibus* (Moscow, 1997), p. 9.
67. M. G. Semenova, extract from unpublished memoir held in Arkhiv Memorial, in S. S. Vilensky, A. I. Kokurin, G. V. Atmashkina, I. Yu. Novichenko (eds) *Deti GULAGa 1918–1956* (Moscow, 2002), p. 252.
68. Vasil'eva, *Deti Kremlya*, pp. 333–5.
69. CKQ-Ox-03 PF1B, p. 7. 11 February 2003 (female informant, b. Moscow, 1936). For a similar story, see CKQ-E-03 PF3B, p. 6, 23 September 2003 (female informant, b. Sverdlovsk, 1931).
70. Anatolii Rybakov, *Roman-vospominanice* (Moscow, 1997), p. 51.
71. N. Korzhavin, 'V soblaznakh krovavoi epokhi', *Novyi Miv*, no. 7 (1992), 207.
72. CKQ-Ox-03 PF1B, p. 7. 11 February 2003 (female informant, b. Moscow, 1936). For a similar story, see CKQ-E-03 PF3B, p. 6, 23 September 2003 (female informant, b. Sverdlovsk, 1931).
73. L. Anninskii, 'Monolog byvshego Stalintsa' in Kh. Kobo (ed.) *Osmyslit' kul't Stalina* (Moscow, 1989), p. 54.
74. On the popular following for the Chelyuskin pilots, see Karen Petrone, *Life Has Become More Joyous, Comrades: Celebrations in the Time of Stalin* (Bloomington, Ind., 2000); for a book about Soviet crack pilots' devotion to Stalin, see G. Baidukov (Geroi Sovetskogo Soyuza), *Vstrechi s tovarishchem Stalinym* (Moscow and Leningrad, 1938).
75. Sheila Fitzpatrick, *Everyday Stalinism: Ordinary Life in Extraordinary Times – Soviet Russia in the 1930s* (New York, 1999), pp. 85–8, p. 224.
76. Cf. the reference in the the text of the 7 April 1935 decree recriminalising juvenile misdemeanours to how children were easily exploited by class enemies to their own anti-state ends. 'Pokonchit' s detskoi prestupnost'yu i ee posobnikami!', *Pravda*, 9 April 1935, p. 1.
77. Marcel Reich-Ranicki (ed.) *Meine Schulzeit im Dritten Reich* (Cologne, 1988), pp. 105–14 (Walter Jens), 93–103 (George Hensel).
78. For an account of teaching in a remote Ukrainian village from the late 1940s to the early 1960s, see Dora Shturman, *Moya shkola* (London, 1990), esp. pp. 112–16, 133.

79. CKQ-E-03 PF1B, p. 4, 14 September 2003 (female informant, b. village, Chelyabinsk province, 1934.)
80. Larry E. Holmes, *Stalin's School: Moscow's Model School no. 25, 1931–1937* (Pittsburgh, 1999).
81. Paola Messana, *Kommunalka: Une histoire de l'Union soviétique à travers l'appartement communautaire* (Paris, 1995), p. 91.
82. Valentina Bogdan, 'Memoirs of an Engineer' in S. Fitzpatrick and Yu. Slezkine (eds) *In the Shadow of Revolution: Life Stories of Russian Women from 1917 to the Second World War* (Princeton, NJ, 2000), pp. 415–16.
83. This is based on personal information, 2000, from a woman brought up in Kazan' in the late 1930s and 1940s for the last case.
84. On fear of standing out as a motive for belief in the Stalin cult, see Anninskii, 'Monolog', p. 55.
85. A. Belousov (ed.) *Russkii shkol'nyi fol'klor: ot 'vyzyvanii' Pikovoi damy do semeinykh rasskazov* (Moscow, 1998), p. 436.
86. On the 1930s, see Gabor Rittersporn, 'Formy obshchestvennogo obikhoda molodezhi i ustanovki sovetskogo rezhima v predvoennom desyatiletii' in T. Vihavainen (ed.) *Normy i tsennosti povsednevnoi zhizni: Stanovlenie sotsialisticheskogo obraza zhizni v Rossii, 1920-e i 1930-e gody* (St Petersburg, 2000), pp. 347–67.
87. CKQ-Ox-03 PF 6B, p. 11, 8 March 2003 (female informant, b. Leningrad, 1931).
88. For an argument of this kind directed at a later period, see Kelli, '"Shkol'nyi val's"'.
89. From a document held in the Volgograd City Archive, 71/37/32 94, quoted here from Polly Jones, *Strategies of De-mythologisation*, chapter 4.
90. See, for example, Mikhail Zhvanetsky's bitter joke: 'This isn't a nation, it's a kindergarten: radio announcers talk as if they were addressing half-wits or children' (1987): in his *God za dva* (Leningrad, 1991), p. 437. And compare Evgeny Dobrenko, 'Vse luchshee – detyam (Totalitarnaya kul'tura i mir detstva)', *Wiener Slawistischer Almanach*, 29 (1992), pp. 159–74, which draws an analogy between totalitarian culture, child consciousness and primitive thinking on the basis of their propensity for authoritarianism, reverence for the heroic, etc., and looks forward to a time when society will have evolved past this stage.
91. For the re-emergence of the 1920s interest in child creativity, see e.g. Vladimir Glotser, *Deti pishut stikhi* (Moscow, 1964).
92. Personal information, 1991.
93. Recited to me by a Leningrad male informant (b. 1935), 1999.
94. See e.g. Oxf/Lev SPb-03 PF 7A p. 50, 15 December 2003 (female informant, b. 1931) (on low retention); CKQ PF 5A, p. 2, 8 March 2003 (informant b. 1931 recalls Kirov's funeral as one of her earliest memories).
95. For the letter by N. Shvetsova, aged 12, see *Kommunist*, 1 (1990), pp. 95–6 (reprinted in M. E. Glavatsky (ed.) *Khrestomatiya po istorii Rossii 1917–1940* (Moscow, 1994), pp. 415–17.)
96. Sarah Davies, *Popular Opinion in Stalin's Russia: Terror, Propaganda and Dissent, 1934–1941* (Cambridge, 1997), pp. 168–82.

7

Georgian Koba or Soviet 'Father of Peoples'? The Stalin Cult and Ethnicity

Jan Plamper[1]

Stalin came from the periphery of the multiethnic Russian empire. Yet for most of his century he was seen as embodying the supraethnic Bolsheviks. Only recently a pronounced trend in scholarship has begun to emphasise Stalin's Georgian background and to regard him as a product of Transcaucasia rather than internationalist Marxism. This trend, which one might call the 'Georgianization' of Stalin, stresses the formative impact of his region on his behavioural patterns, rhetorical style and personality structure. Specifically, Georgianising scholars have foregrounded the role of Georgian literary models in shaping his rhetoric,[2] the socialising impact of the lower-class culture of violence of the Georgian village,[3] the continuing dominance of the Caucasian principle of blood vendetta, and the power of personal networks along the lines of Transcaucasian clan relations.[4]

In contrast to the historical Stalin there was the Stalin as depicted in the cult. Here we explore the ethnic dimension of Stalin's portrayal in multiple media and focus in greater detail on two – oil portraiture and folklore. We shall look at the involvement of the periphery in the Stalin portrait competitions of the 1930s, which were usually organised in conjunction with the large-scale exhibitions with a Stalin focus. For folklore production, we will narrow the focus further and examine the case of Karelia, a centre of Stalin folklore. We first describe the structural features of folklore production and then concentrate on Stalin's image of 'father of peoples'.

The Soviet Union was not a nation-state but a federation composed of territories delimited according to ethnolinguistic criteria. At the same time every Soviet citizen was ascribed a nationality, which (almost) always matched one of the territories of the federation. Rogers Brubaker has described this bifurcated Soviet conception of ethnicity, which was to a large extent formulated by and under Stalin, with the terms 'ethnoterritorial federalism' and 'personal nationality'.[5] The incongruity of these two principles belonged to the genetic code of Soviet nationalities policy, and phenotypic tensions, which contributed to the implosion of the USSR in 1991 and have dominated the post-Soviet realm to this day, were pre-programmed.

Under Stalin the dissolution of the Soviet Union would have been impossible. Not, one could argue provocatively, because of his terror regime, but because of his ethnic symbolic politics, above all the Stalin cult. The personal nationality of Stalin was Georgian, and yet he personified the federation of the ethnoterritories, the Soviet Union. The cultic Stalin functioned as the representation of the federation *above* the ethnoterritories and thereby overcame the tension between the two principles of 'ethnoterritorial federalism' and 'personal nationality'. To push this point even further, the cultic Stalin largely filled the representational vacuum of Soviet national identity, that is, of the roof that spanned the various ethnoterritories. Since the symbolism of the federation was underdeveloped, especially if compared with that of the ethnoterritories, one could claim that Stalin not only embodied the federation but quite simply *was* the federation. As the Soviet Union, Stalin was metaphor and object, signifier and signified, merged into one.

The concept of ethnicity in the Stalin cult was deeply dialectical. The explosive potential of ethnic particularism (that is, personal nationality) – Stalin belongs to his ethnoterritory, Georgia! – was defused in supra-ethnoterritorial Soviet universalism. Therefore Stalin was never depicted as a Georgian. Georgia, when appearing in representations of Stalin, only did so as locally coloured background, as a folkloric wallpaper in one of the many rooms of the 'USRR as a communal apartment'.[6] This dialectic was analogous to, perhaps even causally linked with, Stalin's 'real' nationalities ideology:

> The dialectic of the Leninist approach to the question of national culture is precisely the blossoming of cultures, national in form and socialist in content, during the dictatorship of the proletariat in one country so that these cultures, when the proletariat is victorious in the entire world and socialism becomes a reality, can merge into one general socialist culture (both in form and content) with a single common language.[7]

Here a temporal dimension complements Stalin's embodiment of the federative Soviet Union: by personifying the USSR, Stalin also personified the future tense of 'socialism', before it 'became a reality' and turned into present tense.[8]

Thus a particularist ethnic representation of Stalin was possible only insofar as ethnic particularism was dialectically transcended in Soviet universalism. Following the formula 'national in form, socialist in content' this implied in practice that the background of a portrait of the young Stalin may well have depicted the Caucasus, the eyes of Stalin on a Kirghiz rug may well have been 'slanted' in Asian-Kirghiz manner, in Russian,

Armenian, and Dagestani Stalin folklore the epithets applied to Stalin may well have mobilised the respective local metaphors epic hero (*bogatyr'*), the sun, and falcon (*sokol*), but the 'essence' of Stalin remained unchanged. This 'essence' or lingua franca was neither Georgian, Russian, Kirghiz, Armenian or Dagestani, but in its textual and visual vocabulary constituted a meta-national amalgam, syncretically drawn from a variety of sources. Stalin's metanational, amalgamated representations were canonised by about 1935 and experienced only minor, if remarkable, change thereafter.

The beginning of the Stalin cult is conventionally dated to 20 December 1929, when on the occasion of his 50th birthday Stalin was glorified on a large scale in various media – first and foremost the central press, especially *Pravda*.[9] This powerful beginning was followed by several years of absence from the public stage, which lasted until the middle of 1932 and is usually explained through the attempt to avoid any association of Stalin with the catastrophic results of forced collectivisation or with his as yet unconsolidated power position in the party.[10] By the mid-1930s his image in the various media had coalesced into a coherent system of signs. This image included in the visual media his benevolent face with the hair brushed back, the black moustache, his unblemished skin (without real-life pockmarks) and friendly eyes, which were always directed at a focal point in the distance outside the picture. His grey-green army overcoat, riding trousers and army boots were also part of this image, just as a number of props, mostly used in films, such as his pipe, the *Pravda* newspaper, and a map. In the textual media the canonic Stalin image included the appellation of 'leader' (*vozhd'*), 'great leader and teacher' (*velikii vozhd' i uchitel'*), 'father of peoples' (*otets narodov*), 'wise father' (*mudryi otets*), 'genius', 'locomotive driver of the revolution', 'builder of communism' (*zodchii kommunizma*), 'fighter and falcon' (*borets i sokol*), as well as the adjectives 'great', 'wise', 'benevolent', and 'all-knowing'. The countless folkloric depictions of Stalin drew upon the stock mythologemes of the pictorial and associative expressive registries of a respective national culture.

These pictorial, filmic, audial and verbal representations of Stalin had solidified by the middle of the 1930s, but never become entirely static. The visualised Stalin, for example, underwent tremendous change during the Second World War and was represented during the post-war era in his white parade uniform with its single 'Hero of Socialist Labour' medal, his parade trousers, low shoes (instead of army boots) and greying hair.

The multimediality and intermediality of the Stalin cult

A great variety of media were involved in the Stalin cult, including cinema, photography, poster art, oil painting, sculpture, songs, poetry, prose, folklore, drama and crafts (from Armenian tapestry weaving to vases from the Leningrad porcelain manufacture). These media were engaged in a continual competition for the status of master medium. It was the master medium in which particular images of Stalin were first formulated and later canonised. Other media followed the master medium. Therefore the intermediality – if defined as the relationship between multiple media – of the Stalin cult can be called multifocal but not multidirectional. Until the second half of the 1930s the visual media, particularly photography and oil painting, were the master media. Director Mikhail Romm's *Lenin in October* (*Lenin v oktyabre*), released in 1937, was the first movie with an actor starring as Stalin, and from then on cinema occupied the status of master medium. Oil painting, however, will be at the centre of much of what follows, since this is the medium that most of my research has concentrated on.

In the battle for the place of master medium the specific characteristics of a genre within a medium played a great role. Socialist Realist novels, for instance, hardly ever featured Stalin as the main hero since they followed the conventions of the genre of *Bildungsroman*. In this genre, the hero moves forward along a linear path by overcoming obstacles and in the end emerges a different and better person – usually a Soviet 'new man'. Stalin, however, could not be shown in the process of becoming, for Stalin had long completed his journey to a higher kind of personhood.[11] Stalin quite simply 'was': he, and only he, embodied the endpoint of the utopian timeline. As such he was beyond time and place.[12]

What is more, certain media were ethnically and religiously coded. Because of their traditional functions they lent themselves more or less for the portrayal of Stalin. It has been recently shown that Stalin was hardly ever depicted in the medium of Palekh lacquer box painting because of the traditional Russian Orthodox connotations of this medium.[13] Cultural producers perceived lacquer boxes as looming in the collective imagination as too Russian and too religious to link them with Stalin. Other media had possessed similar connotations but were perceived as having been successfully recoded and as having acquired different meanings.

In a particular medium the portrayal of Stalin changed over time. Sometimes these changes were connected directly with the ethnic factor. In film, for instance, the Jewish actor, Semen Gol'dshtab, played Stalin in the first two movies with an actor starring as the Soviet leader, *Lenin in October* (1937) and *Man with a Rifle* (1938). After these movies Gol'dshtab was replaced by the Georgian actor, Mikhail Gelovani, and transferred to a provincial theatre in Kirov. This may coincide with an upsurge of anti-Semitism ushered in by the Hitler–Stalin pact. However, Gol'dshtab was reactivated to play Stalin in the film *Aleksandr Parkhomenko* (1942).[14] At any rate, Gelovani succeeded Gol'dshtab in the role of Stalin and left a deeper imprint on the screen image of the *vozhd'* than anyone before or after him. Gelovani resembled his real-life alter ego in the Kremlin not only physically but also in speaking Russian with a strong Georgian accent. In the 1948 movie *The Third Blow* he was replaced for a while by the former Gulag convict and ethnically Russian actor of the Moscow Art Theatre, Aleksei Dikii. Dikii is said to have been installed at Stalin's personal behest in order to Russianize his image at the height of the 'anti-Cosmopolitanism' campaign and the battle against 'groveling before the West'.[15] But movie-goers had a hard time accepting the new actor. 'Why, when you play I.V. Stalin, do you speak without the characteristic accent?' asked the author of an anonymous note written on scrap paper and passed forward to the stage at a public 'celebratory evening' (*tvorcheskii vecher*) with Dikii.[16] Another note read: 'because we want to know comrade Stalin, we want to know him in detail down to his accent'.[17] It was not just the accent that set the Russianised Stalin apart from his Georgian predecessor. Gelovani played Stalin as hardly moving, as static, whereas Dikii's body language was wild in comparison – he began unexpectedly waving with his hands or suddenly turning his head. The combined problem of canon and popular reception was a serious one. In one of the last Stalin movies, *The Fall of Berlin* (1949), Mikhail Gelovani returned to his habitual role as the *vozhd'* – at the will of the people or the whim of Stalin?

After Stalin's December 1935 pronouncement of the 'friendship of peoples' the Kremlin, with Stalin at its head, began receiving delegations from Caucasian and Central Asian republics and turned these receptions into public celebrations. The several months of receptions were followed by a newly prized vehicle for demonstrating the friendship of the Soviet family of nationalities, the Moscow-based 'weeks of national art' (*dekady natsional'nogo iskusstva*). These celebrations included art exhibitions and theatre performances from a given national republic. A first Ukrainian *dekada* in March 1936 was followed by *dekady* from Kazakhstan (May 1936), Georgia (January 1937), and Uzbekistan (May 1937).[18] Stalin made an appearance at every one of these events, including the Georgian reception and *dekada*, yet in the elaborate symbolic presentations in multiple media he was not connected with his republic of origin, Georgia, in any special way whatsoever. His personal nationality, again, was downplayed while his embodiment of the federation, the Soviet Union, overshadowed everything else.

The 1930s also witnessed a number of monumental art exhibitions, some connected with the *dekady*, some not, but most with at least a Stalin cult art component if not a Stalin focus.[19] In the first half of the 1930s, when the canon of Stalin depictions was still evolving and relatively few pieces of artwork were available, these exhibitions were more open-ended and invariably connected with competitions. The newspaper of the artistic intelligentsia, *Sovetskoe iskusstvo*, served as the semi-public arena where such competitions were announced and submissions sometimes even judged and criticised.[20] In the second half of the 1930s, after the canon had stabilised and a significant amount of Stalin artwork had already been produced, exhibitions more often collected available art and placed it in specific thematic contexts.

The stellar exhibition *I. V. Stalin and the People of the Soviet Country in the Fine Arts* opened on Stalin's birthday, 21 December 1939; thanks to extensive documentation, it is a good window on the Stalin cult proper, the ethnic dimension of the cult, and the large exhibitions of the 1930s more generally.[21] In April 1939 the visual section of the Council of People's Commissars (Sovnarkom) Committee for Arts Affairs had already sent out a barrage of letters to individual artists, to local artist unions in places as far away as Leningrad, Turkmenistan and Kiev, to museums and publishing houses, and to the directors of the 1939 *Industry of Socialism* exhibition and the Pushkin Fine Arts Museum, asking about any artistic representations of Stalin that the artist or institution might have in stock.[22]

In the end, the Tretyakov Gallery was chosen as the single location for the exhibition. To pool resources, another initially separate exhibition on 'famous people of the country' (*Znatnye lyudi strany*), devoted to images of Stakhanovites and other 'heroes' of the 1930s, was fused with the Stalin exhibition. The artwork was to be assembled from existing Stalin iconography 'plus a small number of works (about 30) that the Committee for Arts Affairs commissioned from great masters'. 'Apart from these commissioned works', the functionary of the Committee for Arts Affairs continued, 'we have collected information in the Union republics – Central Asia, Georgia, Armenia, Ukraine'.[23]

Indeed, the involvement of the periphery in this exhibition was significant.[24] In the spring, central art functionaries visited artists in the Caucasus republics, Leningrad, Siberia, Central Asia and the Ukraine. Everywhere these functionaries communicated with local artists through the regional artists' unions, all of which were subordinate to the Moscow Union of Artists (MOSSKh) anyway (despite the fact that a single Artists' Union, *Soyuz khudozhnikov*, was founded only in 1957). Functionaries toured the republics and reported back to Moscow on the various types of artwork being produced.[25] In October Moscow again wrote to local artists' unions, inquiring, for instance, if paintings by a number of Kiev artists (inspected during the spring) were nearing completion; Moscow 'asked to send photographs of these works as soon as possible'.[26] Or, an individual Leningrad artist received the following warning: 'The State Tretyakov Gallery is informing you that after 9 November the commission for the selection of artwork for the Stalin exhibition will be in Leningrad. This commission will visit your studio and inspect your paintings'.[27] This was in line with the organisers' goal of 'convincing the [artists] that this [exhibition] is a very important political enterprise'; it was also consonant with the intention to 'implement stricter control'.[28] 'On the one hand it is indispensable to prod [*shevelit'*] the artists', echoed Aleksandr Gerasimov, 'on the other hand we need to offer them help when they encounter difficulties. What, for example, if we have commissioned a portrait but the painter has no model'?[29]

Artists responded to the written October inquiries of the Committee with letters and photographs, showing the state of completion of their work. After the news of the exhibition had spread widely in artistic circles, some artists who were not invited proposed to submit Stalin busts and paintings at their own initiative.[30] In late November and early December a jury, composed of famous artists and culture bureaucrats, met in Moscow and judged the art that had been gathered. Certain works were accepted unconditionally, others were designated for changes, and yet others were rejected outright.[31] As was to be expected, given the short notice, many commissions were late.[32]

One of the complaints of participating artists was the difficulty of getting the *znatnye lyudi* – the Stakhanovites, arctic explorers, biologists and kolkhoz milkmaids – to pose. 'I was ordered to do a portrait of Ostuzhev', ventured one artist. 'He came to my studio, I tried to win him over . . . He looked at everything and left – I do not know why, but perhaps my art did not convince him'.[33] A certain Isaev of the Committee for Arts Affairs agreed that getting *znatnye lyudi* to pose often was problematic: famous scientists or Bolsheviks 'believe that if they pose, they will be accused of laziness, of wasting time on modeling, therefore they escape posing or pose at their desk'. The Stakhanovites and decorated kolkhoz farmers were 'easier to get to pose, but they want to keep the painting as a token of remembrance. That is why the Committee . . . must give a public explanation'.[34] Meanwhile artists accused artists, and art functionaries accused artists, of not trying hard enough to get their intended models to pose. 'As far as Fadeev, the writer, is concerned', sniped one artist, 'I suspect that Yakovlev did not look for him seriously. He is such a man of culture, understands so much, that he is always helpful'.[35]

Just before the opening of the exhibition in late December 1939, powerful culture functionaries and party members probably walked round the rooms to see if anything needed to be changed at the last minute.[36] Several artists inquired with the organising commission why their pictures had been rejected, others wanted their rejected artwork back more quickly, and yet others were interested in the success of their paintings in the exhibition:

> Is the exhibition well attended? Do you have a visitor comment book and do they criticize me a lot there? Were there any remarks from the government commission? These questions interest every painter, not just me, so please do not think that I am an exceptionally ambitious painter.[37]

Once it was on, the Tretyakov Gallery was actively involved in propagandising the exhibition. In general, a lot was done so that these exhibitions reached as many people as possible from all stretches of the vast Soviet empire. Not only were people brought from the periphery to the exhibitions in the centres in organised groups, but the main provincial towns organised their own exhibitions or hosted mobile exhibitions from the centre, both mainly showcasing reproductions.[38] One sure way to boost an exhibition's visitor statistics, according to the artists, was to get Stalin to visit it.[39] But clinging to his image of modesty and allegedly only grudging tolerance of his genuinely 'popular' cult, Stalin did not make an appearance at his anniversary exhibition; in his lifetime he only visited one (or two) of the large exhibitions of the 1920s and 1930s: the tenth AKhR exhibition in 1928 and perhaps the 1933 exhibition in honour of the Red Army's fifteenth anniversary.[40]

Stalin as 'Father of Peoples': folklore in Karelia and beyond

> Collect your folklore,
> make a study of it,
> work it over.
> *Maxim Gorky, 1934*

One of Stalin's key images – in fact, the image connected most prominently to the question of ethnicity – was that of 'father of peoples' (*otets narodov*). In this image Stalin presided as a patriarchic father over a harmonious family of Soviet nationalities. The primary medium for the communication of this image was poetry, in particular folklore, which had been redefined effectively as a genre of poetry in 1934 at the First Congress of Soviet Writers, and in English is sometimes referred to as 'fakelore' or 'pseudofolklore' because of its artificiality.[41]

The collection of folklore in Russia began in the early nineteenth century, when the academic discipline of folkloristics (*fok'loristika*) was established. After the Bolsheviks came to power the discipline of folkloristics entered into a period of lively theoretical debates, the boundaries of which were demarcated by the givens of the collective (over individual authorship), 'science' (over art), and materialist history (over individual genius). From the beginning, however, the coexistence of rural folklore with the urban socialist utopia and the active propagation of proletarian culture (through the Proletkult movement, for example) was perceived as an uneasy marriage. Between 1929 and 1931, literary organisations spearheaded efforts to terminate this misalliance of 'rural backwardness' with 'urban progress', clamoring for an all-out abandonment of folklore as a discipline.

All of this changed radically with Stalin's rise to power. Following the Great Break the plenitude of literary organisations was subsumed into the monolithic Union of Soviet Writers, founded in 1932. In 1934 Maxim Gorky, addressing the First Congress of Soviet Writers, strongly supported efforts by

Soviet folklorists to ascribe to folklore a meaning not of a dated art form, but of a new, national-cum-traditional, art form.[42]

Gorky's proclamation ushered in the 20-year-long Golden Age of Soviet folklore during which Socialist Realist centrepieces such as 'Glory to Stalin shall be eternal' (in the traditional Russian epic *bylina* genre) and 'To immortal Lenin' (in the traditional lament [*plach*] genre) began appearing in *Pravda*, Karelian performers in Moscow's largest concert halls, and a Kazakh poet, Dzhambul Dzhabaev, on Kremlin photographs with Stalin. The *bylina* was reintroduced as the composite neologism, *novina*, meaning a half-sung, half-recited oral poem in the *bylina* genre on new, Soviet subjects. While the Golden Age peaked between 1936 and 1941, the first voices doubting Soviet folklore's authenticity and branding it 'pseudofolklore' appeared in 1939. Two years later Yurii Sokolov, then the premier folklorist, publicly regretted the manipulation of performers by folklorists like himself, for the folklorist-guided reworking of their folklore resulted in 'horrifying falsifications of the traditional and Soviet folklore'.[43]

It was this new, Soviet folklore that transported one of Stalin's images as 'father of peoples'. The image of Stalin as a father *per se* was launched in 1935 when during the summer he was pictured in the print media together with the 11-year-old pioneer girl, Nina Zdrogova, on the tribune of the Lenin mausoleum saluting a physical-cultural parade. From then on until the beginning of the Second World War he was frequently shown with young girls, all of non-Russian background such as Buryat-Mongolia's Gelya Markizova and Turkmenistan's Mamlakat Nakhangova. Consonant with his father image, Stalin 'kissed babies, shook hands with fathers, and visited almost every children's home in Moscow at least once'.[44] His biological daughter, Svetlana, was shown with her father once in a 1935 photograph, but only to fade from the public eye for decades. Few people were as appropriate to support the image of Stalin as father in the 'myth of the great family' of Soviet peoples as non-Russian, preadolescent girls.[45] For their distance to the father could not have been greater: belonging to the 'weak gender' and coming from 'backward' republics, they constituted the ideal antipode to Stalin.[46]

Likewise it was not the famous male folklore performers from Central Asia or the Caucasus who lauded Stalin as 'father of peoples', but female folklore poets (*skazitel'nitsy*) from Karelia. Surprisingly, much of the folklore from Karelia was not by Karelians or Finns, but by Russophone Russians (the majority of Karelia's population in 1926), and Russian women in particular.

There are various reasons for the predominance of these Russophone *skazitel'nitsy* from Karelia. First of all, compared with folklore performers from other parts of the Soviet Union, there were logistical advantages, since Karelia had been the chief site of pre-revolutionary folklore since the second half of the nineteenth century and since it was conveniently located in the micro-periphery, just 400 kilometres northeast of Leningrad.[47]

Second, the genre of Russian Karelian folklore lent itself particularly well because it could be easily deployed as *ersatz* Russian Orthodoxy. By the time of the 'Great Retreat' the urban, socialist utopia – with its machine metaphors in Socialist Realist novels – was abandoned in favour of nature and pastoral harmony – reflected, for instance, in a switch to garden metaphors in novels.[48] The natural choice of a symbolic system for representing this shift would have been religion, but Russian Orthodoxy was unavailable for obvious reasons (the Bolsheviks' general atheist stance and Russian Orthodoxy's particular association with tsarism). Russian Karelian folklore was a good substitute because (*a*) it represented timeless tradition (as opposed to the utopian, time-shattering dreams of the 1920s), offering a whole stock of seemingly ancient genres (in truth invented in the nineteenth century) as well as folklore performer dynasties with their descendants of the 1930s and 1940s – Marfa Kryukova, Karelia's star performer, and Petr Riabinin-Andreev; (*b*) certain genres, such as the *bylina* genre with its emphasis on patrilineal male heroes (*bogatyri*), lent themselves extremely well to celebrate lines of Bolshevik male heroes; (*c*) language and genres were Russian, yet the veneer was non-Great Russian, which allowed for the fortification of the *de facto* national-ethnic hierarchy of the Soviet Union – the partiarch Stalin on top, Great Russians and their greatest 'sons' right below (aviation heroes, arctic explorers), followed by the rest of the children (non-Great Russian nationalities); and finally (*d*), it allowed for the redeployment of the father image outside the religious framework.

Folklore production

During the first Five Year Plan authors and their texts were often publicly reworked on the pages of journals and newspapers. Such tactics served pedagogical and disciplinarian purposes: publicly enacted individual textual (and social) engineering was to induce larger segments of society to follow. Public pedagogy was abandoned in 1931–32, when 'Soviet Man' was expected to have emerged (if not, the penal system coercively 're-educated'), and cultural products began appearing publicly in their final form only. This shift did not signal the end to a reworking of texts, it merely pushed the process outside public purview.[49]

In 1938 the folklore section of the Union of Soviet Writers passed a resolution that lambasted the infiltration of 'enemies of the people' in folklore and the resulting falsification in translations and reproduction (printing). It proposed the creation of 'a single leadership of all folklore work in the USSR' as an urgent task.[50] A 24-point list of 'necessary measures' listed, among other things, 'the systematic registration of folklorists and masters of folk art according to a single plan'. It proposed 'the complete harmonization of working plans of the central and local folklore institutions with regard to expeditions, publications, forms of systematization, cataloguing and storage of folklore materials'.[51]

Folklore centres in the Soviet periphery were indeed drawing up annual plans for folklore production. The 1937–38 plan of the folklore section at the Karelian Scientific and Research Institute for Culture was entitled 'The Flourishing of Folk Arts in Soviet Karelia' and listed various objectives in publishing, exhibitions, recordings of folklore performers, including the following targets: collection of civil war folklore; recording of folklore on 'the building of socialism'; 'folk art of the post October period'; 'tales about Lenin'; 'urgent recording of major performers and Soviet material at hand'.[52]

It is unclear who exactly – a Moscow or Leningrad folklore institute, or a higher party institution – ordered the folklore institute in Petrozavodsk to publish a 'series of collections of tales, runes, and *byliny* in Karelian and Russian'.[53] But we know that the Karelian folklore institute then either tapped its pool of available performers to elicit the planned folklore, or it recruited additional performers. This took the form of a memorandum sent out around 1938 to the village soviets, in which institute director Mashezerskii lamented that 'all bearers [*nositel'*] of folk arts have yet to be found . . . in spite of a series of . . . expeditions.' According to Mashezerskii, performers 'creating their songs, *byliny*, runes, and tales about our leaders Lenin-Stalin, and about the achievements of the Soviet Union' were particularly scarce. Therefore the institute asked the village soviet to conduct a search for '(*a*) citizens, who know many tales, *byliny*, runes, sayings, and songs' and '(*b*) talented citizens, who compose these songs and tales themselves'.[54]

Individual work 'on' a performer took place either in the village or in Petrozavodsk. One documented case involved a Petrozavodsk folklorist, A. D. Soimonov, who sent the following instruction to kolkhoz accountant Prokhor Novozhilov:

> Take upon yourself or order some young person to read and explain to the old man Zhuravlev the following books: 'Voroshilov, Stalin, and the Red Army' and 'Budennyi – warrior, citizen,' as well as the biographies of the leaders: Stalin, Lenin . . . Perhaps Zhuravlev will be able to create *byliny* about our leaders on the basis of this material. Talk to him, so that he remembers old *byliny*, too. The old man has nothing to do anyway, so let him work on *byliny*. Inform the institute about your results around May. Then we could summon him to Petrozavodsk or visit him.[55]

In print the performers were represented in precisely the synthetic fashion that from 1939 onwards periodically aroused the criticism of Soviet folklorists. A list of performer biographies appended to the collection, *Byliny Pudozhskogo kraya*, on the one hand stresses a performer's creative, poetic talent, on the other hand accentuates the influence of contemporary themes disseminated in the mass media.[56] It seems very likely that this type of folklore production differed little in other parts of the Soviet Union. This is not to claim that regional differences in Stalin cult production in the multiethnic state were completely erased. Research on this topic is still lacking, but one could speculate that the making of the Stalin in cult in Muslim Central Asia, for example, with Islam's prohibition of the depiction of human faces, bore some specific features.

Folklore products

> Stalin loves all people
> and you small children
> lulla, lullaby, I'll sing you a song
> sleep my grandson.[57]
>
> *From a Karelian lullaby*

In Soviet representations Stalin received power (and legitimacy) not only from the people or by virtue of his deeds, but also from Lenin. Some *noviny* rehearse the theme of Stalin as Lenin's legitimate heir, encapsulated in the formula 'Stalin is the Lenin of today'. As Anna Mikhailovna Pashkova, Karelia's second most prominent *skazitel'nitsa*, who saw her husband in his seventies dekulakized in 1930,[58] recited in 1939, 'Lenin and Stalin, / Were not brothers by blood, / But they were equal talents. / What Lenin had planned, / Stalin has fulfilled.'[59] In this *novina* Stalin and Lenin are figured as brothers, in others Lenin is 'grandfather' to Stalin, who is 'father' to the peoples of the Soviet Union. Indeed, 'father' (*otets*) is one of the most common appellations used for Stalin in folklore, even if without the genitive object 'of peoples' (*narodov*). 'Thank you, father Stalin, / For your good thoughts. / You have done good for the world / You have fixed life,' sounded one typical folk verse *chastushka*.[60] 'Stalin, leader of the world, / Mountain hawk-falcon, / He cares for the workers, / Just like a father for his children', proclaimed Georgian folklore, using regionally coloured imagery ('Mountain hawk-falcon').[61] Above all, however, Stalin was 'father' in the Russian folklore of the female performers from Karelia: 'In the Kremlin lives our close father Stalin, / Oh, father close, dear Stalin / Oh, his eyes are so sincere, / His hair shines golden, / Oh, he has a silken beard (sic), / Yes he has a wise head / How from his wise head / Everywhere grow factories and enterprises, / And in the villages grow kolkhozes.'[62]

Alongside the appellation 'father,' the traditional Russian term *batyushka* (father), previously used in popular parlance for fathers, priests and tsars, reappeared. It was, for example, applied to Stalin in 1938 – in the context of the Papanin-led polar expedition: 'Oh you, hail to you, father [*batyushko*]

Stalin . . . / You care about all of us. / Father [*batyushko*] Stalin will not leave you / On the faraway ice – / He will take care of you, too, / He will hurry to save you.'[63] And Karelia's Evdokiya Kokunova composed an epic tale, entitled 'How We Saw Off our Falcons,' about Soviet mothers sending their sons to the 'Great Patriotic War', in which the mother protagonist, upon hearing of her son's death in the war, receives consolation from the fact that, 'After all, we have the Red Army, / We have our close father [*rodnoi batyushka*] / Iosif light Vissarionovich.'[64] By the late 1930s, then, the word *batyushka* had been stripped of its tsarist and Russian Orthodox connotations to such an extent that it could resurface in the context of Stalin.

It was, as we have seen, the Russian-language female folklore performers from Karelia who were vital in glorifying Stalin as their 'father' and therefore cementing the image of Stalin as 'father of peoples', presiding over a Soviet mythic family of nations connected by the 'friendship of peoples'. Poems in which Stalin was identified as Georgian are almost completely missing, even (or especially?) in Georgian folklore. One of the very rare pieces of folklore that connects Stalin to Georgia is an Evenk song from Siberia, in which Stalin is called a 'son of the Georgian people' and further, by implication, designated as 'father of the Soviet Union': 'Take pride, Georgian people, / In your beloved, great son! / Take pride, our country, mother of Soviets, / In the name of comrade Stalin!'[65] In another piece, entitled 'Lavrentii Beria in the Mountains', Beria is referred to as 'leader of Georgia'. Stalin, who also makes an appearance, is marked as Georgian in no way whatsoever.[66] National ascriptions were carefully kept apart, lest Stalin's personal nationality interfere with his embodiment of the federation of ethnoterritories.

Was everything this clean, one might ask, or was there dissonance in the harmonious, pastoral symphony of the great family, performed by the *skazitel'nitsa*? At times incestuous undertones crept into the harmony, creating a competing strand of Stalin as man/sexual object. *Skazitel'nitsa* Khoteeva, for example, composed: 'How happy would I be / If I suddenly came / To Moscow. I would see / Lenin's Mausoleum! / Well, but if I met / The most beloved, / The songs would melt, / Of the song I'd sing for Stalin!'[67] However, erotic tensions and energy were never channelled and instrumentalised as they were in the symbolic celebration of the relationship between Hitler and the female part of the German people.

Conclusion

In the beginning I introduced a dichotomy between a 'real' Stalin and a 'cultic' Stalin. Just as this dichotomy is above all heuristic, the Soviet conception of nationhood was infinitely more complex and dynamic than described at the outset with the terms 'ethnoterritorial federalism' and 'personal nationality'. During the 1920s the Soviet regime actively developed national, non-Russian cultures and installed national cadres in positions of political power in the ethnoterritories of the Soviet Union.[68] In symbolic politics the significance of the federation, the Soviet Union, and of the largest national republic, the Russian Federation, were downplayed, lest bad memories of Great Russian chauvinism or the tsarist Russifying empire resurface. During the 1930s ethnosymbolic politics switched to more primordial concepts and began celebrating folkloristic, exoticised national cultures with ancient national poets and heroes. In February 1936 Stalin declared the danger of Great Russian chauvinism overcome and reintroduced Russian national culture in the privileged position of a 'first among equals'. At the same time, the Soviet Union proper remained remarkably underdeveloped in the national rhetoric. As I have argued, Stalin compensated for this symbolic deficit by embodying the Union. In so far as the Soviet Union itself was celebrated at all, it was the sum of the national cultures. In other words, the symbolism of the federation (the Soviet Union) was equal to the sum of its parts (the ethnoterritories). Since the Russian ethnoterritory, the RSFSR, was allowed a publicly promoted national culture only in 1936, it was not until then that it began contributing to the supranational Soviet ethnosymbolism. Since the Russian ethnoterritory, the RSFSR, began, however, playing first fiddle among the various ethnoterritories, its part in the sum that made up Soviet rhetoric was greater than that of others.[69]

Up to Stalin's very death his oldest party friends used his early pseudonym, Koba, borrowed from the hero of the romantic Georgian nationalist Alexander Kazbegi's novel, *The Patricide*, when joining an underground leftist group in Tbilisi in 1898. Only on rare occasions, however, did this particularist Georgian ethnic designation enter public discourse. There he was known under his Russianised pseudonym of 'Stalin'. For photographs Stalin might dress in the folkloric costumes of the national republics, but these costumes belonged precisely to the world of costumes – they were but masquerades.[70] Underneath these costumes Stalin wore his army uniform and boots. He represented the supraethnic 'father of peoples' and in this paternal role stood in symbolically for the Soviet Union, the roof spanning the various ethnoterritories that belonged to the first socialist – federal – state. Stalin's belonging to any of the ethnoterritories by virtue of his Georgian personal nationality was carefully censored. If representations of Stalin exhibited any kind of ethnic particularism it was Russian. But Russian only to the extent that the symbolism of the Soviet Union was the sum of its ethnoterritorial parts, and that the Russian part in this sum was larger than that of others.

Notes

1. Many thanks to Chad Bryant and Malte Rolf for their comments.
2. Mikhail Vaiskopf, *Pisatel' Stalin* (Moscow, 2001), pp. 130–1, 181–98.

3. See Jörg Baberowski, *Der Rote Terror: Die Geschichte des Stalinismus* (Munich, 2003), pp. 15, 24–5, 32–3, 42–3, 88–93; id., *Der Feind ist überall: Stalinismus im Kaukasus* (Munich, 2003), pp. 17–18.
4. Alfred Rieber, 'Stalin, Man of the Borderlands', *American Historical Review*, 106, no. 4 (December 2001), pp. 1651–91.
5. Rogers Brubaker, 'Nationhood and the National Question in the Soviet Union and Post-Soviet Eurasia', *Theory and Society*, 23: 1 (1994), pp. 47–78.
6. I borrow this phrase from Yuri Slezkine, 'The USSR as a Communal Apartment, or How a Socialist State Promoted Ethnic Particularism', *Slavic Review*, 53: 2 (summer, 1994), pp. 415–52.
7. Stalin's report to the 16th Party Congress, *Pravda*, 29 June 1930, reprinted in I. V. Stalin, *Sochineniya*, 12 (Moscow, 1952), p. 369.
8. Jan Plamper, 'The Spatial Poetics of the Personality Cult: Circles Around Stalin' in Evgeny Dobrenko and Eric Naiman (eds) *The Landscape of Stalinism: The Art and Ideology of Soviet Space* (Seattle, 2003), pp. 36, 44.
9. Jeffrey Brooks, *Thank You, Comrade Stalin! Soviet Public Culture from Revolution to Cold War*, (Princeton, NJ, 2000), pp. 59–77; Benno Ennker, 'Politische Herrschaft und Stalinkult 1929–1939' in Stefan Plaggenborg (ed.) *Stalinismus: neue Forschungen und Konzepte* (Berlin, 1998), pp. 152, 166; Reinhard Löhmann, *Der Stalinmythos: Studien zur Sozialgeschichte des Personenkultes in der Sowjetunion (1929–1935)* (Münster, 1990), pp. 27–32.
10. James L. Heizer, 'The Cult of Stalin, 1929–1939', PhD diss., University of Kentucky, 1977, pp. 80, 99, 138.
11. I owe this point to a conversation with Hans Günther in Berkeley, 1998. Also see Rolf Hellebust, 'Reflections of an Absence: Novelistic Portraits of Stalin before 1953' in Nina Kolesnikoff and Walter Smyrniw (eds) *Socialist Realism Revisited: Selected Papers from the McMaster Conference* (Hamilton, Ont., 1994), pp. 111–20. On the Socialist Realist novel as *Bildungsroman* see Katerina Clark, *The Soviet Novel: History as Ritual* (1st edition Chicago, 1981), pp. 16–17, 57.
12. There are exceptions to Stalin's absence in Socialist Realist prose. Kazimir Lisovskii, *V Turukhanskoi ssylke* (Novosibirsk, 1947), deals with Stalin's escape from his Siberian place of exile. Many Stalinist novels include a trip of their hero from the periphery to Stalin in Moscow, the centre. See Rosalind Marsh, *Images of Dictatorship: Portraits of Stalin in Literature* (London, 1989), p. 39.
13. Andrew Jenks, 'Russia in a Box: The Production of Russian and Socialist Identity, 1814–2001', PhD diss., Stanford University, 2002.
14. During the openly anti-Semitic late 1940s Gol'dshtab's name was often suppressed. See Nikolas Hülbusch, *Im Spiegelkabinett des Diktators: Stalin als Filmheld im sowjetischen Spielfilm (1937–1953)* (Alfeld, 2001), p. 78.
15. See the television documentary by Oksana Bulgakova, Frieda Grafe and Enno Patalas, *Stalin – Eine Mosfilmproduktion* (WDR, 1993).
16. Rossiiskii Gosudarstvennyi Arkhiv Literatury i Iskusstva (RGALI), 2376/1/197 34.
17. RGALI, 2376/1/197 33.
18. Terry Martin, *The Affirmative Action Empire: Nations and Nationalism in the Soviet Union, 1923–1939* (Ithaca, NY, 2001), pp. 439–40.
19. Major exhibits of the 1930s included, among others, *Artists of the RSFSR over the Past 15 Years* (1932); *On the History of the Bolshevik Organisations of Transcaucasia* (1937); *Industry of Socialism* (1939); *V. I. Lenin and I. V. Stalin in Sculpture* (1939); *I. V. Stalin and the People of the Soviet Country in the Fine Arts* (1939).

20. Plamper, 'The Spatial Poetics of the Personality Cult', pp. 31–2.
21. Jan Plamper, 'The Stalin Cult in the Visual Arts, 1929–1953', PhD diss., University of California, Berkeley, 2001, pp. 120–30.
22. Susan E. Reid, 'Socialist Realism in the Stalinist Terror: The *Industry of Socialism* Art Exhibition, 1935–41', *Russian Review*, 60: 2 (April 2001), pp. 153–84.
23. Otdel Rukopisei Gosudarstvennaya Tret'yakovskaya Gallereya (OR GTG), 8.II/993 21–21ob. Stenographic record of the 'meeting for the preparation of the exhibit' of 7 October 1939.
24. Artwork from the periphery was always judged in the centre, if the exhibit took place in Moscow. The judging was then done by a commission according to majority voting (with the painter, if present in the jury, abstaining from voting). OR GTG, 18/183 3, 8. Stenographic record dated 1 October 1940.
25. OR GTG, 8.II/993 8 (Report by Veimark on his visit to Armenia). On his visit to Central Asia Veimark reported as follows: 'The art in the Central Asian Republics is more random. So far we do not see the kind of great activity as in Georgia, Armenia, and Azerbaijan, where artists were mobilized for Stalin themes . . . In Turkmeniya we have the portrait carpet. . . . In Kazakhstan and Kirghiziya we also have something: Kazakh tapestries with portraits. . . . In Tadzhikistan we have murals . . . In Buryat-Mongolia, I believe, there should also be something fitting . . . I think that we could thus get a minimum of 100 pieces of artwork out of the national republics for this exhibit, even if we select rigorously.' OR GTG, 8.II/993 11–2.
26. OR GTG, 8.II/994 3.
27. OR GTG, 8.II/994 115.
28. OR GTG, 8.II/993 22ob.
29. OR GTG, 8.II/993 23.
30. See, for example, the Leningrad artist Vladimir Kuznetsov's letter in OR GTG, 8.II/993 62.
31. See the protocols of the jury in OR GTG, 8.II/993 89–92, 94–9, 105–7, 142–52.
32. For telegrams of individual artists or local artists' unions saying that their contributions were going to be late, see OR GTG, 8.II/993 119–22.
33. OR GTG, 8.II/993 25.
34. OR GTG, 8.II/993 28ob.-29.
35. OR GTG, 8.II/993 28.
36. Thus the chairman of the Committee for Arts Affairs, Platon Kerzhentsev, made last-minute changes in the way pictures were hung at the 1937 *Art of the Georgian SSR* exhibit, removed several pictures from the exhibit, and had details changed in others. The painting of M. I. Toidze, *Stalin at Lenin's in Gorki* was removed. The artist U. M. Dzhaparidze was ordered to correct the position of the hand of Stalin in his picture, *Comrade Stalin and V. Ketskhoveli*, and I. A. Vepkhvadze was told to change Kirov's chin in his *Portrait of S. M. Kirov*. OR GTG, 8.II/763 3.
37. OR GTG, 8.II/993 191–2.
38. In 1938–39, for example, a 'mobile exhibition Lenin-Stalin in the fine arts', consisting mostly of reproductions and plaster casts of existing artwork, was prepared by the Tretyakov Gallery for travel through the Soviet Union. See OR GTG, 8.II/888. In 1949, the Irkutsk art museum organised an exhibit entitled *Stalin and the Stalin Era in Works of Art*, which dealt in part with Stalin's experience of Siberian exile. See the catalogue, *Vystavka: Stalin i Stalinskaya epokha v proizvedeniyakh izobrazitel'nogo iskusstva* (Irkutsk, 1949).

39. At a discussion of the organising Committee about how to increase the recently opened *Industry of Socialism*'s attractiveness to visitors, one participant suggested that 'Iosif Vissarionovich Stalin should find time to visit the exhibition'. OR GTG, 18/136 28–9. Stenographic record dated 14 April 1939.
40. Evgenii Gromov, *Stalin: vlast' i iskusstvo* (Moscow, 1998), pp. 59–60.
41. See Frank J. Miller, *Folklore for Stalin: Russian Folklore and Pseudofolklore of the Stalin Era* (Armonk, NY, 1990).
42. Ibid., p. 8.
43. Ibid., p. 22.
44. Heizer, 'The Cult of Stalin, 1929–1939', p. 169.
45. On 'The Stalinist Myth of the "Great Family"' see Clark, *The Soviet Novel*, chap. 5.
46. Eric Naiman, *Sex in Public: The Incarnation of Early Soviet Ideology* (Princeton, 1997), p. 15.
47. Karelia's regional folklore institute was ranked in importance only after those of Moscow and Leningrad in the 'chronicle' (*khronika*) section of the journal *Sovetskii Fol'klor*. See e.g. P. G. Shiryaeva, 'Fol'klornaya rabota v SSSR za poslednie tri goda,' *Sovetskii Fol'klor*, 7 (1941), p. 266.
48. Clark, *The Soviet Novel*, pp. 99, 105.
49. There were, to be sure, cases of textual reworking that entered the pages of journals even after 1931, but they are exceptions. They are also kept in a different format, in which public pedagogy is abandoned in favour of an author's 'natural' improvement upon an older version of a text. See, for example, V. Kravchinskaya, 'Novyi variant skazki M. M. Korgueva', *Sovetskii Fol'klor*, 7 (1941), p. 273. Here the Karelian *skazitel'*, Korguev, presents the folklorist with an 'improved' version of his tale 'O Chapae' ('About Chapaev').
50. 'Rezolyutsiya', *Sovetskii Fol'klor*, 7 (1941), p. 249.
51. Ibid., pp. 249–50.
52. T. I. Sen'kina, 'Zabytaya stranitsa iz istorii russkoi fol'kloristiki Karelii (30–40-e gody XX veka)' in N. A. Krinichnaya and E. S. Kyuru (eds) *Fol'kloristika Karelii* (Petrozavodsk, 1991), p. 133.
53. Ibid., p. 130. The targeted year is 1938.
54. Ibid.
55. Ibid., p. 131.
56. P. N. Parilova and A. D. Soimonova (eds) *Byliny Pudozhskogo kraya* (Petrozavodsk, 1941).
57. Composed by E. S. Zhuravleva, 23 October 1932. Arkhiv Karel'skogo Nauchnogo Tsentra Rossiiskaya Akademiya Nauk (AKNTs RAN), 1/1/9/15 51. Original: 'Stalin lyubit vsekh lyudei / i vas malen'kikh detei / bayushki bayu ia te pesenku spoyu / spi vnuchek ty moi.'
58. Sen'kina, 'Zabytaya stranitsa iz istorii russkoi fol'kloristiki Karelii (30–40-e gody XX veka)', p. 136.
59. Miller, *Folklore for Stalin*, p. 165.
60. *Chastushka*, no. 285, recorded in Kotchura, 1938. Typescript in AKNTs RAN, 1/39/62 50.
61. I. V. Megrelidze, 'Iz gruzinskogo revolyutsionnogo fol'klora', *Sovetskii Fol'klor*, 6 (1939), p. 106.
62. A. V. Belovanova, 'Lenin i Stalin v tvorchestve skazitelei sovetskoi Karelii', *Izvestiya Karelo-Finskogo Filiala AN SSSR*, 2 (1950), pp. 43–52; AKNTs RAN, 1/45/78 14.

63. A. Soimonova, *Geroi Arktiki* (preface, typescript draft, 1938); AKNTs RAN, 1/39/87 2–3.
64. Belovanova, 'Lenin i Stalin v tvorchestve skazitelei sovetskoi Karelii', pp. 43–52; AKNTs RAN, 1/45/78 16.
65. 'Pesni o Lenine i Staline' in G. M. Vasilevich and S. D. Magid, 'Novaya evenki-iskaya pesnya', *Sovetskii Fol'klor*, 7 (1941), pp. 72–81; here song no. 9, pp. 77–8.
66. Megrelidze, 'Iz gruzinskogo revolyutsionnogo fol'klora', p. 106.
67. Belovanova, 'Lenin i Stalin v tvorchestve skazitelei sovetskoi Karelii'; AKNTs RAN, 1/45/78 17.
68. Martin, *Affirmative Action Empire*, pp. 432–61.
69. The catchword after 1936, 'Soviet patriotism', is seen by some scholars as Russocentric nationalism packaged as multiethnic identity. See Alan Bullock, *Hitler and Stalin: Parallel Lives* (London, 1991), p. 2; David Brandenberger, *National Bolshevism: Stalinist Mass Culture and the Formation of Modern Russian National Identity* (Cambridge, Mass., 2002).
70. Miklós Kun, *Stalin: An Unknown Portrait* (Budapest, 2003), pp. 220–1.

8
Working Towards the Centre: Leader Cults and Spatial Politics in Pre-war Stalinism

Malte Rolf

The Soviet Union of the 1930s saw the emergence of a new culture. Stalin's 'building of Socialism' not only meant the radical political and economic transformation of the country. The dawn of the new era also manifested itself in the fundamental reshaping of culture. Stalin's cultural revolution was not a 'great retreat' but rather an attempt to realise the utopian vision of the new socialist person and to define the new aesthetics of a brave new world. It was less a time of 'war on the dreamers' than a period of new dream weavers who reinvented culture, and by this the Soviet Union.[1]

The most emblematic cultural expression of this time was the ubiquitous leader cults. The leaders were lauded as assistants of the 'birth pangs of Socialist culture'[2] and were praised as the fathers of all change. Cult production in the 1930s mainly orientated towards Stalin: he was at the centre of public praise and expressions of emotionality. But Stalin was by no means the only object of veneration. His 'dearest comrades' and 'close friends' always stood next to him in such public worship and on the regional level it was the local representatives who built up a cult of the lesser leaders. As even factory directors had themselves lauded by their workers, Stakhanovites were portrayed as guiding figures, and the production of art and literature built on the narrative of the spiritual leadership of outstanding artists, it is fair to say that leader cults were an overall mode of communication in the 1930s. Worshipping the leader was at the core of the ethic and aesthetic of the new emerging culture.[3]

In these representations leaders figured as the 'unmoved movers' of the fundamental transformation that the country and its culture underwent in those years.[4] They were depicted as the source of all change, as leaders who could reshape vast landscapes with a pencil's sketch on a drawing board.[5] In this staging the leaders occupied the centres of authority and represented the eye of the cyclone: While everything was tempestuously moving the leaders stayed motionless. The whole country was twisted in circles around them. In the official Soviet cosmos the leaders occupied the centre of gravity, and by this embodied the core place within a Soviet spatial hierarchy.[6]

Their privileged position in the official mental map was ensured by an active spatial politics conducted by the Stalinist party-state.[7] A set of techniques and mass media tried to establish a new order of space as part and parcel of the reconstructed Soviet culture of the 1930s. It was a time of general centre-building when new Soviet centres had to be marked, leaving an older pre-Revolutionary hierarchy of space behind. City planning and mass festivals were powerful tools of this spatial politics as they visualised the redefinition of space, territorialised the Soviet new centre and placed the leaders in this newly created space. Just like leader cults they were part of the Stalinist 'synthesis of arts' that expressed the emergence of a new era.[8] They were intertwined in many ways and permanently interacted, enforcing each other but also conflicting to some extent. These different media shared the same orientation towards a new centre and expressed a Stalinist notion of centrality.

In the 1930s a general culture of centre-orientation was predominant not only in spatial dimension but also in an abstract ubiquitous fixation towards a centre of authority in all cultural fields. In Stalin's times official culture was not only 'working towards the leader' but it also worked towards the centre as a space and a notion.[9] In the 1930s regional elites copied Moscow's efforts to restructure the order of space and fix it on new Soviet centres. They actively participated in the invention of a new culture and proved to be quite creative and self-referential. As they developed leader cults of their own and a focus on the local centre they contested Moscow's monopoly of authority. Taking a closer look at the regional landscapes – Voronezh and Novosibirsk in this chapter – thus reveals much about the tricky nature of centre-building in the Soviet Union.

Building utopia: the era of 'General Reconstruction Plans'

The 1930s were a period when *utopia* was to be territorialised and what had been *no-space* before was fixed on the spot: in official discourse the 'building of Socialism' made the Soviet Union the place on earth where the bright future of mankind dawned. The birth of a new culture and the new person took place on Soviet territory. Architecture and city planning were prominent media of the regime's self-representation and its vision of the future in that time. As a true Socialist Realist artefact, monumental architecture and the town's topographical reconstruction represented the better tomorrow in the present and allowed a first glance at how beautiful Socialism would be.[10]

The socialist city (*sotsialisticheskii gorod – sotsgorod*) – an older vision of socialist architects and city planners – was now finally supposed to be realised under Stalin's regime. But as Politburo and other party members engaged in city-building, the vision of what a 'socialist city' was to look like changed fundamentally. The era of the General Reconstruction Plans saw a strict spatial orientation towards a new centre that was capable of representing the extraordinary quality of Stalin's reign.[11]

The reshaping of Moscow is the most famous case of the country's reconstruction. Investment was poured into reconstructing the infrastructure and economy of the capital, symbolised most clearly by the construction of the Metro and the Moscow-Volga Canal.[12] Varying projects culminated in the General Plan for the Reconstruction of Moscow that was approved in a final version in 1935. Political leaders like Stalin, Molotov and Kaganovich were portrayed as the master minds behind Moscow's reconstruction. They were displayed as the source of all change and acted as Soviet Haussmanns, cutting new avenues through the city's ground-map and tearing down historical buildings that did not match with their new aesthetics. But the power elite's aesthetics of style and spatial order differed fundamentally from older avant-garde visions of the 'socialist city'. All concepts of de-urbanisation, not to mention the anti-urbanist projects, were abandoned in favour of a strict centre-building that built on the traditional radial structure of Moscow but orientated a system of concentric circles and aisles towards the newly defined centre. This core spot of the political and symbolic order was to be marked by the monumental Palace of the Soviets that was projected but never built.[13]

No doubt, Moscow underwent fundamental reconstruction. But in comparison with provincial cities that mushroomed during the first Five Year Plans it was certainly not the most radical change in urban topography. The General Plan of Moscow had rejected radical models of reshaping the city's ground-map and approved a change that compromised with the traditions of spatial order. By contrast, in towns like Voronezh and Novosibirsk the city's body was resculptured in a much more radical and iconoclastic fashion.

During the period of the New Economic Policy (NEP) 1921–28 local officials in Voronezh mainly tried to sovietise the pre-revolutionary heritage of space. They erected a small monument for the 'Victims of the White Terror', ornamented the facades of traditional official buildings with Soviet symbols and rebaptised older houses with revolutionary names.[14] All in all the changes were not substantial, they did not aim at redrawing the whole city's ground-map.

This changed fundamentally in the 1930s. Now, Voronezh officials invested much more resources to relocate the city's centre. They created a new Soviet Voronezh with a new spatial hierarchy. The General Plan of Voronezh that was worked out by local city planners and economists in 1931–32 chose the somewhat remote *Starokonnaya ploshchad'* (Old horse square) as the future main square. The project was accepted by Moscow and by the local authorities in a final version in 1935, and within two years the architectural landscape of Voronezh was changed fundamentally. The new buildings of the district party and Soviet Executive Committee were erected by 1937. Soon, the city's opera and ballet theatre was to follow. A look at the city's map in 1936 in contrast to the ones of 1903 or 1910 demonstrates the fundamental spatial renovation Voronezh had under gone within one decade: the nodal point of the urban infrastructure was now located at the old *Starokonnaya ploshchad'*, a place that had been at the former periphery of the town. In 1937 it was renamed as *Ploshchad' 20i-letiya Oktyabrya* (Square of the 20th Anniversary of October) and in 1940 a Lenin monument was unveiled. Name and monument equipped the square with the symbolic capital of one of the most sacred Soviet symbols.

One can spot a very similar development in Novosibirsk, even though basic conditions and prerequisites were quite different from those in Voronezh. Novo-Nikolaevsk/ Novosibirsk, as a bigger town, was very much a post-revolutionary product. The capital of Western Siberia was one of those boomtowns that mushroomed in the Soviet Union during the first Five Year Plan. Before 1917, no traditional centre had been established in Novo-Nikolaevsk. The main buildings of the railway management and the nearby station, the most important cathedral and the corpus of the city's representatives were scattered throughout the city. Therefore, there was no centre that the Bolsheviks needed to take over after the seizure of power. A 'Lenin-house' was built in 1925 on the traditional main avenue – the *Krasnyi Prospekt* (Red Boulevard) – but the first Lenin monument was erected in 1927 on the *Barnaul'skaya ulitsa* closer to the railway station and quite distant from the main boulevard. Until the end of the 1920s Novosibirsk was still lacking a clearly defined centre.[15]

The 1930s brought about a fundamental change in Novosibirsk just as in Voronezh. Now, the city planning of the General Reconstruction Plan aimed at fixing the centre, and 'virgin' territory was chosen to build this central square of the rapidly growing city. As in Voronezh, the city's former market place suited for the new sacred centre of Soviet Novosibirsk. The vast space of the *Bazarnaya ploshchad'* (Market Square) was chosen for the construction of a huge opera house, which started in 1931. The centrality of the square was even more emphasised by the opening of the Stalin Park of Culture and Rest that was located some distance up the main avenue and the new theatre building *'Krasnyi fakel'* (Red Torch) closer to the railway station. Now, the theatre and the railway station, the district's administrative building and the recreational park created a radial around the *Bazarnaya ploshchad'*. Toponymical change also expressed and enforced this new quality as the market square was re-baptised Stalin Square in 1935.[16]

A comparison of the city's maps of 1919, 1928 and 1935 shows the same spatial renovation of Novosibirsk as in Voronezh. The town's ground-map and the main buildings were now orientated towards a new renamed central square. So, a similar tendency can be observed in Novosibirsk and Voronezh for the 1930s. Spatial policy of that time reached out to so far underdeveloped areas. The new era that was dawning was in need of blank territories to draw the new outlines of the 'Socialist city' to come. It distanced itself from the past – both pre- and early post-revolutionary times – and aimed at creating something completely new. In the provincial towns of Voronezh and Novosibirsk spatial politics created a new urban topography in an even bolder iconoclasm than in Moscow. But it was common to all towns of the Soviet Union that city planning in the era of 'General Reconstruction Plans' was working towards a new Soviet centre.

Creating ceremonial landscapes: 'ornaments of the masses'[17]

Reshaping Moscow, Voronezh, Novosibirsk and other cities in the Soviet Union was not only the result of the architectural changes initiated by the General Plans. The relocation of the city's centre, which was the most important spatial renovation of the period, needed other media if it wanted to inscribe itself into the mental map of the town' inhabitants. In order to endow public space with new meaning the Bolsheviks invested much effort in crafting a festive 'ornament of the masses'.[18] In the clear hierarchy of regions and cities in the USSR, the reconstruction of regional centres was intended to bolster municipal pride. The ability of regional centres to put on impressive festive displays and to outdo their rivals served to foster local identity.

Mass festivals gained importance in mapping out the new topography of the town since, in times of tight budgets, resources for monuments or other forms of architectural representation were rather limited. Changing the topography of a city was an expensive and slow undertaking. Mass celebrations were easier and cheaper to organise. The reconstruction of the town's landscape was accompanied by the renovation of ceremonial space. Soviet ceremonial choreography witnessed a similar development as city planning in the two post-revolutionary decades. While the 1920s saw a period of irritation about the nature and the place of a festive centre, the 1930s were dominated by the notion that celebrations needed to have *one* centre and by the general agreement about where this centre was supposed to be located. There had been a few years of experiment in the early post-revolutionary period, when it was discussed whether Soviet festivals should have a central point at all (since the masses were supposedly demonstrating for and to themselves only), different stages were equally evaluated and the leadership commuted between various places of symbolic action.

At the end of the NEP official festival, experts articulated harsh criticism of this plurality and de-centrality of Soviet holidays.[19] In the time of general plans they also called for a centrally organised and controlled 'standardised ceremonial plan' that would give the festival a uniform character. And they called for a strict centre-building of the choreography focusing on the central *meeting* and the reviewing stand with the leaders of the party-state.

But it was not until 1932 that the debate about the orientation of Soviet celebrations towards a single centre was ended. During the violent clashes of the Culture Revolution the Soviet regime's self-definition developed only in forms of a counter-subject and in a self-perception of being isolated within society's backwardness and hostility.[20] It focused on its political and cultural enemies and became self-aware mainly in contrast to cultural antagonisms, for example with regard to the campaign against religion. But such a strong reference towards the enemy hindered the coming to terms with what the vision of socialism should be. The 1930s saw the destruction of church buildings and of other monuments deemed incompatible with the new order.[21] It was a time more of destruction and denial of cultural alternatives than a period of agreement on Soviet cultural standards. The heated debates in all kinds of political and cultural fields, the general culture of harsh criticism and the lack of an overall accepted source of authority during the years of the Great Break illustrated the Bolshevik's insecurity about the centre. This also holds true for the regimes' celebrations that were to a large degree 'ritual of the counter-faith'.[22] During the Great Break no consensus was reached on how a Soviet ceremonial space should be created and where the centre of it could be fixed. The polemical debates on the nature of Soviet ceremonies only ended when a new 'positivism' and public praise of the 'achievements' of socialism-building was canonised from above in 1935 and a satisfaction with the present was made obligatory.

The 1930s also saw a fundamental break with the ceremonial choreography of the first post-revolutionary decade. A closer look at the ceremonial choreography in Voronezh reveals some of this new spatial order of Soviet festivals and shows how it interacted with the town's architectural renovation during these years. In the mid-1930s the new central point of Soviet festivals in Voronezh was marked by the *Starokonnaya ploshchad'*. Columns of demonstrators from the town's districts approached the square from different directions, drawing a star-like marching order on the town's map. They met on the new central square, marching past the reviewing stand that was set up for the local leadership.

The festive choreography also included the construction site of the new Voronezh to display the 'building of Socialism' as a work in progress. The marching order included these objects in the cartography of Soviet festivals and connected the nodal points of a still wide-meshed net of Soviet achievements in the city's horizontal landscape. Celebrations referred to architecture, but architecture as well took festive arrangements into account: the main avenue leading to the future central square was built especially wide to allow impressive masses of demonstrators to enter the place synchronically. Soviet ceremonial processions and city planning jointly reinforced the new centre-building.

But the festivals' choreography and the redefinition of the town's landscape also corresponded in other ways. In the vertical dimension Soviet festival decoration aimed to enforce the bridging of still isolated symbols of the new era: buildings along the marching routes were decorated with banners, slogans, illuminations and portraits of the leaders. Festival organisers attempted to create ceremonially privileged areas and festive boulevards. Facades of Soviet core symbols and the leaders' faces along these streets covered the older building structure, and all traces of ancient Voronezh were supposed to be eliminated, so that columns ideally would move in a fully Sovietised space.[23]

To create a ceremonial space of extraordinary quality, the everyday and profane needed to be repressed. Streets were collectively cleaned before the holidays, flowers were planted and personal belongings on balconies along the parades' paths, like clotheslines, were strictly forbidden. Collective cleaning of the streets also had a symbolic meaning and had a long tradition in Lenin's engagement in the collective work on the *subbotnik*. But in the 1930s cleaning also meant 'cleansing' and all 'social aliens' such as beggars, prostitutes or stray children were removed from the festive space.

The hectic activities unfolded before the festive date aimed at creating a ceremonial space that was set apart from the usual profane use of streets and places. The festival was portrayed as being the exception from the everyday – so, space had to correspond with this exceptionality. Both, ritually cleaned boulevards of decor and the columns of marchers, had their anchorage point in the *Ploshchad' 20i-letiya Oktyabrya* and, thus, linked the isolated and peripheral Soviet achievements with the new heart of Soviet Voronezh, the central square with the Lenin monument, the platform and local officialdom.

What was said about Voronezh holds true for Novosibirsk as well, showing an even sharper contrast between the 1920s and subsequent decades. By the mid-1930s the *Bazarnaya ploshchad'* had established itself as the fixed final point of all ceremonial processions. The platform was now always erected on this square to which the demonstrators marched from the different regions of the town.[24] The huge theatre under construction provided the backdrop for the reviewing stand of the Western Siberian leadership and seemed to demonstrate the constructive quality of the new era. And the avenues leading to the square were widened to enable a complicated marching order to enter the central square.

Staging the leader as the 'unmoved mover'

In the 1930s this centre was embodied by a small group of leaders. The elite of the party-state stood side by side up on the platform that marked the core space of the ceremonial arrangements. Here they awaited the masses and oversaw them from their elevated reviewing stand. The festive crowd reflected them like a mirror: the leaders looked into their own faces carried as posters by demonstrators, or read their own names spelled out by the bodies of physical culture activists. The platform's personage was thereby staged as the 'unmoved mover', the core group of power that had the force of making things and people move without moving themselves. Their stolidity symbolised a gravity of those who oversaw the course of history and guided the masses on the right path just as they sketched out the marching routes of the festive crowd.

Making things and people move without moving oneself was a clear expression of authority. But it also legitimised this power. The choreography of Soviet festivals had always ensured the privileged position of the leaders. In the 1930s, though, a new model of the relationship of those who led and those who were led was played out. It is worth noting that it was only during the years of the first Five Year Plan when the model of parading past by the platform became the general form of Soviet ceremonial movement. What had been a meeting around a platform in the 1920s became a demonstrators' procession past the reviewing stand in the following decade. The unorganised movement of the festive crowd turned into a military-like parade where every choreographic detail was planned and violations of the conventions were punished. The 'ornament of the masses' that unfolded under the leader's eyes was a carefully crafted stage-event.[25]

The strict order of movement enforced the focus on the moment of passing by the leaders. The scenario of Soviet festivals tried to establish this bypassing as the anchorage point of festive emotions: all activities beforehand were depicted as an anticipatory state, that culminated in the great moment of entering the central square. Public discourse portrayed it as the very sacred core of the whole festive arrangement and anxiousness before presenting oneself to the views of the leaders was part of the official rhetoric: it was frequently stated that columns tended to rush towards the leaders, thereby disturbing the strict marching conventions. And Soviet citizens often remembered, in published narratives, the short moment when they had been so close to the leader and when he seemingly had looked at him or her personally or when he even had met them.[26]

In the first post-revolutionary years Lenin had still commuted between different festive locations, and he had climbed improvised platforms, that were surrounded by the crowd, to address them with his speeches. The pictures of that time demonstrate – and were intended to demonstrate – the leader's closeness to the people. Although the reviewing stand was institutionalised in the early post-revolutionary years as an expression of the leaders' outstanding status, the form of a meeting around this locus still ensured the staging of a collective symbiosis in one large festive crowd. The years of the Great Break also saw a representation of the leader as one being close to ordinary people. Pictures, posters and paintings tried to catch the massive scale (*massovost'*) of the festive and other crowds and their fusion with the leaders. And leaders themselves moved to come in contact with 'the masses': they queued up in bread lines, travelled the country, climbed on dirty construction sites and rode on the trams.

These displays of direct contact between the leaders and the led came to an abrupt end in the 1930s. The elite of the party-state retreated into their freshly built fortresses – the new administrative buildings with their closed-up facades. Now, they called for meetings and bestowed the rare privilege on small groups of elected people to attend one of the leaders' receptions. They themselves made rare public appearances and by this the short moment of a glance upon them was ever more extraordinary. Withdrawing their *person* from public sight was accompanied by flooding the public space with representations of their *persona*. As pictures, images and spoken words, they became omnipresent in the 1930s: a light was always left burning in one of the windows of the Kremlin to symbolise Stalin's limitless care. He himself as a person stayed out of sight, but thousands of posters portrayed him sitting at his desk and working for 'the good of the people' at night-time.

The dates of Soviet holidays were the few occasions the leaders showed themselves to a public and the rare moment the public could make itself visible to the leaders' eyes. But even here ceremonial arrangement manifested the remoteness of the leaders as the marching columns passed by the reviewing stand in growing distance and the altitude of the platform increased in these years. Few moments of contact and direct communication between the leaders and the people were displayed: the figures on the platform waved their hands and pointed at the festive crowd, or children brought flowers to the leaders. The leaders marked the centre of Soviet ceremonial space, which in the 1930s gained much of its authority by being untouchable. It was a taboo space that the ordinary person could never enter and was only allowed a glimpse of.[27]

The leaders' authority built on their own central position in the spatial order. Making political decisions, being in charge of military forces and the secret police or forging industrialisation were all expressions of the power statutes of the party-state elite. But to make a social system work required some form of acceptance of the authority of those in power. Even in a totalitarian dictatorship, some legitimacy of the privileged status of the leaders was required – if no one believed or at least accepted that they were supposed to be in the position of making political and other decisions, enforcing these decisions became an almost impossible task. Legitimising authority, therefore, was at the core of a regime's self-representation even in a period when fear and terror secured Bolshevik rule. It was in the nature of the Stalinist regime that it conducted a policy of brutal oppression of all deviant behaviour and the use of 'soft forms' of forging the New Soviet person and making people believe in the superiority of the system at the same time. Stalin's regime was at the same time both a police and a propaganda state, that made people fear, but simultaneously wanted to convince them of the legitimacy of the system, its leaders and their politics. So, in the 1930s, parallel to policing, monitoring and murdering people, the power elite applied forms of making their rule legitimate. The rhetoric of revolution, the recourse to the 'will of the masses' or the rituals of elections and constitution campaigns were all part of this strategy.

As Edward Shils and Clifford Geertz have convincingly argued, occupying the accepted centre of a symbolic system is a powerful source of legitimacy. Decisions coming from such a centre seem much more legitimate that any coming from the peripheries.[28] Nevertheless, the locus of the centre still needs to be permanently re-established as any symbolic mapping-out becomes stable only by ritual re-enactment.

City planning and ceremonial choreography introduced a new spatial centre within the urban landscape and placed the leaders within this symbolically privileged spot. In consequence, the leaders' self-claimed extraordinary status was reinforced by their sheer occupation of this most sacred terrain. The leaders also portrayed themselves as the founding fathers of the new urban landscape. Stalin and Kaganovich in Moscow and the lesser leaders in the regional capitals were displayed as the masterminds behind the architectural renovation and the sculptors of the new aesthetic. They were the 'unmoved movers' of a spatial revolution and changed the towns' topography with a pencil. It was a representation of an artist-leader who with his almighty will could sculpt the raw material of society into the beautiful piece of art of socialism.[29] As the reconstruction of the cities symbolised the beginning of a new era, the leaders figured as midwives at the birth of a new epoch. They made spatial renovation possible and ensured that the new spatial order worked towards the centre they embodied themselves. The logic of such a representation worked like a self-fulfilling prophecy: the leaders' claim of being the source of all legitimate authority in the country was backed up by their self-positioning within a self-made centre created by spatial politics.

This highly political quality of spatial politics made it a contested field in the 1930s. As demonstrated, spatial politics was by no means a privilege of Moscow. The provincial leaders engaged in an active centre-building in the regional context and placed themselves within this centre. The provincial cities' reconstruction and ceremonial space lauded the role of the regional first party secretary. Local official discourse presented Iosif Vareikis in Voronezh – and later in Stalingrad and the Far East – or Robert Eikhe in Novosibirsk as the initiators of all reconstruction. A wave of renaming public institutions in their honour swept the districts and the festival crowds carried their portraits in even greater numbers than those of Stalin and Molotov. Vareikis and Eikhe were the 'unmoved movers' in the regional context. And they too organised receptions to give a small group of privileged subjects access to this taboo zone of power. In Voronezh and

Novosibirsk there existed little courts with courtiers encircling the centre embodied by the regional leader. By exploring the same media and methods of placing themselves in the centre of a spatial order, they created on a regional level what Moscow's power elite did on a Union-wide scale.

This parallelism of central and peripheral spatial politics and leader cults had ambivalent effects. On the one side it reinforced the party's effort of centre-building since it made it a common, recognisable Union-wide phenomenon. Only because local leadership also pushed the orientation towards a fixed centre did this become a Soviet cultural standard of the 1930s. The different centres were located in a spatial hierarchy that seemed to secure the extraordinary status of Moscow and Stalin as the centre of all centres. Many public rituals tried to ensure this outstanding quality of Moscow as the Soviet Rome, the cult of Stalin and his 'close friends' being the most prominent one. Stalin's name was to be lauded in all peripheral places in order to symbolise the connection of the most remote places with and the devotion to him as the source of all change and the ultimate 'unmoved mover' of Soviet socialism-building. Scientists out on the ice of the Arctic were rebound to the will and care of Moscow and Stalin just as the construction sites in the vast lands of Siberia symbolically referred to the main leader.[30] 'Stalin's falcons' followed the 'Stalin-route' crossing the Soviet Union and the 'whole country' sent their 'thanksgiving' towards the Kremlin that sent people out to seize the peripheries in its name.[31] The official mental map of the Soviet Union was constructed in 'circles around Stalin' in a 'hierocentric' order.[32] In this Soviet adoption of the notion that 'all roads lead to Rome' the large 'family of the peoples' looked towards the father figure:[33] He was symbolically seated in the presidium of local festive galas to manifest the presence of the far-distant. Here again, his staged absence reinforced his central authority. The capital's and Stalin's privileged position seemed to be secured by a set of rituals and symbols that all worked towards Moscow.

But on the other hand this position of Moscow and Stalin was threatened by the ambitious projects of centre-building in the regional contexts. The hierarchy of space seemed to be questioned by such competitive definitions of where the most relevant centre was to be fixed on the spot. At least, this was the perspective of Moscow that viewed regional self-centredness with growing mistrust in the middle of the 1930s. One rationale behind the Great Terror of 1937–38 was to eliminate the regional elite as networks that had partly withdrawn themselves from Moscow's tight control and, in Stalin's perception, had proved to be disobedient. The important issues of contest stemmed from the fields of political and economic decision-making, but the symbolic practices of regional centre-building were a clear expression of such threatening local autonomy and 'misuse of power'. This accusation figured prominently during the raging campaign against the regional elite that led to their almost complete destruction in the years 1937–38.[34] It was a struggle between conflicting centres in which Moscow violently subordinated all regional self-focus and centre-building.

The Great Terror eliminated most of the well-known regional leaders of the 1930s. Their followers were more careful with placing themselves in the centre of a regional spatial order. They rather tried their best in playing out Moscow's and Stalin's superiority in symbolic practices. The regional *Stalinyada*-production was raised: Stalin portraits grew in size and numbers on festival dates, his birthday in 1939 was a Union-wide staged celebration of the 'father of Soviet family of the peoples', and the renaming policy that erased the toponyms of the 'enemies of the people' from the country's map focused even more on the small canon of Moscow's power elite.

Making Russian cities Soviet: spatial politics in a *longue durée*

The 'unmoved mover' of the 1930s proved to be mortal in 1953. But Stalin's spatial politics continued to dominate the Soviet order of space long after his death. The cities' reconstruction in the General Plans of the 1930s and the post-war reconstruction had changed the urban ground-maps fundamentally and had created a totally new topography.[35] And the festive 'ornament of the masses' of Stalin's times lingered on under his successors. Although the ceremonial landscapes were de-Stalinised, his portraits removed and his name erased, the choreography of Stalin's celebrations was kept largely unchanged. Festive columns continued to march past the platform on which the leadership still marked the centre of the procession. The new leaders themselves tried to restrain to some extent cultic veneration in other cultural fields. In the ceremonial landscapes of mass festivals they still embodied the symbolic core of the spatial order.[36]

But what proved to be most influential was the general centre-building effect of spatial politics in Stalin's times. The common denominator of city planning, ceremonial stage management and the production of leader cults was the notion that every cultural practice and any discourse needed to bear a reference towards a centre of authority. In the 1930s, it was mainly a fixation on the leadership that was fostered by this mental mapping: almost every event needed to be rebound to one of the leader's initiatives. But it was also a more general cultural mode of orientation towards a centre of authority. It expressed itself in such forms as the devotion towards a 'spiritual father' in Soviet high culture, the praise of Peter the Great as state-builder, the lauding of Pushkin as the master poet and Gor'ky as a literary role model or the citing of canonical texts of Marxism-Leninism and Stalin's 'genius elaboration' of Marxist-Leninist ideology. It was a patriarchal order and a paternalistic pattern of rule at display that enforced a fixation on the centre not only in concrete spatial but also in abstract terms.[37] The leader cults of the 1930s were a prominent expression of centre-orientation but they were embedded in a larger frame of cultural practices that all worked towards the authority of the centre. This notion of a centre did not wither away with the dictator's death. His successors promoted a model of authoritarian culture that was no less centre-orientated than the totalitarian predecessor. The methods to enforce obedience towards such a model were different and the centre was no longer embodied by one person. But the veneration of Lenin as the founding father, the omnipresence of the party, the emphasis on canonical text and the fixation on core symbols all articulated the continuum of centre-orientation in Khrushchev's and Brezhnev's Soviet Union.

After de-Stalinisation it was the *Soviet* nature that remained as the essence of the centre. In terminology, 'Stalinist' and 'Stalin's' were replaced by 'Soviet'. In spatial politics the Soviet heritage of change was emphasised while Stalin's role was downgraded then suppressed. The reconstruction of urban topography and reshaping of ceremonial order that had taken place in the 1930s continued to be proudly presented as expressions of the 'heroic building of socialism' in the country. Only Stalin was withdrawn from this picture. The fundamental change cities had seen in this period was now depicted as the successful Soviet transformation of old backward Russia. The re-location of the centre still served as representations of the increasing quality of the 'Soviet way of life' (*zhit' po sovetski*).[38]

So, in the long run the reconstruction of Russian cities in the 1930s appears to be rather a Sovietisation than a Stalinisation. The post-Stalinist regime continued to build on the new order of space that was originally introduced in the pre-war decade, and managed to integrate the changes into a Soviet master narrative. It was a form of 'inner Sovietization' that expressed itself not only in colonising the cities with the Soviet core symbols but in recreating them as a new urban landscape according to Soviet aesthetic standards and a Soviet notion of a centre-orientated order of space. Making Russian cities Soviet in this narrative was the 'achievement' of the 1930s general reconstruction of society.[39]

How this enforced reshaping of urban topography and rebuilding of the centre were perceived by those who inhabited the cities is hard to judge. The regime was undoubtedly successful in crafting the 'ornament of the masses' according to the new spatial order. And it is important to say that it was one of the main potentials of public ritual to show how much the party-state was able to make the people march along the marks of the official ceremonial landscapes. This was a powerful expression of authority as it proved the scale of obedience in public displays of loyalty. But as the regime also wanted people to like to march, it aimed at the internalisation of the aesthetic standards and spatial arrangements. It wanted to bring people's perception of space into line with the new Soviet topography. For the 1930s expressions of city dwellers or travellers being impressed by the new aesthetic and the beauty of socialism stand side by side with a stubborn popular reluctance to accept the city's new centre. Also, older meanings of the territory colonised by Soviet city planners lived on in the form of anecdotes and rumours. The seemingly 'doomed character' of the place determined for the Palace of the Soviets in Moscow is only the most famous example.[40] Legends like these transmitted an unofficial collective memory and knowledge of former meanings of space. They at least prove that redefining a town's mental map was not an easy and immediate outcome of official spatial politics.

In the long run, though, the Soviet mental and physical reconstruction of cities did not fail to have a formative effect on the people's perception of space: today, in cities like Voronezh and Novosibirsk the *Ploshchad' Lenina* is the place where the annual Christmas market is located, just as it is the spot where demonstrations of varying political movements still meet.[41] This is not only due to the size and functionality of the squares: rather, they have become 'the centre' for most city dwellers. Even though they often do not agree on the content of these political demonstrations and cultural activities, they do agree that it should be the *Ploshchad' Lenina*, where such activities take place. In a process of *longue durée* the new Soviet centres of Voronezh and of Novosibirsk that were fixed in the 1930s did manage to establish themselves as the anchorage point of urban focus. Soviet spatial politics in the long run proved to be rather successful in working towards the new centre and thereby making Russian cities Soviet.

Notes

1. N. S. Timasheff, *The Great Retreat* (New York, 1946) and for 'war on dreamers', see Richard Stites, *Revolutionary Dreams: Utopian Vision and Experimental Life in the Russian Revolution* (New York, 1989), pp. 225–52.
2. Stephen Kotkin, 'Birthpangs of Socialist Culture', *Slavic Research Center, Hokkaido University, Occasional Papers*, 46 (1993), pp. 1–24.
3. Malte Rolf, 'The Leader's Many Bodies: Leader Cults and Mass Festivals in Voronezh, Novosibirsk, and Kemerovo in the 1930s', in Kaus Heller and Jan Plamper (eds) *Personenkulte im Stalinismus* (*Personality Cults in Stalinism*) (Gottingen, 2004), pp. 86–97.
4. The 'unmoved mover' is a representation well known from medieval kingship. See Horst Wenzel, 'Repräsentation und schöner Schein am Hof' in Hedda Ragotzky and Horst Wenzel (eds) *Höfische Repräsentation. Das Zeremoniell und die Zeichen* (Tübingen, 1990), pp. 171–208.
5. For the notion of the artist-leader who sculpts the raw material of society see Boris Groys, *Gesamtkunstwerk Stalin. Die gespaltene Kultur in der Sowjetunion* (Munich, 1988), pp. 7–8.
6. Jan Plamper, 'The Spatial Poetics of the Personality Cult: Circles Around Stalin', in Evgeny Dobrenko and Eric Naiman (eds) *The Landscape of Stalinism: The Art and Ideology of Soviet Space* (Seattle, 2003), pp. 19–43; James von Geldern, 'The Centre and the Periphery: Cultural and Social Geography in the Mass Culture of the 1930s', in Stephen White (ed.) *New Directions in Soviet History* (Cambridge, 1992), pp. 62–80.

7. For the concept of spatial politics see Maoz Azaryahu, *Vom Wilhelmplatz zum Thälmannplatz. Politische Symbole im öffentlichen Leben der DDR* (Gerlingen, 1991).
8. Boris Groys has used the Wagnerian concept of a 'synthesis of arts' to interpret the pictorial arts of the Stalin era as part of larger cultural matrix. See Groys, *Gesamtkunstwerk*.
9. Ian Kershaw, '"Working Towards the Führer": Reflections on the Nature of the Hitler Dictatorship' in Ian Kershaw and Moshe Lewin (eds) *Stalinism and Nazism: Dictatorships in Comparison* (Cambridge, 1997), pp. 88–106.
10. Greg Castillo, 'Peoples at an Exhibition: Soviet Architecture and the National Question', *South Atlantic Quarterly*, 94: 3 (1995), pp. 715–46; Chans Gjunter and Evgenii Dobrenko (eds) *Socrealisticheskii kanon* (St Petersburg, 2000).
11. Anatole Kopp, *Town and Revolution: Soviet Architecture and City Planning 1917–1935* (New York, 1979).
12. E. A. Rees, 'Moscow City and Oblast' in E. A. Rees (ed.) *Centre–Local Relations in the Stalinist State, 1928–1941* (Basingstoke, 2002), ch. 4.
13. In 1934 Boris Iofan, V. A. Shchuko and V. G. Khelfreikh were commissioned to design the projected palace. Now, the monumental style of neo-classicism was officially set as the aesthetic standard that was capable of representing the growth of the powerful socialist party-state. See Sona Stephan Hoisington, '"Even Higher": The Evolution of the Project for the Palace of Soviets', *Slavic Review*, 62: 1 (2003), pp. 41–68.
14. G. A. Chesnokov, *Architekturno-planirovochnoe razvitie goroda Voronezha* (Voronezh, 1998), pp. 8–21, 48–53.
15. *Nasha malaya rodina. Khrestomatiya po istorii Novosibirskoi oblasti 1921–1991* (Novosibirsk, 1997), pp. 25–36.
16. *Novosibirsk 100: Istorichesko-geograficheskii atlas* (Novosibirsk, 1993), pp. 22–4. Before the park was opened a church was demolished and a cemetery was 'secularised'.
17. Siegfried Kracauer, *Das Ornament der Masse* (Frankfurt/Main, 1977).
18. On mass festivals in the Soviet Union, see James von Geldern, *Bolshevik Festivals, 1917–1920* (Berkeley 1993); Karen Petrone, *'Life Has Become More Joyous, Comrades': Celebrations in the Time of Stalin* (Bloomington, Ind., 2000); Malte Rolf, 'Constructing a Soviet Time: Bolshevik Festivals and their Rivals during the First Five-Year Plan', *Kritika*, 1: 3 (2000), pp. 447–73; Stites, *Revolutionary Dreams*, pp. 109–23.
19. M. Danilevskii, *Ulitsa i ploshchad' v Oktyabr'skie dni. Scenarii masovikh deistvii i metodika ikh provedeniya* (Moscow, 1927), pp. 5–15.
20. On a Bolshevik 'fortress mentality', see David Joravsky, 'Cultural Revolution and the Fortress Mentality' in Abbott Gleason, Peter Kenez and Richard Stites (eds) *Bolshevik Culture: Experiment and Order in the Russian Revolution* (Bloomington, 1985), pp. 93–113.
21. For the brutal fury against the Church and believers of all denominations, see e.g. Jörg Baberowski, *Der Feind ist überall. Stalinismus im Kaukasus* (Munich, 2003), pp. 553–668; Daniel Peris, *Storming the Heavens: The Soviet League of the Militant Godless* (Ithaca, NY, 1998).
22. Stites, *Revolutionary Dreams*, pp. 109–14.
23. 'Oktyabr'skaya demonstratsiya v Voronezhe', *Kommuna*, no. 258 (10.11.1936), p. 3; 'Gorod prinimaet prazdnichnyi vid', *Kommuna*, no. 99 (29.4.1940), p. 1. For such thoughts on vertical arrangements of Stalinist celebrations, see also Pawel

Sowinski, 'Der 1. Mai als totalitäres Theater in der Volksrepublik Polen', *Zeitschrift für Ostmitteleuropa-Forschung*, 48: 3 (1999), pp. 352–3.

24. 'Oktyabr'skaya demonstratsiya v Novosibirske', *Sovetskaya Sibir'*, no. 260 (10.11.1937), p. 2.
25. Petrone, *Life Has Become More Joyous*, pp. 28–32. On physical culture, also see David L. Hoffmann, 'Bodies of Knowledge: Physical Culture and the New Soviet Man', in Igal Halfin (ed.) *Language and Revolution: Making Modern Political Identities* (London, 2002), pp. 269–86.
26. Seeing or meeting the leader during a Soviet holiday was part of the official narrative. This is partly reflected in contemporary diaries: see Nina Kosterina, *Tagebuch* (Munich 1973), pp. 20–1.
27. And those whose right of presence in this privileged spot was redrawn soon fell victims to the purge. For example, Nikolai Ezhov was forced to leave the mausoleum *during* the celebration in 1938. He lost his position a month later and was shot in 1940. See Marc Jansen and Nikita Petrov, *Stalin's Loyal Executioner: People's Commissar Nikolai Ezhov* (Stanford, 2002), p. 162.
28. Edward Shils, *Center and Periphery: Essay in Macrosociology* (Chicago, 1975), pp. 3–16, 273–6; Clifford Geertz, 'Centers, Kings, and Charisma: Reflections on the Symbolics of Power' in Sean Wilentz (ed.) *Rites of Power: Symbolism, Ritual and Politics since the Middle Ages* (Philadelphia, 1985), pp. 13–40.
29. Groys, *Gesamtkunstwerk*, pp. 7–8; Plamper, 'Spatial Poetics'. See also David L. Hoffmann and Peter Holquist, *Sculpting the Masses: The Modern Social State in Russia, 1914–1941* (Ithaca, 2002).
30. Iwan D. Papanin, *Das Leben auf einer Eisscholle. Tagebuch* (Berlin, 1947), pp. 322–33. Also John McCannon, *Red Arctic: Polar Exploration and the Myth of the North in the Soviet Union* (Oxford, 1998). In Siberia in 1932 Kuzneck was renamed Stalinsk in the honour of the remote leader and special 'Stalin-grants' were given to students.
31. For the orientation of the periphery towards Moscow in official discourse and the colonisation of Moscow-sent 'volunteers', see Geldern, 'The Center and the Periphery', pp. 65–8; Elena Shulman, 'Soviet Maidens for the Socialist Fortress: The Khetagurovite Campaign to Settle the Far East', *Russian Review*, 62: 3 (2003), pp. 387–410.
32. Plamper, 'Spatial Poetics'.
33. On the official discourse of the 'family' and the 'friendship of the peoples', see Terry Martin, *The Affirmative Action Empire: Nations and Nationalism in the Soviet Union* (Ithaca, 2001), pp. 432–59.
34. For the criticism of regional 'vozhdizm' on the February–March CC plenum in 1937, see E. A. Rees, 'The Great Purges and the XVIII Party Congress of 1939' in Rees (ed.) *Centre–Local Relations in the Stalinist State, 1928–1941* (Basingstoke, 2002), pp. 191–2.
35. The post-war construction plans of the almost completely destroyed Voronezh did not change the ground-structure introduced in the pre-war years and expressively spoke of the city's 'restoration' (*vosstanovlenie*) or 'rebirth' (*vozrozhdenie*). See Chesnokov, *Razvitie goroda Voronezha*, pp. 65–110.
36. This only changed in 1981, when for the first time party leaders in Poland took a walk-about in the demonstration. It is not accidental that this renovation came from the periphery of the Soviet empire. Detailed research on festivals in the post-war and post-Stalinist Soviet Union are still wanting. On the importance and quality of mass festivals in the 'peoples' democracies' extensive research already

exists. On Poland, see Izabella Main, 'The Weeping Virgin Mary and the Smiling Comrade Stalin: Polish Catholics and Communists in 1949' in Gabor T. Rittersporn, Malte Rolf and Jan C. Behrends (eds) *Zwischen partei-staatlicher Selbstinszenierung und kirchlichen Gegenwelten: Sphären von Öffentlichkeit in Gesellschaften sowjetischen Typs (Between the Great Show of the Party-State and Religious Counter-Cultures: Public Spheres in Soviet-Type Societies)* (Frankfurt/Main, 2003), pp. 255–78. On Hungary, see Árpád von Klimó, 'The King's Right Hand: A Hungarian National-Religious Holiday and the Conflict between the Communist Party and the Catholic Church' in Karin Friedrich (ed.) *Festive Culture in Germany and Europe from the Sixteenth to the Twentieth Century* (Lewiston, NY, 2000), pp. 343–62.

37. On state-socialism as a paternalistic form of rule, see e.g. Jeffrey Brooks, *Thank You, Comrade Stalin!: Soviet Public Culture from Revolution to Cold War* (Princeton, 2000), esp. ch. 4; Stephen Kotkin, *Magnetic Mountain: Stalinism as a Civilization* (Berkeley, 1995), pp. 11–13.
38. 'Tam, gde zhivut po sovetski', *Voronezhskaya Kommuna*, no. 159 (15.7.1927), p. 2.
39. This phrase 'inner Sovietization' is borrowed from Lewis Siegelbaum, who describes the process of making Russian workers Soviet. See Lewis Siegelbaum and Ronald Grigor Suny (eds) *Making Workers Soviet: Power, Class, and Identity* (Ithaca, NY, 1994).
40. In Novosibirsk similar legends were told as the local Park of Rest and Culture was built on a former cemetery. Popular belief knew of numerous accidents in this park and considered it to be bewitched.
41. Today, skate-boarders use the Lenin statue for their art. But it still is Lenin who marks the centre of the town's topography.

Part III

Beyond Moscow: The Cult's Peripheries

9

Exporting the Leader: The Stalin Cult in Poland and East Germany (1944/45–1956)

Jan C. Behrends

> The Centre will shape everything, though individual countries will retain a few ornaments in the way of folklore.
>
> *Czesław Miłosz, 1953*

Stalin's 70th birthday in 1949 was the most extensive celebration of his leader cult.[1] After months of campaigning, the attention of the entire Socialist Bloc was focused on Moscow, the Stalinist Rome, where communist dignitaries from around the world had assembled to pay their tribute. No efforts had been spared: throughout autumn the mobilisation for the event had left its mark on public life in the Soviet empire. The official public celebrations as staged by the party-states concentrated on building up excitement for the event. The whole socialist camp became one giant display case showing the love of its peoples for the leader. The jubilee provided an opportunity to spread and solidify Stalin's image as *the* leader and symbol of unity of the post-war Soviet empire. In contrast to the celebrations of his 50th and his 60th, Stalin's 70th birthday was an international affair: *Pravda* showed the leader not only amongst his Soviet lieutenants, but amidst a host of foreign guests such as Mao Zedong and Walter Ulbricht. Highlighting the campaigns around Stalin's 70th birthday campaign and his death in 1953, this chapter will explore how the cult was exported to and indigenised in Poland and East Germany. How were the narratives of the cult changed? And, finally, what can we say about reactions to the Stalin cult in these countries?

Before the war, Stalin's charisma rested mainly on four pillars: his close relationship to Lenin, his role as the creator of the Five Year Plans, the authority of his words and writings and his close, paternalistic ties with the Soviet people.[2] These themes remained when the communists seized power throughout East Central Europe and imposed the cult on their societies. The Polish and the East German regime used the 1949 birthday campaign to highlight their achievements on the path of sovietisation and their efforts in the re-education of their population. Using their control of the official public, both regimes made their subjects participate in the celebrations.[3] They ordered the populace to demonstrate their emotional ties to the leader through the 'economy of the gift' which had been a part of Soviet culture since the 1930s.[4] The inclusion of the Soviet satellites in the birthday celebration signalled their full integration on the Soviet side in the Cold War. Thus, the campaign also served as a show of force for the international public.

So far, the post-war heyday of the Stalin cult in and outside the USSR has been largely neglected by historical research.[5] Attempts to adapt Stalin's cult for different ethnic groups had already existed in the multinational USSR.[6] The Polish and East German party-states imported this Soviet practice of adjusting parts of Stalin's persona while keeping the main pillars of the cult. The 1930s master narrative had to be supplemented to create new bonds between the leader of both the German and Polish nations, which had long been considered enemies of the Soviet Union.[7] New bonds of trust and affection for Stalin had to be constructed in order for him to be conceived as a charismatic leader, that is, a leader whose authority derived, as Max Weber put it, from 'personal trust in [the leader's] manifestation, heroism and exemplariness'.[8]

As the 1930s had seen the rise of the idea that the multiethnic Soviet Union rested upon the *friendship of the peoples* that were united in their love of Stalin, the 1940s witnessed the invention of the friendship of the Central European nations with the USSR.[9] Stalin was portrayed as the founding father of this great friendship. He represented the epicentre of the friendship propaganda and as such he symbolically occupied the centre of the Soviet cosmos.

In order to understand how the Stalin cult was perceived, we must take into account the history of the countries where the cult was introduced. Before the establishment of communist regimes, both Poland and Germany had experienced their own domestic modern leader cults, which were initially not totalitarian in nature. In the German Empire, Chancellor Otto von Bismarck and then in the Weimar Republic Field Marshall Paul von Hindenburg had been portrayed as charismatic leaders of the nation.[10] The pre-war Polish republic created an extensive cult of Józef Piłsudski. The victor of the 1919–21 Polish–Soviet war, whose charisma derived from the fact that he had defeated the Bolsheviks, was the object of widespread cultic veneration.[11] At least the older generations of Poles and Germans were still familiar with the paternalistic cults around absolute monarchs such as the German or Austrian Kaiser or the Russian Tsar.[12]

Finally, and perhaps most significantly for their attitudes towards modern leader cults, Poles and Germans had been exposed to Hitler's charismatic image.[13] In Nazi politics, the Führer embodied the German Reich like no other symbol; in his persona the National Socialist propaganda fused the personal and the political. While Hitler, like Stalin, represented a state with totalitarian aspiration, participation in his cult was limited by racial restrictions. Hitler was *the* Führer of the Germans and the Aryan 'master race', he was a conqueror and brutal oppressor of the Poles. While the Führer cult and Hitler's personal charisma helped to stabilise Nazi rule until the weeks of chaos and defeat in early 1945, the catastrophic outcome and legacy of the Third Reich served to discredit the whole idea of charismatic and dictatorial rule.[14] To understand how the Stalin cult was perceived in both Poland and East Germany this historical context is vital.

Stalin's image abroad was tainted before his cult was ever introduced. Polish society traditionally defined itself as Catholic, anti-Russian and anti-communist. The country was traumatised by the Hitler–Stalin pact of 1939, which was followed by the annexation and Sovietisation of her eastern provinces, by mass deportations to Siberia, the NKVD's murder of Polish officers at Katyń and the Soviets' refusal to aid the Poles in the 1944 Warsaw uprising. These events lingered in the Polish collective memory and in addition tarnished the reputation of the Soviet leader. To the Germans, Stalin was the feared commander of the Red Army. These collective experiences and memories meant that the regimes faced the task of building a new *fama* for the Soviet leader. Poles and Germans had to be re-educated along the lines of the Soviet master narrative that portrayed Stalin as the wise and caring father. With the tensions of the Cold War growing, it became the regimes' utopian goal to install the kind of unconditional trust and quasi-religious belief in the Soviet leader in their societies that devoted communists had long internalised.[15]

'Poland's unbending friend'

In 1944–46, nationalistic, pan-Slavic and anti-German themes dominated communist propaganda in Poland. A regime, which was widely perceived as having been imposed from abroad, tried to gain legitimacy through this populist approach.[16] Although Stalin initially did not loom large in Polish propaganda, some cultic materials were released early on: in 1945, a small biography of the Soviet leader was published in Polish.[17] The short text stressed Stalin's role in saving the Soviet Union through his supreme military skills. During 1945, many Polish cities thanked Stalin in letters and telegrams for their liberation from German occupation. Immediately after the Nazis had withdrawn from Warsaw, one of the main arteries of the Polish capital, *Aleje Ujazdowskie*, was renamed *Aleja Marszałka Stalina*. In most instances, Stalin's significance as the Soviet commander was highlighted. He was shown wearing his uniform and addressed using his rank as 'Marshall Stalin' or 'Generalissimo Stalin'. Clearly, he was granted the charisma of the victor and bore the marks of a Soviet Bonaparte.[18] The propaganda ascribed to him the role of the liberator, but throughout 1945 he was portrayed as a friendly foreign statesman, not as the leader of Poland.

In *Przyjaźń* (*Friendship*), the monthly journal that officially promoted Polish–Soviet friendship, the Soviet leader's persona initially did not play an outstanding role. On Red Army Day 1946 he was hailed as a military genius and portrayed as the creator of the Polish communist army, the partisans of the *Armia Ludowa* (People's Army).[19] The relative scarcity of Stalin portraits at mass-meetings and celebrations is a clear indicator of the absence of a Soviet-style cult before 1947. Even at manifestations of Polish–Soviet friendship, where one might expect the symbolic presence of the Soviet leader, initially no pictures of him were displayed. In official speeches, it was not yet commonplace to end addresses with 'long live Stalin'.[20] In December 1947, *Przyjaźń* still mentioned his 68th birthday in a rather modest way.[21] Gradually, however, Stalin's portrait gained prominence; it became customary to show the Soviet leader next to Poland's president Bolesław Bierut.

As the Cold War began to take shape, the propaganda began to tie Stalin's persona to Polish issues. When in September 1946 American Secretary of State James F. Byrnes questioned in Stuttgart the permanence of Poland's new western border, Polish communists instantly found a new propaganda theme and turned against the United States.[22] In October 1946 Stalin publicly contradicted Byrnes and stated that the Soviet Union saw Poland's border as 'permanent'. Stalin's statement about Polish territorial integrity was displayed on posters and boards throughout the country.[23] The high significance that was attached to Stalin's words marked a visible shift towards making his persona more prominent and tying it to Polish issues.[24]

The new narrative portrayed Stalin as the protector of the new Poland. He was credited with standing up to defend the new Polish borders against American-sponsored German revanchism. Communist propaganda claimed that Stalin personally represented Polish interests in the international arena. Furthermore, a historical dimension was added to the official narrative. According to the propaganda, Lenin and Stalin had decreed Polish independence during the October Revolution. Thus they were the legitimate fathers of Polish sovereignty, and Polish statehood was a prime example of 'Soviet nationality policy'. In the Stalinist view, Piłsudski's White Poles had merely hijacked the Polish state to turn it against the Soviet Union. This political folly of Piłsudski's clique led straight to the catastrophe of 1939.[25] Still, despite all setbacks and disappointments, Stalin had kept his trust in the 'Polish workers and peasants' and helped them regain independence and assume power in 1944/45. He was credited with having always demanded a 'Poland free, strong and independent'.[26] This official narrative assigned Stalin the role of the wise protector and 'unbending friend' of the Polish nation.[27] In the Stalinist view of Polish history, Piłsudski was a traitor while Stalin's persona was tied to the core values of Polish nationalism: independence [*niepodległość*] and liberty [*wolność*]. The discursive bond between Stalin and the Polish nation was, however, highly fragile because it coincided with the strict taboo on the discussion of Poland's loss of its eastern territories and the fate of her citizens in the USSR.

During the course of 1948 and 1949, pictures of communist leaders became a prominent part of public life. The reports of the May Day demonstrations noted explicitly which portraits were carried.[28] Expressions of love and gratitude to Stalin became a regular feature in official mass culture. The harsh reactions of the party-state to the frequently reported instances of iconoclasm – deliberate destruction of portraits – exemplified that these portraits were of high symbolic significance. Information on such iconoclasm in the provinces was reported to the Central Committee and passed on to the party leadership. The local authorities usually assured the centre that 'the security organs are conducting a search for the villains'.[29]

The campaign around Stalin's 70th birthday marked the point at which the Stalin cult in Poland reached Soviet proportions.[30] The party-state now aimed to penetrate all layers of the society. The entire population was supposed to be reached and play a role in the festivities. The campaign constituted nothing less than an effort of total physical and emotional mobilisation. As the Central Committee's instructions stated, the goal was to 'familiarise the Party, the working class and the whole society with the life and struggle of the Great Leader and teacher'.[31] The party-state ordered local officials to organise lectures and classes on Stalin's life not only for party activists, but also in all towns, villages, collective farms, workplaces, universities, schools and even nurseries. Workers, farmers, women, youth and pupils were asked to write collective letters of gratitude to Stalin, thanking him for his helping hand in rebuilding Poland.[32] The party-state attempted to mobilise all strata of society for these collective acts of symbolic communication with the leader. To contribute to a festive mood, public places were supposed to be decorated with portraits of Stalin and Polish and Soviet flags. VOKS, the Soviet agency for cultural exchange and propaganda abroad, sent 1455 portraits of Stalin to Poland.[33] When the daily *Wolność* (*Freedom*) exclaimed in large letters on 21 December, 'Long live *our* beloved Stalin!'[34] the headline expressed the obvious: Poland had turned Stalinist, and the Stalin cult formed an integral part of her political culture. The Soviet leader had been indigenised.

As in the USSR, the birthday campaign in Poland consisted of central festivities in Warsaw, well-orchestrated acts of symbolic communication with the leader in the form of letters, telegrams and presents, a concerted campaign of 'voluntary' economic mobilisation – the *Praca Stalinowska* – and a multitude of mass-meetings. Additionally, youth were mobilised to participate in a motor-rally to Warsaw. Young motorcyclists brought presents from all corners of Poland to the capital where they were loaded on a special train and accompanied the official Polish delegation on its way to the centre of celebrations, Moscow. Thus the order of festivities mirrored the political order of communist Poland and the strict hierarchy of the empire: all roads led to Moscow. While Poles focused on their capital Warsaw, which formed a sub-centre in the Stalinist universe, a handful of activists were chosen to go on a pilgrimage to the Soviet Rome. To be sent on such a journey and to come that close to the leader was one of the highest honours a Stalinist regime could bestow.

Internal reports to the Central Committee paint a picture of a very successful campaign. Festivities in the major cities and towns and in the countryside were well attended. Internal statistics claimed that 811 presents, specially selected, were shipped to Moscow where they would be displayed in the Pushkin museum. Furthermore, 2,100,000 youth were mobilised for the motor-rally and 563,340 letters were sent to Stalin.[35] The 'voluntary' *Praca Stalinowska* was described as a major contribution to the economic rebuilding of Poland. Schools, factories and collective farms had adopted the name '21 December'. As one outstanding example, the report singled out Poznań where all public buildings had been decorated with portraits of Stalin, and Soviet and Polish flags: 'Poznań has never been decorated and illuminated as on the 21st of December. The festivities proved that comrade Stalin is close and dear to our people. The name 'Stalin' is most respected and revered.'[36] Clearly, Polish communists could congratulate themselves on their success in mobilising the nation. It seems as if this internal jubilation was just another part of the Stalinist mode of communication: on the leader's jubilee one could not write about anything less than joyful celebration. Considering the small social base of the regime and the strong anti-Russian sentiments, there is reason to be sceptical about the emotional and educational impact of the Stalin campaign on ordinary Poles. We do not know how many were touched by the staging of this exceptional event. But in any case the party-state demonstrated that it had the means to mobilise society for these festivities. To the communist leadership that was probably an achievement in itself.

From 1949 until Stalin's death in March 1953 the Stalin cult remained an integral part of Polish mass culture. Although no other campaign could compare to that of December 1949, the Stalin cult thrived in the party, in the mass organisations and amongst communist intellectuals. Efforts to promote the study of Stalin's writings and his biography continued and the publication of new volumes of his collected works as well as his rare interviews were extensively featured in the press. At official rallies, the Polish leadership was often represented as a troika with Stalin as *primus inter pares* shown alongside portraits of Bolesław Bierut and Russian-born minister of defence Konstanty Rokossovskii.

From internal reports two characteristic responses to the Stalin cult may be isolated. First, people wondered why a *foreign* head of state should be venerated. This argument was often recorded at mass-meetings and was even articulated within the ranks of the party. The Stalin cult and the dogma of Soviet superiority in many ways contradicted the populist nationalist rhetoric of the party. In a variation of this argument, Poles drew a comparison between tsarist times and Stalinism. After the appointment of the Soviet Marshall Rokossovskii as Polish minister of defence in the autumn of 1949, a Lublin resident stated: 'Tsar batiushka gave us Prince Konstantin, and now Stalin has sent us Konstantin Rokossovkii.'[37] Here, Stalin is seen as the new representative of Russian imperial rule over Poland, a Soviet tsar. This view corresponds to the widespread fear of these years, that Poland would lose her fragile sovereignty and become the 'seventeenth republic' of the USSR.[38] The Stalin cult was not perceived as something genuinely Soviet, but the continuation of Russian imperial domination over the Poles. The paternalistic and pseudo-religious notions of the cult as well as the policies of (self-) sovietisation lent this interpretation plausibility.

Secondly, there is evidence that some viewed the Stalin cult as a typical feature of a totalitarian system. In opposition leaflets and street rumours, the prominent role of the leader cult in communism was perceived as resembling Nazism and the Hitler cult. In a sort of *totalitarian theory from below* Poles compared Stalin and Hitler and pointed to the anti-Polish policies, the cruelty and the dictatorial nature of both regimes.[39] Many saw the United States as the antithesis of totalitarian rule and, under the influence of John Foster Dulles' liberation policy, hoped that the Americans would eventually liberate them.

'The best friend of the German people'

As the USSR's enemy in its 'Great Patriotic War', Germany constitutes a special case. The Red Army's invasion of the eastern German lands in the course of 1945 was a traumatic experience for Germans. Plunder, mass rapes and random violence by Soviet soldiers characterised the spring and summer of that year.[40] During the early years of Soviet occupation, the relationship between Germans and Russians was ruled by mistrust. A British communist visitor to Germany remembered that in 1947 'hatred and fear' dominated the attitude towards the Russians.[41] Until the beginning of the Cold War, the Soviets were eager to uphold a democratic facade in their zone, which, along with the looming shadows of the Hitler cult, might have initially prevented them from introducing Stalin worship. But as in Poland, fragments of the cult could be found early on, for example, in *Tägliche Rundschau*, the Soviet-edited Berlin daily, which partly consisted of articles and editorials translated from Soviet publications. Victor Klemperer, Jewish victim of Nazism and after the war professor of philology in Dresden, who had analysed Nazi speech in his famous *Lingua Tertii Imperii* (*LTI*), noted in his diaries as early as July 1945 the striking parallels between Nazism and Bolshevism, and commented on the way Stalin was portrayed:

> Analogies between Nazi and Bolshevist speech: in Stalin's speeches, which are now regularly published, Hitler and Ribbentrop are beasts and cannibals. In articles about Stalin he is the generalissimo of the Soviet Union and the greatest commander of all times, the most ingenious human being alive.[42]

Although Klemperer later became a staunch GDR-supporter and joined the Communist Party, his diary shows that as an intellectual he was appalled by the re-emergence of the leader cult. It must be noted, however, that throughout the years of occupation, the Stalin cult was merely exhibited in the Soviet zone, and the Germans – not yet admitted to the Stalinist family of peoples – were not supposed to participate in it.

In 1947, propaganda efforts in the Soviet zone increased. The Russians became increasingly worried about their reputation amongst the German public. Gradually, the controlled media began to spread the message that Germans should put their trust in Stalin because he was in favour of German unity and sovereignty. As in Poland, the propaganda narrative claimed that Stalin's friendship extended back before the war and had persisted even during the bloody conflict. The Soviet leader's ties to the German people were usually demonstrated by quoting a wartime speech, in which he had stated that the Red Army did not seek the destruction of the German people but the defeat of Hitler. He continued: 'The lessons of history show, that the Hitlers come and go, but the German people, the German state remain.'[43]

While Stalin's care for German interests was emphasised throughout 1947 and 1948, one can only speak of a leader cult in 1949 when the German Democratic Republic (GDR) was founded.[44] Stalin's congratulatory telegram on the occasion of the establishment of the Communist German state deserves special attention. It became the first canonical text of his cult in Germany. On 14 October 1949, Stalin declared:

> The foundation of the German Democratic Republic is a turning point in European history. There can be no doubt that the existence of a peaceful and democratic Germany besides the Soviet Union will end the possibility of war in Europe . . . The experience of the last war has shown that the German and the Soviet people had borne the greatest sacrifices and that both these peoples have the greatest potential to accomplish deeds of world-wide significance.[45]

Thus, Stalin had publicly acknowledged the potential greatness of the German people and even indirectly lauded them for their war effort. The East German Communist Party (Sozialistische Einheitspartei Deutschlands – SED) immediately ordered that Stalin's telegram should be posted in all classrooms and all 'Houses of German–Soviet Friendship' and all *Freundschaftsecken* (corners of friendship) that existed in many workplaces. Until 1953, authors referred to Stalin's telegram in countless articles and speeches; it was given the status of the GDR's founding act. The text marked the essence of the GDR's Stalin cult: the Soviet leader as the guardian of the German nation and the paternal friend of the GDR.

Stalin was portrayed as the only leader of a great power who genuinely supported German unity. As unity (*Einheit*) was a central term in German nationalism, the SED's propaganda apparatus tried to denounce the Western 'puppet government' in Bonn as separatist, and accused Chancellor Konrad Adenauer of preparing for war against the USSR. This was contrasted with the 'tireless efforts' of the Soviet government, headed by Stalin, to solve the German question. This theme became especially vibrant with Stalin's proposal for German reunification in 1952. Clearly, GDR propaganda tied Stalin's persona to its nationalistic rhetoric.[46] As in Poland, the populist nationalistic appeal was used to reach people's emotions while the contradictions of being at once nationalist and pro-Soviet remained unresolved.

Immediately following its foundation the GDR joined the celebration of Stalin's 70th birthday. This event also symbolised the integration of the Germans into the Stalinist family of peoples. The Germans, now included in the *friendship of the peoples*, could and were expected to honour the *father of the peoples*. Under the auspices of the SED's Politburo, the party-state tried to mobilise the whole society to celebrate Stalin as the new *Übervater* of the reborn nation. While gifts were assembled throughout East Germany and ceremoniously shipped to Moscow, the SED leadership outdid the ritualised participation in the economy of the gift with a highly symbolic present. The party-state decided to present Stalin with a state-of-the-art Carl Zeiss planetarium that was to be built in his city, Stalingrad. This present had various symbolic dimensions. First of all, it stood for the high significance the SED wished to attach to the celebration of Stalin's 70th birthday. By choosing the planetarium and locating it in Stalin's city, site of the decisive battle, the SED offered symbolic compensation and atonement for the destruction the Wehrmacht had left behind. Additionally, the German communists hoped to construct a potent symbol of the newly declared 'German–Soviet Friendship'. On another level, though, the planetarium may also be interpreted as a sign of the regained self-confidence of the German communists. Being a technically advanced apparatus, the planetarium stood for supreme German craftsmanship that was – possibly – even superior to Soviet technology. Therefore, the gift implicitly questioned the Stalinist dogma of absolute Soviet superiority.[47]

The celebration of Stalin's birthday in the GDR's provincial cities was organised according to instructions from Berlin, using material the Soviets had provided through VOKS.[48] A newly composed Stalin cantata was premiered in Berlin's opera house. While central festivities took place in the capital, every small town or village was supposed to have its own mass-meeting. At these gatherings, people would be able to learn the official narrative about the Soviet leader or to join others in *speaking Bolshevik* (Stephen Kotkin) when reciting Stalin poems or singing Soviet songs. As in the Soviet Union, there was a strong artistic and folkloristic component to the cult. Communist writers such as Erich Weinert or Johannes R. Becher wrote Stalin poetry. At local meetings Stalin was not only present through his portrait, but he was often – unanimously – elected to the 'honorary presidium' of the meeting and a chair was left free for him. This ritual aimed to create a sense of the leader's omnipresence. Local celebrations combined elements of bourgeois festive culture with religious or liturgical overtones as in the music, the recitation from the scriptures or the leader's spiritual presence in the empty chair. An internal document stated that the goal of the celebration was to thank Stalin for his continued struggle for German unification and to teach the population that 'the Soviet Union, under the leadership of Stalin, has always defended the true interests of the German working people' and that 'the struggle of the Soviet peoples under Stalin's leadership teaches us many important lessons.'[49]

In the midst of the Stalin campaign, on 16 December 1949, Victor Klemperer again noted that 'the horrible similarities with Nazi methods is obvious in the propaganda of the society [for German-Soviet Friendship], in the noise around Stalin's birthday'. And on 22 December he summarised: '*Stalin*. The presents from all over the world: reminds one partly of the Jesus-child, everything a bit too oriental. . . . Everything is now "national front".'[50] To Klemperer, the mixture between leader cult and nationalist rhetoric seemed all too familiar. But while he criticised the GDR's totalitarian political culture in the privacy of his diary, he too learned to *speak Bolshevik* in public and gave public lectures on German–Soviet friendship.

It is interesting to note that, when Stalin was publicly honoured, on most occasions the person who sang his praises was not the veteran communists and SED-leaders Walter Ulbricht or Wilhelm Pieck who had both been in exile in the Soviet Union, but former Social Democrat and GDR prime minister Otto Grotewohl.[51] Possibly, the SED's propagandists wanted to add extra credibility to their message by making a recent convert to communism a central speaker of the cult. Grotewohl ideally represented a German successfully re-educated along Stalinist lines. For the next years, Stalin would be the god-like super-leader towering over the GDR, and Otto Grotewohl was his prophet.

Until Stalin's death, his cult thrived in the GDR, and produced more than its share of *Staliniana*. But the attitude of large segments of the population towards the 'Russians' in general and to Stalin in particular remained at best ambivalent. The continuing attempts of the party-state to re-educate the populace could not stem the anti-Soviet tide. Whilst the propaganda succeeded in creating a small group of believers in and around the party, it could for the most part not overcome the hurdles posed by collective memory about the final months of the war and national sentiment that refused to accept the loss of territory in the east. As in Poland, the rulers were trapped between their nationalistic rhetoric and the realities of Soviet domination. The attempt to legitimise SED-rule by exploiting Stalin's charisma as the 'best friend of the German people', and as the only foreign statesman working for reunification, had its limits. As time progressed, the advantages of the Western political and economic system became ever more apparent. To most people, the deficiencies of Communist rule were hardly outweighed by the charismatic elements of the cult.

This did not mean, however, that the German people of the 1950s no longer cherished charismatic leadership or the warmth of paternalistic rule. Just the opposite: in the West, much of the Christian Democrats' success was certainly due to both the charisma and the paternalism of Konrad Adenauer. To most Germans, who needed to fill the void left by Hitler, Adenauer not Stalin seemed to be the prime choice.

Stalin's last role: 'the warden of peace'

With the onset of the Cold War the *leitmotif* of the post-war Stalin cult changed once more. The Soviet Bonaparte disappeared and the 'warden of peace' appeared centre stage. In the Stalinist peace narrative, it was the Soviet leader who prevented the outbreak of yet another world war, which was pursued by the 'Anglo-American warmongers' and their 'German henchman'. In the Cold War, the peace theme was designed to create a sense of moral superiority of the Soviets over the Western powers. The 'struggle for peace' was fought on the usual fronts: at demonstrations, in schools, at the workplace and at mass-meetings where people were expected to sign the 1950 Stockholm peace petition. Stalin was the representative of the Soviet-controlled peace movement. In his rare interviews he commented on the necessity of the 'struggle for peace'. The propaganda implied that trusting Stalin and hating the Americans could save the world from the perils of all-out war. To 'struggle for peace' did not mean being a pacifist; on the contrary, it meant being ready to 'defend socialism'. The peace campaign was tied to the leader cult and constituted another attempt by both regimes to reach the people's feelings and mobilise the population. Intellectuals – both Western and from the Bloc – who lent their name to the endeavour could expect to be awarded the 'Stalin Peace Prize' in Moscow, a sort of 'Nobel Prize' in the parallel universe of High Stalinism.

In the Soviet Union, Poland and the GDR, the intensified peace propaganda could, however, lead to ambivalent results. While it obviously played on the fears that another war would bring disaster, it did not rally everyone around Stalin's banner of peace. Widespread rumours often connected the intense peace propaganda with the onset of another war that led to panic purchases of food.[52] These reactions emphasise that Stalin's final role, as the patron of peace, was not an unproblematic one.

The aims of the regimes in Poland and in the GDR were similar. In their Stalinist phase, the official culture of both regimes was focused on Moscow. They were expected to imitate the centre and thereby tried to achieve a maximum degree of conformity. The introduction of the Stalin cult was the most visible form of the process of (self-) Sovietisation. The aims of the party-states were totalitarian in aspiration, in the sense that they tried to re-educate and mobilise entire populations through the leader cult. They wanted to transform their people into Stalinist believers. This utopian goal was not achieved; nevertheless, for those living in a Stalinist society it was hardly possible to keep out of the cult's reach.

This omnipresence of Stalin's persona coincided with his personal remoteness. Stalin's portraits and biography and his writings; the songs, poems, and books about him; his statues and photos – all that assured an almost unprecedented presence in the public arena. The renaming of streets and places, the whole culture of producing *Staliniana,* the language of the cult and the art of joining in the chorus of veneration was learned in the party and throughout society. Yet the leader himself remained distant, virtually inaccessible and untouchable. In contrast to the 1930s, when audiences in the Kremlin were frequent, Stalin never received a delegation of Polish or German activists. This distance contributed to the strong religious overtones of the cult in the years and months before his death. His portraits became icons. Their magic aura was part of the cult. For Stalin's 73rd birthday in 1952, the popular Polish women's journal *Przyjaciółka* (*Girlfriend*) ran a cover with a peasant woman, in solemn pose before a Stalin bust, looking up to the leader, with hands clasped as in prayer. The title read: 'The name of Joseph Stalin is the dearest name to millions of working people worldwide.'[53] In this last stage of the cult, the official narrative proclaimed that Stalin's cult was becoming universal: 'There is no place in the whole world, where the name Joseph Stalin is unknown . . .'; the Soviet peoples pronounce his name with 'pride and love', and, as the propaganda exclaims, with 'confidence and hope': the French proletarian, the Chinese coolie, the Italian unemployed and the partisans of Greece and Indonesia. In analogy to the Bible, it was stated that 'Stalin's books are read on the whole planet [*na całej kuli ziemskiej*] in all languages of the world.'[54]

Stalin's death: campaigning amidst confusion, uncertainty, grief and joy

Stalin died twice, first physically then spiritually. In March 1953, the Soviet leader suffered a stroke and passed away, and in February 1956, Nikita Khrushchev destroyed Stalin's persona in his 'Secret Speech' at the 20th congress of the Soviet Communist Party. In a stagnant, ideologically immobile system such as High Stalinism, the leader's death unforeseeably interrupted the established order. The leadership in both Poland and the GDR reacted quickly and mobilised the apparatus to master the situation. The task was to display grief for the passing of the great leader *in extensio* while at the same time controlling people's emotions and preventing 'the enemy' from openly rejoicing. Both regimes passed this test and managed to stage both shows of national mourning and contain possible unrest. The stage-managed official mourning resembled in many ways the birthday campaign – there was just a reversal of emotions: sorrow took the place of joy. The instruments of mobilisation and the codes of communication – collective letters, telegrams, obligations to work overtime – remained.

What do we know about popular reactions to Stalin's death? Internal reports and diaries from both Poland and the GDR show a great variety of responses. Analysing the sources, the official picture of a people united in grief falls apart. Some were surely in deep despair, many felt a loss, and others enjoyed secret satisfaction. Out of fear and caution, many abstained from publicly showing emotion. Many statements expressed a sense of uncertainty about the future. Most anticipated a change – be it for better or worse.[55] Years of exposure to the narrative about Stalin's persona had left a mark on people's minds. In the GDR, a young generation of communist intelligentsia had internalised the values of the regime. To them, Stalin had symbolised the system that promised them a new, a better Germany. GDR-historian Walter Markov remembered the sense of loss he felt when Stalin died: 'I think it is fair to say that there was some sort of sincere grief, accompanied by a sense of emptiness in the politically engaged circles of youth . . . and amongst students.'[56] The same holds true for young believers in Poland.[57] To a generation of young communists Stalin had personified socialism like no other symbol.

In these days, the eyes and ears of the party-state carefully recorded hostile voices. A Leipzig resident declared 'this is the best thing in the papers since 1945', and a worker in Weißenfels mocked the stage-managed mourning: 'I cannot work today, I'm exhausted and down because our father [*Väterchen*] Stalin has died.'[58] Both in Poland and the GDR large attendances at memorial meetings were reported, while other sources recorded the deliberate destruction of Stalin portraits, wreaths, flowers and the like. In the end, one may conclude that while the introduction of the cult had probably failed to create a positive picture of Stalin amongst the wider populace, it had most certainly provided a point of attachment for those who sympathised with communism. Like no other symbol, Stalin had represented the USSR and its utopian mission. But even in this totalitarian setting, most people seem to have pieced together their own picture of the Soviet leader that was probably composed of pre-war memories about him, combined with parts of the official master narrative and information from Cold War Western sources such as Radio Free Europe, BBC or RIAS.

Throughout the spring of 1953 Warsaw and Berlin misinterpreted the signals from the centre. While Moscow started gradually to back away from the adulation of Stalin, the Silesian industrial town of Katowice was renamed Stalinogród and the SED christened Germany's first socialist city Stalinstadt. Warsaw's Soviet-style Palace of Culture, one of the most prominent symbols of the new Poland, was named after the deceased and declared the Soviet leader's gift to the Polish people. The propaganda claimed: 'Never in history has one nation built for another a similar present.'[59] Thus, the last peak of the cult's toponymical extravaganza and of the economy of the gift took place at the peripheries of the empire.

Certainly, Stalin's death and the subsequent dismantling of his charisma by Khrushchev played an important role in the crises in 1953 in the GDR and in 1956 in Poland.[60] As both regimes had differed in the pace at which they had introduced the Stalin cult, so they differed when it came to dismantling Stalinism. How far the void and uncertainty after Stalin's death contributed to the East German crises of 1953 is still an open question. In the aftermath of the June crises and again after the 20th party congress, the SED suppressed any open discussion about Stalin. During the spring of 1956, the Polish regime went in the opposite direction and tried to gain new legitimacy by opening up this subject for restricted debate. The discussion about Stalin, however, proved to be hard if not impossible to control. By the autumn of 1956, this campaign had almost destroyed the regime's fragile legitimacy and only by stirring up nationalist sentiments against the Soviets and using the anti-Soviet charisma of Władysław Gomułka could they regain control.

After 1956, the void left by Stalin was partially filled by other cults. There was a strong revival of Lenin adulation and of the cult of the 'party'. The renewal of these forms of cultic veneration shows that the communist regimes did not choose to abandon elements of charismatic legitimisation altogether. The renewed Lenin cult flourished and cults of local Communist martyrs such as Karol Świerczewski and Ernst Thälmann gained prominence. But these cults could never match the extravagance of Stalin's cult. To those who had participated in the making of the cult, its demolition and the revelations about Stalin's crimes constituted a moral disaster. The German singer of the cult and former exile to the USSR, Johannes R. Becher, noted after the 20th congress: 'I have venerated this man like no one else among the living. . . . but in the same way that I loved him I was shaken by the horror because of certain things I witnessed in the Soviet Union. I cannot say that I had not known about these things'.[61] At last, it seems, Becher could put the puzzle together and his picture of Stalin became complete.

After Krushchev's deliberate deconstruction of Stalin's charismatic authority in 1956 and again at the 22nd congress of the CPSU (Communist Party of the Soviet Union) in 1961, his name disappeared from public life and official texts. There could be neither debate about his crimes nor about his cult. Again, history was carefully rewritten and texts edited.[62] The parties declared an almost complete *damnatio memoriae* on Stalin. In official discourse, the recent past vanished behind the euphemism 'cult of personality'. While Stalin's shadow continued to haunt the regimes, once anathematised national heroes such as Piłsudsksi or Bismarck gradually resurfaced. The grip of the centre had loosened.

Notes

1. Many thanks to Jan Marcin Kula (Warsaw) and Eric D. Weitz (St Paul, Minn.) for their comments.
2. Sarah Davies, *Popular Opinion in Stalin's Russia: Terror, Propaganda and Dissent*, (Cambridge,1997), p. 148.
3. The highly fragmented nature of the public sphere in Soviet-type societies is discussed in Gábor T. Rittersporn, Malte Rolf and Jan C. Behrends, 'Open Spaces and Public Realm: Thoughts on the Public Sphere in Soviet-Type Systems' in id. (eds) *Sphären von Öffentlichkeit in Gesellschaften sowjetischen Typs* (*Public Spheres in Soviet Type Societies*) (Frankfurt/ Main, 2003), pp. 423–52.
4. This term was coined by Jeffrey Brooks, *Thank You, Comrade Stalin. Soviet Public Culture from Revolution to Cold War* (Princeton, NJ, 2000).
5. But see for Poland as a first assessment, Robert Kupiecki, *'Natchnienie Milionów' Kult Józefa Stalina w Polsce* (Warsaw, 1993); for the GDR: Katharina Klotz, 'Führerfiguren und Vorbilder – Personenkult in der Ära Ulbricht' in Dieter Vorsteher (ed.) *Parteiauftrag. Ein neues Deutschland. Bilder, Rituale und Symbole der frühen DDR*, (Munich, 1997), pp. 322–41; Jan Plamper, '"The Hitlers Come and Go . . .", the Führer Stays: Stalin's Cult in East Germany' in Klaus Heller and Jan Plamper (eds) *Personality Cults in Stalinism* (Göttingen, 2004).
6. See Jan Plamper's contribution in this volume (chapter 7).
7. On the treatment of Poles and Germans in the USSR and their status as 'enemy nations' before the war, see Terry Martin, 'Origins of Soviet Ethnic Cleansing', *Journal of Modern History*, 70 (1998), pp. 813–61, and on their image in Soviet culture: David Brandenberger, *National Bolshevism: Stalinist Mass Culture and the Formation of Russian National Identity* (Cambridge, Mass., 2002).
8. Stalinist dictatorships cannot be characterised as fitting the Weberian ideal type of 'charismatic rule'. The Stalinist narrative, however, emphasised the extraordinary [*außeralltäglich*] qualities of the leader and thus tried to add charismatic elements to stabilise communist power. Cf. Max Weber, *Wirtschaft und Gesellschaft: Grundriß der verstehenden Soziologie* (Tübingen, 1980), pp. 140–8, 654–87, quotation p. 124.
9. On the Soviet friendship of the peoples see Terry Martin, *The Affirmative Action Empire: Nations and Nationalism in the Soviet Union*, (Ithaca, NY, 2001), pp. 432–61; on German-Soviet friendship, see Jan C. Behrends, 'Sowjetische 'Freunde' und fremde 'Russen'. Deutsch-Sowjetische Freundschaft zwischen Ideologie und Alltag (1949–1989)' in id. *et al.* (eds) *Fremde und Fremd-Sein in der DDR* (Berlin, 2003), pp. 75–100.
10. Lothar Machtan, 'Bismarck Kult und deutscher National-Mythos 1890–1940', in Lothar Machtan (ed.), *Bismarck und der deutsche National-Mythos* (Bremen, 1994), pp. 14–67; Noel D. Cary, 'The Making of the Reich President, 1925: German Con-

servatism and the Nomination of Paul von Hindenburg', *Central European History*, 23 (1990), pp. 179–204.
11. Heidi Hein, *Der Piłsudski Kult und seine Bedeutung für den polnischen Staat 1926–1939* (Marburg, 2002).
12. For the case of the Russian tsars, see Michael Cherniavski, *Tsar and People: Studies in Russian Myth* (New Haven, Conn., 1961).
13. See Ian Kershaw, *The Hitler Myth: Image and Reality in the Third Reich* (Oxford, 1987).
14. For a recent influential interpretation of the Third Reich as an example of charismatic rule in the Weberian sense, see Hans-Ulrich Wehler, *Deutsche Gesellschaftsgeschichte. Vierter Band 1914–1949* (Munich, 2003).
15. On the Soviet leader as an icon of trust, see Jan C. Behrends, 'Soll und Haben. Freundschaftsrhetorik und Vertrauensressourcen in der staatssozialistischen Diktatur' in Ute Frevert (ed.) *Vertrauen. Historische Annäherungen* (Göttingen, 2003), pp. 336–64.
16. Marcin Zaremba, *Komunizm, legytimizacja, nacjonalizm. Nacjonalistyczna legitymizacja władzy komunistycznej w Polsce* (Warsaw, 2001).
17. Józef Stalin, *Marszałek Związku Radzieckiego* [1945].
18. Max Weber points to the specific charisma of military leaders, see id., *Wirtschaft und Gesellschaft*, p. 864.
19. 'W 28-mą rocznicę Armii Czerwonej', *Przyjaźń*, 1946 (1), pp. 3–6.
20. 'Kongres tow. Przyjaźni Polsko-Radziekiej', *Przyjaźń*, 1946 (5), pp. 1–14.
21. 'W Stalinie Polska ma wypróbowanego przyjaciela', *Przyjaźń*, 1947 (1), p. 1.
22. Krystyna Kersten, *The Establishment of Communist Rule in Poland 1943–1948*, (Berkeley, Cal., 1991), p. 301ff.
23. 'Czy Związek Radziecki uważa granicę Polski za ostateczną? Stalin: Tak jest', *Przyjaźń*, 1946 (10), p. 10ff.
24. Kupiecki, *'Natchnienie Milionów'*, p. 103ff.
25. See e.g. Aleksander Zawadzki, 'Życzenia z głębi serca', *Przyjaźń*, 1949, no. 50/51, p. 3.
26. 'Uchwała Biura Politycznego KC PZPR w sprawie obchodu 70. lecia urodzin Towarzysza Józefa Stalina', *Nowe Drogi*, 1949, no. 5 (17), p. 3ff.
27. 'O Józefie Stalinie', *Przegłąd Wydarzeń*, 16 (1949), pp. 7–35, p. 30ff.
28. Archiwum Akt Nowych (Archive of New Acts), Warsaw (AAN), KC PZPR, 237-VII-113, pp. 83–126.
29. AAN, KC PZPR, 237-VII-343, p. 25.
30. For a case study of Stalin's 70th birthday in Lublin, see Izabella Main, 'The Weeping Virgin Mary and the Smiling Comrade Stalin: Polish Catholics and Communists in 1949' in Gábor T. Rittersporn *et al.* (eds) *Sphären von Öffentlichkeit in Gesellschaften sowjetischen Typs* (*Public Spheres in Soviet-Type Societies*) (Frankfurt/Main, 2003), pp. 255–78.
31. AAN, KC PZPR, 237/ XXI-25, pp. 70–3, quotation on p. 70.
32. Many such collective letters to Stalin can be found in AAN, KC PZPR, 237/ VIII-190.
33. *Polsko-radzieckie stosunki kulturalne 1944–1949. Dokumenty i materiały* (Warsaw, 1984), p. 627.
34. *Wolność*, 21 December 1949.
35. AAN, KC PZPR, 237/ VII-343, pp. 38–9.
36. AAN, KC PZPR, 237/ VII-113, pp. 4–38, quotation on p. 29.

37. AAN, KC PZPR, 237/ VII-199, p. 141.
38. Dariusz Jarosz and Maria Pasztor, *W krzywym zwierciadle. Polityka władz komunistycznych w Polsce w świetle plotek i pogłosek z lat 1949–1956* (Warsaw, 1995), p. 121ff.
39. AAN, MIP, Nr. 964; AAN, KC PZPR, 237-VII-2696.
40. Norman M. Naimark, *The Russians in Germany: A History of the Soviet Zone of Occupation* (Cambridge, Mass., 1995), pp. 69–204.
41. Eric J. Hobsbawm, *Interesting Times: A Twentieth Century Life* (London, 2002), p. 179.
42. Victor Klemperer, *LTI: Notizbuch eines Philologen* (Berlin, 1947); Victor Klemperer, *So sitze ich denn zwischen allen Stühlen. Tagebücher 1945–1949* (Berlin, 1999), p. 38.
43. Joseph Stalin, *Über den Großen Vaterländischen Krieg der Sowjetunion* (Berlin, 1951), p. 49f.
44. On the divided Germany, see Christoph Kleßmann, *Die doppelte Staatsgründung. Deutsche Geschichte 1945–1955* (Bonn, 1991).
45. *Neues Deutschland*, 14 October 1949.
46. On GDR nationalist discourse, see Sigrid Meuschel, *Legitimation und Parteiherrschaft. Zum Paradox von Stabilität und Revolution in der DDR, 1945–1989* (Frankfurt/ Main, 1992).
47. On the dogma of Soviet superiority: Jan C. Behrends, 'Besuch aus der Zukunft. Sowjetische Stachanov-Arbeiter in der DDR', *Jahrbücher für Geschichte Osteuropas*, 50 (2002), pp. 195–204.
48. Gosudarstvennyi Archiv Rossiskoi Federatsii (GARF), Moscow, 5283/16/142; Stiftung Archiv der Parteien und Massenorganisationen der ehemaligen DDR im Bundesarchiv, Berlin (SAPMO-BArch) DY 32–10072.
49. SAPMO-BArch DY 34 - 2/-/431.
50. Klemperer, p. 708, p. 711.
51. Otto Grotewohl, 'Rede zum Tag der Befreiung. 8. Mai 1950' in id., *Im Kampf um die einige Deutsche Demokratische Republik*, vol. II (Berlin, 1954), pp. 48–54; id. 'Eine historische Lehre. 22. Juni 1950' in ibid., pp. 84–88; 'Deutscher Patriot sein heißt Freund der Sowjetunion sein. Aus der Rede zur Feier des 71. Geburtstages Stalins. 21. Dezember 1951' in ibid., pp. 306–19; id.: 'Stalin und das deutsche Volk. März 1953', in id., *Im Kampf um die einige Deutsche Demokratische Republik*, vol. III (Berlin, 1954), pp. 256–67.
52. SAPMO-BArch DY 32–11345; DY 34–22666; AAN, KC PZPR, 237/ VII-3865 and Jarosz and Pasztor, *Wkrzywym zwierciadle*, pp. 72–80.
53. *Przyjaciółka*, 21 December 1952.
54. 'O Józefie Stalinie', p. 7.
55. See the well-documented popular reaction in: AAN, KC PZPR, 237/ VII-132, pp. 376–547.; SAPMO-BArch DY 34 - 15/56/1196; Marcin Zaremba, 'Opinia publiczna w Polsce wobec choroby i śmierci Józefa Stalina' in Andrzej Friszke (ed.), *Władza a społeczeństwo w PRL. Studia historyczne*, (Warsaw, 2003), pp. 19–53; Plamper, 'The Hitlers Come and Go'; Karl-Heinz Schmidt, 'Als Stalin starb. Die Reaktion des SED-Regimes und der Bevölkerung im Spiegel interner Berichte' in Klaus Schroeder (ed.) *Geschichte und Transformation des SED-Staates. Beiträge und Analysen* (Berlin, 1994), pp. 85–111.
56. Werner Mittenzwei, *Die Intellektuellen. Literatur und Politik in Ostdeutschland, 1945–2000* (Berlin, 2003), p. 104.
57. Zaremba, 'Opinia publiczna', p. 29ff.

58. SAPMO-BArch DY 34 – 15/56/1196.
59. O Nowej Hucie i o warszawskim Pałacu Kultury i Nauki im. J. Stalina dwóch pomnikach wielkiej Przyjaźni, TPPR, pogadanki propagandysty, Nr. 12/53.
60. On these events in the GDR, see Christian Ostermann (ed.) *Uprising in East Germany 1953* (Budapest 2001); on Poland, Pawel Machcewicz, *Polski rok 1956* (Warsaw, 1993).
61. Mittenzwei, *Die Intellektuellen*, p. 125.
62. For the GDR, see Siegfried Lokatis, *Der rote Faden. Kommunistische Parteigeschichte unter Walter Ulbricht* (Cologne, 2003), pp. 33–53.

10

President of Poland or 'Stalin's Most Faithful Pupil'? The Cult of Bolesław Bierut in Stalinist Poland

Izabella Main

This chapter analyses the ways in which the communist regime in Poland created and propagated the cult of Bolesław Bierut. The Polish Communist party faced a formidable obstacle in seeking to legitimise its rule in Poland. The party at the end of the war was numerically small and had only a very limited base of popular support. It had been devastated by the Great Purges in 1937–38, its leadership shot and, on Stalin's instructions, the party itself was disbanded.[1] It was only re-established during the war. Coupled with this it faced the problem of winning the support of a Polish public that was strongly antithetical to the Russians and to the whole communist experiment. Socialism was brought to Poland in the wake of the Red Army. It is against this background that we need to examine the role of Bierut's cult as a device intended to overcome this antipathy and to broaden the base of public support for the reconstruction of Poland along socialist lines.

Who was Bolesław Bierut?

Bolesław Bierut became the most important political leader of the immediate post-war era in Poland: He was chairman of the National Council between 1944 and 1947 and president of Poland between 1947 and 1952, when the office of president was abolished. Until 1954 he served as prime minister, and was first secretary of the ruling Communist Party from 1948 until his death in 1956.[2]

Bierut was born in the village of Rury Brygitkowskie, near Lublin, in south-eastern Poland on 18 April 1892. In his youth he became a member of the left wing of the Polish Socialist Party (PPS). During the First World War he remained in Lublin, and took no part in the fighting. When the Communist Party of Poland (KPP) was created in 1918, he immediately joined but did not yet play an important role in politics. In the 1920s, Bierut was active in various co-operatives. He was then arrested for the first time but quickly released. In 1925, Bierut undertook a short training course in a Soviet party school, returning to Poland the following year. After another arrest in January 1927, he escaped to the Soviet Union, where he attended the International Lenin School.

In the autumn of 1932, Bierut returned to Poland and became a professional revolutionary. He was arrested in December 1933 and sentenced to eight years in prison. This may well have saved his life, as he spent the years of the Great Terror and Stalin's purge of the KPP in the relative safety of a Polish prison. In 1936, he was expelled from the KPP; but this decision was rescinded in 1940. Bierut was released from prison in December 1938. During the Second World War he lived in Minsk, where he probably worked as a Soviet spy.

At the end of 1943, Bierut was invited to join the leadership of the newly created Polish Workers' Party (PPR), the successor to the KPP. When on 31 December 1943, the National Council (KRN) was created in Warsaw, he became its chairman. The National Council, functioned as a provisional parliament until the parliamentary elections in January 1947. These elections were rigged in favour of communist candidates.[3] In September of 1944, the National Council passed a bill that appointed Bierut as president.[4] At this time he was not the only leader of Polish communism – Władysław Gomułka was general secretary, Jakub Berman was the *éminence grise* of the party, whilst Edward Osóbka-Morawski was prime minister. The power was not yet concentrated in Bierut's hands.

The beginnings of Bierut's cult

Although the power of the communist government was established only gradually, early celebrations already portrayed Bierut as the leader of Poland. During the celebration of the anniversary of the Bolshevik Revolution in Lublin, on 7 November 1944, Bierut delivered the address.[5] On 11 November, when the pre-war Independence Day (regained in 1918) was celebrated, Bierut, who was the main speaker, talked about the new guarantees of Polish independence, with the Soviet Union as the chief guarantor.[6] During the celebration of 3 May 1945 (the anniversary of the of the 1791 Polish constitution), Bierut's portrait was displayed above the portraits of commander-in-chief Michał Rola-Żymierski and Osóbka-Morawski on the parade stand. He was continually presented as the most important figure in Poland. His leading position was emphasised by placing his persona at the centre of state celebrations. During the first post-war years Bierut did not officially belong to the Communist Party, but he was the president of the National Council, and he was often called 'the president' in the press and in the documents of the period, implying that he represented the whole nation.

On 5 February 1947, the parliament elected Bierut as president. The swearing-in followed the rites of the pre-war ceremony, and concluded with the reference to God.[7] *Rzeczpospolita* printed Bierut's picture, the speech he delivered on the occasion, together with a short biography.[8] The strong similarity with the pre-war ceremony had a clear goal. The communists promoted many revolutionary changes, notably the introduction of the planned economy and the collectivisation of agriculture, which were imported from the Soviet Union. In order to obtain legitimacy they claimed to represent the continuity of the Polish nation through the invocation of traditional symbols and institutions. The office of president was intended to provide Bierut, and the communist regime, with this symbolic capital and social support.

In the autumn of 1948, Bierut became first secretary of the PPR, after the previous secretary, Gomułka, had been purged. In December 1948, after the forced merger of the PPR with the Polish Socialist Party PPS, Bierut was also elected first secretary of the new Polish United Workers' Party (PZPR). This was his moment of triumph in the power struggle. The press referred to Bierut as 'the prime citizen of the state,' and even one of the newly opened schools in Cracow was named in his honour in December 1948.[9]

On 18 April 1949 the press mentioned Bierut's birthday for the first time. On the second page of *Rzeczpospolita* a picture of 'president Bierut' and his biography were printed. This portrayed Bierut's life as a continuous series of patriotic deeds. He took part in an anti-tsarist school strike in 1905, he participated in the defence of Warsaw against the Germans in September 1939, and he had worked for Poland since the war, establishing personal contacts with people, and fighting for national and social aims.[10] On May Day 1949, *Trybuna Ludu* printed his picture with a biographical note, and referred to him as 'President of the People's Poland and the chairman of the Central Committee'.[11] Even after his elevation to the post of first party secretary, Bierut was still referred to mainly as president; this was a deliberate choice.

In 1951, Bierut's 59th birthday was reported on the front page of *Trybuna Ludu*. A short note read:

> On April 18, 1892, Bolesław Bierut was born. Today, on the day of His birthday, the working masses of Poland wish comrade Bolesław Bierut, President of the Polish Republic and the Chairman of the Central Committee of the Party, good fortune and success in His dedicated work in the fight for peace, for the victory of socialism, the happiness of the Polish nation and the flourishing of People's Poland.[12]

Two days later, the same newspaper described a meeting in Berlin, at which Bierut's birthday was celebrated. The director of the information office of the German Democratic Republic expressed his best wishes and stressed the importance of Polish–German friendship.[13] The Bierut cult had gained prominence within the Bloc.

It is revealing to compare the visual representations of Stalin and Bierut in the press of this period. On May Day 1949, in *Trybuna Ludu*, Bierut's picture was placed below the portraits of Marx, Engels, Lenin and Stalin, indicating the strict hierarchical order among communist leaders and their cults.[14] In 1951 and 1952, on 21 April (the anniversary of the signing of the post-war friendship treaty between Poland and the Soviet Union) and on May Day the press published photos of Bierut and Stalin of the same size.[15] The number and size of the pictures of the two leaders corresponded to their increased presence in the official public sphere. The peak of public veneration came for Stalin on his 70th birthday in 1949 and for Bierut on his 60th birthday in 1952. Comparing the issues of *Trybuna Ludu* published throughout 1951, Bierut's picture was published more often than Stalin's was. In official rhetoric, however, he was assigned a lower standing in the hierarchical order of the cults: Bierut was now called 'the first and the most faithful pupil of Stalin in Poland'.[16]

Celebrating the Polish leader: Bierut's 60th birthday

The first climax of the Bierut cult was the celebration of his 60th birthday on 18 April 1952. As was typical with such communist leader cults it included special publications, the renaming of streets and factories, various pledges, and symbolic greeting to the leader through collective letters and telegrams. His persona dominated the public realm in early 1952; Bierut's New Year address with his portrait featured on the front page of *Trybuna Ludu*; on the seventh anniversary of the liberation of Warsaw greetings were sent to him; on the adoption of the new constitution (Bierut was chairman of the constitutional commission) several publications praised his achievements; on the fifth anniversary of his election as president further compliments were showered on him; and from 4 March, daily press updates were published about new commitments undertaken by workers to honour him.[17]

A special birthday anthology of poems, entitled *The Poems About Bolesław Bierut*, and a book for young readers, entitled *President Bolesław Bierut – the Great Friend of Youth*, were published and occasional radio broadcasts were prepared. The Polish scholar Michał Głowiński analysed the cult poetry, which included 14 panegyrics by well-known Polish authors. Głowiński notes the absence of any personal element in these poems, and the attempt to create a sense that the leader was praised by 'the whole of progressive humanity, by the working class, by the working people of towns and villages.'[18] In this way the regime tried to create the impression that Bierut was venerated by the entire nation.

In connection with his birthday the authorities decided to rename two factories (the Lublin truck factory and the Częstochowa steelworks) and the university in Wrocław in his honour. A mountain village was renamed 'Bierutowice' – a name it still bears today.[19] The choice of Lublin for a factory named after Bierut was intended to cement his links with his native town. However, renaming the steelworks in Częstochowa can be interpreted as a calculated step in the struggle against the Catholic Church because the city was the spiritual capital of Catholic Poland, the site of the Jasna Góra Monastery and home of the famed icon of the Virgin Mary, the symbolic Queen of Poland. Through renaming the steelworks the regime attempted to bolster its presence in Częstochowa, and to present it as a symbol of the new, industrial, socialist Poland.[20]

Renaming the university in Wrocław, situated in Poland's western territories which had been gained from Germany after the Second World War, was equally important for the regime.[21] The university had previously borne the name of Prussian king Friedrich-Wilhelm III. The renaming was intended to underline the Polishness of the city. In their propaganda the Polish communists claimed that these territories were ancient Polish lands. The 'regaining' of the western territories was popularised as a sign of Soviet support for 'Poland's historical rights'. Obviously, neither the loss of the Poland's eastern territories to the Soviet Union nor the fate of the former German population that had been forcibly expelled were mentioned. In all cases, the press reported that the initiatives for the renaming came from inhabitants, workers or students. The party-state authorities used these imagined or orchestrated popular initiatives to camouflage its complete domination of the public sphere.

To honour Bierut's birthday, special pledges to boost output were made by workers, farmers, women and youth, and these were reported in *Trybuna Ludu*.[22] Stakhanov-style promises to boost productivity were made in numerous factories and institutions. In Cracow province alone, according to a party report, meetings were organised in 238 factories prior to 25 March 1952, during which workers proposed various ways of honouring Bierut. The same report stated that 54,000 workers out of 69,000 employees in Cracow undertook honouring activities in various work collectives in transport, education, health services, construction, commerce and administration. The commitments included increasing the production of trucks, cars, and so on, raising the 'ideological level' of a group or a party unit, taking part in special training for workers, cleaning factories, draining swamps, and conscientious learning by pupils and students.[23] These commitments were the most visible and significant part of Bierut's birthday celebrations because they were supposed to be organised in all workplaces. The aim was to trigger and demonstrate respect and admiration for Bierut; yet, additionally they aimed at the economic mobilisation of the workforce.

Another element in the celebration of Bierut's birthday was the extensive practice of sending congratulatory letters to him. Some letters were reprinted in the press, and some are preserved in party documents. A typical example reads:

> Our achievements in the construction and industrialisation of the country, in education, culture and other socialist accomplishments are

> all thanks to You, Our Beloved President – the creator of the National Council and the Polish United Workers' Party. We have achieved these successes under Your leadership, thanks to the help of the Soviet Union and the Great Friend of the Polish Nation, Comrade Stalin.[24]

Bierut's and Poland's achievements were discursively tied to the cult of Stalin and the Soviet Union. But Bierut's persona remained subordinated to the demi-god in the Kremlin. Certain epithets were reserved for Stalin: only the Soviet leader could be described as 'the engineer of history', 'the genius architect of communism' or 'the great genius of mankind'.[25] Bierut was more modestly described as 'the faithful and the best student of Stalin in Poland'. This phrase, however, did not appear very often in the press. The most common titles in the published letters were as before: 'President', 'Mister President', or 'Comrade President'.

In official discourse Bierut was also called 'the First Citizen and Host of the State', 'the Leader of the State and the Party', 'the Teacher of the working masses', 'the Helmsman of the Polish nation' or 'the Fighter for the happiness of the Polish people'. These titles were often written in capital letters.[26] The different roles of Bierut's persona were reflected by different ways of publicly addressing him. Students and pupils called him 'the teacher and caretaker of youth', 'beloved leader', 'great friend of children and youth', and images often portrayed him surrounded by children; for mine-workers he was 'the friend of miners' and artists dubbed him 'the caretaker of Polish culture'. As the reconstruction of Warsaw, devastated by the war, was an important way of gaining legitimacy for the communist regime, Bierut was praised as 'the initiator of the enthusiastic building of the new beautiful Warsaw', 'the reconstructor of Warsaw', 'the beloved constructor of the united independent People's Poland'.[27] The birthday celebrations for Bierut were also an occasion to celebrate the regime and its achievements.

Furthermore, Bierut was promoted as an inspirer and creator of the new constitution, which was approved on 22 July 1952 – he was 'the author of the project of the Constitution, the *Magna Carta* of the achievements and accomplishments of the Polish people'. On other occasions, official discourse elaborated on Bierut's personal character. He was a simple man and – like many of his fellow countrymen – 'the son of a small-holder'.[28] Whilst a man of great deeds, he was yet a modest and down-to-earth person.

Many of the epithets ascribed to Bierut were connected to Polish nationalism. The emphasis on his Polishness was intended to highlight the image of Polish sovereignty and independence. Of course, the role of the Red Army and of Stalin himself in liberating Poland was mentioned and celebrated on various anniversaries. But in the Stalinised national master narrative this was not seen as a contradiction. National symbols and songs, national heroes, and strong national leaders were important components in the regime's quest for legitimacy.[29]

Portraits of Stalin, and occasionally of Lenin, were also present during the celebrations. During the main ceremony in the Polish Theatre in Warsaw, on the evening of 18 April, a large portrait of Bierut hung above the presidential table, and two smaller busts – of Stalin and Lenin – stood behind it. Bierut stood in the middle, surrounded by the members of ruling elite.[30] Even though Bierut's power in Poland was limited by Stalin and his advisors, the Polish regime wanted to convey the clear message to the Polish public that Bierut was ruling the country.

In spite of the multiple virtues assigned to Bierut, there was one missing component: the charisma of the successful military leader, although his participation in the defence of Warsaw in September 1939 was stressed.[31] Yet, he was not popularised as a military figure, as Józef Piłsudski, the prewar leader had been. Other figures had to fill this gap in the official narrative – notably Marshall Konstanty Rokossovskii, the Soviet commander who was made Polish minister of defence, and General Karol Świerczewski ('Walter'). On 28 March, during the preparations for Bierut's birthday, the fifth anniversary of the death of Świerczewski-Walter was observed – he was named 'a patriot and revolutionary, and the constructor of the Polish People's Army'.[32]

The international dimension of the Bierut cult was very visible during these birthday celebrations. At the ceremony in the Polish Theatre in Warsaw the first greeting read was that from Stalin, and then telegrams from Mao Zedong, Kim Il-sung, Ho Chi Minh, Klement Gottwald, Wilhelm Pieck and Mátyás Rákosi were read. These messages were published in the press the next morning. The media also reported various celebrations of Bierut's birthday throughout the Bloc, emphasising his inclusion amongst the self-proclaimed ruling group of the 'progressive world and mankind'.

After his 60th birthday, Bierut's cult was propagated mainly by displaying his portraits during state holidays. With Stalin's death the leader cult became more tempered. Bierut's birthdays in 1953 and 1954 were observed in a more modest way.[33] In 1955, Bierut's birthday was not even mentioned in *Trybuna Ludu*. On May Day in 1955, the press did not print his portrait; instead he was pictured together with other political leaders, emphasising the collective nature of the leadership.[34] This decline of the Bierut cult may be related to political changes in Poland after 1954: an increasing criticism of the system, the release of his rival Gomułka from prison, the dissolution of the Ministry of Public Security and the appointment of moderate communists to leading positions in regional committees.

'The nation says good bye to its Faithful Son'

The death of Bierut on 12 March 1956, in Moscow, spared him from having to respond to Khrushchev's 'Secret Speech', and from facing the June 1956 protests and a further political turmoil in Poland. After the announcement of his death, days of national mourning were proclaimed until his funeral on 16 March in Warsaw. His corpse was brought to Poland on 14 March, the coffin was draped with a Polish flag and carried in a funeral procession to the building of the Central Committee. On 14 and 15 March people were allowed to pay their last respects to the deceased leader. His coffin was surrounded by members of his family and a guard of honour, made up of members of the Central Committee, and representatives of the Polish people.[35] *Trybuna Ludu* wrote 'in silence and concern the people of Warsaw are passing by the coffin, paying their last respects to the Great Son of the Polish Nation. Workers, constructors, clerks, railwaymen, soldiers, students, young people, women with children are passing by.' The pictures of the crowds underlined this description.[36]

The day of his funeral was proclaimed a non-working day in Warsaw, and the entire country halted for three minutes of silence. At the beginning of the funeral, a procession was formed next to the building of the party's Central Committee. The inhabitants were asked to gather on Stalin's Square, the place of the main ceremony, and then to process to the Powązki cemetery. The coffin was first carried by the party secretaries of regional branches of the party, then by generals, and finally it was placed on a special funeral car and covered by the white-and-red national flag – 'as a scarf with which a mother wraps her beloved son'.[37] The cortege was followed by Bierut's family, by members of the Politburo, by foreign leaders, such as Nikita Khrushchev himself, and by other members of the central and regional committees, ministers, members of mass organisations, veterans of the working-class movement, men of science and culture, and so on. The order of the procession reflected the hierarchy of authority in communist Poland.

On Stalin Square, next to the Palace of Culture and Science, 'the gift of the Soviet people to the Polish nation', the next stage of the funeral took place. The coffin was placed on a red catafalque and the *Internationale* was played. The chairman of the State Council Aleksander Zawadzki, Prime Minister Józef Cyrankiewicz and Nikita Khrushchev gave speeches about Bierut. At the end of this farewell ceremony, the bells of Warsaw rang as the procession continued, passing Dzerzhynskii Square and the Warsaw citadel, 'recalling the death of several generations of revolutionaries', before it finally reached the cemetery. There the national anthem was played, the artillery fired salutes and factory sirens hooted. The solemn character of the funeral ceremony was reinforced by the gloomy winter weather.[38] In the following days the press was filled with expressions of grief. The funeral ceremony, like the earlier celebrations, combined national and revolutionary symbols and traditions, the former to satisfy national sentiments, and the latter to express the ideology of the state and the official narrative of friendship with the Soviet Union.

Opinions about Bierut

It is difficult to sketch a clear picture of the way in which Bierut was viewed by his comrades and contemporaries; only a very small number of such opinions have survived in print. As his fellow communist Andrzej Werblan pointed out, Bierut's personality was not well suited for the role of dictator: he was quiet, shy and polite.[39] Moreover, Zygmunt Mycielski, a composer and music critic, wrote in his *Memoirs 1950–1959* that 'Bierut seemed to be embarrassed during parties'.[40] Bierut's son, Jan Chyliński, and a few party members who knew him personally believe that he objected to the creation of his own cult.[41] Jerzy Morawski, a PZPR activist, recalls that at the time of Bierut's 60th birthday, the construction of a square in Warsaw was nearing completion, and a few members of the Central Committee of the PZPR proposed to name the square in his honour. Bierut, however, objected and, on his insistence, the square was named Constitution Square.[42] The opinions of Bierut among the party leadership reflected the knowledge that he was Stalin's intermediary in Poland; Roman Zambrowski in his *Memoirs* in 1970 wrote that this was clear to everyone in the Politburo.[43]

There are a few instances of critical views of writers and intellectuals. Karol Estreicher, an art historian, believed that

> Bierut's career in Poland was stunning even for him. He was not popular. There was little clapping in the Parliament after his election as president. He made few and short public appearances.[44]

Another writer, Maria Dąbrowska, who attended the celebrations of Bierut's 60th birthday, wrote in her memoirs that she did not understand why the party put so much effort into this celebration. Furthermore, she compared the celebration with the pre-war birthday anniversary of Piłsudski, and criticised the whole idea of the leader cult.[45]

The attitudes of ordinary people towards Bierut are difficult to analyse. Throughout the late 1940s and early 1950s, there were a few hostile actions directed against portraits of Bierut, displayed on the occasion of state holidays. For example, on Stalin's 70th birthday in 1949, the secret police reported hostile actions in Lublin province: 'Cases of destroying decorations and portraits of Stalin, Bierut and Rokossovskii took place in Łuków, Kraśnik, and Krasnystaw'.[46] These iconoclastic actions, directed against both Polish and Soviet leaders, were clearly politically motivated. Bierut was opposed because he was perceived as a representative of Soviet domination.

Various internal party documents list examples of similar hostile action before and during Bierut's 60th birthday celebrations. There were cases of iconoclasm, with the destruction of his portraits, as well as cases of industrial sabotage.[47] Some of the letters sent to Bierut pointedly included no commitments, or included pledges that were irrational or improper. In many factories, it proved difficult to encourage workers to make any commitments.[48]

There are also examples in which Bierut's official persona was perceived in a positive light. The already mentioned writer, Dąbrowska, stated that the only moment of society's acceptance occurred after his unexpected and mysterious death in Moscow, when last crowds attended his funeral in Warsaw.[49] She also argued that for uneducated people, such as her servant, Bierut was the president of Poland, and they respected him for that. For her, however, Bierut was primarily the leader of the party. It is clear that the office of president commanded greater public respect than the post of party leader. Both Dąbrowska and Estreicher mentioned rumours that Bierut was poisoned in Moscow, and died as a result of this; these views increased his popularity. Some believed that he was poisoned because he did not force agricultural collectivisation or the inclusion of Poland into the Soviet Union.

There are also a few other indications that Bierut was popular and respected during his life. For example, a woman working in a textile factory told her own story of meeting the leader:

> In the 1950s, I participated in the production competitions in 1950 or 1952 . . . I don't remember exactly. I was chosen as the best Stakhanovite in my factory. I did 250 percent of the quota. I don't like to boast about it but I was invited by President Bierut for a Stakhanov-movement ball. So . . . one day I went to work, of course in my daily clothes, because you did not go to work in Sunday clothes. And they gave me a ticket saying that I am going for the Stakhanov-movement ball. I said that I was not going because I was not dressed up but they ordered me to go. So I went with the others. It was an amazing experience. Me, an ordinary worker of a sewing department, visited President Bierut himself. Bierut welcomed us, and thanked us for our good work. I received a letter of commendation. We returned home in the morning, it was nine o'clock. My mother started to shout at me – where had I been? I showed her the letter but she didn't believe me. I wept and tried to convince her that I was in Warsaw, with Bierut! After some time she started to believe me. And when she started to believe, she was so proud of me, so proud.[50]

Other examples of positive feelings towards Bierut are provided by letters sent to him which asked for help. In many cases people asked him to save the life of their family members, to reduce the sentence, or to help financially – these letters reflected desperate appeals.[51] Yet there are also letters expressing genuine expectations. For example, Bronisława Kołodziejczykowa sent Bierut numerous requests, which people addressed to her, after she was photographed standing next to him. She explained that the picture was taken during a meeting of working women on Mothers' Day, and after this fact many people asked her for help.[52] In many letters people described their difficult situation, often mentioned the case of relatives who had been apprehended by the security services, indicating that they hoped that Bierut might intervene, might reverse official decision, and implying that other people, not he, were responsible for abuses and miscarriages of justice. These letters clearly illustrate the patriarchal element of the cult.

These diverse voices do not allow us to reconstruct what were the dominant social attitudes towards Bierut. Many of the memoirs were written and published decades after the events in question and the security agency's reports of anti-regime actions might reflect a tendency to exaggerate out of institutional self-interest. But these sources do provide an additional understanding of socialist realities and supplement (or sometimes question) the officially produced discourse.[53]

Analysing the above views, it seems that some intellectuals questioned and criticised Bierut and his cult, yet did not oppose it openly. Dąbrowska for example was very critical in her memoirs but received various government privileges and a state award on the tenth anniversary of People's Poland in 1954. Many complied with the regime's expectations and participated in activities honouring Bierut, in order to sustain their position or privileges. The memoirs of other party members point to Bierut's personal attributes and lack of charisma, and to Stalin's role in choosing him as the leader of Poland.

Workers and farmers faced continual propaganda that exalted Bierut as the president and father of the nation; some opposed it by destroying his portraits, others trusted and respected him. Obviously, the absence of public opinion polls or statistical data make it impossible to precisely estimate the prevailing views. However, these accounts point to possible reasons why people may have supported Bierut; their attitudes to him were linked to their attitudes to the regime, and to an instrumental calculation of personal gains and/or losses under the new People's Poland. For a young woman, brought up in a traditional community, becoming a Stakhanov-worker meant a change of social status (gaining respect, earning a higher salary, winning the chance for education, travel and promotion), and it was probably followed by respect for and admiration of the leader.

Conclusion

Bierut had been chosen as the leader of post-war Poland by Stalin during the war, yet this was not immediately obvious to the Polish people. His power was only gradually established and progressively more and more elements of his cult were organised by the party-state. The extended celebration of his 60th birthday in 1952 was the peak of the Stalinist leader cult in Poland. The stage-managed celebrations of Bierut's 60th birthday probably did not increase his popularity, especially since many honouring actions were imposed and superficial. The strong ties to the Soviet Union and Stalin, moreover, were a somewhat counter-productive factor because the majority of Polish society maintained deeply rooted anti-Soviet attitudes.

However, an important component of Bierut's cult was that he was presented as a president, and this strategy had higher chances of success: for some people, any president was a person to be respected. The restoration of the presidential office and the traditional swearing-in ceremony using even religious formulas are clear examples of the attempt to create a sense of continuity with the pre-war Polish state. National symbols and values were constantly used, and Bierut was often called 'the leader, the son, etc. of the nation'. Thus, nationalism was a fundamental element of the cult.

The most characteristic feature of a hero, according to the Polish sociologist Stefan Czarnowski, is that he represents a concrete virtue, an embodiment of a collective ideal or hope of greatest significance for a certain community.[54] Thus the question of the status of Bierut's cult is also a question about the nature and depth of support for the communist regime in Poland during the time of his leadership. Historians' views vary on this matter. Many place the emphasis on terror, repression and manipulation, and highlight the few cases of opposition to the Communist Party. Few historians point to the enthusiasm for rebuilding post-war Poland or to the gradual improvement of living and working conditions – all elements that created a degree of support for the regime. More research is needed to better understand the attitudes of society towards the regime, and these attitudes were certainly very diverse.

There was therefore a certain ambiguity surrounding Bierut. The cult, as expressed in the press and organised by the party-state, centred on the image of the great Pole, a constructor of the country and a teacher, had higher chances of achieving support than basing it on his friendship with Stalin and the ideals of Marxism-Leninism. However, even these officially promoted elements of the cult proved to be too short term. Bierut's image was too ambiguous to gain the widespread support that would have led to a genuine rise of popular feeling, suggesting that the cult had only a very limited social base.

Post-script: the Bierut monument in Lublin

In 1979, the party-state celebrated the 35th anniversary of the *July Manifesto*, the official founding act of the post-war regime. As part of this celebration, a monument of Bolesław Bierut was unveiled in Lublin. The idea was mooted in April 1978, and the Committee for the Construction of the Monument was established by the City Council. The monument was intended to celebrate Bierut's associations with Lublin, although his pre-war activities there were not very significant.

The idea of building the monument, however, was by no means universally welcomed. The attitude of Lublin's citizens towards it was not well articulated, though some voices of discontent were expressed. For example, on 30 March 1978 a few members of an illegal organisation, the Movement in Defence of Human and Civil Rights, addressed a protest letter to the Province Governor that was published in *Kronika Lubelska*, a *samizdat* newspaper.[55] They stated that the construction of the monument was an expensive and unnecessary endeavour, given the difficult economic situation in Poland, and criticised the fact that forced money collections were made in schools and factories.

Edward Gierek, then Bierut's successor as the leader of Communist Poland, participated in the unveiling ceremony. There were, according to some witnesses, not many participants; pupils and students were not obliged to participate; in any event it was during the summer vacation. Besides the authorities, some representatives of factories and institutions participated. *Trybuna Ludu* reported that the ceremony was attended by 'dozens of thousands of city inhabitants, and representatives of factories and schools from the entire country'.[56] A party document noted simply that there were 'no incidents'.[57]

The monument of Bierut was erected at the entrance to an apartment complex in the suburbs. It was designed by the sculptor Bronisław Kubica. It featured a standing figure of the leader with his right arm outstretched, and the left hand holding a sheet of paper; the plate was engraved with a shape of an eagle and bore the inscription 'Bolesław Bierut'.[58] The sheet of paper probably represented the *July Manifesto*; though the symbolism of the monument was not elaborated upon in the press. The monument immediately became an object of derision because the statue's coat was too short and buttoned in the female style.[59]

The idea to build the monument of Bierut with the intention of reinvigorating his cult occurred at a very sensitive moment. The election of the Polish Pope John Paul II and his first pilgrimage to his homeland left no doubt as to who was genuinely venerated by Polish society. The unveiling of the monument to Bierut occurred a month after the Papal visit, and for this reason alone the revival of Bolesław Bierut's cult was doomed to fail. The monument quickly fell into complete neglect, no acts of vandalism were directed against it, not because it was socially accepted, but rather because it was completely ignored. Paradoxically, the fate of the devastated monuments of Lenin or the Soviet soldiers was better: at least they were noticed and the acts of vandalism were discussed and opposed by some as provocation or iniquity. Polish sociologist Aleksander Wallis suggested that when monuments lose social significance they are no longer monuments but simply sculptures.[60] Lublin's Bierut monument was removed in 1990. One hand of the statue is now displayed in the Museum of Socialist Realist Art in Kozłówka, near Lublin.

Notes

1. William J. Chase, *Enemies Within the Gates? The Comintern and the Stalinist Repression, 1934–1939* (New Haven, Conn., 2001), pp. 217–92.
2. Andrzej Garlicki, *Bolesław Bierut* (Warsaw, 1994).
3. Andrzej Albert (Wojciech Roszkowski), *Najnowsza historia Polski 1918–1980* (London, 1991).
4. Stanisław Karboński, *W imieniu Kremla* (Paris, 1956), p. 257.
5. Archiwum Państwowe w Lublinie (APL), WUIiP 64.
6. *Rzeczpospolita*, 13 Nov. 1944.
7. Karboński, *W imieniu Kremla*, p. 257.
8. *Rzeczpospolita*, 6–8 February 1947.
9. *Trybuna Ludu*, 16 December 1948.
10. *Rzeczpospolita*, 16–18 April 1949.
11. *Trybuna Ludu*, 16 April 1949; *Trybuna Ludu*, 1 May 1949.
12. *Trybuna Ludu*, 18 April 1951.
13. *Trybuna Ludu*, 20 April 1951.
14. *Trybuna Ludu*, 1 May 1949.
15. *Trybuna Ludu*, 21 April 1951; 1 May 1951.
16. Stalin's picture appeared in *Trybuna Ludu* on May Day, 21 April, 21 December, and from time to time in relation to the international political situation.
17. *Trybuna Ludu*, Jan.–April, 1952.
18. Michał Głowiński, *Rytuał i demagogia. Trzynaście szkiców o sztuce zdegradowanej* (Warsaw, 1992), pp. 110–13.
19. *Trybuna Ludu*, 18 April 1952, p. 1; *Życie Lubelskie*, 30 April 1952, p. 5; Krzysztof Mazurski, *Karpacz i okolice* (Wrocław, 1978), p. 14.
20. The physical and symbolic competition between the party-state and the Catholic Church continued throughout the entire period of communist rule. See Izabella Main, 'National and Religious Holidays as the Clashing Point of the State, the Church and Opposition between 1944 and 1989: The Case of Lublin', PhD dissertation, Central European University, 2002; on Częstochowa: Damien Thiriet, *Marks czy Maryja? Komuniści i Jasna Góra w apogeum stalinizmu (1950–1956)* (Warsaw, 2002).
21. On the reinvention of Wrocław as a Polish city after 1945, see Gregor Thum, *Die fremde Stadt. Breslau 1945* (Berlin, 2003).
22. See *Trybuna Ludu*, February–May 1952.
23. Archiwum Państwowe w Krakowie (APK), KM PZPR 39, pp. 70–6.
24. Ibid., p. 71.
25. Robert Kupiecki, '*Natchnienie Milionów Kult Józefa Stalina w Polsce* (Warsaw, 1993). pp. 76, 79.
26. *Trybuna Ludu*, March–April 1952.
27. David Crowley, 'People's Warsaw/Popular Warsaw', *Journal of Design History*, 10: 2 (1997), pp. 203–23.
28. *Trybuna Ludu*, March–April 1952.
29. Marcin Zaremba, *Komunizm, legitimizacja, nacjonalizm. Nacjonalistyczna legitimizacja władzy komunistycznej w Polsce* (Warsaw, 2001).
30. *Trybuna Ludu*, 19 April 1952, p. 1.
31. *Trybuna Ludu*, 4 March 1952, p. 1; *Trybuna Ludu*, 15 April 1952, p. 3.
32. *Trybuna Ludu*, 28 March 1952, pp. 1, 3. On the cult surrounding Karol Świerczewski ('Walter'): Jerzy Kochanowski, '". . . doch diesen Namen werden sie preisen": Der General Karol Świerczewski' in Silke Satjukow and Rainer Gries (eds)

Sozialistische Helden. Eine Kulturgeschichte von Propagandafiguren in Osteuropa und der DDR (Berlin, 2002), pp. 193–202.

33. See the reports in *Trybuna Ludu*, 28 March 1953 and *Trybuna Ludu*, 19 April 1954.
34. *Trybuna Ludu*, April, 1955; *Trybuna Ludu*, 1–3 May 1955.
35. *Trybuna Ludu*, 14–16 March 1956.
36. *Trybuna Ludu*, 16 March 1956, p. 1.
37. *Trybuna Ludu*, 18 March 1956.
38. Ibid.
39. Interview with Werblan cited in Piotr Lipiński, 'Bolesław Niejasny', *Gazeta Wyborcza. Magazyn*, 25 May 2000. Andrzej Werblan (born 1924) was member of the Central Committee of the PZPR between 1948 and 1981.
40. Quoted in Lipiński, 'Bolesław Niejasny', p. 27.
41. Lipiński, 'Bolesław Niejasny', pp. 26–7; Jan Chyliński, *Jaki był Bolesław Bierut. Wspomnienia syna* (Warsaw, 1999).
42. Lipiński, 'Bolesław Niejasny', p. 26.
43. Ibid., p. 18.
44. Karol Jr. Estreicher, *Dziennik wypadków 1946–1960* (Cracow, 2002), p. 97.
45. Maria Dąbrowska, *Dzienniki powojenne 1945–1949* (Warsaw, 1996), p. 285.
46. Instytut Pamięcy Narodowej, MBP, GM 330, p. 243.
47. Paweł Machcewicz, 'Urodziny Bolesława Bieruta', *Karta*, 7 (1993), p. 50; APK, KM PZPR 39, p. 73.
48. APK, KM PZPR 39, pp. 78–9.
49. Dąbrowska, *Dzienniki powojenne 1955–1959*, p. 89. This brief moment of popularity is also pointed out by Paweł Machcewicz, *Polski rok 1956* (Warsaw, 1993), pp. 42–51.
50. Interview with Irena L. I would like to thank Małgorzata Fidelis for sharing this interview.
51. Józef Stępnień (ed.) *Listy do Pierwszych Sekretarzy KC PZPR* (*1944–1970*) (Warsaw, 1994).
52. Ibid., p. 57.
53. Robert Perks and Alistair Thompson, *The Oral History Reader* (London, 1998). See also Katherine Lebow, 'Nowa Huta 1949–1957: Stalinism and the Transformation of Everyday Life in Poland's "First Socialist City"', PhD dissertation, Columbia University, 2002.
54. Stefan Czarnowski, *Kult bohaterów i jego społeczne podłoże. Święty Patryk bohater narodowy Irlandii* (Warsaw, 1956).
55. The Movement in Defence of Human and Civil Rights (the Polish acronym is *ROPCiO*) was organised by Leszek Moczulski, the founding declaration was signed on 26 March 1977.
56. *Trybuna Ludu*, 10 July 1979, p. 1.
57. APL, KW PZPR 100/VII/31/15, p. 43.
58. Anna Wójcik (ed.) *Lublin w fotografii Zbigniewa Zugaja* (Lublin, 1988), photograph 77; APL, KW PZPR 100/VIII/15/4, p. 32.
59. The ceremony was attended by his children, probably by his daughter Krystyna and son Jan. See Chyliński, *Jaki był Bolesław Bierut*, pp. 44, 49; Garlicki, *Bolesław Beirut*, p. 12.
60. Aleksander Wallis, *Socjologia przestrzeni* (Warsaw, 1990), p. 229.

11
Georgi Dimitrov: Three Manifestations of his Cult

Markus Wien

The cult of Georgi Dimitrov, first secretary of the Bulgarian Communist Party, long predated his appointment as leader of the communist state of Bulgaria in 1945. He was one of the few non-Soviet communists who had achieved a high degree of international popularity, at least among their own movement from his revolutionary, illegal activity mainly in Austria and Germany during the 1920s and 30s. Dimitrov's popularity was mainly associated with his performance at the Reichstag trial in Leipzig in 1933. The trial helped him to make a career in Soviet exile as the general secretary of the Communist International (Comintern) from 1935 to 1943. In this position he became an object of a cult within the framework of public celebrations in Moscow – to a lesser degree than Stalin himself, but on a similar level with other high Soviet functionaries.

In Dimitrov's case the biographical elements of the cult had real foundations to a higher degree than the cults of other post-war communist leaders. Three main periods of Dimitrov's cult can be distinguished: first, as the general secretary of the Communist International (1935–43), second, as the head of the Bulgarian state (1945–49), and third, the cult after his death. Each of these periods had a particular promoter of the cult. During the first period, the cult was basically part of the official Soviet state cult around Stalin, from which Dimitrov, as one of his closer satraps, profited, too – a kind of sub-cult within the general framework of the Soviet leader cults. After 1945, the centre of the promotion of the cult switched from Moscow to Sofia; it became the official state cult of communist Bulgaria. This function of the cult virtually remained the same beyond his death. Posthumously, the cult worked as the main national source of legitimacy for the communist regime during the following decades. The study of Dimitrov in Bulgaria was for a long time highly politicised. Only in recent years has a more objective assessment of his life become possible.[1]

Dimitrov's biography as a central element of the cult

As with all communist movements, wherever possible, attempts were made to emphasise the leader's proletarian origins.[2] When Dimitrov was born in 1882 Bulgaria was predominantly an agrarian country, without an industrial proletariat as a stable and significant social stratum, but with a substantial artisan stratum.[3] Dimitrov's social origin was amongst the artisans and traders. His father was a hat maker and he owned a fur-hat shop in Sofia.[4] An early biography says that his father subsequently became a worker. In Marxist categories he would be defined as petty bourgeois subject to proletarianisation.

As an adolescent, he had opposed his parents' wish for him to become a pastor and joined a printing house in Sofia as an apprentice typesetter, becoming active in the printers' union. As was typical of working-class revolutionaries of his generation he was an autodidact. He studied the ideas of Marx, Lenin, Chernyshevskii and the prominent Bulgarian socialist leaders Christo Botev and Dimităr Blagoev. In 1901, at the age of 19, he was already the secretary of the Printers' Trade Union in Sofia. In 1902, he joined the Bulgarian Workers Social Democratic Party (Narrow Socialists) or BRSDP, the antecedent of the Communist Party, led by Blagoev. Seven years later, he was admitted to the party's Central Committee (CC). In 1913 he became member of parliament and there he took a strong anti-war stance. At the end of the First World War he was imprisoned for inciting disobedience, having defended a group of wounded soldiers in a conflict with their commanding officer.[5] In the 1920s he was active in the trade union movement and communist party in Bulgaria.

An event, which was subsequently hailed as the first nation-wide anti-fascist uprising, was the Bulgarian Communist Party (BKP) putsch of September 1923, organised by Dimitrov and Vasil Kolarov. After the Second World War the communist Bulgarian regime made this uprising part of the myth of the Bulgarian revolution, regardless of the fact that it had been ill prepared and, thus, had resulted in a disastrous failure. However, Dimitrov was mythologised as its heroic leader.[6] In reality, the putsch had been conducted only due to pressure on the BKP from the Comintern, after the Bulgarian communists had failed to support the government of Aleksandăr Stambolijski against the military coup d'état of June 1923, which had brought Aleksandăr Tsankov to power. Being seriously criticised by the Comintern for its passiveness, the BKP had initiated the September putsch.[7]

Thus, from this point of view, the idea of a united anti-fascist popular front was, at least at that time, imposed on Dimitrov and the BKP. It was not his own original idea, although he did develop it further later on. After the communist attempt to assassinate Tsar Boris III at the Sveta Nedelja church in Sofia in 1925, he was sentenced to death and, thus, was forced to escape from Bulgaria.[8] Thereafter he worked as a Comintern agent carrying out illegal activity mainly in Austria and Germany.

It was actually this defeat, which put Dimitrov on the track of an international communist career, that became a fundamental element of the myth created around his biography. Since this myth focused on the creation of an image of Dimitrov as an eminent revolutionary theoretician and a communist leader of international rank, his personal development in these fields – which was dated to his years in exile, his 'European period', his work in the Balkan Communist Federation, then in the West European Bureau of the Comintern – that occupied a central position in the biographical elements of his cult.[9]

The Leipzig trial

Dimitrov's fame derived primarily from his performance in the Reichstag trial, held in December 1933 in Leipzig. He was accused with other communists of having set the parliament building on fire. Dimitrov's success stemmed from his ability to confound the testimony of the main prosecution witness Hermann Göring. The Reichsgericht acquitted him. The trial marked one of the last instances of the relative independence of the German courts. He was released and moved to the USSR, which then granted him citizenship, since a return to Bulgaria was impossible because of the pending death sentence against him.[10]

In 1934 a Russian language biography of Dimitrov by Stella Dimitrova Blagoeva had been published, and an English language edition was immediately issued.[11] The biography was unashamedly propagandistic, depicting him as a 'a great Bolshevik', one of a family of revolutionaries, whose three brothers (Konstantin, Nikola and Todor) had already died for their convictions. His revolutionary services in the underground in the 1920s and his central role in the Leipzig trial was outlined, with a copy of his speech to the court. He was a model Bolshevik – a man of humble origin, largely self-made, intelligent, with a strong will, courageous with a powerful presence, someone who had dedicated himself to the revolutionary movement, as theorist, organiser and powerful orator. Notwithstanding the hagiography, Dimitrov undoubtedly was a figure of real charismatic power.

The Reichstag affair and subsequent trial was immortalised in various publications.[12] In 1936 the Soviet Communist Party published extensive documentation of the trial, including photographs of Dimitrov and Stalin, facsimiles of letters by prominent figures sent to Dimitrov, and even a song composed in his honour by 'German workers' – 'Das Dimitrofflied'.[13] Dimitrov was also credited with exceptional intellectual qualities. A persistent myth was that he had learnt the German language within the relatively short period of his imprisonment prior to the Leipzig trial. He mastered it so well that he was able to defend himself in front of the court without the help of a lawyer.[14] In fact Dimitrov had worked in German-speaking circles since 1925. As a result of the Reichstag trial Dimitrov emerged as the icon of the anti-fascist struggle. The anti-fascist struggle from 1933 onwards became one of the basic legitimising concepts of communism.

General secretary of the Communist International

In late February 1934 Georgi Dimitrov arrived in Moscow; he was then 52 years of age and a veteran of the communist movement. He was welcomed by Dmitrii Manuilski, a member of the Political Secretariat of the Comintern. He wrote:

> Before the Leipzig trial, Dimitrov was known outside of Bulgaria only to a broader circle of party activists: illegal Bolsheviks do not need to be very famous. The great masses of the working class first got to know him in Leipzig. From the very first words he spoke into the excited silence of the hall at the Leipzig trial his enemies as well as his friends felt the power of G. Dimitrov.[15]

In April 1934 Dimitrov joined the Comintern leadership on Stalin's invitation. From this time he was its head although not formally appointed as general secretary until the Seventh Congress in August 1935.[16] Stalin instructing the Politburo to approve a list of the Soviet members of the Executive Committee of the Communist International (IKKI) and the appointment of Dimitrov.[17] Comintern policy was now initiated and implemented by direct contact between Stalin and Dimitrov and his deputy Manuilskii. Dimitrov played a key role in persuading Stalin of the need to abandon the 'ultra left' policy of the past and to pursue the strategy of 'popular front' with left-wing and liberal parties to combat the fascist threat. From their correspondence it is clear that Dimitrov saw close relations with Stalin as vital to the Comintern's work.[18] Stalin on occasions offered reassurance that he, Dimitrov, had the Politburo's (i.e. Stalin's) confidence.[19] The publication of Dimitrov's letters with Stalin confirms his close connection with the Soviet leader.

His international standing was reinforced by his performance at the Seventh World Congress of the Comintern in July and August 1935, where he took a leading role in emphasising the struggle against fascism and war as the main task of the international communist movement. He endorsed the definition of fascism, already approved by the Comintern in December 1933, as the 'open terrorist dictatorship of the most reactionary, most chauvinistic and most imperialist elements of finance capital'. Additionally, he redefined the strategy of this struggle. He argued for nothing less than a twofold change in the traditional communist view of fascism and class struggle themselves. First, he insisted that communists, under the pressure of fascism, had to join together with other anti-fascist forces within society, including social democrats and liberals, and form so-called 'popular fronts'. In addition he argued that the nations, especially the European ones, should find their own way to socialism and that the motifs of patriotism and national pride had been neglected for too long.[20]

Dimitov was a huge international celebrity. One Soviet memoir account of the 1930s reports that Dimitrov in his visits to factories and towns in the USSR spontaneously drew large audiences of people anxious to see this famous personality.[21] Whether this reflected mere idle curiosity or ideological commitment is unclear.

The Great Terror of 1936–38 was fierce in the Comintern. Dimitrov's high standing with foreign communists gave him some immunity, but it also placed him under suspicion when Stalin began to perceive these individuals as spies. Dimitrov's diaries contain hints of Stalin's fear of a military coup in the summer of 1937, but it is the great silences on the terror in his writings that are most revealing.[22] He recorded in his diary Stalin's ominous remark: 'All you in Comintern are serving the enemy.' When in 1937 Dimitrov sent Stalin a draft Comintern resolution for disbanding the Polish Communist Party, the leaders of which had already been shot, Stalin commented acidly: 'The dissolution is about two years too late.'[23]

Dimitrov was certainly complicit in the terror that devastated the ranks of foreign communists based in the USSR and those attached to Comintern. As general secretary of Comintern he lent his personal authority to the carnage.[24] He rationalised the terror by the analogy that the need to cut out the gangrene from inside the party inevitably meant cutting into the healthy flesh. As with other high functionaries, their participation in the terror was a test of their loyalty to Stalin.

The Nazi–Soviet pact of August 1939 delivered a further blow to the Comintern's standing. Soviet foreign policy was increasingly dictated by Soviet state interests. Dimitrov's position and that of Comintern depended critically on their place in Stalin's operational plans – especially after the beginning of the German invasion in June 1941, when the Soviet war propaganda shifted away from communist internationalism towards the more patriotic line of 'healthy nationalism'. The wartime alliance with Britain and the USA dicated that the revolutionary strategy associated with Comintern be temporarily suspended.[25] With the war, Dimitrov was evacuted to Kuibyshev. In 1941 in his diary he records the main report by Stalin, broadcast from Moscow on 6 November ('remarkable document') and Stalin's speech in Moscow on the 7th and K. E. Voroshilov's speech in Kuibyshev the same day. Dimitrov was elected to the honorary presidium in Kuibyshev but not that in Moscow. His entry for 7 November wistfuly noted 'Like yesterday, was not in the parade today. – No *need* to emphasize the Comintern!'[26]

Dimitrov's decline in the cult hierarchy stemmed primarily from Stalin's decision to dissolve the Comintern in 1943. Thereafter Dimitrov worked as a leading official in the Central Committee's department, responsible for contact with foreign communist parties, which assumed some of the functions of Comintern. This was true especially in terms of eventual future plans to control East Central and South East Europe – and even more so since Dimitrov was the most prominent supporter, and to some extend even the creator, of the idea of an autonomous path of each nation towards socialism, according to its specific circumstances, conditions and traditions. Additionally, he argued for the application of the so-called tactic of 'National Fronts' in the struggle against fascism and for socialism. This idea, whose essentials had been developed by Dimitrov himself, included also a temporary co-operation with bourgeois non-fascist forces. This was the new official line with which Stalin was in full agreement, with the policy of national roads to communism that held sway from 1944 to 1947.

As the fortunes of war shifted with the Soviet victory at Stalingrad, the question of the liberation of Eastern Europe increasingly preoccupied the thinking of the Soviet leadership. In Bulgaria the 'Fatherland Front' (OF) was established in 1942 to conduct the partisan struggle. In the propaganda of the OF during the second half of the Second World War, Dimitrov constantly stood in the centre of the hopes that were directed towards Moscow in the expectation of a 'liberation' or at least of substantial support for the fight against 'fascism'. The OF played a major role in mobilising popular support against the Bulgarian monarchical authoritarian regime, and in organising the armed coup which overthrew the government on 9 September 1944. The communists dominated the OF government between September 1944 and November 1945, in expectation of Dimitrov's return from Moscow. The presidium of the Supreme Soviet of the USSR awarded Dimitrov the Order of Lenin for his work in the OF. As the only Bulgarian communist with international popularity, he was an integrative figure for the communists, who conducted illegal underground activities during the war. Considering the question of power in post-war Bulgaria, there was apparently no alternative to Dimitrov as head of the state.

As leader of the Bulgarian state

Dimitrov returned to Bulgaria in November 1945, more than a year after the occupation of the country by the Red Army and the seizure of power by the OF had already insured the implementation of the socialist state system. It was Stalin who decided precisely when Dimitrov should return to Bulgaria, insisting that he stay in Moscow despite his demands to be allowed to return home. The reason for the delay was Stalin's fear that Dimitrov's arrival in Sofia would be interpreted by the Western allies as a signal that Bulgaria was to be turned into a Soviet satellite.[27] The September 1946 referendum, organised under the auspices of the new communist dominated government, approved the abolition of the monarchy and the proclamation of a people's republic.

Connected with this image as the inventor of the popular front strategy and his conviction of a national way to socialism, assigned to him by the cult, Dimitrov also was celebrated as the father of the concept of 'people's democracy'. This was something different from the bourgeois as well as from the Soviet state. It included a parliamentarian transition from bourgeois democracy to socialism instead of a proletarian dictatorship.[28] This notion was intended to take account of the particular circumstances in the newly conquered countries of Eastern Europe. It was a notion which had Stalin's approval. The people's democracies represented a less developed stage than socialism, which had already been attained by the USSR. It was intended also to serve the strategic interests of effecting a transition to socialism in these countries, supposedly under the flag of democracy, without provoking the Western allies.

The new period in Dimitrov's political career, which began in November 1945 with his return to Bulgaria and his take-over of the state leadership, also brought about a change in the quality of his cult. With Stalin's backing, Dimitrov was the undisputed leading personality in his country, although behind the scenes his position was challenged, with power struggles between the so-called 'Home Communists' and the 'Muscovites', headed by Dimitrov. His opponents, the Home Communists, claimed more political influence, since, in their view, it was they who had fought as an underground movement against fascism, who had carried the burden of partisan warfare, in contrast to the Muscovites, who had lived in relative safety throughout the war in the Soviet Union. Despite that, they were unable to defeat Dimitrov, who had Stalin's support, including the Soviet troops in Bulgaria since September 1944, and, thus, had the power to eliminate not only the representatives and sympathisers of the monarchy, but also his rivals within the Communist Party. The most prominent ones, who were executed on Dimitrov's initiative, were the leader of the Peasant Union, which was part of the OF, Nikola Petkov, in 1947, and the Home Communist Trajčo Kostov in 1949. Kostov was accused by Dimitrov of treason but was in fact executed after Dimitrov's death.[29]

Notwithstanding Dimitrov's high authority in the international communist movement he needed to retain Stalin's confidence. From 1945 onwards Dimitrov developed a close relationship with Tito, and both were intent on pressing forward their own policies for socialism in the Balkans and Eastern Europe. This became the basis for the rift between Tito and Stalin and the expulsion of Yugoslavia from the Cominform in 1948. The degree of autonomy allowed the East European communist leaders was strictly limited. Milovan Djilas reports how in 1948 the leaders of the Yugoslav and

Bulgarian communist parties were summoned to Moscow for a top-level meeting with Stalin and other Soviet leaders. At this meeting Stalin stingingly rebuked Dimitrov for his scheme to create a federation of East European socialist states and to set up a customs union between Bulgaria and Romania, without Soviet consent. Djilas reports that the rebuke left Dimitrov embarrassed and humiliated in the company of other senior communist leaders.[30] Dimitrov's death in 1949 may have been fortuitous. He was not subject to the execration heaped on Tito.

Dimitrov's cult became a constitutive element of the socialist statehood until its end in 1989. During the period 1945–49 the cult was enriched by new myths, in addition to the Leipzig one, focusing on Dimitrov's image as a revolutionary theoretician and a socialist state builder. Accordingly, the socialist constitution, which was ratified in December 1947 and replaced the Tărnovo Constitution of 1879, was named 'Dimitrov Constitution' in emulation of the Soviet 'Stalin Constitution' of 1936. Modern Bulgarian historiography tends towards a characterisation of the Dimitrov cult as very similar to Stalin's. At the end of 1947 Bulgaria, like other East European states, refused the reconstruction aid of the Marshall Plan, joined the Communist Information Bureau and began the process of Sovietisation of the economy, society and political regime. Also other parallels of this kind reveal to what extent the cult and its form were 'borrowed' from the Soviet example. This was most clear, for instance, in the famous attribute, which was added to Dimitrov's name – practically a literal translation of its Soviet equivalent: 'Leader and teacher of the Bulgarian people'.[31]

Dimitrov's stature within the Bulgarian Communist Party and the international communist movement derived in large measure from his political record. What is striking is the extent to which Dimitrov's standing was based on his stature as a theorist, which he maintained without ever courting the accusation of posing a deviation to Marxism-Leninism. There was never a Dimitrovist deviation, unlike Titoism or Maoism. His standing within the Bulgarian Communist Party was built on a powerful revolutionary tradition, and a political tradition that was Russophile.

Dimitrov died on 2 July 1949 at a spa near Moscow. The public manifestations of the Dimitrov cult were relatively modest. The full development of leader cults in Eastern Europe was in the late Stalin years, 1948–53. His name was given to the new town of Dimitrovgrad, which was built by Bulgarian youth in 1947. Factories, schools and streets were named after him. His name was conferred on the Bulgarian Communist Youth Movement. The Order of Georgi Dimitrov was instituted as the highest honorary award and the Dimitrov prize was instituted for achievements in science, technology, literature and art. His home was turned into a museum. In 1951–54 his collected works in 14 volumes were published.

The cult as a whole found its visible expression in the mausoleum that was erected in the centre of Sofia opposite the former royal palace. His embalmed body was placed in the mausoleum, which was partly modelled on the Lenin mausoleum, but based on the classical style. During the following decades, the mausoleum itself developed its own myth and cult. After his death his cult, Nikolaj Poppetrov argues, was transformed from a Stalin-type cult into a type which was similar to the Lenin cult[32] – a change that might be characteristic of 'posthumous' cults in general. The transformation corresponded to a natural change in the purpose of the cult, from an instrument of the preservation of power for the object of the cult to a source of legitimacy and a symbol of tradition, stability and continuity for the regime itself and the following leader generations. According to Poppetrov, the myths created along with the Dimitrov cult after 1949 included all the elements from the previous periods, but were extended by various new myths created around and connected to his death. This process corresponded to a gradual decline of the concrete functionality of the cult of Georgi Dimitrov after 1949. Poppetrov writes:

> Exclusively functional at its beginning, the cult turned into a dysfunctional routine, separating itself from any original contents and losing any enthusiasm as well as any political influence.[33]

The posthumous cult

Dimitrov was succeeded briefly by Kolarov who died in 1950, and then by Dimitrov's own son-in-law Vulko Chervenkov. Chervenkov initiated an intense leader cult around himself, and was dubbed 'Little Stalin'. Under Chervenkov political controls were still further tightened up. A major purge was instituted within the party to expel deviationists. Agricultural collectivisation was put in train from 1950 onwards, and a drive to develop heavy industry was instituted. With Stalin's death in March 1953 the 'New Course' policy was instituted in Bulgaria as in the USSR and other Eastern European countries. The emphasis on heavy industry was reduced with increased emphasis placed on the production of consumer goods, and investment in agriculture was increased. Political repression was eased and in 1955 around 10,000 political prisoners were released. Chervenkov's cult was also moderated. In 1954 he gave up the post of party leader but retained the post of prime minister. Khrushchev's attack on the Stalin cult in February 1956 was followed in April 1956 by a similar attack on the cult at the plenum of the Central Committee of the Bulgarian Communist Party. Chervenkov was accused of cultivating his own cult and of 'brutality'.[34] Chervenkov resigned as prime minister and was replaced by Anton Yugov, and Todor Zhivkov assumed full powers as party first secretary.

Zhivkov remained in the leading position of the Bulgarian state until 1989. He projected an authoritarian image, but at the same time the image of a fatherly patriarch of the country ('Bai Tosho'). Nevertheless, the

Dimitrov cult served an important function, to link the Bulgarian regime with the earlier, more idealistic aspect of the struggle for socialism. Dimitrov could be lauded as the representative of the Bulgarian tradition of revolutionary politics, with deep national roots, but also as part of an international Marxist-Leninist tradition. After 1962 the close links binding Dimitrov to Stalin were suppressed.

In the 1960s and 1970s various works were published in his honour in the USSR and in the Eastern European communist states.[35] The Dimitrov cult had a particular following in the GDR. There he was celebrated alongside other communist figures who were icons of the anti-Fascist struggle, such as Ernst Thälmann and Julius Fucik. In Leipzig the former Reichsgericht was partially turned into a Dimitrov museum.[36]

One work which deserves being singled out is that by Louka Zoulamski and Georgi Stoichev, entitled *You, I and Dimitov*, published in Sofia in 1968. It was issued to commemorate the Communist International Festival of Youth held in Bulgaria that year. It was an invocation to youth to give themselves to the great communist cause, outlining Dimitrov's exemplary life as revolutionary, with extracts from his speeches on youth, notably his speech 'We shall not surrender our youth to Fascism' delivered on the 15th anniversary of the Komsomol. It is constructed in the form of inspirational homilies. We shall quote just one of these homilies, entitled 'In the Storm', whose quasi-religious undertones are very clear.

> Such is the truth of History!
>
> History cannot be distorted. It is mercilessly just, but its justice must be understood. History does not interpret events, its lessons are self-explanatory. History tells us tersely: Dimitrov tore the accusations against communism into shreds.
>
> At the time, many of his contemporaries only saw his victory, without comprehending how it was reached.
>
> At present, the danger exists that this misapprehension may arise in our midst, within the world youth movement. Fascism, imperialism, the forces of war – they are more than paper tigers; they are infinitely more powerful than certain short-sighted people would have us believe. But they can be crushed, if there is a timely struggle against them, if hazards are met with counter blows, and not shirked, if instead of timid boastfulness, ranks are united to confront them.
>
> At the time, there were some who overestimated and others who underestimated the forces of fascism. Fascism was very terrible, but it was possible to sweep it away.
>
> After Leipzig, Dimitrov struggled, heart and soul, to make this clear to everybody. Many of the people admired him for it, but they did not understand him.
>
> Let us at least try to follow his example.[37]

In this we see the attempt to transmit communist traditions to a younger generation through an appeal to moral values, and by invoking the authority of Dimitrov as a leading figure and thinker within the Bulgarian and international communist movement.

At an international conference held on the 13 June 1972 in Sofia on the occasion of Dimitrov's 90th birthday, Zhivkov lauded him as 'a true son of the Bulgarian working class, as a passionate patriot and strict internationalist and real Marxist and Leninist'. He laid emphasis on Dimitrov's contribution as a theoretician in elaborating the concepts of popular fronts and people's democracy, and his role in the formation of the BKP as a Leninist party. He was

> a globally renowned politician, as a man with an undisputed authority and as real leader of the people, Georgi Dimitrov directed the struggle in a superior way against all attempts to restore the bourgeois order in Bulgaria. Dimitrov's maturity and his talent as a theoretician, organiser and constructor of the new society were revealed on all fields of the socialist transition.[38]

Dimitrov could be lauded by Bulgarian and Soviet authorities as a model Leninist.[39] The centenary of Dimitrov's birth in 1982–83 prompted the publication of a number of studies, issued in Moscow and Sofia, in his honour. The most notable was a collected memoir by Todor Zhivkov, and two luminaries of the Soviet Politburo and noted guardians of ideological orthodoxy – M. A. Suslov and B. N. Ponomarev. The volume included the memoirs of Zhivkov, Suslov and Ponomarev, and memoir accounts from 58 other figures, including prominent leaders of the international communist movement such as Jacques Duclos, O. V. Kuusinen, Palmiro Togliatti, Maurice Thorez and Dolores Ibárruri.[40]

A conference commemorating his life was held in Moscow on 17 June 1982, organised by the Institute of Marx-Engels-Lenin, the Soviet Academy of Science, and the Soviet Academy of the Social Sciences.[41] His reputation as a contributor to revolutionary theory continued to be upheld, right up to the end of the communist era.[42]

The posthumous cult and the official memory of Dimitrov became idiomatic and was dominated by clichés. A book published in Sofia on the occasion of the centenary of Dimitrov's birth in 1982 contains speeches and articles about him written ten previously, for his 90th birthday, by Todor Zhivkov. In Bulgaria the Dimitrov cult was conducted with considerable, if not extraordinary propagandist efforts, and was inseparably linked to socialist statehood. It was an institutional part of socialist public life. With the collapse of the socialist state order in Bulgaria in 1989, the cult lost its *raison d'être* as well as its institutional support. Therefore, it virtually disappeared from the country's socio-political agenda.

However, the carriers of the cult and its supporters did not disappear so suddenly, and the successor party of the BKP, the Bulgarian Socialist Party (BSP), remained the strongest political power in the country long after the change of 1989, in fact until 1997, with a short interruption in 1992. The BSP's dominance was challenged by Union of Democratic Forces (Săjuz na Demokratičnite Sili). Dimitrov's body was removed from the mausoleum in July 1990. A prolonged public discussion followed as to what should be done with the mausoleum. Finally in July 1999 Dimitrov's mausoleum in Sofia was blown up.[43]

The 120th anniversary of Georgi Dimitrov's birth on 18 June 2002 provided an occasion for a broader public commemoration of his life. The remembrance and celebration of his personality, however, was confined almost exclusively to the communist, nominally the socialist, party. It was virtually ignored by the mass media and by the broader public. A conference organised by the Centre for Historical and Political Studies of the Supreme Council of the Bulgarian Socialist Party entitled 'Georgi Dimitrov – between admiration and rejection' attempted a partial rehabilitation of his reputation. Dimitrov, it was asserted, could not be extinguished from the national memory. His standing in the history of the Bulgarian and international labour and communist movemernts was assured, although his record was not free from certain 'deficiencies and mistakes'.[44]

The only chapter of Dimitrov's biography that inevitably required a re-evaluation was his time as prime minister of Bulgaria, 1945–49. The purges within his own party as well as the prosecution of non-communists and representatives of the old regime had been too serious to be ignored. Apologists, such as Tanja Turlakova, argued that the violence was the result of 'mistakes', due to the 'difficult times', and 'naturally human weaknesses' of Dimitrov.[45] Others, such as Aleksandăr Lilov, political scientist and member of the Bulgarian Academy of Sciences, acknowledge his responsibility for the excesses, but argued that his merits outweighed his faults:

> his historical merits should not prevent us from viewing and reflecting some serious mistakes he made – especially during the final period of his life . . . The objective analysis of the mistakes cannot darken either Dimitrov's historical merits, or his national and global importance, or his personality. History does not even know one great politician or statesman without any mistakes.[46]

All these activities, however, evoked little public interest; their effect remained restricted to socialist circles. Therefore, it seems that neither Dimitrov himself nor his cult left any traces in the public historical memory which would have been deep enough still to be visible 13 years after the end of communist rule. The persistence of his influence and cult is remarkable, for a politician who ruled the country for less than four years and whose image throughout the decades had not been much more than an institutionalised cliché. It still was what it had been during most of the socialist era: an abstractum. The demise of the cult was associated with the general crisis of legitimacy of the system of communist rule in 1989, and the rise of new politics in a society where the aspirations and idealism of the early communist movement were but a remote memory.

Notes

1. One of the main studies was published by the Centre for Historical and Political Research in Sofia: *Georgi Dimitrov – meždu văzchvalata i otricanieto. Studii i statii* (Sofia, 2003).
2. A. Lilov, 'Teoretičeskite i političeskite prinosi na Georgi Dimitrov', *Ponedelnik. Spisanie za teorija, politika i kultura*, 7–8 (2002), p. 10.
3. M. Wien, 'Arbeitsbeziehungen in Bulgarien vor 1944 und ihr Fortwirken in der Periode des Sozialismus' in *Arbeit im Sozialismus* (Conference in Munich, April 2002, forthcoming).
4. I. Banac (ed.) *The Diary of Georgi Dimitrov 1933–1949* (New Haven, Conn., 2003), pp. xvi–xvii.
5. Ibid., pp. xvii–xix.
6. Ibid.
7. Ibid.
8. Ibid., p. xxvii.
9. Lilov, 'Teoretičeskite i političeskite', pp. 11–12.
10. *Diary*, p. xxvii.
11. Stella Dimitrova Blagoeva, *Dimitrov: A Biography* (New York, 1934).
12. *Protess o podzhoge Reikhstaga i Georgii Dimitrov* (Moscow, n.d.).
13. *G. Dimitrov: Pered Fashstskim Sudom* (Moscow, 1936).
14. E. Savova, *Georgi Dimitrov. Letopis za života i revoljucionnata mu dejnost* (Sofia, 1982), p. 7.
15. Cited by L. Revjakina, 'Georgi Dimitriov v bălgarskoto i meždunarodnoto komunističesko dviženie (1919–1934)' in *Georgi Dimitrov – meždu văzchvalata i otricanieto. Studii i statii*, p. 5.
16. A. Dallin, and F. I. Firtsov (eds) *Dimitrov and Stalin, 1934–1943: Letters from the Soviet Archives*, translated by Vadim A. Staklo (New Haven, Conn., 2000), p. 6.
17. Ibid., p. 23.
18. Ibid., pp. 13–16.
19. Ibid., pp. 18–22.
20. *Diary*, pp. xxviii–xxix. On Dimitrov's role at the Seventh World Congress of the Comintern see E. H. Carr, *The Twilight of Comintern, 1930–1935* (London, 1982), ch. 7.
21. N. Kuznetsov, *On the Eve of the War* (Moscow, 1966).
22. In the *Diary*, p. 45, he records Stalin's assertion that the military commanders were preparing a coup for July 1937.
23. Ibid., p. 32.
24. William Chase, *Enemies Within the Gates: The Comintern and the Stalinist Repression, 1934–1939* (New Haven, Conn., 2001).
25. *Diary*, pp. xxxv.
26. Ibid., p. 204.
27. Milovan Djilas, *Conversations with Stalin* (London, 1962), p. 107.

28. Lilov, 'Teoretičeskite i političeskite', pp. 16–17.
29. *Diary*, p. xliv.
30. Milovan Djilas, *Conversations with Stalin*, p. 159.
31. N. Poppetrov, 'Georgi Dimitrov kato obekt na integralen izsledovatelski podchod' in *Georgi Dimitrov – meždu văzchvalata i otricanieto. Studii i statii*, p. 164.
32. Ibid.
33. Ibid.
34. Zbigniew K. Brzezinski, *The Soviet Bloc: Unity and Conflict* (Cambridge, Mass., 1967) p. 201.
35. For a survey of Soviet works on Dimitrov see V. P. Gruzdeva, 'Sovetskaya istoriografiya o G. Dimitrov' in *Georgii Dimitrov: Vydayushchiisya revolyutsioner i teoretik* (Moscow, 1982), pp. 407–31.
36. See also E. Kalbe, *Freiheit für Dimitroff. Der internationale Kampf gegen die provokatorische Reichstagsbrandstiftung und den Leipziger Prozeß* (East Berlin, 1963).
37. Louka Zoulamski and Georgi Stoichev (eds) *You, I and Dimitrov*, edited by Pauline Pirinska, translated by Mikhail Todorov (Sofia, 1968), p. 67.
38. T. Shiwkow, *Ein großer Sohn Bulgariens. Reden, Beiträge, Aufsätze und Gedanken über Georgi Dimitroff* (Sofia, 1983), pp. 188–90.
39. Vaselin Khadzhinikov, *Georgi Dimitrov i sovetskaya obshchestvennost, 1934–1945*, translated from Bulgarian by A. N. Krishevskoi and A. M. Koren'kova (Moscow, 1975; Bulgarian edn pub. Sofia, 1972); Nedelcho Ganchovskii, *Georgii Dimitrov, kakim ya ego videl i zapomnil* (Moscow, 1975) (original in Bulgarian): this work has many photographs on Dimitrov's meetings with children and young communist constructors.
40. Todor Zhivkov, M. A. Suslov and B. N. Ponomarev, *Vospominaniya o Georgii Dimitrov*, translated from the Bulgarian by V. N. Grebnnikova (Moscow, 1982); Elena Savova, *Georgi Dimitrov: Letopis za zhivota i revolyutsionnata mu deinost* (Sofia, 1982); A. I. Sobolev, F. I. Firsov, D. Sirkov and P. Boev (eds) *Georgii Dimitrov: Vydayushchiisya revolyutsioner i teoretik* (Moscow, 1982); Yu. A. L'vunin and V. A. Kuz'ko, *Georgii Dimitrov i mezhdunarodnoe profsoyuznoe dvizhenie* (Moscow, 1983).
41. P. A. Rodionov (ed.) *Zhizn' otdannaya bor'be za sotsializm (100–letie so dnya rozhdeniya G. Dimitrova* (Moscow, 1983).
42. *G. Dimitrov: voprosy razvitiya revolyutsionnoi teorii* (Moscow, 1987).
43. Lilov, 'Teoretičeskite i političeskite', p. 21.
44. T. Turlakova, 'Introduction' in *Georgi Dimitrov – meždu văzchvalata i otricanieto. Studii i statii*, pp. 3–4.
45. Ibid., p. 4.
46. Lilov, 'Teoretičeskite i političeskite', pp. 14–15.

12

Leader Cults in the Western Balkans (1945–90): Josip Broz Tito and Enver Hoxha

Stanislav Sretenovic and Artan Puto

The geographical configuration of the Balkans, the relative absence of direct interests of the great powers in this region and the existence of well-organised communist parties loyal to Moscow favoured, during the Second World War, the development of communist resistance movements fighting for 'national liberation and social revolution'. The South Slav communist resistance movement, which fought in the mountains of the Western Balkans, co-operated and influenced the Albanian communist partisans. In 1941 the Communist Party of Yugoslavia, headed from 1937 on by Josip Broz Tito (1892–80), supported Enver Hoxha (1908–85) to become the leader of the Albanian Communist Party and helped establish the Albanian resistance movement, with Hoxha as general commander. The successful outcome of this partisan struggle created communist regimes in Yugoslavia and Albania quite different from those in other Eastern European states. These were regimes that came to power largely by their own efforts. Both regimes were legitimised by the partisan struggle, and the struggle against the Nazi occupiers and their domestic 'collaborators'.

The ideology of two communist leaders and parties brought Yugoslavia and Albania into the Soviet sphere of influence in the immediate post-war period (1945–48). In this period, both for Tito and Hoxha, the image of Stalin was untouchable and was the most important element in building up their own cults. In that same period, moreover, Hoxha referred to Tito as a model. After his break with Stalin in 1948 Tito developed his own autonomous cult. By contrast, Hoxha's fear of being charged as 'Titoist' strengthened his attachment to Stalin. Thereafter, the cults of Tito and Hoxha were shaped by very different domestic and international factors.

The cult of Josip Broz Tito

The cult of the Yugoslav communist leader Josip Broz, better known under his nickname Tito, emerged in the context of the Second World War of the

Yugoslav Civil War. It developed during the Cold War in parallel with the internal difficulties of the young communist state, which he ruled, and it continued after his death. This evolution was shaped by the internal social conditions of Yugoslavia, including its cultural traditions, and by the international situation. The Communist Party of Yugoslavia (CPY), renamed the League of Yugoslav Communists in the 1960s, in seeking to legitimise its rule, promoted the cult of Tito, but the cult also had a spontaneous side to it.[1]

The 'reflection' of Stalin's cult (1945–48)

It is not possible to analyse the emergence of Tito's cult without making reference to Stalin's cult. Following the military victory in the Second World War, the Soviet Union represented the ideal of the construction of the socialist state and Stalin was an incontestable authority figure in all newly emerging socialist countries in Eastern Europe. From the pre-war period, the communist leaders contributed to the development of Stalin's cult because winning Stalin's confidence was of decisive importance in gaining ascendancy within national communist parties. In his writings and speeches in the post-war period Tito glorified Stalin, referring to him as a 'leader and teacher', a 'successor of Lenin' and the 'great leader of all free-minded people'.[2] The glorification of Stalin was very strong in the Yugoslav press.[3] Stalin was projected as the supreme authority for the whole socialist world. Leading Yugoslav communists, up to 1948, held Stalin in genuine awe.[4]

In Yugoslavia the Communist Party, headed by Tito, came out of the war as victor after a long and bloody period of resistance to the German occupation and the Civil War. This experience created genuine support and benevolent acceptance of Tito's authority among the common people in the regions where the communist movement appeared as the only liberation movement (notably in those parts of Croatia, Bosnia and Herzegovina which had suffered the crimes of the Ustashas). Tito's authority was also a constructed phenomenon; the role of the royalist resistance in the war was largely ignored; the struggle against the external conqueror was represented at the same time as a struggle for the socialist revolution against the local bourgeoisie who were charged with betrayal.

Yugoslav propaganda reconstructed the former worker Josip Broz as the persona Tito, a war strategist of genius and a heroic commander-in-chief of the partisan forces. Tito took the title of *maréchal*, the highest possible decoration in communist Yugoslavia. He was called 'the best son of our people', 'the creator of the war victory', 'organiser of the people's army'.[5] He was represented as wise, far-sighted, resolute, proud, generous and sensitive. During the war, these qualities allowed him to 'understand the essence of reality' and to always take the 'right' decision. At the same time, he was never represented as alienated from 'the basis', from the common people of his country, and he was depicted as very susceptible to human relationships.

His attachment to the party ('organiser', 'teacher') and his ties with the people ('creator', 'son of the people', 'leader') were emphasised on all occasions.[6] Tito was his partisan pseudonym. It conveyed resoluteness (from the Serbo-Croat words *ti to* which prosaically means *You do this*, often used by Josip Broz in issuing orders during the war). During the guerrilla war he was always attentive to people, especially the wounded partisans. The first statue of Tito had been created during the war by the sculptor Antun Avgustincic.

The emphasis of Tito's worthiness during the war in the immediate post-war period was explained by the political needs of the moment. During the war Yugoslavia did not exist. New Yugoslavia emerged from the war having suffered large losses in human lives and serious material damage. The atrocities perpetrated during the German occupation and the Civil War were still fresh. Under international pressure, free elections were anticipated and the royalist movement was still present in the country. Yugoslavia's western border was not fixed and the 'crisis of Trieste' underlined its insecure international position. The political, economic and social life of the country were to be reorganised entirely.

In this context, the 'great' and 'genial' but distant Stalin appeared as a guarantor of the international position of the new and weak socialist Yugoslavia. Overshadowed by Stalin in international politics, Tito emerged as a unifying force internally, as the only person able to guide the country towards reconstruction and stability. Thus, Tito's cult grew on the belief that if he was able to lead the people during the war, the country should give him their support in building socialism in the post-war period.

The cult of an autonomous leader (1948–61)

A crucial event, which contributed to the strengthening of Tito's cult, was the Yugoslav break with Stalin and the Soviet Union in 1948.[7] Until the end of 1948, despite Soviet accusations of 'deviations', Tito and his party collaborators kept on stressing Stalin's worthiness in building socialism throughout the world. Stalin was elevated to the level of Marx, Engels and Lenin, and he was even thought to have developed the principles of the founding fathers of Marxism-Leninism.[8] The representation of Stalin was paradoxical: Yugoslav communists fought against Stalin in the name of Stalin. At meetings convened to support Tito and the Communist Party of Yugoslavia, Yugoslav communists agreed to send telegrams to Stalin asking him to exert his influence upon Soviet communists to withdraw the unfair accusations against Yugoslavia. In the initial phase of the crisis with Stalin, Tito had to move cautiously. Stalin was still respected among communists in Yugoslavia. Tito needed time to show to the 'masses' that Stalin was behaving unfairly towards his country and to break the internal pro-Stalinist opposition. At the international level, Tito had to carefully negotiate with the West to secure economic and military assistance.

From the end of 1948 onwards, the Soviet Union and Stalin himself started to be openly criticised in Yugoslavia. In his speeches, Tito avoided using Stalin's name and avoided any reference to him as one of the founding fathers of Marxism-Leninism. From that period, Tito talked frequently about the specificity of 'our revolution' and 'our way of revolutionary development in the future'. In 1949, Tito's closest collaborator, the ideologist of the Yugoslav Communist Party, Edvard Kardelj, proposed a new model of direct participation of workers in the management of enterprises, known as 'Workers Self-Management', which should have effectively detached Yugoslavia from the Soviet economic model. Tito spoke about the 'liberation of Marxism-Leninism from the chains of slavery imposed by Soviet bureaucrats and Cominform dogmatics' and about the defence of the 'lively science of Marxism-Leninism from Stalin's and Soviet bureaucrats' revisionist points of view'.[9]

The rift between Stalin and Tito, and the expulsion of Yugoslavia from the Communist international movement (Cominform), represented a threat to the very independence of the country. Soviet troops were posted on the eastern border and a military intervention seemed imminent. This atmosphere of uncertainty strengthened Tito's cult. The eyes of most of the Yugoslav people were on their leader and his decisions. The press represented Tito as the defender of 'pure Marxist thought'. The message was clear: it should demonstrate that Stalinism was a deviation from Marxism-Leninism and that the politics of Tito and the Communist Party of Yugoslavia was the consistent application of this thought. In May 1950, *Politika* published an article where Tito was compared to Marx, Engels and Lenin. His name appeared together with adjectives like 'great' and 'genius', previously reserved for Stalin. In this text, Tito was represented as a 'great leader, irreconcilable combatant for the defence of Marxism-Leninism and proud leader of the most progressive forces in the world'. Tito's partisans during the war, such as Mosa Pijade,[10] and writers like Miroslav Krleza, contributed to the exaltation of Tito's persona.[11] The most important indicator of the strengthening of Tito's cult was the celebration of his 60th birthday on 25 May 1952. *Politika* dedicated its first six pages to the event and nine photographs to Tito. Telegrams of congratulations and good wishes appeared in the press. This celebration was the turning point. Never before had such attention been lavished on Tito's jubilee. From then on, all Tito's jubilees were celebrated on the date of his birthday. Devotion to Tito was symbolised by the so-called 'Tito's staff', a baton which was carried around the country before being ceremonially presented to him on his birthday.

The normalisation of the Soviet–Yugoslav relations after 1953 was a major international event, but also a personal triumph for Tito. In 1953 he became President of Yugoslavia, a post he held until his death. According to Milovan Djilas, from this time, Tito's capacity for self-criticism gradually declined.[12] Khrushchev's visit to Yugoslavia in 1955 and the recognition that the 'harsh accusations against the Yugoslav party leadership' were 'created by the enemies of the people that entered in our party' demonstrated an important approval of Tito's policy.[13] In this way, Khrushchev clearly recognised Tito's authority as a leader of the opposition and critics of Stalinism. Thus, the basis for the new component of Tito's cult, his anti-Stalinism, was established. Khrushchev's criticisms of Stalin's 'cult of personality' in 1956 had echoes in Yugoslavia.[14] Yugoslav propaganda sought to emphasise Tito's human side. To avoid the unpleasant analogies with Stalin, Tito ordered that from 1956 the 'Tito's staff' be renamed as the 'Youth's staff'. Similarly, from that year, Tito's birthday was designated as 'Youth day', to symbolise the link between Tito and the Yugoslav youth. Tito's biography was much more present in textbooks and his photographs were permanently on the first pages of schoolbooks.[15]

The international fame of Tito as the dominant component of his cult (1961–66)

Tito used the credit, which he had built up in the anti-Stalinist struggle, to develop an active foreign policy with the countries which belonged neither to the Warsaw Pact nor to the North Atlantic Treaty Organisation (NATO). He was one of the founders of the Non-Aligned Movement, together with Nasser and Nehru, and organised the first conference of this movement in Belgrade in 1961.[16] The movement, which was heterogeneous, lacking any significant military force, and assembling the poorest countries in the world, was tolerated by the two superpowers. Even though diplomatically closer to the Soviet side, the movement became an area of contention between the two opposite blocs. Tito presented his foreign policy as part of his personal mission to promote peace in the world. In his traditional New Year messages to the Yugoslav citizens in 1960s, he stressed his activity and his devotion to international peace. As one of the founding fathers of the Non-Aligned Movement he travelled extensively overseas. He sometimes sent his New Year messages from abroad, when he was on this mission, thus underlying his peace objectives. In Africa and Asia, he would often wear local costume and appear on television surrounded by crowds crying out his name. The leaders of friendly countries gave him decorations and several universities of the Third World proclaimed him honorary Doctor of Philosophy for his role in the struggle for peace. Through Tito's personality, the small country of Yugoslavia was known all over the world.

In the introduction to Tito's book *1941*, published in 1961, the writer Dobrica Cosic described Tito's foreign policy as the logical continuation of his struggles for peace since 1945. Always inspired by the 'universal humanitarian meaning of freedom', Tito moved logically, according to Cosic, from the anti-fascist and the anti-Stalinist struggle to the 'principle of active peaceful co-existence, maximum engagement in the anti-colonial liberation struggle of all enslaved and exploited peoples, struggle for democratic and equal co-operation between peoples, political movements and working class parties and defence of the principles of universality of the United Nations'.[17] The celebration of 'Youth Day' in 1962 showed how the strengthening of Tito's cult was founded on his international reputation. On that occasion, Tito received the 'Charter of the Yugoslav communes' which proclaimed him the most honoured citizen of all Yugoslav municipalities and the 'Letter of the Central Committee of the Communist Party of Yugoslavia' which, with emotional tones, identified Tito's personality, his qualities and his activity as the personification of the 'fundamental interests and wishes of all Yugoslavs'.

The Communist Party of Yugoslavia had a crucial role in glorifying Tito's personality. Party officials competed in promoting elaborate celebrations of Tito's personality. The leader's importance in the life of the party became essential and the maintenance of his cult represented the guarantee of the legitimacy of the party hierarchy. Like the party, the class and the people, the leader became a source of sovereignty. Even the lowest party bureaucrats glorified Tito. The 'Charter of the people of Vis', published in 1964 during Tito's visit to this Adriatic island, described the leader as a saint:

> The place where you stayed, the roads where you walked, are today true sanctuaries of reason and human dignity. Today, the stone on which you rested and the bench on which you worked for the happiness and welfare of the working people is more precious than gold.[18]

Thus local officials expressed their loyalty to Tito, ensuring their political positions in the 'great world' that his international work was forging.

Internal crises and the peak of the leader's cult (1966–80)

The year 1966 marked the end of Yugoslavia's post-war consolidation and the beginning of a period of internal instability. The key event was the fall of Alexandar Ranković, Yugoslavia's vice-president and Tito's heir apparent. Ranković was one of the high party officials who favoured increased centralisation of the Yugoslavian state. Tito dismissed Ranković and sent him into retirement. It was the first time that a disagreement on internal policy issues touched the top of the Communist Party of Yugoslavia. The move strengthened those party leaders from the different Yugoslav Federal Republics and created powerful factions within the party.

Tito had a crucial role in the resolution of the social and political crises that shook Yugoslavia after the fall of Ranković: the student demonstrations in 1968, the Croatian separatist movement in 1970–71 and Serbian demands for economic liberalisation in 1971.[19] His handling of the student demonstrations in 1968 shows how his cult was widespread among the population and how he could use it for the concrete political needs of the moment. Following sharp clashes between the students and the police, Tito went on television and declared that not only did he support the students, but that he had been blocked in his work by the country's bureaucracy, and hinted at resignation. There was jubilation at the university and the students went home. Two weeks later, Tito ordered a purge of the university of those professors who were 'corrupting' the nation's youth. In a similar way, Tito used his personal reputation to eliminate the opposition in Croatia and Serbia.

During the period of internal crises from 1966 to 1972 there was a relative decrease in the intensity of the glorification of Tito's personality by high party officials. Nevertheless, the messages of support for Tito's actions against the opposition from various lower level party organisations, such as the Conference of Belgrade Communists or the Committee of the Communists of the Autonomous Regions, indicated strong support for his leadership. These messages were intended to overcome internal instability, by denying the leader's responsibility for the failures and the conflicts within the country and showing that the 'masses' and the rank and file party members were still loyal to him. The messages of support to Tito justified all his actions in the name of the 'people' and of the 'working class'.

In 1972, Tito emerged from this period of crisis as victor. Thereafter, as well as being exalted as a war commander, revolutionary, anti-Stalinist and non-aligned peacemaker, a new element was added to his cult – the saviour of the unity of Yugoslavia. The constitution of 1974 included a provision, which contemplated no limitation of the mandate of the President of the Republic. In doing so, the constitution referred only to Tito. In the mid-1970s Yugoslav propaganda promoted Tito as a candidate for the Nobel Peace Prize, but this initiative was used only for internal purposes and had no impact abroad.

As the Tito cult developed he was awarded all the highest awards and decorations that socialist Yugoslavia could bestow. In 1977, he received, for the third time, the award of the People's Hero of Yugoslavia.[20] The celebration of his birthday on 25 May 1977 was unprecedented, with the main celebrations organised at the Stadium of the Yugoslav Army in Belgrade and with many speeches delivered on the occasion of the 'Youth Staff'. The newspaper *Politika* dedicated its first 12 pages to the event and published 14 photographs of Tito. Stane Dolanc, a top party official, wrote the panegyrics to Tito and concluded that he 'was the most exceptional, the greatest personality in our history and one of the most important personalities of our era'.[21]

The cult of Tito increased as he advanced in age and reached a climax at the moment of his death. This reflected in part a deep anxiety about the future of this heterogeneous, multinational state; this was an anxiety shared by governing circles and by sections of the broader public. At the end of his life, the integrative function of Tito's cult was underlined and, thus, his posthumous cult was developed as a guarantee of the unity of Yugoslavia. This was the sense behind the monumental funeral of Tito in 1980. The Tito cult received a new impetus with his death. It was summarised in the slogan 'After Tito, Tito'. Its symbolic centre was the Memorial Centre, the site of his tomb at his former residence. In the ten years after his death more than 14 million people visited it. At his death four towns carried his name. By 1983 there were eight 'Tito towns', one in every republic and region. Hundreds of books were published on Tito.[22] In 1984 a special law was enacted regulating the use of his name and likeness, with terms of imprisonment laid down for violations.

With the oil price shock the Yugoslav economy was precipitated into a major economic crisis, which gradually uncoupled the links binding the various federal units of the state. The cult of Tito at the same time came under attack, as with Vladimir Dedijer's book *New Contributions to a Biography of Josip Broz Tito* in 1981.[23] The demystification was spurred by the contest over the ownership of the assets of the former president between his family and the state, and by revelations concerning his life-style, his residences, his yacht, his foreign travel, his mistresses and his illegitimate children.[24] Complaints were raised over the costs of maintaining the Memorial Centre. The planned 60-volume edition of his collected works was halted, only half completed, because of costs and unsold stocks. Support for the cult seems to have persisted longest in the Yugoslav Army. However, on 4 May 1990 *Politika* announced 'The myth of Tito is today to all intents and purposes totally dead'.[25]

With the collapse of communism a much more critical assessment of his legacy was undertaken. Kosta Cavoski, in his study of the technology of power, stressed the machiavellian devices used by Tito in consolidating his power and in establishing his cult.[26] Todor Kuljic, in the most comprehensive study of the cult phenomenon, analysed the Tito cult in terms of the model of the 'Balkan traditional charismatic leader'. The unstable political and economic situation of the Balkans in the nineteenth and twentieth centuries, he argues, created within Serbian peasant society a particular political culture, characterised by the acceptance by the peasants of the authority of the warrior leader, who became a monarch with absolute power. This, Kuljic argues, was typified by a succession of rulers in Serbian history from the first modern ruler-warrior Karadjordje (1768–1817) to Alexander I Karadjordjevic (1888–1934), King of Yugoslavia.

Kuljic argued that the Tito cult was strongly supported by the high party bureaucrats, the high army and state officials, the partisan and war veterans and amongst the party rank and file because of a combination of material interests and emotional ties to Tito.[27] It was not accepted by non-party intellectuals, nor by the small owners, and those parts of the peasantry and the rests of the bourgeoisie who had lost out. Close to 90 per cent of the Yugoslav population at the end of the 1930s were peasants. From 1945 to 1990 about seven million peasants moved to the cities and took positions in military, state and economic institutions.[28] This uprooted population, Kuljic argues, represented the social base for the leader cult. The Tito cult represented the 'traditional combination' of the peasant chief, protector and the legendary hero. For the 'new' population of semi-peasants, semi-citizens, it was a surrogate for God, the king and the father of the family.

The cult of Enver Hoxha

After the Second World War Albania became part of the communist camp and was ruled with an iron hand by the communist leader Enver Hoxha. His dictatorship dominated the country from 1944 until his death in 1985. He was elected head of the Albanian Communist Party in 1941 (renamed the Albanian Party of Labour at its first congress in 1948), and during the war he was also general commander of the communist-led Albanian National Liberation Army. He retained during his rule the position of the first secretary of the Albanian Party of Labour. In the first post-war years he occupied also the position of prime minister and minister of foreign affairs.

Until 1948 Albania was under strong Yugoslav influence, with heavy pressure to have Albania included in the Yugoslav federation. Hoxha benefited from the Soviet–Yugoslav split in 1948 and broke with Belgrade, and moved to eliminate the pro-Yugoslav faction within the Albanian Communist Party. The most prominent victim of this extensive purge was Koçi Xoxe, the Party's organisation secretary. After the breach with Belgrade the Albanian leadership further reinforced its links with Moscow. Stalin and the USSR were projected as the guarantors of Albanian statehood, and the cult of Stalin was strongly promoted.[29]

Albania followed the Soviet model of development closely. Hoxha was highly critical of the de-Stalinisation process, initiated by Khrushchev in 1956, which he saw as a direct threat to his dominion over the Albanian Labour Party. In the autumn of 1960 Hoxha liquidated a pro-Soviet faction within the party. At its Fourth Congress in February 1961 the party proclaimed its fidelity to Moscow, but strongly supported the Chinese position on imperialism, war and on Yugoslav revisionism. Hoxha strongly attacked Titoist alleged aggressive intentions towards Albania. At this congress Hoxha was warmly supported by the North Vietnamese, North Korean, Malayan and Indonesian communist parties, but he earned the disapproval of the Soviet Communist Party (CPSU), whose delegation was headed by P. N. Pospelov and Yuri Andropov, and was censured by the delegates from the Eastern European parties.[30]

After the congress relations with the USSR deteriorated sharply. The USSR suspended its economic aid to Albania and withdrew its personnel, as they had done with the Chinese Communist Party over the 'Great Leap Forward'.

At the 22nd Congress of the Soviet Communist Party in October 1961 Khrushchev renewed his attack on the cult of Stalin, and Stalin's body was removed from the mausoleum. This marked a watershed in Albanian-Soviet relations.

The Albanian Labour Party was thus increasingly drawn into the Chinese sphere, and saw in communist China an alternative source of economic and technical assistance. Hoxha shared with Mao Zedong a strong distaste for the anti-Stalinist rhetoric coming from Moscow. He shared with the Chinese a commitment to a strong anti-imperialist struggle against the West, and a resolute stance against revisionism, especially Titoism. He was motivated by a similar ideological puritanism, with its emphasis on political zeal and will to overcome material and cultural backwardness as a compensation for present privations. Both Chinese and Albanian communists saw in Stalin the model of strong, effective leadership.

Inspired by the Chinese Cultural Revolution, launched in 1964, Hoxha undertook further tough measures to tighten his grip of the situation in the country and to radicalise policies. In 1967 all religious practices were banned and all religious institutions were closed down. Albania officially declared itself to be the only atheistic country in the world. A Museum of Atheism was established in Shkodra (northern Albania). The period of revolutionary transformation continued with severe attacks on the intelligentsia. Hundreds of specialists were removed from the capital to the country, to assist in various campaigns and to be re-educated with 'the revolutionary spirit of the working class and co-operativist peasantry'. Through the 'revolutionising of the school' political ideology was firmly injected into the curricula of educational institutions. The Albanian economy was rapidly socialised and agriculture collectivised: its small private sector disappeared in the early 1970s.

The period of warm relations with China ended in 1978, when the Albanian leadership decided to break with Beijing, after clear signs that China was gradually opening up to Western capitalism. During the isolation period in the late 1970s and 1980s Albania became the centre of the so-called Marxist-Leninist parties, which were minor militant groups advocating radical ways to fight capitalism. These groups, financed by the Albanian Labour Party, were expected to propagate the cult of Hoxha through distributing his translated works and promoting the image of Albania as the only true socialist country in the world.

The period of Albania's political and economic isolation saw the regime's efforts to promote the international dimension of Hoxha's cult. He was hailed as a great international Marxist, a great theoretician and intellectual. He was often pictured in his study reading and writing, or even just thinking. In the 1970s and early 1980s He was projected as a major theorist of Marxism-Leninism.[31] In that period Hoxha wrote 'Imperialism and Revolution', as an echo to Lenin's book 'State and Revolution', and 'Euro-

Communism is Anti-Communism', as a response to the book by Spanish communist leader Santiago Carrillo 'Euro-Communism and the State'. He also wrote *With Stalin Memoirs*, which sought to reinforce his own personal connections with Stalin, by recounting his five meetings with the *vozhd'*. In *The Krushchevites* he bitterly denounced the 'revisionism' of Khrushchev and his successors.[32]

The cult of Stalin was one of Hoxha's greatest ideological investments. The cult of Stalin was kept alive, and it performed two functions: (*a*) propagandistic and (*b*) pragmatic.[33] Through Stalin's cult Hoxha was promoted as the communist leader who remained firm to pure Marxist principles, and thus he was set apart from all other communist leaders in Europe and in the world. His perseverance in protecting Stalin's cult was made also with the aim of preserving the national sovereignty of the country. The break with China accentuated further the nationalistic propaganda inside the country and the need to be self-reliant in the task of building socialism.

The only rival to the leader cult of Hoxha was provided by the cult of the party. He himself used to say that he was obeying party orders. He was careful to present himself not as an absolutist leader, nor as a saint, but as a mortal, who was subject to a higher authority. Nevertheless, his portraits were everywhere on display, making him omnipresent. In the end it was he who decided matters on behalf of the party, reducing the party only to an abstract image.

In his memoirs Hoxha offers his own, sometime insightful, sometimes idiosyncratic, views on the operation of leader cults in communist states. He perversely denied that any such cult had existed under Stalin, whilst bitterly denouncing the cults around Tito and Khrushchev. His real venom was directed at the cults of Mao and Kim Il-sung, notwithstanding the fact that his own cult resembled these cults and was partly based on them. The cult around Mao he saw as a denigration of the stature of a great figure: 'In reality they are turning the cult of Mao almost into a religion . . . Are we dealing with Marxists or with religious fanatics?' On his own leader cult in Albania, in a note dated January 1977, he offered this following self-vindication:

> We have condemned the cult of the individual and condemn it to this day about anybody at all. On this question we follow the view of Marx, and for this reason amongst us, in our leadership, there is Marxist-Leninist unity, affection, sincerity, Marxist-Leninist respect towards comrades . . . Amongst us there is no *idolâtrie*. Above all we speak about the Party, while we speak about Enver only as much as the interests of the Party and country require, and when from the base and the masses there has been some excess in this direction, the Central Committee, the leadership of the Party and I personally, as much as I can and to the extent that they have listened to me about it, have always taken and always will take measures to proceed on the right course.[34]

Hoxha died in April 1985, the last surviving Stalinist leader of Eastern Europe. His body was buried in the cemetery of the 'Martyrs of the Nation'. On his death his cult received a new impetus. In 1988, on the 80th anniversary of his birth, the government built an impressive mausoleum in Tirana, where his remains were interred, and a monumental statue of Hoxha was erected in the centre of the capital. In 1988 the state publishing house issued a two-volume collection of memoirs of Hoxha with contributions by Politburo members, scientists, writers, sculptors, painters, and linguists, who extolled his expertise in every field of human endeavour.[35]

This campaign was orchestrated by his successor as party leader Ramiz Alia (1985–91) who had an interest in trying to legitimise his succession. He sought to invoke the name of Hoxha to bolster up his own authority with his book on Hoxha entitled *Our Enver*.[36] This is less a biography than a panegyric on Hoxha as a Marxist-Leninist, a leader of great political acumen, someone closely connected to the Albanian people and a staunch Albanian patriot.

Here a parallel might be drawn between the cult of Enver Hoxha and that of King Zog I, who ruled Albania from 1928 to 1939. Ahmet Zogu was at first President of the Republic (1924–28) and then ruled as the self-declared King of the Albanians (1928–39). In 1937 Kristo Dako, an Albanian professor of history in a lycee of Tirana, published a book entitled *Ahmet Zogu, the King of the Albanians*.[37] Here the parallels between the two leaders can be clearly seen. Hoxha, like King Zog, sought to cultivate Albanian nationalism, to preserve his power and to strengthen the cultural and social cohesion of the society.[38] This was done through the extension of state control over society, through centralising power, through developing public administration and a national army, and by extending the educational system in the native language.[39] Like Zog, Hoxha faced the problem of ruling a small country, deeply divided amongst its Moslem, Orthodox and Catholic communities and one vulnerable to encroachment by its more powerful neighbours.

Enver Hoxha and King Zog were often presented as fathers of their nation and state-builders. King Zog 'made a nation out of tribes and a state out of a nation'.[40] In his turn Enver was 'the most beloved teacher and leader of the whole Albanian people'.[41] Both leaders used the historical past to legitimise their power in the eyes of the people. King Zog tried to represent his rule as the rebirth of the tradition of the Albanian national hero Gjergj Kastrioti Skanderbeg (1403–68), who fought against the Ottoman armies for almost 25 years. The communist regime similarly used Skanderbeg as the symbol of resistance to the external threat, and the connection with the past grew in importance as Albania's political isolation increased.[42]

But Hoxha's method of rule followed the model of the Stalinist system. The party structures, the so-called 'base-organisations', were used to keep this cult alive and present in the family life of the Albanians, as part of a general mechanism of indoctrination and control. They were present in the collective farms, in the factories, in schools, universities and hospitals. They were responsible for organising festivities, parades, conferences, and all kinds of mass expressions, hailing the role of Hoxha and the party in the history of the country. They continued their role after Hoxha's death. They organised the so-called 'Enver's days', when festivities, conferences, or mass participation in public works were organised. These days coincided either with the date of Hoxha's birthday or some important occasion.

These celebrations declined in importance and faded away in 1990, when Ramiz Alia was forced to make the first and timid reforms in response to growing internal and external pressure after the fall of the communist regimes in Eastern Europe. In December 1990 the Council of Ministers ruled that Stalin's name and statues be removed from state institutions and public places.[43] In February 1991 the crowd toppled the great statute of Hoxha in the centre of Tirana. In May 1992 his body was removed from the mausoleum to the cemetery of the 'Martyrs of the Nations' and the mausoleum was designated as an international cultural centre.

The cult of Hoxha was that of an absolute ruler constructed with the help of a quasi-religious ideology that celebrated his central role in socialist Albania for almost half a century.[44] His was a totalitarian regime, which borrowed elements from other similar ones in communist Eastern Europe. It was consolidated during his long, highly personalised rule over the country and was reinforced by the deep isolation of Albania. The patriarchal and 'clannish' character of the Albanian society, based on clique and factions, not simply on kinship networks, may have played their part too. The society had inherited from the past a respect for the strong, and 'the first of the first', and a hatred for adversary groups. Unlike in other countries of Eastern Europe, repressive measures were not confined to the accused person but were extended to the family and relatives. This collective culpability was a mechanism of control, aimed at dissuading people from any form of 'subversive' action or thought.

Hoxha's cult can be compared with the cult of the long-standing communist leaders like Stalin, Mao and Ceauşescu. Hoxha was venerated as an all-powerful figure and as a supreme authority in all the fields of human activity. As Arshi Pipa has written:

> Hoxha was decisive in producing a cultural atmosphere totally dominated by a doctrinaire propaganda exalting nationalism. Linguistics, literature, history, geography, folklore, and ethnology have been cultivated, not only to give the people a sense of their own past, but also to spread and inculcate xenophobia, slavophobia, isolationism, ethnic compactness, and linguistic uniformity.[45]

His was a 'state-of-siege nationalism', which intensified the xenophobic feelings of Albanians, but on the other hand homogenised further the Albanian community within the state borders. His cult was built on the credo 'terror as a precondition for ruling'.[46] He strangled at birth the slightest forms of doubt on the veracity of the party's line. His image inculcated among people a strange mixture of fear, veneration, belligerence, fatalism and apathy. Finally, the cult called on the people to endure present sacrifices for a brilliant future. With time, that future looked more like a mirage and people became worn-out looking for it.[47]

Conclusion

The careers of Tito and Hoxha at the outset shared many striking similarities. Both were brought to power through the anti-Nazi struggle of their respective partisan movements, they shared the reputation of military commanders as well as revolutionary party leaders and state-builders. In the immediate post-war period both took a strongly pro-Soviet stance and were fervent admirers of Stalin, and emulated his leader cult. From 1948 onwards their paths diverged dramatically. Tito became the outspoken critic of the Stalinist model of communism, the arch-revisionist, promoting his own brand of socialism, which was dubbed by his critics 'Titoism'. Hoxha remained an ardent Stalinist and broke with the Soviet leadership after 1961 on the question of de-Stalinisation. Increasingly he sought to promote himself as the true guardian of Marxist-Leninist orthodoxy in its Stalinist variant.

Notwithstanding the radically different policy courses adopted by both leaders, and their very different leadership styles, both fostered their own brand of leader cult, which survived for nearly half a century. This reflected an attempt to find a basis for legitimising the one-party socialist state, and to preserve the unity of their fragile states, beset by internal divisions and external threats. Both cults may also have reflected a tradition of leadership politics in the Balkan region, and of societies still deeply infused with the values of peasant patriarchalism. With the deaths of both Tito and Hoxha, similar attempts were made to use their cults posthumously to legitimise the rule of their successors. In neither case was the integrative power of the cult able to withstand the corrosive influences set in train by the opening up of their political systems. The crisis of legitimacy in both states saw the rise of new political forces that sought to use populist and nationalist rhetoric to create a new basis of legitimacy.

Notes

1. For biographies and studies of Tito see: Arsa Lazarevic, *Slobodan Nesovic, Svijet o Titu* (*The World of Tito*) (Zagreb, 1966); Vladimir Dedijer, *Tito* (New York, 1972); Auty Phyllis, *Tito: A biography* (Harmondsworth, 1974); Nora Beloff, *Tito's Flawed*

Legacy: Yugoslavia and the West since 1939 (Boulder, 1985); Savo Krzavac, *Tito na raskrscima istorije* (*Tito on the Crossroads of History*) (Belgrade, 1985). For a critical view, by a former colleague, see Milovan Djilas, *Tito – The Story from Inside* (London, 1981).

2. Kosta Cavoski, *Tito-tehnologija vlasti* (*Tito: the Technology of the Power*) (Belgrade, 1991), p. 13.
3. Dusan Mojic, 'Evolucija Kulta Josipa Broza Tita 1945–1990: analiza stampe' (The Evolution of the Cult of Josip Broz Tito 1945–1990: The Analysis of the Press), *Srpska politicka misao* (*Serbian Political Thought*), 2: 1 (1995), p. 136.
4. See for example Milovan Djilas, *Conversations with Stalin* (London, 1962).
5. *Politika*, 1 May 1945.
6. Mojic, 'Evolucija Kulta Josipa Broza Tita', p. 137.
7. G. R. Swain, 'Tito – The Formation of a Disloyal Bolshevik', *International Review of Social History*, 34 (1989), pp. 248–71; G. R. Swain, 'The Cominform, Tito's International', *Historical Journal*, 35 (1992), pp. 641–63.
8. Cavoski, *Tito-technologija vlasti*, p. 15.
9. Ibid., p. 17.
10. *Politika*, 25 May 1951.
11. No author/no editor *Knjizevnici o Titu* (*The Writers about Tito*) (Sarajevo, 1984).
12. Djilas, *Tito – The Story from Inside* (London, 1981), p. 64.
13. G. Swain and N. Swain, *Eastern Europe Since 1945* (London, 1998), pp. 76–9.
14. Veljko Micunovic, *Moscow Diary* (London, 1980), pp. 77, 78.
15. Mojic, 'Evolucija Kulta Josipa Broza Tita', p. 145.
16. Duncan Wilson, *Tito's Yugoslavia* (Cambridge, 1979), pp. 132–4.
17. Dobrica Cosic, *Tito u zapisima savremenika* (*Tito in the Records of the Contemporaries*) (Zagreb, 1965).
18. *Tito medju nama* (Tito Among Us) (Ljubljana, 1972).
19. G. Swain and N. Swain, *Eastern Europe Since 1945*, pp. 136–7.
20. Mojic, 'Evolucija Kulta Josipa Broza Tito', p. 149.
21. Cosic, *Titu u zapisima savremenika*.
22. Other significant political-propanadistic works on Tito were: *Tito ocima sveta* (*Tito in the Eyes of the World*) (Belgrade, 1977); *Nas Tito* (*Our Tito*) (Zagreb, 1980); *Secanja na Tita* (*Memories of Tito*) (Belgrade, 1985).
23. Vladimir Dedijer, *Novi prilozi za biografiju Josipa Broza Tita* (*New Contributions to a Biography of Josip Broz Tito*) (Zagreb, 1980).
24. Filip Raulovic, *Ljubavi Josipa Broza* (*The Loves of Josip Broz*) (Belgrade, 1990).
25. Stevan K. Pavlowitch, *Tito: Yugoslavia's Great Dictator, A Reassessment* (London, 1992), p. 93.
26. Cavoski, *Tito – tehnologija vlasti*.
27. Todor Kuljic, *Tito* (Belgrade, 1998), p. 321.
28. *Ibid.*, p. 291.
29. See the main party newspaper *Zëri i Popullit* (*The Voice of the People*), 7 November 1948, p. 2. Academic conference on the occasion of the October Revolution, *Zëri i Popullit*, 30 November 1948, p. 1. Enver Hoxha was bestowed the award 'Hero of the People', *Zëri i Popullit*, 21 December 1948, p. 1. Telegram of wishes sent to Stalin by Albanian Prime Minister and Foreign Minister Enver Hoxha, on the occasion of his birthday.
30. Zbigniew K. Brzezinski, *The Soviet Bloc: Unity and Conflict* (Cambridge, Mass., 1967), pp. 414–15.
31. Bashkim Shehu, 'The Red and Black Hoxha', article published in the Spanish newspaper *Vanguardia*, 10 December 2000.

32. Enver Hoxha, *Me Stalinin, kujtime* (Tirana, 1979); Enver Hoxha, *With Stalin: Memoirs* (Tirana, 1979): the book carries the dedication 'On the occasion of the centenary of the birth of the great Marxist-Leninist Joseph Stalin'; Enver Hoxha, *Hrushovianët* (Tirana, 1980). Albania was the only country in the Eastern Europe after 1960 to have a town called 'Qyteti Stalin' (Stalin's Town). It was changed into its old name 'Kuçova' in 1990 with the fall of the regime.
33. Alex Standish, 'Enver Hoxha's Role in the Development of Socialist Albanian Myths' in Stephanie Schwandner-Sievers and Bernd J. Fischer (eds) *Albanian Identities, Myth and History* (London 2002).
34. *The Artful Albanian: Memoirs of Enver Hoxha*, ed. Jon Halliday (London, 1986), p. 372.
35. *Memoirs of Enver* (Tirana, 1988).
36. Ramiz Alia, *Enveri ynë* (Tirana, 1988).
37. Kristo Dako, *Ahmet Zogu, mbret I shqiptarëve* (Tirana, 1937).
38. Bernd Fischer, 'Albanian Nationalism in the Twentieth Century' in Peter F. Sugar (ed.) *Eastern European Nationalism in the Twentieth Century* (Washington, 1995), p. 44.
39. Piro Misha, 'Fenomeni i nacionalizmit dhe kriza shqiptare' The Phenomenon of Nationalism and the Albanian Crisis), *Përpjekja*, nos 15–16 (Tirana, 1999), p. 30.
40. Dako, *Ahmet Zogu*, p. 142.
41. *Historia e Partisë së Punës së Shqipërisë* (*History of the Albanian Party of Labor*) (Tirana 1982), p. 122.
42. See also Fatos Lubonja, 'Midis lavdisë së një bote virtuale dhe mjerimit të botës reale' (Between the Glory of a Virtual World and the Misery of a Real World), *Përpjekja*, nos 15–16 (Tirana 1999), p. 147. For more see Brend Fischer, 'King Zog and the Struggle for Stability in Albania'. In Brend Fischer, *Zog I, the King of the Albanians* (New York 1984), ch. 7.
43. Miranda Vickers, *The Albanians* (London and New York, 1995), p. 218.
44. Alex Standish, 'Enver Hoxha's Role in the Development of Socialist Albanian Myths' in Schwandner-Sievers and Fischer, *Albanian Identities, Myth and History*, p. 121.
45. Arshi Pipa, *Albanian Stalinism: Ideo-Political Aspects* (Boulder, Colo., 1990), quoted in Brend Fischer, 'Albanian Nationalism in the Twentieth Century'.
46. Todi Lubonja, *Nën peshën e dhunës* (*Under the Burden of Violence*) (Tirana, 1993), p. 278.
47. Fatos Lubonja, 'Tetë karakteristikat e totalitarizmit' (Eight Characteristics of Totalitarism) in 'Liri e kërcënuar' (*Threatened Freedom*), published by '*Përpjekja*' (Tirana, 1999), p. 59.

Part IV

The Dilemmas of De-Stalinisation: Change and Continuity in Leader Cult Patterns in the Post-Stalin Period

13
'I've Held, and I Still Hold, Stalin in the Highest Esteem': Discourses and Strategies of Resistance to De-Stalinisation in the USSR, 1953–62

Polly Jones

Leader cults rarely go quietly, fading into obscurity after the demise or removal of their central figure. The comprehensive claims which they make about their object's authority, coupled with their dominance of the public sphere, characteristically undergo a difficult transition into the new era. Historically, however, societies experiencing the aftermath of such cults have tended to underestimate the difficulties of this transition, and have used inadequate methods to deal with the leader's legacy. These have included a flat refusal to interrogate the past, de-mythologisation by fiat (N. S. Khrushchev's 'Secret Speech'), highly controlled forms of historical reassessment, also 'from above' (the moderate new history of Maoism authorised by the Chinese Communist Party in the 1970s), and relatively uncontrolled, often sensationalist, historical revelations released into a freer public sphere (the flood of revelations about Stalin, and then Lenin, in the *glasnost'* and early post-Soviet period).[1] It is clear that all of these methods, whilst they have their political uses, signposting the transition from one regime to another, signally fail to confront the enduring social and cultural legacies of the cult. A single historical narrative imposed 'from above', or even a multitude of stories of the past from above *and* below, cannot substitute for, or dispense with, the complex of mythologies propagated by leader cults.

In this regard, the legacy of the Stalin cult, an exceptionally well-developed cultural system, may be the most challenging of all the 'post-cult' situations mentioned above. In the decade after Stalin's death, his cult was subjected, albeit with very different degrees of official sanction, to all of the above methods. The authorities at different times attempted to ignore the problem of the Stalin cult, even as it renounced many Stalinist *policies* (1953–56), to dispense with it at one fell swoop (Khrushchev's 'Secret Speech' of 1956), to provide a highly controlled and balanced account of Stalin's good and bad points (the official party resolution issued a few months after the 'Secret Speech'), and to contain a potential flood of popular, often sensationalist, narratives about the Stalinist past. All of these methods represented efforts to get to grips with the Stalinist past, and each was constrained by different factors in the emerging post-Stalinist system. To ignore the Stalinist past was not long viable, given the pressures on the system (from below, and from within the leadership) to emerge from out of the shadows of Stalin, in both a political and a moral sense.[2] Imposing a narrative on the Stalinist past 'from above', whether a scandalous and secretive exercise in de-mythologisation, or a more measured public assessment, however, was also inadequate to the task of confronting Stalin's legacy.

This uncertainty with regard to the cult set the party on a collision course with sectors of public opinion which owed their new-found boldness on the subject of Stalin precisely to the erosion of the totalitarian edifice of the Stalinist dictatorship. This chapter will examine one, overlooked section of this popular response to de-Stalinisation, namely that group of people – most of them authors and perpetrators of anonymous protests against the new leadership – whose militant protest against the new account of the Stalinist past issued from a conservative, or an 'anti-anti-Stalinist' position.[3] It is this sector of public opinion which epitomised many of the specific weaknesses of official policy on de-Stalinisation, as well as indicating more broadly some of the inherent problems of 'de-cultification' alluded to above. The militant protest of Stalin's supporters testified to the persistence of the discourse and attitudes of the cult, and it pointed to some of the most basic problems of legitimacy and authority which would confront the post-Stalinist leadership in their efforts to 'de-mythologise' the Stalinist past.

It is often argued that leader cults contribute to the strengthening of state order, both at its apex (being the expression, and guarantee, of an end to political in-fighting), and in the broader mass of society, where the single mythic narrative of personal power helps to integrate, or to conceal, centrifugal social forces.[4] The Soviet cults of Lenin and Stalin cults fulfilled both these aims. The Lenin cult played an important role in the transition from Leninism to Stalinism, providing an 'interim icon' during a time of fierce infighting.[5] The Stalin cult, which first built on the Lenin cult, before overshadowing it in the 1930s and 1940s, emphasised and consolidated Stalin's one-man rule, whilst also inscribing into Soviet culture a 'master narrative' reiterating the unbreakable ties between leader and people.[6]

These insights into the functions of the cult still need to be complemented by a thorough examination of the ways in which the leadership's intentions for the cult actually played out in Soviet society. Nevertheless, studies working within the evident confines of Stalin-era source materials already suggest that the cult did, broadly, penetrate into the mind-set of the Soviet people, not least because it syncretically assimilated older traditions from popular culture.[7] Its dominance of the Soviet public sphere heavily influenced the modes of expression, or 'Soviet speak', employed in communications between people and party, such as letters, and the language used in public settings, such as party meetings.[8] Disingenuous as these recitations of the cult's epithets may have been, repeated usage ingrained certain linguistic and rhetorical habits, if not always certain attitudes of deference and worship. Further, new research into 'Soviet subjectivity' has begun to deconstruct the boundary between 'private' and 'public', showing that 'official' language interacted in complex ways with the narration and formation of 'individual' identities.[9] Although it is virtually impossible to quantify contemporary public opinion about the Stalin cult, scrutiny of the types of language used in the available sources, however apparently 'contaminated', can at a minimum allow us to assign to the Stalin cult an important 'discursive' influence in shaping popular modes of expression, if not always popular sentiment.

If the Stalin cult was to a degree 'successful' in penetrating popular culture, it follows that the 'success' of de-Stalinisation would depend on a thorough extirpation of the cult from that same arena. However, the difficulties of rooting out both the discourse of the cult, and the genuine sentiments – as well as, it must be said, self-serving motivations – which sometimes lay behind its usage, were not fully acknowledged by the Soviet leadership, and a surprisingly similar oversight has been common amongst historians of the post-Stalin era. To a large degree, the story of de-Stalinisation has been seen by both as a struggle waged by the new Soviet leadership with pro-Stalinists in its ranks (V. M. Molotov, G. M. Malenkov and L. M. Kaganovich, deemed to be members of the 'anti-party-group' in 1957) and with anti-Soviet dissent outside them, in the USSR and the Soviet Bloc.[10] These problems from the 'internal left' and the 'external right' were apparently decisive influences on the course of de-Stalinisation.[11] However, the focus on these opposing forces ignores a third constituency lying between them, namely adherence to the cult beyond the narrow confines of Stalin's supporters in the Khrushchev leadership. The leadership's attempts at de-Stalinisation roused some listeners not only to mount a reflexive defence of Stalin, but also to deploy in that defence the language and rituals of the cult itself. In these appropriations of the cult's discourse as a weapon *against* the current leadership, rather than as a reassurance of the bond between ruler and ruled, there emerged a striking hybrid of defiance and deference towards authority, and towards the historical and political prerogatives of the Soviet leadership.

One of the most striking manifestations of the power of the Stalin cult after Stalin's death was also one of the earliest: Stalin's death on 5 March 1953 provoked a nearly unanimous outpouring of grief.[12] The Central Committee received a record number of letters from grief-stricken members of the public, full of the language of the cult (especially its paternalist imagery), and shot through with apparently genuine heartfelt sentiment.[13] Clearly, the fear of what was to come after the removal of the regime's main source of stability played its part, but so too did the deeply ingrained habits of the cult. Nonetheless, some were startlingly quick to recover, amongst them L. P. Beria, an influential architect of 'de-Stalinising' reforms, such as the criminal amnesties, until his arrest and subsequent execution in late 1953.[14] These policies, along with Malenkov's 'New Course', the more relaxed tenor of public life and, most striking of all to observers, the virtual disappearance of Stalin from public discourse, all suggested that the Stalin cult had collapsed, both rapidly and painlessly.[15] Certainly, the broader Stalinist legacy had been targeted in its constituent parts by these changes to economic policy, criminal justice and the forms of politics (the shift to 'collective leadership'). All of these moves suggested that there had been a pent-up desire for reform in the last years of Stalin's life, which had been held in check by Stalin's dominance of the Politburo.[16] However, whilst Stalin's death and these reforms did signal his decreasing influence over party policy, these changes did not overtly tackle the broader issue of the cult of Stalin's authority, which had, especially latterly, permeated every domain of Soviet public life.

Khrushchev, and A. I. Mikoyan, were amongst those in the Soviet leadership who recognised that the cult would survive until decisively confronted, compromising the post-Stalin regime's political and moral legitimacy.[17] Most analysts of the Khrushchev era have rightly seen Khrushchev's delivery of the 'Secret Speech' to a closed session of the 20th Party Congress as a turning point, marking a radically new stage in the understanding of the Soviet past, and in the forms of Soviet state–society relations.[18] It is tempting to view these two developments as mutually compatible, and many accounts of the aftermath of the speech have emphasised the ways in which new narratives of the Stalinist past were able to emerge through the new (or perhaps revived) channels of public opinion which opened up during the early years of de-Stalinisation.[19] As has been copiously, perhaps even disproportionately, recounted in the new literature on de-Stalinisation, the Secret Speech provoked the emergence of new forms of 'anti-Soviet' dissent, especially in some quarters of the intelligentsia, with which the regime could only deal through resorting to quasi-Stalinist forms of repression.[20] However, the interaction of the new content of official rhetoric and the new forms of state–society relations could also work in other ways, for example by allowing old narratives (preserved from the cult) to be voiced with unprecedented vigour.[21]

'Conservative', rather than 'radical', dissent did feature in the constellation of opinion about the party's new wave of de-Stalinisation, and its arguments in favour of retaining the cult emerged in paradoxical, hybrid forms combining Stalinist and newer, post-Stalinist norms. Conservatively minded letters to the leadership in response to the Secret Speech reflected in their language the tenacity of the Stalin cult (and, in their anonymity, residual fears of repression), yet their form exploited the emergent changes to the 'Soviet public sphere', taking advantage of the apparent opening of channels between party and people, sanctioning greater freedom to express oneself 'from below'. Another, less common, form of conservative dissent examined here – statements in party meetings – inhabited a similarly unstable middle ground between the language and rituals of high Stalinism, and the post-Stalinist sense, however illusory, of being able to speak back to the party. Meanwhile, 'rituals' of the cult, such as the retention of 'personal' Stalinist iconography or the protection of public portraits and symbols of the Stalin cult, exploited the party's own evident discomfort and uncertainty with regard to the Stalin cult, rightly claiming that there had been no specific prohibition issued to outlaw preservation.

In a broad sense, the vast majority of recorded responses to the Secret Speech bore witness to the persistence of the language and imagery of the Stalin cult in 'the Soviet political mind'.[22] The key terms *vozhd'*, *uchitel'*, *korifei* and *generalissimus* (respectively, leader, teacher, coryphaeus and generalissimo) were widely used to interpret the Secret Speech; many questions, for example, enquired whether the above terms should, or indeed could, continue to be applied to Stalin after Khrushchev's revelations.[23] They functioned as anchors for the incipient discourse of de-Stalinisation, which, after all, lacked the requisite clarity for confident replication even amongst those willing to subscribe to it. In a broad sense, therefore, even the most apparently well-intentioned responses to the Secret Speech reflected the greater strength and coherence of the language of the Stalin cult. Indeed, a frequent criticism of de-Stalinisation pointed to the failure of the Secret Speech as *propaganda*, that is, as an easily decipherable, palatable message for the people. A collective farm chairman in Stalingrad *oblast'* worried that his farmers, who had taken Stalin's death very much to heart, would not adjust to the abrupt shift from worship to rejection of the *vozhd'*.[24] In Saratov, one conversation monitored by observers included a criticism that 'all of this will inflict grievous trauma on the hearts of the workers'.[25]

In a similar way, anxieties were frequently expressed on behalf of another group directly targeted by the cult's propaganda – children. An anonymous letter to Molotov, for example, argued that the speech should not have been recounted to children, as the changes to Stalin's image were likely to be distressing to the young who 'from their earliest years know the words Lenin and Stalin'.[26] Another anonymous letter, also to Molotov, also advised strongly against reading the speech out to young people, alleging that 'the young . . . love Stalin, their lives are linked to his name'.[27] Occasionally, children themselves would confirm these fears, as in a letter to Molotov from a group of schoolchildren in Zhukovskii, in the Moscow province.

> It's really hard for us to get used to the idea that Iosif Vissarionovich Stalin is not at all the way we imagined him to be. We never once doubted that he was the true, the best pupil of Vladimir Il'ich Lenin. Our teachers at school are telling us that we should 'forget his name forever'. They're taking down and ripping his portraits. We're left with a really

> horrible feeling, as though we're losing Stalin all over again, and this time, it's for good.[28]

All of these concerns suggested not so much an unwillingness to dissociate from the Stalin cult, as an *inability* to abandon the intensely inculcated images of the leader as wise, strong and worthy of the gratitude offered to him by the Soviet populace.[29] By emphasising heartfelt sentiment rather than objective and rational judgement, such statements argued that the regime's new narrative of the Stalinist past was incommensurate to the task of tackling the Stalin cult; the hearts *and* minds of the cult's 'target audience' still remained to be fully 'de-Stalinised'.

However, the language and rituals of the Stalin cult also functioned in less benign ways in the aftermath of the Secret Speech, providing a weapon for those less *willing* to subscribe to the new imagery of the *vozhd'*. Strategies of opposition to de-Stalinisation included letter-writing, often emboldened by the cover of anonymity and by the prediction that the addressee might share the sentiments expressed within it. Letter-writing as a channel between state and people had had a lengthy pedigree in Russian culture, surviving, albeit in progressively emasculated forms, throughout the Stalin era.[30] In the Khrushchev era, the genre took on a renewed importance, and was used to a multitude of ends; however, in the aftermath of the Secret Speech, letters to the leadership (at least those currently available to researchers) were to a striking degree dominated by *conservative* opposition to de-Stalinisation.[31] In addition, there were also occasional public statements of dissatisfaction, and rituals of resistance such as the protection or retention of Stalinist icons (e.g. portraits) and Stalinist rituals (e.g. the recitation of cult epithets). All these methods benefited from the temporal proximity of the cult – that is, the all too recent saturation of Soviet culture with obligatory cultic worship – and also from the weaknesses of the discourse of de-Stalinisation, which seemed ill-equipped to replace it, either as a coherent narrative of the past, or as a usable mythology for the Soviet present.

In letters and statements expressing dissatisfaction with the Secret Speech, arguments against de-Stalinisation proceeded most simply from the assumption that the cult reflected objective truth, and consequently repeated key phrases and images from the cult to dispute the Secret Speech's version of events. Most appealing were the military imagery of the cult (the claim that Stalin's leadership had assured the victory in the Second World War) and the broader tendencies towards monumentalism in the cult (the depiction of Stalin as superhuman). Military imagery, unsurprisingly, featured strongly in the overwhelmingly negative opinions of de-Stalinisation monitored in the Moscow military garrison.[32] A retired colonel, Chursin, responded to a reading of the speech in March 1956, with a militant refusal to renounce the cult, saying, 'I've held, and I still hold, Stalin in the highest esteem. His merits are great in every regard, our people believed in him as in a God, and it was thanks to that that we won the war'.[33] He defended his right to maintain 'his own' representation of Stalin, whilst also arguing for the wider benefits of this cultic image as a totemic symbol and spiritual anchor within popular culture. This defence was echoed in the reaction of a lieutenant-colonel and political instructor:

> All the Soviet people put their trust in Stalin, believed in him, Stalin was a symbol of the whole Soviet people and all humanity. The party generated his authority and over a long period praised him, took pride in him, and yet now they're saying he's talentless . . . but, you know, history's history, and there's a lot in it that's linked to him, and it isn't so easy just to erase it from the historical record.[34]

Again, the cult of Stalin was represented as a universal system of belief and, accordingly, a means of identification for the Soviet people. Against the vagaries of de-Stalinisation, with its abrupt shifts from worship to criticism, however, the speaker set the objective narrative of history, which naturally placed Stalin at its very centre. However, the rest of this speech underlined the subjective beliefs underpinning these 'historical' claims. He claimed, for example, that the iconoclastic practice of renaming towns and factories could not be brought to bear on Stalingrad ('that city's not so easy to rename'), because of its associations with victory in the Second World War.[35] This speaker equated commemoration in history with a positive subjective assessment of the object in question.

We therefore see that the military arguments above protested against de-Stalinisation by asserting Stalin's place in history and in the national psyche. This type of argument was not unique to military circles, although the myths surrounding Stalin in war probably possessed the greatest resonance in that domain. Non-military people also repeated epithets from the cult, used to denote Stalin's military prowess and his rightful dominance of the war effort, as in one letter to Malenkov describing Stalin as 'commander and chief and genial commander of the troops (*genial'nyi polkovodets*)'.[36] Others alluded to Stalin's alleged steadfastness in the face of the Nazi attack – 'loyally, he stood at his post, and his every word inspired the party and people' – claiming that this (apocryphal) image of Stalin had been crucial to victory and was inseparable from current commemorations of the victory; indeed, the party authorities noted in their commentary that many other similar letters had gone so far as to claim that rejecting Stalin's leading role meant 'rejecting the victory altogether' (*otritsat' pobedu voobshche*).[37] Whilst this contention may have reflected a sincere belief in the inextricable links between the Stalin myth and the war myth, it also strategically targeted one of the most vulnerable points in the party's policy, namely the risk of sacrificing 'good', useful myths from the Stalinist past along with the 'bad' myths of the Stalin cult.

These obstinate repetitions of party cant occasionally translated into physical protest against de-Stalinisation. The Georgian incidence of this has been well documented; however, other incidents of stubborn attachment to the cult's symbolism were also recorded.[38] A letter to Molotov, from a lieutenant in the Moscow garrison, claimed that – 'In my apartment, I had a portrait of Stalin, it's still there, and will remain there until there's a direct order from the Central Committee to take it down'.[39] According to letters and party records, at a Moscow military base, a Ukrainian factory, a Moscow school, to take a few examples, there were more public attempts to resist the removal of portraits.[40] Collective rituals of protest also focused on other, suspended symbols of the cult, such as the Soviet national anthem's verse about Stalin, which was applauded by students in Dagestan in March, or the habitual praise offered to Stalin in academic settings (whose disappearance from lectures at one Moscow university elicited a 'roar of disapproval' from the assembled students).[41] Letter writers meanwhile expressed their distress or outrage at such violent, disrespectful actions on a local level, as in one anonymous letter to Molotov from Moscow, which recounted that, 'now people are shaming Stalin, they're breaking his monuments and tearing his portraits. This shouldn't be allowed'.[42] Similar feelings of disgust or trepidation were aroused by the rumoured plans to remove Stalin from the Red Square mausoleum.[43]

This seemingly uncritical respect for the cult's verbal and visual symbolism was often grounded, however, in an astute sense of the workings of political mythology. In the view of many protesters, Stalin's merits consisted precisely in the fact that his character and deeds had been amenable to mythic representation, providing a set of images capable of inspiring the populace at difficult times. The power of Stalin's 'name' (*imya*) and its symbolic and mythic associations was accorded primary importance in war; people were said to have fought, and died, in battle proclaiming Stalin's name, a slogan that had been extremely prevalent in wartime propaganda.[44] A particularly vivid elaboration on these slogans came in a letter to Molotov from a party member in April, who called the speech 'an affront to all the people (*narod*), including those who, proclaiming Stalin's name, went to fight the Germans, threw themselves beneath German tanks'.[45] Furthermore, it was alleged that those who had lived through the war would never renounce their feelings for Stalin ('we loved, love and will love Stalin').[46] This highly rhetorical identification of Stalin's name with Soviet patriotism and indeed with the Soviet people themselves meant that Khrushchev's attacks on Stalin had insulted the Soviet people, and threatened to deconstruct the war myth along with the Stalin cult ('where's the sense now in our trampling that banner into the mud?').[47]

In such arguments, there appeared a paradoxical acceptance that Stalin may not have been exactly as depicted in official propaganda, but that the burnished and magnified images of the cult still fulfilled an important cultural function, as argued in an anonymous letter to Molotov: 'The time has not yet come to exchange a leader (*vozhd'*) for collective leadership (I'm talking about the popular psyche). People still needed a leader (*vozhd'*). Lenin was that kind of leader, and Stalin too became one.[48] In this argument, the myths constructed around Stalin answered a psychological need in the Soviet people and spurred them on to succeed in his name. Indeed, authors frequently were quick to admit their own helpless need for leadership, as in one *anonimka* to Molotov, which claimed that 'the people without a leader is like a flock of sheep'.[49]

However, the very fact that the *new* leadership, Khrushchev chief amongst them, was willing to ignore, and even denigrate, these myths dramatically affected popular trust in the post-Stalin regime. In these statements, alongside the reverent attitude to the Stalin cult, and his past leadership, there emerged a strikingly *irreverent* attitude to the post-Stalinist leadership. One letter to Malenkov, for instance, was categorical in its disdain for party attempts to impose a new narrative of Stalinism 'from above' (*sverkhu*), claiming that the masses were more than capable of independent judgement (which would, naturally, reject Khrushchev's 'stupid, vulgar and cynical speech').[50] Another letter similarly claimed retrospective revisionism was doomed to failure – 'what's past is past. In the people's memory, he remains a great leader (*velikii vozhd'*)'.[51]

Elsewhere, the new leadership and its supporters were accused of wilful or unintentional amnesia; one group of Muscovite women urged Molotov to help Stalin 'who of late has been mercilessly slandered. It's clear that the Soviet people *have forgotten* Stalin's merits'.[52] This amnesia would have to be 'cured' by the robust health of popular memory, and its maintenance of Stalin's 'glorious memory':

> By tarnishing the glorious memory of Iosif Vissarionovich Stalin, they're cutting the ground from beneath themselves (*sami rubiat suk, na kotorom sidiat*). Now everything's being blamed on a dead man, there's nothing simpler, they're smearing him and forgetting his merits . . . nothing good will come of this persecution of Stalin, except disgrace for the party.[53]

This letter reminded Khrushchev that the success of his project to write the old images of Stalin out of history was dependent on the consent of the people in whom popular memory resided.

Consenting to de-Stalinisation meant, at the most basic level, conceding that the official imagery had been a cult. However, this leap of faith, or away from the former faith, was often refused, as in another letter to Molotov:

> They're claiming that, you know, Stalin was always propagandising himself in works of art, that this, you know, caused great harm, and all

> kinds of other rubbish (you see, the people loved Stalin, and they love him still!)[54]

Without this basic assent to the revisionist view of the cult *as cult*, it was the authorities' narratives of de-Stalinisation which would be seen, and ridiculed, as a complete fiction (or 'cock-and-bull story', in the words of one letter), whilst the old views of Stalin would be perpetuated as sincere and genuine popular traditions.[55] In all of these arguments, therefore, the 'people' were not only represented as more responsible *custodians* of the national past and its invented traditions, but also as stalwart *defenders* of those memories against the leadership's assaults on them.

The rejection of the historical narrative imposed 'from above' led to some quite radical revisions of relations between party and people. One writer claimed, for instance, that 'we are not puppets, who can be twisted this way and that . . . but the thing is, people aren't used here to taking account of the opinion of the masses (*'schitat'sia s mneniem mass*)', whilst another echoed this call for public opinion surveys by suggesting that any decision on removing Stalin from the mausoleum ought to be decided by a secret national referendum.[56] In some ways, this binary opposition of people banded together against the party and defiant in their independent version of history was at least as controversial as the type of rightist dissent which was punished. The provenance of these anonymous letters was assiduously investigated, which suggests that they aroused concern in the leadership, but a more reliable indication of the authorities' attitude to this kind of dissent lies in the party's response to public statements of conservative sentiment, at party meetings.

Tellingly, these elicited mild rebukes and were chalked up to propaganda failures. In the Tatar republic, for example, a communist worker at a construction trust spoke out at a closed party meeting, using language strikingly similar to that used in the above letters:

> As far as Comrade Stalin's cult of personality is concerned, I don't entirely agree. Under Stalin's leadership, we won the fatherland war, and he has many merits and we can't take them away from him, and Stalin's not to blame in all this, it's enemies who are responsible.[57]

Comrade Alsaeva compounded her offence after the meeting by acting 'tactlessly' and becoming agitated. At the next meeting of the organisation, she was roundly condemned by her fellow communists for her 'incorrect' speech and behaviour, although she repented sufficiently to limit her formal punishment to a mark on her party card. The way she was treated confirms that the language of the cult was no longer acceptable, but also suggests, however, that its deployment was a less serious offence than so-called 'anti-Soviet dissent'.

This was confirmed by the mild rebuke issued to another public defender of Stalin, a collective farm chairman (and former KGB officer), who used a familiar battery of arguments in his defence of Stalin:

> No-one approves of these accusations, the people are up in arms . . . we know Stalin as a former political exile, as a party theorist, as the writer of a whole host of works, for having routed anti-Leninist groups, and to insult him would be totally incorrect and unacceptable![58]

Although this language was largely indistinguishable from the militant claims made under cover of anonymity, its public articulation only earned the speaker a mild rebuke for 'misunderstanding' the import of de-Stalinisation. Attachment to the cult was therefore viewed as a sign of backwardness, which could be corrected with further propaganda, rather than as a sign of ideological deviation. This was certainly true of the groups, such as the young, whose more intense exposure, and potential vulnerability, to the cult was of particular concern to the leadership, as well as the caring representatives of the *narod* mentioned above.[59] It is difficult not to agree with the Russian Scholar M. Zezina that the threat from this end of the political spectrum was significantly under-estimated.[60]

The corollary to this disdain for the current leadership was an equally scandalous willingness to engage in bruising verbal attacks against their beliefs *and* characters. This kind of transgressive discourse, as it emerged *from the opposite side of the political spectrum* over this period, has been amply documented.[61] However, 'anti-Soviet' attackers of the Soviet system shared much common ground, in terms of their aggressive language and scandalous attitudes, with those who longed for its complete restoration along high Stalinist lines. In fact, the discourse of opposition to de-Stalinisation closely resembled Stalin-era letters of denunciation, one of the great 'epistolary genres' of high Stalinism.[62] In their denunciations *of* the regime (rather than *to* it, as had usually been the case in the Stalin era), the most ardent defenders of the former faith viciously attacked the new regime's discourse of de-mythologisation and aggressively refused to recognise the authority of the post-Stalinist leadership.

Thus, the absolute belief in the tropes of the cult was often complemented by an absolute refusal to believe the claims contained in the Secret Speech. The speech was often described as untrue (*lozh'*, or the more bruising colloquialism, *lipa*), or, less strongly, but with the same sense of indignation, as nothing more than slander (*kleveta*) or tittle-tattle (*boltovnia*).[63] A letter from a certain Petrov in Polotsk, for instance, made a bold stand 'against slander and lies on [*sic*] Stalin', and criticised Khrushchev's attempts to 'slander' thirty glorious years of Soviet history.[64] By belittling the status of this 'official' discourse, making it seem the very opposite of objective, rational assessment, such accusations also aimed to maintain the monumental myths of Stalin intact and lend them the appearance of objective truth.[65] Similar terms appeared in anonymous notes and leaflets picked up by the KGB in the wake of the Secret Speech, in Gomel' ('enemies of the people ... are besmirching Stalin's name ... Comrades, don't believe it, it's a *lie*')[66], and in Vologda (describing the speech as 'tittle-tattle').[67]

At other times, the speech came in for more colourful criticism, again reminiscent of the derogatory language of Stalinist denunciation. The trope of 'dirt' or 'muck' (*griaz'*) was frequently used to dismiss de-Stalinisation as a 'smear campaign', and its perpetrators as similarly dirty and immoral. In a letter to Molotov, one critic pointed out that the people were 'extremely unhappy' with official attempts [to] 'sully Stalin's reputation' (*oblivat' griaz'iu Stalina*).[68] Another, to Malenkov, lamented the presentation of Stalin's life and works 'in such a sordid (*griaznyi*) way'.[69] At the meeting of Chelyabinsk provincial party committee (*obkom*), held to discuss the 20th Party Congress, the chairman mentioned one question submitted to the meeting by a communist, asking 'was it necessary to do all of this muck-raking?' (*sleduet li podnimat' vsiu etu griaz'?*)'.[70] His commentary on the question gives a clue to the earliest party line on the cult, and on this particular form of criticism – 'surely we're not muck-raking? We're raking over a bitter tragedy, which was the result of our having raised the cult of personality up to a God, a dictator'.[71] Other related terms used to describe the campaign included rough equivalents of the English expressions, 'smear campaign' (*oblivanie pomoiami*) and 'airing dirty laundry' (*sor iz izby ne brosaiut*).[72] All of these accusations implied that the Stalin cult had, as many scholars have argued, a significant 'aestheticising' function, although in these letters, the façade of the Stalin cult was usually imagined as a genuine source of pride and joy.[73] By contrast to the joyous technicolor rituals of Stalinist public culture, the sordid ritual of raking over the Stalinist past was a poor performance indeed, made all the more so by the uneasy, underhand way in which the revelations had been 'performed' to the public.

At other times, as so often when accusations of smear campaigns are bandied around, the perpetrators of the campaign themselves – that is, Khrushchev, and occasionally Mikoyan – came in for severe criticism, variously as 'bastards'[74] , prostitutes, bog-dwellers, and alcoholics.[75] Additionally, because de-Stalinisation had been a posthumous campaign, Khrushchev and his cronies came in for criticism as cowards who hit a man when he was down, took up the fight when the physical danger had passed (*posle draki kulakami ne mashut*),[76] 'were fighting a dead man',[77] or, worse still, had violated the sanctity of the memory of the dead, as forbidden by proverbs such as 'shame on he who violates his father's grave' (*pozor tomu pakhariu/chto ottsa mogilu vspashet*)[78] and 'don't hit a man when he's down' (*lezhashchego ne b'iut*).[79] Such violations were bound to haemmorrhage popular support for the regime; one letter from a certain Kharitonov in Odessa claimed 'the people (*narod*) are outraged by this', whilst an anonymous letter from Sverdlovsk also pointed out that 'the people (*narod*) are unhappy that all sins have been heaped on the deceased Stalin'.[80] In all cases, these statements drew a deliberately worrying picture of popular national tradition and moral norms gathered in concert against the ill-advised, even immoral, activities of the new Soviet leadership. By replacing, or supplementing, subjective political arguments with apparently objective, 'civilised' norms, these letters presented the preservation of the Stalin myth as natural and necessary. However, they also pointed out the appeal of stability and tradition, rather than disruptive revisionism, an insight which exercised more and more influence on the Soviet authorities' stance as the year went on.

Naturally, this rhetoric hardly reflected the true scale of opposition to de-Stalinisation – these were, after all, people who were concerned enough to write in to the leadership and more likely to invent supporters. Nevertheless, it does suggest that the Khrushchev administration's policies on the Stalin cult satisfied *neither* the more radical 'democrats', *nor* the more conservative defenders of Stalin. In this sense, the cardinal dynamic of de-Stalinisation, and arguably its most damaging consequence, was the bifurcation of the Soviet public 'into two camps', leaving the party occupying an isolated middle ground.[81] In the matter of reassessing Stalin, it might be said, there could be no half measures. However, half measures were exactly the course pursued by the leadership until at least 1961, in the party's published resolution on the cult in July 1956, the partial rehabilitation of Stalin in public discourse thereafter, and the decision – or non-decision – to leave cult sites, such as the Stalin mausoleum, statues and museums, as they were before February 1956.[82]

However, this irresolute stance on everything from mentioning Stalin's name, to hanging his portrait, to reading his works, did nothing to satisfy the supporters of the cult, for whom equivocation on the matter of Stalin's status was tantamount to treason. This is evident from the continuing flood of correspondence to the leadership, even after the July resolution, a concession which had gone some way to satisfying conservatives *within* the leadership, according to Kaganovich's memoirs.[83] Letters, however, continued to arrive at the Central Committee, containing the same kind of critiques of de-Stalinisation, and claiming that Stalin was as great as ever.[84] The Hungarian and Polish crises only added grist to their writers' mill. Numerous letters to the Soviet leadership and the journal *Kommunist* in autumn and winter 1956 scolded the leadership for allowing these crises to arise, by destroying Stalin's authority, the linchpin which had kept the Soviet empire together. One non-anonymous letter to *Kommunist* found in the centrifugal chaos of late 1956 ample justification for the 'strong hand' stance of:

> THE GREAT LEADER, whose unbreakable will, diamond-hard and precise mind, was able to unite into one great, united force one half of the globe

> ... could not be a 'humble little man' ... a 'nice old granddaddy' (*lichnost' skromnenkii ... dobrenkii diadushka*)[85]

In the same file, another writer was not quite so bold, not affixing his name to a similar claim that the crisis in Hungary would not have happened had Stalin still been alive.[86] The blame for the Hungarian crisis was placed firmly on the Secret Speech in numerous other letters to the Soviet leadership.[87] Furthermore, despite the leadership's decisive response (which, to many, looked quintessentially Stalinist), these letters lamented the regime's *inability* to respond in a Stalinist manner (*po-Staliniski*),[88] and claimed that 'everywhere, in every place, we need Stalin's iron word (*Stalinskoe zheleznoe slovo*)'.[89]

For these writers, then, there was no way back from the 'original sin' of having penned the Secret Speech. In fact, the July resolution, and subsequent retractions of the worst of Khrushchev's criticisms induced at least one observer to *intensify* his attacks on the current leaders for their past errors of judgement:

> If Stalin *has* been unjustly, undeservedly slandered and insulted ... then Stalin's name should be lifted up, cleaned of all the muck and dirt that Khrushchev, Mikoyan and others hurled at him, and the people who perpetrated this dreadful deed [the Secret Speech] should be sacked from the leadership.[90]

Like most of the letters examined here, the author of this anonymous letter from Krasnodar harboured a sincere faith in Stalin *and* in the possibility of the purification and resurrection of the Stalin myth. Like most of our authors, too, he viewed the restoration of the Stalin *faith* as fundamentally incompatible with the political survival of those who had condemned it as a *cult*. However minor the threat posed by 'Stalin's army', this argument went to the heart of the post-Stalinist authorities' struggle to construct a new political order. It presented Khrushchev with the stark choice between the resort to Stalinist bases of legitimacy, impossible for a man so closely identified with the campaign against the cult, and a definitive abandonment of the cult.

In the end, the mobilisational power of de-Stalinisation won out over half-hearted concessions to the implacable defenders of Stalin. The public denunciation of Stalin at the 22nd Party Congress was motivated by a complex combination of political and moral calculations, but its effect in the public sphere was to make clear for the first time that militant protest against de-Stalinisation *was* the greater evil, and that a commitment to 'overcoming the cult' was the only acceptable stance on the Stalin question.[91] As a more easily readable, and less shocking discourse of de-Stalinisation, the Congress's criticisms of Stalin provoked far less public tumult. However, where objections to the party's course did emerge, as they did, for example, in

Stalingrad during the city's renaming, the party was quick and decisive in its intervention, subjecting the remaining defenders of Stalin to a combination of intensive propaganda and strict disciplinary measures.[92] For a few years, the Stalin question was closed; only in the Brezhnev era did the leadership begin to sound out the possibility of ceasing, or perhaps even reversing, de-Stalinisation, appealing to a pronounced sense of dissatisfaction with de-Stalinisation, both within its own ranks and in some sectors of Soviet society (notably the army).[93] The fact that some 're-Stalinisation' could be countenanced suggests, at least, that there remained a constituency within the Soviet leadership in favour of building upon remnants of the Stalin myth which had survived de-Stalinisation. At most, it suggests that the Stalin myth still enjoyed some popularity, and could fulfil a useful function in the Soviet public sphere, both in providing a more stable foundation for party legitimacy, and also in sealing off intractable questions of culpability for the crimes of the Stalin era.

In analysing the discourse of protest against de-Stalinisation, we cannot hope to gain a good sense of the *quantitative* importance of conservative sentiment during the anti-Stalin campaign. Instead, however, it can be read *qualitatively*, as an expression of 'post-cult malaise', which raised larger questions about the viability of rewriting myth using historical narrative 'from above'. In many cases, the sincere faith in Stalin's authority, expressed through repetition of the cult's epithets, was counterposed to a transgressive negation of present-day authority, expressed through a combination of Stalinist-style denunciation, proverbial wisdom and an insistent invocation of the alleged spirit of the *narod*. Whilst professing the need for strong leadership, therefore, those below (the *nizy*) began to question the prerogatives and authority of those on high (the *verkhy*). During de-Stalinisation, therefore, the Soviet leadership was attacked from two sides whose differences in ideology should not mask the similarities in their strategies and discourses of resistance. As has been shown here, protest against the party's specific course of de-Stalinisation issued not only from those whose faith in *Soviet socialism* had been shaken, but also from those whose faith in *Stalin* remained, to the end, unshakeable.

Notes

1. R. Thompson, 'Reassessing Personality Cults: The Case of Stalin and Mao', *Studies in Comparative Communism*, 21: 1(1988), pp. 99–128. On the revision of Stalinist, and later Leninist, history, see R. W. Davies, *Soviet History in the Gorbachev Revolution* (London, 1989).
2. A. Pyzhikov, '"XX s"ezd i obshchestvennoe mnenie', *Svobodnaya mysl'*, no. 8 (2000), pp. 76–85. Khrushchev, in his memoirs, emphasised the moral over the political motivations: N. S. Khrushchev, *Khrushchev Remembers*, trans. Strobe Talbott (London, 1971).
3. Term from S. Cohen, 'The Stalin Question Since Stalin' in id., *Rethinking the Soviet Experience: Politics and History Since 1917* (New York, 1986), pp. 93–127.

4. J. Held (ed.) *The Cult of Power: Dictators in the Twentieth Century* (Boulder, New York, 1983); G. Gill, 'The Soviet Leader Cult: Reflections on the Structure of Leadership in the Soviet Union', *British Journal of Political Science*, 10:2 (1980), pp. 167–86; B. Ennker, 'The Origins and Intentions of the Lenin Cult' in Ian D. Thatcher (ed.) *Regime and Society in Twentieth Century Russia (*Basingstoke, London 1999), pp. 118–28; J. Brooks, *Thank You, Comrade Stalin! Soviet Public Culture from Revolution to Cold War* (Princeton, NJ, 2000).
5. Ennker, 'Origins and Intentions'; also N. Tumarkin, *Lenin Lives! The Lenin Cult in Soviet Russia* (Cambridge, Mass., 1997) and O. Velikanova, *Making of an Idol: On Uses of Lenin* (Göttingen, 1996).
6. Brooks, *Thank You, Comrade Stalin!*; V. Bonnell, *Iconography of Power: Soviet Political Posters under Lenin and Stalin* (Berkeley, Cal., 1997).
7. Notably Tsarist paternalism – S. Fitzpatrick, *Everyday Stalinism: Ordinary Life in Extraordinary Times – Soviet Russia in the 1930s* (Oxford, 1999), p. 15; E. Gromov, *Stalin. Vlast' i iskusstvo* (Moscow, 1998), p. 172; S. Davies, 'The "Cult" of the *Vozhd'*: Representations in Letters from 1934 to 1941', *Russian History*, 24: 1–2 (1997), pp. 131–47.
8. S. Kotkin, *Magnetic Mountain: Stalinism as a Civilization* (Berkeley, 1995); Brooks, *Thank You, Comrade Stalin*; Davies, 'The "Cult" of the *Vozhd'* '; K. Petrone, *Life Has Become More Joyous, Comrades: Celebrations in the Time of Stalin* (Bloomington, Ind., 2000).
9. J. Hellbeck, 'Fashioning the Stalinist Soul: The Diary of Stepan Podlubnyi (1931–1939)', *Jahrbücher für Geschichte Osteuropas* (1996), no. 3, pp. 344–73; see also I. Halfin, *Language and Revolution: Making Modern Political Identities* (London, 2002).
10. V. Naumov, 'K istorii sekretnogo doklada N. S. Khrushcheva na XX s"ezde KPSS', *Novaya i noveishaya istoriya*, no. 4 (1996), pp. 147–68. On 'anti-Soviet' dissent see R. Pikhoya, *Sovetskii Soyuz: istoriya vlasti, 1945–91* (Moscow, 1998); M. Gorshkov, O. Volobuev and V. Zhuravlev (eds), *Vlast' i oppozitsiya: Rossiiskii politicheskii protsess dvadtsatogo stoletiya* (Moscow, 1995).
11. M. Kramer, 'New Evidence on Soviet Decision-Making and the 1956 Polish and Hungarian Crises', *Cold War International History Project Bulletin*, no. 8–9 (winter 1996), at http://www.wwics.si.edu.
12. H. Salisbury, *Moscow Journal: The End of Stalin* (Chicago, 1961), pp. 335–55; Yu. Polyakov, 'Pokhorony Stalina. Vzglyad istorika-ochevidtsa', *Novaya i noveishaya istoria*, nos 4–5 (1994), pp. 195–207; L. Alekseyeva and P. Goldberg, *The Thaw Generation: Coming of Age in the Post-Stalin Era* (Toronto, 1990).
13. Polly Jones, 'From Stalinism to Post-Stalinism. De-Mythologising Stalin, 1953–56' in H. Shukman (ed.) *Redefining Stalinism* (London, 2003), pp. 127–45.
14. A. Knight, *Beria: Stalin's First Lieutenant* (Princeton, NJ, 1993).
15. R. Service, 'The Road to the Twentieth Congress', *Soviet Studies*, no. 2 (1981), pp. 232–45; V. Saechnikov and G. Sagatelian, 'Sovetskoe obshchestvo: politicheskie kampanii 50-kh godov' in V. Lelchuk and G. Sagatelian (eds) *Sovetskoe obshchestvo: budni kholodnoi voiny. Materialy 'kruglogo stola', Institut Rossiiskoi istorii. RAN 29 Marta 2000 g* (Moscow-Arzamas, 2000), pp. 305–35.
16. M. Zezina, 'Crisis in the Union of Soviet Writers in the Early 1950s', *Europe-Asia Studies*, 46: 4 (1994), pp. 649–62.
17. A. Mikoyan, *Tak bylo: Razmyshleniya o minuvshem* (Moscow, 1999).
18. Yu. Aksiutin and A. Pyzhikov, *Poststaliniskoe obshchestvo: problemy liderstva i transformatsiia vlasti* (Moscow, 1999), which describes the speech as 'crossing the rubicon'; and Vol'noe ekonomicheskoe obshchestvo Rossii, *Kruglyi stol, '40 let*

zakrytogo doklada N. S. Khrushcheva XX s"ezdu O kul'te lichnosti i ego posledstviyakh', 24.2.96 (Moscow, 1996).

19. Gorshkov, Volobuev and Zhuravlev (eds) *Vlast' i oppozitsiya*; Alekseyeva, and Goldberg, *The Thaw Generation*; c.f. E. Zubkova, *Russia After the War: Hopes, Illusions and Disappointments, 1945–57* (Armonk, NY, 1998).
20. On intelligentsia dissent, see e.g. M. R. Zezina, *Sovetskaya khudozhestvennya intelligentsiya i vlast' v 1950–60-e gody* (Moscow, 1999). On the resumption of repression of political dissent, see e.g. V. Naumov, 'Diskussii i obsuzhdeniya – N. S. Khrushchev, lichnost', vremya, reformy', *Svobodnaya mysl'*, no. 10 (1994), pp. 27–32; examples of punishment of anti-Soviet dissent can be found in Pikhoya, *Sovetskii Soyuz*, and in P. Jones, 'Strategies of De-Mythologisation in Post-Stalinism and Post-Leninism: A Comparison of De-Stalinisation and De-Leninisation', DPhil. diss., University of Oxford, 2002, pp. 116–24.
21. Iurii Aksiutin in his 'Popular responses to Khrushchev' in A. Gleason, S. Khrushchev and W. Taubman, *Nikita Khrushchev* (New Haven, Conn., 2000), pp. 177–208, concludes that the Secret Speech was not well received or understood by the people, after so many years of exposure to the cult.
22. Term taken from R. Tucker, *The Soviet Political Mind. Stalinism and Post-Stalin Change* (London, 1972).
23. See Jones, 'From Stalinism to post-Stalinism'.
24. Rossiiskii Gosudarstvennyi Arkhiv Noveishei Istorii (RGANI) (Russian State Archive of Contemporary History), 5/32/43 9.
25. RGANI, 5/32/45 62.
26. RGASPI (Russian State Archives of Socio-Political History), 82/2/1467 52.
27. RGASPI, 82/2/1470 59.
28. Ibid.
29. Brooks, *Thank You, Comrade Stalin!*
30. Davies, 'The Cult of the *vozhd'*'. Concrete examples of letters to the authorities can be found in A. Livshin and I. Orlov (eds) *Pis'ma vo vlast' 1917–1927: zayavleniya, zhaloby, donosy, pis'ma v gosudarstvennye struktury i sovetskim vozhdyam* (Moscow, 1998).
31. S. Bittner, 'Local Soviets, Public Order, and Welfare After Stalin: Appeals from Moscow's Kiev Raion', *Russian Review*, 62: 2, pp. 281–93. Letter-writing was actively encouraged in the Khrushchev era, as a (strictly limited) form of 'criticism from below' (*kritika snizu*), e.g. 'Ne otmakhivat'sia ot pisem', *Pravda*, 3.8.58, p. 2. One of the most frequent uses of letters was to request rehabilitation: see M. Dobson, 'Refashioning the Enemy: Popular Beliefs and the Rhetoric of De-Stalinisation, 1953–64', PhD diss., School of Slavonic and East European Studies, London, 2003. Letters are mostly drawn from the following *fondy/opisi*: RGASPI, f.82 (Molotov); f. 83 (Malenkov); f.599 (*Kommunist*); RGANI, 5/30/140 (materials, including newspaper correspondence, dating from discussion of July resolution and other published materials on Stalin cult from 1956).
32. RGANI, 5/32/46 202–11.
33. RGANI, 5/32/46 204.
34. RGANI, 5/32/46 205–6.
35. RGASPI 82/2/1470 59.
36. RGASPI, 83/1/35 130–8.
37. RGASPI, 82/2/1470 66.
38. Materials on Georgia in V. Kozlov, *Massovye besporiadki v SSSR pri Khrushcheve i Brezhneve* (Novosibirsk, 1999), pp. 155–83 and e.g. RGANI, 5/30/140 52–68.
39. RGANI, 5/32/46 210.

40. RGANI, 5/32/46 209; GARF, 7523/75/16 197.
41. RGANI, 5/3245 88; TsKhDMO, 1/32/810 8.
42. RGASPI, 82/2/1470 .56.
43. RGASPI 82/2/1467 26; RGASPI, 82/2/1467 3; Ibid., 1.27.
44. RGASPI, 82/2/1467 30.
45. RGASPI, 82/2/467 17.
46. RGASPI, 82/2/1470 63.
47. RGANI, 5/30/140 183; see another use of banner trope RGASPI, 82/2/1467 30 (a non-anonymous letter from Leningrad).
48. RGASPI 82/2/1467 48.
49. RGASPI, 82/2/467 22.
50. RGASPI, 83/1/35 130–8 (letter entitled 'This is what the Soviet people think'). See an anonymous letter from Stalingrad sent to Molotov 'in connection with this campaign . . . *conjured up from above* of slander against the Great Stalin' (RGASPI, 82/2/1467 1; my italics).
51. RGASPI, 82/ 2/1470 24.
52. RGASPI, 82/2/1470 63.
53. RGASPI, 82/2/1470 56 (my italics) and 19.
54. RGASPI, 82/2/1467 2.
55. RGASPI, 82/2/1467 28.
56. RGASPI, 82/2/1467 25, 27.
57. RGANI, 5/32/46 195.
58. RGANI, 5/32/45 86.
59. The Komsomol monitored youth reaction to the speech, and found significant reserves of 'cultic' sentiment amongst, for example, young factory workers. Tsentral'nyi khranitel' dokumentov molodezhnykh organizatsii (Central Document Repository of Youth Organisations- TsKhDMO), 1/32/810 7 ('Stalin has such great merits').
60. M. Zezina, 'Shokovaya terapiya: ot 1953-go k 1956 godu', *Otechestvennaya istoriya,* no. 2 (1995), pp. 121–35.
61. V. Kozlov and S. Mironenko (eds), *58–10. Nadzornye proizvodstva Prokuratury SSSR po delam ob antisovetskoi agitatsii i propagandy. Mart 1953–1991* (Moscow, 1999).
62. S. Fitzpatrick and R. Gellately (eds) *Accusatory Practices: Denunciation in Modern European History, 1789–1989* (Chicago, 1997).
63. RGANI, 5/31/54 10.
64. RGASPI, 82/2/1470 66.
65. RGASPI, 82/2/1467 1; Ibid., 1.15.
66. RGANI, 5/31/54 11.
67. RGANI, 5/32/45 5.
68. RGASPI, 82/2/1467 26.
69. RGASPI, 83/1/35 30–8.
70. RGASPI, 556/1/1195 148.
71. Ibid. Note, however, the mild incoherence of the response (raising the cult, rather than Stalin), typical of local authorities' improvisational responses to difficult questions.
72. RGANI, 5/30/141 114 (letter to Pospelov).
73. See, for example, Petrone, *Life Has Become More Joyous*; B. Groys, *The Total Art of Stalinism: Avant-Garde, Aesthetic Dictatorship and Beyond* (Princeton, NJ, 1992).
74. RGANI, 5/30/140 8.
75. RGASPI, 82/2/1467 5; RGASPI, 83/1/35 138; RGASPI, 82/2/1470 70.

76. RGASPI, 82/2/1467 24. This trope remained common: see a letter to *Pravda* after the July resolution, RGANI, 5/30/140 92.
77. RGASPI, 82/2/1470 62.
78. RGASPI, 82/2/1467 4.
79. Ibid., 1.24.
80. RGASPI, 82/2/1470 67–8.
81. As alleged in a letter to Molotov, RGASPI, 82/2/1467 22.
82. See Jones, 'From Stalinism to Post-Stalinism'. Dissatisfaction with the July resolution was widespread on both sides, being seen as too mild and ambiguous by both conservatives and radicals. For a sample of this range of opinion, see letters to *Pravda* in RGANI, 5/30/140.
83. L. Kaganovich, *Pamiatnye zapiski rabochego, kommunista-Bol'shevika, profsoiuznogo, partiinogo i sovetsko-gosudarstvennogo rabotnika* (Moscow, 1996), pp. 429–527.
84. RGANI, 5/30/140 100.
85. RGASPI, 599/1/101 7–10.
86. RGASPI, 599/1/89 32.
87. RGASPI, 82/2/1470 .80; RGASPI, 82/2/1467.58; RGANI, 5/30/140 196.
88. RGASPI, 82/2/1470 73; cf. ibid., 1.74, 81, 90.
89. RGASPI, 82/2/1467 64.
90. RGASPI, 82/2/1470 80.
91. H. Achminow, 'A Decade of de-Stalinization', *Studies on the Soviet Union*, 5: 3 (1965), pp. 11–20.
92. Tsentr dokumentatsii noveishei istorii Volgogradskoi oblasti (Volgograd party archive, TsDNIVO), 594/1/31; TsDNIVO, 71/37/32 98.
93. Cohen, 'The Stalin Question'; V. Zaslavsky, *The Neo-Stalinist State: Class, Ethnicity and Consensus in Soviet Society* (Brighton, 1982); and N. Tumarkin, *The Living and the Dead. The Rise and the Fall of the Cult of World War II in Russia* (New York, 1994), which indicates the importance of stabilising Stalin's image in order to stabilise the myth of the Second World War.

14

Surviving 1956: Gheorghe Gheorghiu-Dej and the 'Cult of Personality' in Romania

Alice Mocanescu

In 1956 Khrushchev's 'Secret Speech', the Polish unrest and the Hungarian uprising created the greatest unrest in Eastern Europe since the establishment of communism. The influence of those events was felt differently in the countries of the Soviet Bloc and local leaders adopted various tactics in their attempts to contain the challenge posed to the status quo by those proceedings. This chapter deals with the impact of Khrushchev's speech in Romania. It attempts to identify the strategies adopted by the Romanian leadership to diminish its influence and to get rid of those who, using this opportunity, attacked the position of the general secretary of the Romanian Workers' Party (RWP), Gheorghe Gheorghiu-Dej. This specific episode has been examined by various scholars. Dennis Deletant analyses it as part of a larger investigation of the role played by the political police during the Gheorghiu-Dej regime, as one of the main charges lodged against him was of the use of terror and intimidation prior to 1956.[1] Stelian Tănase and Vladimir Tismăneanu approach the events of 1956 in terms of individual and interest group conflicts within the party.[2] This chapter focuses primarily on the investigation of the accusations regarding strictly the 'personality cult'. Furthermore, it will explore the strategies adopted by Gheorghiu-Dej to restrain the consequences of the speech and its employment by his opponents.

In order to understand better the focus of the accusations brought against Gheorghiu-Dej by his critics following Khrushchev's 'Secret Speech', as well as his response to those allegations, a short investigation of the extent of the leader cult in Romania prior to 1956 is essential.

The communist leader cult in Romania before 1956

As in the other countries of the Soviet Bloc, the dominant leader cult in Romania before 1956 was that of Stalin. Imposed simultaneously with political and economic Soviet patterns, the cult of Stalin was the most visible method of Sovietising Romania, ending up by gradually encompassing all other aspects of the process. The name of Stalin became through time synonymous with the idea of constructing socialism, a guarantee of communism's future growth in Romania, and the defence of peace and socialism. At the beginning, this was a more concrete image, which proved easy to disseminate, without arousing immediate negative attitudes from ordinary Romanians. Whilst the replacement of the political elite, forced industrialisation and the collectivisation of agriculture generated massive social disturbance, the dissemination of Stalin's cult was seen as a less harmful way to induce positive feelings towards the Soviet Union. Furthermore, it was far easier to accept a reluctant and, at the same time, paternal figure rather than the myth of 'the liberating Red Army'.

This is not to say that a cult of Gheorghe Gheorghiu-Dej did not exist in Romania at all before Stalin's death. On the contrary, it emerged shortly after the communists came to power and carefully carved out its own sphere, emulating and mimicking the cult of Stalin, whilst Gheorghiu-Dej continued to proclaim himself as a promoter of the Stalin cult. It covered, all the main forms of mass adulation (chanting of his name during mass demonstrations, renaming places in his honour, the sending of letters of congratulation, and so on).[3] Furthermore, Gheorghiu-Dej's domestic cult grew particularly powerful from the late fifties. In other words, Dej gradually moved to a central and unchallenged position within the top of the party hierarchy, and projected himself as such in his relationships with the other members of the leadership. In point of fact, this manoeuvring was at the crux of allegations made against him by his opponents in 1956.

The comparison of two important anniversary moments – the anniversary of Stalin's 70th birthday in 1949 and that of Dej's 50th birthday in 1951 – offers a good opportunity to assess the two cults in parallel. The comparison is based on the analysis of the manner in which these two events were treated in *Scînteia* (*The Spark*), the official daily of the Romanian Workers' Party. It becomes quickly evident from reading *Scînteia* that the space devoted to Stalin's anniversary was disproportionally larger than that allocated to Dej's 1951 anniversary. Nevertheless, it is evident that the same scheme was employed and the same repertoire of formulas used in both celebrations.

The official celebration of Stalin's 70th anniversary began well in advance of 21 December 1949. A campaign of 'socialist competition' between all important industrial units and branches had been launched on 25 October.[4] Prior to this date, Stalin's image was constantly present in the party's newspaper, being linked to different events and celebrations. For instance, a similar competition to that launched for Stalin's birthday celebration was initiated for the anniversary of 7 November. Stalin was presented in the materials devoted to this event as the closest collaborator of Lenin during the days of the revolution, as well as the one who continued and implemented Lenin's ideas successfully. Consequently, in the articles describing the great achievements registered since the revolution, Stalin was portrayed as the main guiding voice, guarantor and example. More often than not these articles featured his portrait. On the other hand, events such as 'The International Day of the Struggle for Peace' were used to extol Stalin's personal merits in the liberation from fascism and imposing peace on Europe.[5] Again, a picture of Stalin was employed to reinforce the article's main idea. In addition, the eleventh anniversary of the publication of Stalin's 'Short History Course' was a good opportunity to praise Stalin. Articles were published on the importance of this work, information regarding the circulation of the publication, as well as statistics on the number of Party members who studied the Course.[6] Apart from constant updates on the socialist competition,[7] Stalin's image was kept in the public eye through references to the opening of an exhibition dedicated to Soviet industry,[8] or to the role that the USSR played in the struggle for peace.[9] Many articles dealt with Stalin's contribution to the development of Marxist-Leninist theory.[10] Starting from December, letters of gratitude to Stalin began to be published in *Scînteia*.[11] On 11 December an article was published on the opening in Bucharest of an exhibition of the gifts that were to be sent to Stalin. The article, entitled 'The exhibition of gifts for Comrade Stalin, token of the love and gratitude of our working people' was accompanied by a photograph showing Gheorghiu-Dej and Ana Pauker attentively studying one of the exhibits.[12] As Stalin's birthday neared, a series of conferences was held that endeavoured to deal with every aspect of Stalin's personality. All this culminated with the special session organised by the Romanian Academy where scientific and cultural personalities competed in praising Stalin.[13] This session was just the climax of a wave of meetings, conferences and talks which took place in factories, 'Red Corners', clubs, cultural houses, schools, military units, and so on.[14] This flurry of discussions about Stalin was accompanied by the publication of his speeches and works, as well as of books about his personality. Everything culminated on 21 December with meetings held in various towns and villages, where speeches praising Stalin were delivered.[15]

The anniversary of Gheorghiu-Dej's 50th birthday was covered in *Scînteia* in a far smaller number of issues. Besides the political necessity of maintaining an appropriate proportion of the space devoted to Stalin's birthday anniversary, Gheorghiu-Dej's date of birth (8 November) fell rather inconveniently between the date of the Great October Revolution and Stalin's birthday in December. In comparison with the space dedicated to these two events, Gheorghiu-Dej's birthday anniversary was covered in slightly more than a week.

The first reference to Gheorghiu-Dej's birthday appeared in *Scînteia* on 6 November 1951. A letter of congratulation signed by the RWP's Central Committee, accompanied by Dej's official photograph, was published on the first page.[16] Epithets were scarce and referred to Dej mainly as a faithful follower of Lenin and Stalin.[17] An article by Chivu Stoica, the vice-president of the Council of Ministers, was also published which underlined Dej's role in the consolidation of popular democracy and socialist economy, without omitting Stalin's role as the true teacher and inspiration of Dej. On the third page of the newspaper, there were poems devoted to Dej, as well as telegrams of congratulation from foreign socialist leaders.[18] There were then two days of silence on this topic – including 8 November itself – which were devoted to the 34th anniversary celebration of the Great Socialist Revolution. On 9 November, alongside a long article on 'The Great Force of the Soviet State – the Bastion of Peace' and another one devoted to 'The Unveiling of the Statue of I.V. Stalin in Stalin Town', there was published the decree conferring on Comrade Gheorghe Gheorghiu-Dej the title of 'Hero of Socialist Labour' and the gold medal 'The Sickle and the Hammer' as a token of recognition for 'outstanding services for our motherland, our people, our working class and our Party'.[19] In the following days, the party's daily newspaper published letters of congratulation from Romanian youngsters,[20] from workers from various factories in the country,[21] as well as requests for renaming various industrial units.[22] Furthermore, *Scînteia* also published photographs and descriptions of the delegations that came to Dej to congratulate him. The photographs showed Dej shaking hands with different people, while the descriptions verged on panegyrics, listing mainly the speeches of the delegations' leaders.[23]

The leader cults of both Stalin and Dej, as manifested during their birthday celebrations, were similar in their forms, but differed in their extent and intensity, as well as in their rhetoric. Whilst Stalin's 70th birthday was an international event that was lavishly celebrated, especially within the communist countries,[24] Dej's birthday celebration was confined mainly to the boundaries of Romania. As a consequence of this internal/international dimension of their birthday celebrations, the rhetoric employed was different. Stalin was portrayed as the defender of the international peace and promoter of world communism. Dej was represented as a disciple of Stalin, who following his example, and strove to put into practice his teachings.

Contesting Gheorghiu-Dej – the uncontested leader of the party

Khrushchev's Secret Speech at the 20th Congress of the Communist Party of the Soviet Union in February 1956 had an important impact upon the Romanian leadership and especially upon Gheorghiu-Dej. Gheorghiu-Dej was in a particularly weak position after such an overt exposure of Stalinism. He was identified by Russians and Romanians alike with the period of high Stalinism. He had been the Soviets' main pawn in the attack launched against Tito. Dej delivered the speech 'The Yugoslav Communist Party in the hands of a gang of assassins and spies' at the Cominform meeting in Bucharest in 1949, where Tito and the Yugoslav Party were labelled as agents of American capitalism and imperialism. He also proved his loyalty to Stalin in the fight against Tito by a series of measures directed towards weakening and limiting the spread of the Yugoslav example into Romania.[25] Dej's position was also vulnerable internally, since his figure was associated with the period of unconditional support for the Soviets, economic dependency,[26] mass terror and imprisonment, and the Sovietisation of Romanian culture.[27] Therefore, Khrushchev's speech gave Dej much cause for anxiety.

Gheorghiu-Dej attended the 20th Congress of the Communist Party of the Soviet Union (CPSU) as the head of the Romanian delegation. The other members of the delegation, equally exposed in the unsettling atmosphere in Kremlin, were Iosif Chişinevski, Miron Constantinescu and Petre Borilă. After his return to Romania, Gheorghiu-Dej adopted a wait-and-see tactic. Officially involved in the resolution of the Greek crisis, Dej maintained silence on Khrushchev's revelations for almost a month.[28] When he broached the subject, he did it only within restricted meetings of party members and only doctored versions of the discussions and their conclusions were published in the press. Two recently published documents allow us access to Dej's handling of the issue of the leader cult. The first one is the Report of the RWP's Delegation at the Soviet Congress, presented by Gheorghiu-Dej at the enlarged party Central Committee plenum on 23–25 March 1956. The second is Dej's assessment of the phenomenon of the 'personality cult' in Romania, presented to a select audience of party members at the 'Griviţa Roşie' club. As the views in the two speeches are similar, I shall analyse them in parallel rather than discussing them separately.

The first thing that is worth highlighting is that no reference was made to the speech of Khrushchev *per se*; the report was directed at the works of the Congress in general. Stalin's abuses in his final years and the influence that his cult had had upon political life in Romania were approached only cautiously. It is also interesting to note that Dej did not launch into an attack against Stalin. He singled out Stalin's erroneous practices (personal leadership, bypassing the Central Committee and the Politburo, ignoring the collective leadership, and so on) and personal defects (lack of modesty, intolerance) while stressing his positive role in other fields (the organising and victory of the socialist revolution, his contribution to the development of Marxist theory, the repression of the deviationists, and so on).[29]

Both speeches tackled the issue of the 'cult of personality' within the framework of Marxist-Leninist theory, reiterating its theories of the relationship between the individual and the masses, and pointing to the opposite, defective practice of elevating individuals above the party:

> It seems that in the activity of the Party organisations, of mass organisations, people worked in such a manner that the cult of personality has been developed to a very serious degree. Is it possible, comrades, that a

> single man, no matter how capable he is, can solve the big problems that the construction of socialism involve . . . ? Can a single person replace the Party? Can he be put on the same level as the Party? Can he be confused with the Party? It is well known that the Party is the leading force. The Central Committee is the collective leading force of the Party. Is this an issue that should be addressed only at special occasions, or in lessons or by our agitators? How has it been possible that, in over a certain number of years in our country, this kind of manifestation around a single person has become so powerful, that the name of that person be celebrated? The character and content of these manifestations are wrong, anti-Marxist, and harmful to our Party.[30]

In the report that Dej presented at the enlarged Central Committee plenum, he went further and identified the forms the cult took in Romania. Nevertheless, he did not forget to stress the influence of the Soviet model, to point to the Romanian case as an outgrowth of the former. Moreover, it is worth noting that the forms of the cult he mentioned were only the external ones. He made no reference to his leadership, to eventual shortcomings in the internal activity of the Politburo, or to more delicate matters such as the role played by the political police in previous years. In general, he portrayed himself as a passive subject of the 'personality cult', if not as a 'victim' of the propaganda machine:

> The influence of the personality cult has been evident in our country, taking different forms. Factories, institutions, districts, streets were given the names of some of the members of the leadership of our Party and State.
>
> In journals and newspapers, there were published fictionalised descriptions of the meetings between the Party's and the Government's leaders and the working people. Pieces of literature and musical compositions contributed to the development of the personality cult. One of the most strident manifestations of the cult – the chanting of the leaders' names – was widespread.[31]

Apart from the superficial and incomplete treatment of the issue of the leader cult, Dej was eager to underline his role in downplaying its most extravagant forms in Romania. Therefore, a different section in Dej's speech was devoted to securing his position, in other words to advancing explanations and highlighting the efforts made to eliminate the influence of Stalin's cult in Romania. He mentioned his initiative in summoning representatives of the press and propaganda activists for a briefing at the Central Committee in 1952, on which occasion he denounced the party's excessive praise of the leader:

> No later then 1952, we summoned to the Central Committee, the editors of the central and local newspapers, correspondents, the activists (*aktiv*) of the Central Committee, the Party cadres in representative positions. We showed them what damage they did to the Party through the improper propaganda they promoted, by presenting the meetings of Comrade Dej with the working people in an idyllic light, in a manner that led to the conclusion that it was enough that Comrade Gheorghiu-Dej meet with those people for the problems raised by them to be solved immediately.[32]

A different tactic employed by Gheorghiu-Dej in order to diminish the impact of Khrushchev's speech was that of finding scapegoats. The so-called 'deviationist group', headed by Ana Pauker, Vasile Luca and Teohari Georgescu, were depicted as the main promoters of Stalin's cult in Romania in the late 1940s and early 1950s, and were also themselves the subjects of lavish praise. Finally, Dej claimed that the trial in 1952, which led to the removal of this pro-Moscow troika from the political scene, was an important step in moving away from high Stalinism and, implicitly, the most excessive forms of the cult.[33] Dej was careful to isolate the issue of the 'personality cult' from the larger context of de-Stalinisation. He focused on the external manifestations of the cult, whilst stressing the measures towards de-Stalinisation that already had been taken (the 1952 trial, the most important of them), and that basically the party, its leadership especially, had been already cleansed of servile and dogmatic Stalinists.

By the same token, the prevailing unresolved problems and excesses in the 'cult of personality' were considered a result of short-comings within the system and not as something promoted or encouraged by the leadership itself. The removal of the 'deviationist group' did not lead automatically to the elimination of all those who could propagate the leader cult. Gheorghiu-Dej identified a different group of culprits in the surviving petit-bourgeois elements bent on undermining the people's achievements:

> It is sometimes disgusting to see and listen to petit-bourgeois elements with their velvet-like tongues or sharp and long ones, who know how to spread this cult of personality. The petit-bourgeois or those persons dominated by petit-bourgeois spirit always need superhumans. When superhumans disappear a kind of vacuum occurs around them, they are seized by despair, confusion, lack of focus. They are not able to see where the force of our Party comes from, the grandiose achievements of our working people.[34]

The tactics adopted by the Romanian leadership amongst the wider public was to mimic debate whilst adopting a more critical approach to the leader cult. Although the text of Khrushchev's speech was not distributed publicly,

Scînteia published materials related to it. One article published in the 3 April 1956 issue of the party daily, stated rather laconically that the RWP approved the decisions of the 20th Congress and condemned the 'personality cult' of Stalin as being 'un-Marxist, foreign to the spirit of Leninism'.[35] In the following months, as a consequence of this implied party directive, debates on the cult were organised in various party organisations across the country. They took different forms and, according to *Scînteia*, they were designed to cover as many themes as possible: from simple discussion of the party communiqué, to the emphasis put on the necessity of links with the masses and open exposures of different leaderships' shortcomings in various party organisations in the country. In an interview given to the Yugoslav newspaper, *Politika*, and also published in *Scînteia* as well, Gheorghiu-Dej was asked what measures had been taken by the Politburo to eliminate the negative effects of the 'personality cult'. Dej responded:

> [the documents of the 20th Congress] have been widely discussed during the months April–July within the entire Party. These debates have taken place with the very active participation of the mass of Party members and it demonstrated the development of the ideological level of Party members and their high sense of responsibility.
>
> Our Party regards the fight for the removal of the negative effects of the personality cult not as a campaign but as a permanent activity for the development of internal Party democracy, the consistent application of the Leninist norms in the activity of every Party organisation.

In addition to this generalised imitation of debate, Gheorghiu-Dej maintained a very low profile during the whole year. On the occasion of the anniversary of the National Day of the Popular Republic of Romania, it was not Gheorghiu-Dej who delivered the main address, but the Minister of Defence, Leontin Sălăjan.[36] The photograph published on 25 August 1956, that depicted the official tribune during the mass parade, showed Dej only indistinctly.

Another way in which the idea of reform was compromised, and intellectuals' reactions contained, consisted in manipulating debates and actors in this area too. Whilst advocating the need for change to the mechanical application of the principals of Socialist Realism, Gheorghiu-Dej carefully chose and supported certain people to act as his mouthpiece.[37]

In this atmosphere, the RWP's Politburo convened on 3, 4, 6 and 12 April 1956, at which Dej came under the attack from two members of the Politburo, both of them old collaborators of his: Chişinevski and Constantinescu. First of all, they demanded an open discussion of the CPSU's leader's speech, after the examples of Poland and Hungary. They argued against the superficial treatment of the problem of the 'personality cult' within the enlarged plenum, pointing to the fact that in the document presented there, the period under investigation was limited to the interval up to 1953. Furthermore, they set the question of the leader cult in a larger perspective, insisting that the external manifestations of the cult were not its only and most harmful components.[38] In his speech, Constantinescu singled out the abuses registered in the activity of the Ministry of Internal Affairs both *before* and *after* 1952, the year asserted in Dej's report as the moment when abuses had ended in the party, once Pauker's group had been removed. Constantinescu further linked all these abuses to Gheorghiu-Dej's persona by pointing to the harmful influence which the Ministry of Internal Affairs had had upon Dej.[39] Besides these accusations, Constantinescu also identified deficiencies in the personal style of Dej's leadership, including putting himself above the party, ignoring others' opinions; these were all argued using concrete examples.[40]

Gheorghiu-Dej's tactics to deal with this sudden attack were again thoughtful and astute. He did not respond to the attacks immediately. He waited and took the measure of the situation. Within the meeting on 4 April, other members of the Politburo addressed the issues raised by Constantinescu and Chişinevski the previous day. Their speeches focused on a few recurrent ideas. Firstly, all of them acknowledged that the phenomenon of the 'personality cult' existed in Romania. Stalin's cult had been predominant, and there was Dej's cult as a result and imitation of the former. Secondly, the speeches focused on the idea that nobody was without guilt (implying that nobody had the right to criticise) the whole party leadership contributed to Stalin's and Dej's cults.[41] Furthermore, Chişinevski (as head of propaganda) and Constantinescu (as director of *Scînteia*) were even more involved in the process of implementing and developing those cults. Thirdly, there was a unanimous consensus to point to the 'Ana Pauker group' as the main supporter of Stalin's cult and to consider that with its removal things started to get better in the RWP.

At the session of the Politburo on 12 April 1956 Gheorghiu-Dej delivered a report that concluded the discussions that had taken place during the previous days. The most important point in Dej's report was that, in spite of errors and shortcomings in the evolution of the party, its unity had been maintained. He did not name those responsible for this, mentioning only 'a healthy nucleus' within the party, who managed to obstruct all deviationist initiatives.[42] Furthermore, he identified the culprits in the introduction of the 'personality cult' in Romania as the members of the deviationist group, and emphasised the cult developed around Pauker. Constantinescu was singled out as one of the most willing collaborators of Pauker, one who did nothing at that time to acknowledge publicly or diminish Pauker's cult. In general, Dej's report linked the 'personality cult' to the influence of Pauker's group, the accusers Constantinescu and Chişinevski with the latter and, implicitly, the victory over it with his initiative in removing this group. On the other hand, already feeling secure about his position, with the large majority of the Politburo on his side, Dej did not hesitate to engage in self-criticism. He viewed the existence of his 'personality cult' as the result of the influence of Stalin's cult and as part of a larger phenomenon that manifested itself in the other countries of the Soviet Bloc as well, but he recognised that he had not taken firm action against it either publicly or within the party's structures. Nevertheless, he did not forget to stress his genuine discomfort with any forms of praise:

> I did not take a public and firm attitude, though. It would have been good and right if I had put the problem openly, within the debates of the Politburo and the Central Committee. That is what I should have done if I had wanted to be consistent with my principles . . . My character is not inclined towards the personality cult. I never wanted to be adulated. I would be wrong, though, if I said that I took a firm attitude against this cult.[43]

The meeting of the Politburo ended with no practical measures against the two challengers of the establishment.

The time was not still ripe for a more drastic movement; the situation in the Kremlin was still ambiguous and there was still the suspicion that Constantinescu and Chişinevski were actually just Khrushchev's pawns; Dej himself did not feel confident enough to undertake a more radical initiative. On the other hand, his opponents were not the most suitable challengers of Dej's supremacy. Their past and their direct link with the darkest moments in the history of the party did not recommend them as potential replacements. Furthermore, they did not succeed in forming a coherent opposition group around themselves. Their attempt to attract to their side other members of the Politburo failed and this episode was the main charge brought against them. They were accused of a 'non-party attitude' because they had tried to co-opt, within private discussions, potential supporters for their planned attack against Dej.[44] Finally, they gave up their combative attitude as soon as they came under attack and found themselves isolated within the Politburo. Their attack seems in retrospect to be an impulsive action that took place without enough preparation and support. Most probably they were only actors who interpreted a script written in Moscow.

The impetus to move against them came after Dej proved his fidelity to the Kremlin as its main supporter in the Hungarian crisis.[45] Emerging from this episode as a reliable collaborator, Gheorghiu-Dej felt strong enough to initiate the removal of his two rivals. This took place at the party plenum on 28–29 June and 1–3 July 1957.[46] This coincided with Khrushchev's expulsion of the hardliners from the Politburo, the so-called 'antiparty group' of Malenkov, Molotov, Kaganovich, and Shepilov that was announced on 4 July. However, no concrete archival documents proving a link between the two events or between the two groups have yet emerged.

Constantinescu and Chişinevski were accused of 'grave anti-party actions against the unity of the Party and its leadership' and expelled from the Politburo.[47] The set of charges brought against them a year earlier was extended further; to it was added accusations that they had contributed to the development of Pauker's and Vasile Luca's cults that they had been complicit in the actions of the deviationist group, they had intrigued with other members of the Politburo against the leadership of the party, they had instigated some members against others, they had sapped the party's unity through these practices, and had shown petit-bourgeois arrogance and condescension in their relationships with others.[48] The most important change that took place within this plenum, from the point of view of the leader cult and of the future career of Gheorghiu-Dej, was the new emphasis put on the role which Dej played in the maintenance of the party's unity in 1956. Speaker after speaker praised Dej for dealing adequately with Khrushchev's speech and avoiding, in this way, a situation similar to that existing in Hungary or Poland. Without any doubt, Gheorghiu-Dej was the main hero of the plenum.

Gheorghiu-Dej successfully survived this challenge to his leadership. He continued to dominate the political scene. It is instructive to compare his low key presence at the celebration of National Day of the Republic in August 1956, with his appearance at these same celebration four years later. In August 1960 *Scînteia* published a photograph captioned 'The Presidium of the Festive Meeting Devoted to the Anniversary of 23 August' where the portrait of Dej was placed above the slogan 'Long Live 23 August, the Day of Romania's Liberation from the Fascist Occupation' and between the portraits of Chivu Stoica, vice-president of the Council of Ministers, and Ion Maurer, the prime minister. The main speech was delivered by Dej this time and published in *Scînteia* along with two photographs of Dej: Dej at the official tribune applauding and Dej reading his speech.[49] In the same issue of the newspaper, on the third page, there were also published the 'first echoes of the country' to Dej's report.[50] It was of course received with 'vivid interest'. A photograph representing people who were listening to the radio was also published under the caption: 'At the Griviţa Roşie Club – around the radio set', while the article asserted that the report was received with 'applause and words of warm approval'.[51] Gheorghiu-Dej continued to dominate Romanian politics until his death in 1965.

Conclusions

Romania was the only socialist country in Eastern Europe (apart from Tito's Yugoslavia and Hoxha's Albania) where the policy initiated by Khrushchev did not lead to change at the very top of the political hierarchy.[52] On the contrary, the leader of the RWP, Gheorghiu-Dej, emerged from that turbulent period even stronger. How was this possible? First of all, by the time

Khrushchev urged a new course and revealed Stalin's excesses, Gheorghiu-Dej had already eliminated his most important potential rivals.[53] Secondly, Dej was experienced and astute enough to be able to assess the situation properly and to deal cautiously with it. He employed diverse strategies in order to keep the situation under control and to make the most out of it when the opportunity arose. He both delayed and mimicked the debate on the issue of the 'cult of personality', he used moments from the history of the party, reinterpreting them according to us need; he offered unconditional support to Khrushchev in the Hungarian crisis, and so on. Thirdly – and this was probably the factor that contributed most to Dej's victory – the Romanian political elite coalesced around Dej and backed him unreservedly. This proved that in Romania, the hard Stalinist nucleus was more powerful than in other socialist countries in the region and more reluctant to embark upon a sustained process of de-Stalinisation. The evolution of Gheorghiu-Dej's leadership, his national-Stalinist orientation in the 1960s, and Ceauşescu's later hybrid of hard Stalinism and nationalism can be better understood through an examination of this episode from the history of the Romanian Communist Party. In 1968 Nicolae Ceauşescu used a compromising revelation to destroy Gheorghiu-Dej's image, one of the leading personalities in the RWP, Lucreţiu Pătrăşcanu, was killed on Dej's direct orders in April 1954. Pătrăşcanu had the reputation as an anti-Stalinist and a moderate, and a rival of Dej. In the 1970s and 1980s the new cult of Ceauşescu flourished in Romania, drawing in part on the cult of Dej, and on the cult of Mao Zedong and Kim Il-sung.

Notes

1. Dennis Deletant, *Teroarea comunistă în România, Gheorghiu-Dej şi statul poliţienesc, 1948–1965* (Iaşi, 2001), pp. 194–7.
2. Stelian Tănase, *Elite şi societate, Guvernarea Gheorghiu-Dej 1948–1965* (Bucharest, 1998), pp. 120–4; Vladimir Tismăneanu, *Stalinism for All Seasons: A Political History of Romanian Communism* (Berkeley, Cal., 2003), pp. 142–4.
3. Appellations such as 'the liberator [of Romania from the Fascist regime]', 'genius', 'token of the fight for peace in the entire world', etc., were entirely reserved for Stalin. They were to be revived during the Ceauşescu leadership and used until they became hackneyed.
4. *Scînteia*, 25 October 1949, 1. For a comparative analysis of Stalin's 70th birthday celebrations in the other socialist countries see Anders Åman, *Architecture and Ideology in Eastern Europe during Stalin Era: An Aspect of Cold War History* (Cambridge, Mass., and London, 1992) p. 28.
5. *Scînteia*, 2 October 1949, p. 1.
6. In 1949 alone 60,000 party members studied the Short Course, *Scînteia*, 1 October 1949, p. 3.
7. 'The élan of the socialist competition devoted to Comrade Stalin's birthday celebration increases. The constructors from Reşiţa will build for Comrade Stalin's birthday 48 apartments for workers.' *Scînteia*, 30 October 1949, p. 3.

8. 'The Exhibition of the Soviet Industry – USSR the Biggest Industrial Power in the World', *Scînteia*, 15 October 1949, 5.
9. 'USSR the Leading Force in the Fight for Peace', *Scînteia*, 2 November 1949, p. 1.
10. S. Titorenko, 'Lenin and Stalin – Initiators and Organizers of the Great Socialist Revolution of October', *Scînteia*, 1 November 1949, p. 3; G. Gak, 'The Theoretical Teaching of Comrade Stalin, a Peak of the Marxist-Leninist Philosophical Thought', *Scînteia*, 24 November 1949, p. 3.
11. The first phase of letter-writing, according to certain figures, was followed by an avalanche of letters from workers, peasants, children, etc.
12. *Scînteia*, 11 December 1949, p. 1.
13. For instance C. I. Parhon spoke about 'I. V. Stalin – The Guide of Science', T.R. Săvulescu chose the topic 'I. V. Stalin – Theoretician and Initiator of Nature's Transformation', whilst M. Sadoveanu gave a talk on 'I. V. Stalin – As Reflected in the Literatures of the World's Peoples', *Scînteia*, 15 December 1949, p. 1.
14. *Scînteia*, 9 December 1949, p. 3.
15. The Cominform's newspaper reported that the meeting in Bucharest was attended by 250,000 people, *Pentru o pace trainică, pentru democraţie populară*, 30 December 1949, 1.
16. In the period when Gheorghiu-Dej was still a *primus inter pares*, that is until 1952, the photographs of him published in *Scînteia* mainly represented him in an official pose. By contrast, Ana Pauker, Vasile Luca or other top members of the party were envisaged in more dynamic postures: while giving a speech, visiting a plant, and so on. It is quite striking that the type of photograph that was employed in his case in *Scînteia* resembled very much the remote, official photograph used in the case of Stalin. After 1953 and especially after 1956, Gheorghiu-Dej's photographs circulated in *Scînteia* depicted a more down-to-earth leader, who met people, visited factories, welcomed official delegations.
17. 'unflinching fighter for the cause of Lenin and Stalin', *Scînteia*, 6 November 1951, p. 1.
18. Palmiro Togliatti, Mao Zedong, Kim Il-Sung and Mátyás Rákosi are among those who sent telegrams. In the following days the list extended with telegrams from Harry Pollitt, Walter Ulbricht and Jacques Duclos (*Scînteia*, 10 November 1950).
19. *Scînteia*, 10 November 1951, p. 1. The same distinctions were conferred to Dej ten years later. That time the reasons enumerated were more detailed and stressed the merits of Dej in maintaining the unity of the party, the main point on which his defenders had insisted in the 1956–57 conflict within the party.
20. 'Letter of congratulation sent by the young people in the RPR' signed by 2,319,933 persons, *Scînteia*, 10 November 1951, p. 1.
21. Under the heading 'The working people congratulate Comrade Gheorghe Gheorghiu-Dej on the occasion of his 50th birthday', hundreds of telegrams were published see the issues of *Scînteia* from 13, 14, 15 November 1951.
22. The metallurgical factory from Hunedoara and the thermo-electric power station from Doiceşti were renamed on this occasion. *Scînteia*, 11 November 1951, 1.
23. *Scînteia*, 13 November 1951, p. 2.
24. Jeffrey Brooks. *Thank You, Comrade Stalin! Soviet Public Culture from Revolution to Cold War* (Princeton, NJ, 2000) pp. 219–23. A first-hand account of the celebrations within the Soviet Bloc can be found in the Cominform's newspaper, *Pentru o pace trainică, pentru democraţie populară*, nos 9 December 1949, 16 December 1949, 21 December, 30 December 1949.

25. Dej ordered the deportation of the population of Serbian origin from the Romanian Banat. He organized troops and supplied them with military equipment, which could have intervened in the eventuality of a military action against Yugoslavia. Furthermore, he allowed Tito's political opponents to settle on the territory of Romania and to lead actions against their rival. Finally, he got involved in and supported diversionary actions aiming to overthrow Tito. Cf. Stelian Tănase, *Elite şi societate*, p. 107. See also Dennis Deletant, *Teroarea comunistă în România*, pp. 109–11.
26. Michael Montias, *Economic Development in Communist Rumania* (Cambridge, Mass., 1967).
27. On the impact of Sovietisation upon Romanian culture in the late forties and the fifties see Marin Niţescu, *Sub zodia proletcultismului* (Bucharest, 1995) and Ana Selejan, *România în timpul primului război cultural (1944–1948)*, vol. I, *Trădarea intelectualilor* (Sibiu, 1992), vol. II, *Reeducare şi prigoană* (Sibiu, 1993). See also Vladimir Tismăneanu, *Arheologia terorii* (Bucharest, 1992).
28. Vlad Georgescu, *Istoria românilor: De la origini pîna în zilele noastre* (Bucharest, 1992), p. 261. See for a more detailed account of the Romanian delegation's participation to the Congress, Tismaneanu, *Stalinism for All Seasons*, pp. 142–4.
29. Alina Tudor and Dan Cătănuş, *O destalinizare ratată, Culisele cazului Miron Constantinescu – Iosif Chişinevschi* (Bucharest, 2001), p. 38.
30. 1956, Cultul personalităţii lui Dej, *Dosarele istoriei*, An VII, Nr. 2(66), 2002, 12.
31. Tudor and Cătănuş, *O destalinizare ratată*, pp. 30–1.
32. Ibid., p. 13. See for the 1952 episode the following books of memoirs: Paul Sfetcu, *13 ani în anticamera lui Dej* (Bucharest, 2000), p. 78; Silviu Brucan, *Generaţia irosită, Memorii* (Bucharest, 1992), p. 60.
33. Georgescu, *Istoria românilor*, p. 246. See also Stephen Fischer-Galaţi, *Twentieth Century Romania* (New York, 1991), pp. 121–3; Dennis Deletant, *Teroarea comunistă în România*, pp. 185–8. For a detailed account of the trial see Robert Levy, *Ana Pauker: The Rise and Fall of a Jewish Communist* (Berkeley, Cal., 2001), pp. 194–219.
34. 1956, Cultul personalităţii lui Dej, *Dosarele istoriei*, An VII, Nr. 2(66), 2002, 13.
35. 'The Propaganda's Problems in the Light of the Decisions of the XXth Congress of the CPSU', *Scînteia*, 3 April 1956, p. 3.
36. *Scînteia*, 25 August 1956. On the National Day itself, 23 August, no image of a party leader was published.
37. Tismăneanu, *Stalinism for All Seasons*, pp. 148–52.
38. 'I am wondering whether these external manifestation [of the cult], such as mass demonstrations and propaganda through poems, songs, pictures, etc, are really the kernel of the problem? Without any doubt, the external manifestations of the cult have an important influence upon the education of the Party members . . . The root of the problem is to what extent the norms of leadership, the norms of Leninist Party life are respected, as the denial of these norms leads to the negation of the Party role and the reduction of the role of collective work.' Miron Constantinescu, 'Minutes of the Meeting of the Politburo of the CC of the RWP, 3 April 1956' in Tudor and Cătănuş, *O destalinizare ratată*, p. 56. Iosif Chişinevschi stressed the same aspect in his speech, ibid., p. 79.
39. Ibid., p. 54.
40. Ibid., pp. 57–9.
41. 'I too was educated in the cult of Stalin. I thought that that was normal and I was proud when I had the opportunity to work with Stalin directly. On different

occasions, I used in my speeches quotations from Stalin and I contributed in this way actively to the development of his personality cult. . . . In time, a cult of personality around Gheorghiu-Dej has been developed in our country and, to a greater or lesser extent, around others too . . . to this every one of us contributed': Emil Bodnăraş, ibid., p. 83). 'All of us, without exception, can affirm that they contributed to Stalin's cult . . . It was almost a law to cite from Stalin, Dej and, in an earlier period, from Ana [Pauker]. Our leaders were undoubtedly influenced by the personality cult of Stalin': Nicolae Ceauşescu, ibid., p. 94.

42. Tudor and Cătănuş, *O destalinizare ratată*, p. 144.
43. Ibid., pp. 154–5.
44. There were lively debates about what label should be used for describing Miron Constantinescu's and Iosif Chişinevschi's attempt to form a coalition against Dej. The labels ranged from 'unhealthy manifestations' (Nicolae Ceauşescu), 'fractionism' (Alexandru Drăghici), 'anti-party attitude' and 'non-party attitude' (ibid., pp. 165–9).
45. Dennis Deletant, *Romania under Communist Rule* (Bucharest, 1998), pp. 133–4.
46. Vladimir Tismăneanu, *Stalinism for All Seasons*, p. 163; Ghiţă Ionescu, *Communism in Romania, 1944–1962* (London, 1964), p. 284; Kenneth Jowitt, *Revolutionary Breakthroughs and National Development: The Case of Romania, 1944–1965* (Berkeley, Cal., 1971), p. 173.
47. Tudor and Cătănuş, *O destalinizare ratată*, p. 250.
48. Ibid., pp. 251–4.
49. *Scînteia*, 31 August 1960, p. 1.
50. The report was linked to the admission of Romania to the organisation of the United Nations and preceded the first participation of Romania to the 15th meeting of this organisation in September 1960.
51. *Scînteia*, 31 August 1960.
52. While in Poland and Czechoslovakia the change took place by natural causes; B. Bierut died in 1956 and K. Gottwald in 1993. In Bulgaria and Hungary the USSR had to intervene and Chervenkov and Rákosi were removed at Moscow's initiative. See Georgescu, *Istoria românilor*, p. 266.
53. Vladimir Tismăneanu, *Fantoma lui Gheorghiu-Dej* (Bucharest, 1995), pp. 115–18; Tănase, *Elite şi societate*, pp. 103–6.

15

The Second Step of a Ladder: The Cult of the First Secretaries in Poland

Marcin Zaremba[1]

In communist Poland not only was Bolesław Bierut surrounded by a cult, but there were also attempts to manufacture an atmosphere of adoration, modelled on comrade Tomasz's cult, around Władysław Gomułka, Edward Gierek and Wojciech Jaruzelski.[2] But between the leader cult of the Stalinist era and the cults of the party secretaries after 1956 there was a significant difference, with an obvious desacralisation of the first secretary's image. One might question as to whether regarding Gomułka's rule in the 1960s it is possible to speak of a leader cult, or perhaps only of a 'specific court culture', more akin to the presumptions of monarchical authority.[3] Was the celebration of Gomułka's birthday in 1965 a renewal of his crumbling charisma, or rather the strengthening of his authority? If one follows Max Weber's definition of charisma, one should consider the creation of an atmosphere of boundless worship, quasi-religious in form, as applying only to Stalin and his Polish 'faithful pupil' Bierut, while the word 'authority' or rather 'authoritarian rule' would apply to Gomułka, Gierek and Jaruzelski better. In reality, however, it is difficult to point precisely to a place where the manufacturing of authority ended and charisma began. In the Polish case the Communist Party's ability to stake a claim to charismatic authority was complicated by the real authority and popular support wielded by the Catholic Church.

The manufacturing of the first secretaries' adoration testifies to the regime's lack of legitimacy. Being reliant on coercion and lacking sources of stability – such as economic success, democratic mandate, traditional authority, authentic charisma – in the end led to the usage of a simple and inexpensive idea: the creation of collective support for the leader of 'the party and the state' by the uncritical idealisation of him. The death of Stalin fundamentally changed the situation.[4] Here we examine the way in which the cult of the first secretary was projected, and how it evolved under successive first secretaries. The problem of the actual social support for the leaders of the party lies beyond the scope of our study. The cult of Bolesław Bierut, which was associated more with the office of president than that of party first secretary, has been examined by the author elsewhere and by others (see Chapter 9).[5] Here we shall examine the way in which three of the first secretaries of the Polish United Workers Party of the post-Stalin era were projected as part of this general legitimisation strategy: Władysław Gomułka (1956–70), Edward Gierek and Wojciech Jaruzelski.[6]

Beloved Comrade Wiesław

Khrushchev's 'Secret Speech' to the 20th congress of the CPSU in February 1956 triggered a very mixed reaction in Poland: hostility, fear, grief, but first and foremost uncertainty. The party leadership was itself divided, and, being under the pressure of public opinion and the new direction signposted by the Congress, it could not evade addressing the issue of the 'cult of personality'. Leading party figures such as Edward Osóbka-Morawski, Jozef Cyrankiewicz, Jakub Berman and Edward Ochab all reflected self-critically on the 'personality cult', emphasising its hierarchical and widespread nature, Stalin's role in its implementation, and its symptoms.[7] The attitude of the party membership towards the leader cult was also characterised by some ambiguity, manifested in the expression of doubt amongst party activists. One opinion compared the cult to other totalitarian leader cults (Hitler and Mussolini), another drew analogy with the cult of 'Emperor Mao'. One party member was not sure whether the dismantling of the cult meant taking down the statues of Copernicus, as well.[8] The authority of the party was further shaken by the fact that the Polish translation of the 'Secret Speech,' meant for internal use, somehow became public and was quickly spread all over the Soviet Bloc, and the West.[9]

In this context, and mirroring later events in Hungary and Poland in the same year, any return to the sacralisation of the first secretary, modelled on the cult of Bierut, was no longer possible. It was blocked by the public hope for the democratisation of the system, the resistance of political elite and first of all by Władysław Gomułka. During the eighth Central Committee (CC) plenum of the Polish United Workers' Party in October 1956 Gomułka pronounced that 'the personality cult' was incompatible with 'socialist humanitarianism, with the socialist sense of freedom of man, with the socialist sense of law and order'. He said:

> The cult of personality cannot be confined solely to the person of Stalin. The personality cult is a system which reigned in the Soviet Union and which was transplanted – probably – to all of the communist parties, as also to a number of countries from the socialist camp, including Poland . . .[10]
>
> The essence of this system consisted in the fact than an individual, hierarchic ladder of cults was created. Each such cult comprised a given area in which it functioned. In the bloc of socialist states it was Stalin

> who stood at the top of the hierarchic ladder of cults. All those who stood on lower rungs of the ladder bowed their heads before him. Those who bowed their heads were not only the other leaders of the Communist Party of the Soviet Union and the leaders of Communist and Workers' Parties of the countries of the socialist camp. The latter, namely the First Secretaries of the Central Committees of the Parties of the various countries who sat on the second rung of the ladder of the cult of personality, in turn donned the robes of infallibility and wisdom. But their cult radiated only on the territory of the countries where they stood at the top of the national cult ladder. The cult could only be called a reflected brilliance, a borrowed light. It shone as the moon does.[11]

Gomulka was anxious to avoid any assertion that the cult reflected on the undemocratic nature of the Soviet regime and its satellites.

> Our enemies assert that the personality cult of Stalin was not engendered by definite historical conditions which have already passed, but by the Soviet system itself, by what they consider its lack of democracy, and so on. Such slanderous assertions are refuted by the entire history of the development of the Soviet state.[12]

This criticism did not lead to the cessation of propaganda activities. Changes related to 'the thaw' did, however, cause it to become less intrusive, less strident. Gomułka himself tried to avoid inflated celebrity. His reputation as a leader who had resisted the pressures of the Kremlin, could not validate the system of ruling for long, particularly as it could not be used in official statements, for obvious reasons. This is why efforts extolling the first secretary's charisma were an important life-belt of the system.

In the 1960s portraits of Gomułka were seen hanging everywhere: in shops, schools and in all state institutions. They were carried during May Day processions,[13] and accompanied all official celebrations and festivals. His quotations were hung up in industrial halls and showcases, in streets and during celebrations. At the National Anti-Alcohol Congress in March 1964 a gigantic portrait of Gomułka hung above the presidential table with his words 'One can achieve serious savings without lowering the existing standard of life only by the decreasing the consumption of vodka and other alcoholic beverages'. Gomułka's speeches, first printed in newspapers, later appeared in book form in several thousand copies. Even Bierut did not have so many editions of his own speeches. In factories, collective listening to important pronouncements from the first secretary were organised for workers. It became a specific kind of tradition to organise public meetings of support for 'the policy of Comrade Wiesław' during which allegedly spontaneously prepared telegrams were read out. After his speech to the UN General Assembly in New York in October 1960, teachers and young people of the Third Elementary School and the T. Kosciuszko General Education High School wrote:

> We whole-heartedly support comrade Gomułka's pronouncement at the XV UN Session. We solidarise with the response, given to Macmillan, who dared to defend the interest of West-German militarists, and with it struck at the vital interests of the Polish nation, our peace and security . . . With beating hearts we listened to You speaking on the radio, and our young minds and hearts were with You.[14]

The staff of the 'Pudliszki' Fruit and Vegetable Processing plant in Pudliszki 'spontaneously organised a mass meeting, to declare that behind the words of Comrade Gomułka stood all the working people of the People's Poland.'[15] Similar actions of support were organised after Gomułka's speech on 19 March 1968.

However, the first secretary's portrayal in the press differed from that of his predecessor in the Stalinist period. In the 1960s he was 'the first among equals', the most important person, but not the only one and not irreplaceable. Press releases always began with him, his name was usually visible in the title, but usually Gomułka was also accompanied by the premier, the chairman of the State Council and other dignitaries, who were mentioned by their name and surname. The first secretary's arrival was, however, described in special terms: he was greeted 'heartily' or with a 'warm ovation', 'stormy applause', 'enthusiastic applause' or even a 'thunderous applause'. It often happened that the 'Live a Hundred Years' song was sung in his honour.[16]

From press summaries and discussions of Gomułka's speeches we can see that the first secretary had 'touched an important problem', 'paid a lot of attention', 'pointed', 'emphasised' and 'extensively discussed' matters. Thus the first secretary's authority, shrewdness and erudition was emphasised. In accounts of *Trybuna Ludu* or *Życie Warszawy* he appears as an unusually versatile person. Unlike his successors, Gomulka, as first secretary, was deemed to have special competence for judging cultural events. For example, at the 13th Central Committee plenum of the Polish United Workers' Party in 1963, he was assigned the role of most important film and literary critic.

The next element of propaganda in the creation of the first secretary's image was the ritual of sending and subsequently publishing of the letters, which he received from different social and professional groups. The propaganda with the greatest meaning for the first secretary and the whole party were the letters from 'the whole society', as in the case of the signing of the new treaty of 'Friendship between Poland and the USSR'. The headline in *Trybuna Ludu* in April 1965 read 'Polish Society fully approves the treaty concluded between Poland and the USSR'; the subtitle read 'Letters from the whole country to comrade Gomułka and to Comrade Brezhnev'. Letters were also sent to the first secretary and to the party on other important occasions. The front pages of *Trybuna Ludu* and *Życie Warszawy* reported the resolutions of the Społem Congress and carried a letter from members of the co-operative to 'comrades Wł. Gomułka and E. Ochab':

> At the end of the congress, letters to Władysław Gomułka and Edward Ochab were warmly applauded. In the letter to the First Secretary of the Polish United Workers' Party's CC, the participants of the congress, were expressing the feelings of two and a half million members of the co-operative society and one hundred and sixty thousand workers, sending warm greetings and assurances that the cooperative movement will do its best, to fulfil the assignments, which were laid out by the IV congress of the party.[17]

As with Bierut, the celebration of Gomulka's 60th birthday saw an intensification of propaganda activity. Gomułka received fewer birthday greetings than Bierut, but still received a lot: from the National Councils, various party offices, the Home Office, the army, the staff of newspapers and periodicals, hospitals and other public services. Even the children's magazine *Świerszczyk* informed its readers about Gomułka's birthday. Pre-school children celebrated the birthday of the first secretary:

> Our Head Mistress told us a lot about Comrade Gomulka being a friend of the children, a very good friend because You love Polish children as well as the children of different countries. Today we drew congratulatory cards, which we have sent in remembrance. Though we live far from Warsaw we think about all of the State dignitaries, whom we know and whose portraits we have.[18]

The description of the birthday celebration that took place on Saturday 6 February in the Central Committee office, was published in Monday's newspapers (the same text was placed in *Trybuna Ludu* and *Życie Warszawy*). A programme prepared by the Secretariat Office provides further detail. At first members of the Politburo and the Secretariat expressed good wishes to comrade Wiesław.[19] The meeting, 'in the presence of press photographers, news teams and TV', took place in a hearty atmosphere. Edward Ochab delivered a speech. Then Gomułka and other leaders met with party activists. From 11:30 a.m. onwards, delegations from all over the country came to the Central Committee, which reflected a specific social hierarchy. First, members of the core party elite had the honour of approaching, then lower party leaders. The turn of the representatives of the allied parties, namely the United Peasant's Party and the Democratic Party were the ones to follow, then the representatives of trade unions arrived, followed by the army delegation. After the soldiers came the scientists, scholars and artists. The list of delegations was long, and included miners, textile-workers, farmers and the representatives of ZBoWiD (the Union of Fighters for Freedom and Democracy). The impression conveyed was that the whole country attached huge importance to the birthday of the first secretary.

As it was the custom, Gomułka received wishes from friendly socialist states. *Trybuna Ludu's* second page heading read: 'Thousands of letters and telegrams from our country and abroad', in order to form in the mind of the reader the conviction that that the birthday of the first Central Committee secretary of the Polish United Workers' Party was an event of international significance. The theme of congratulatory telegrams was still present in the issue of *Trybuna Ludu* on 8 February. This is mentioned in the press in the context of the Eighth Congress of the Democratic Party on 9 February. *Życie Warszawy* reported that the people present sang 'Live a Hundred Years' to honour the first secretary, while *Trybuna Ludu* printed Gomułka's thanks for birthday wishes. However, Gomułka was a somewhat ascetic figure, who disliked ostentatious celebrations. Consequently the propaganda apparatus tried to create an atmosphere of charisma not so much around Gomułka's person, but around the office of the first secretary.

From press accounts the one-dimensional figure of the first secretary appears through the recital of old themes – his person as first (but among many), omniscient, interested in the problems of people and able to formulate solutions to problems. His position in the international communist movement was emphasised; he took a strongly pro-Soviet line, as can be seen in his defence of the Soviet and Warsaw Pact invasion of neighbouring Czechoslovakia in 1968. These exertions to kindle the charismatic aura around Gomułka were subverted by the schematic style and content of official propaganda. This is visible even in the descriptions of Comrade Wiesław's meetings with the workers, where the sense of spontaneous expressions of sympathy for the first secretary – which cannot after all be excluded – was disappearing.

The good manager

The rule of Edward Gierek saw a renewal of the first secretary's image. The use of force to quell workers' strikes in December 1970 humiliated both the party and its leader, Gomułka, providing clear proof that the Polish United Workers' Party owed its position to force, and that it lacked legitimacy. The principal objective of the new team was to rebuild Polish society's trust in authority, which was in the main identified with the person of the first secretary. Józef Tejchma, one of the most intelligent members of the Politburo, spoke openly of this tactic at a Politburo session on 14 December 1971:

> The VI Congress strengthened two mobilising and integrating factors active in 1971: the first of them was the programme of the party which

> obtained general acceptance, the second was the authority of the central management, and especially the Central Committee's First Secretary as a person and as an institution. After the Congress the issue is to transform the authority of the CC's First Secretary into the authority of the party, as an institution and as an authority of the state. This is the guarantee of the system's continuation.[20]

During the 1970s, in all Eastern Bloc countries there was a turn towards ritualisation and paternalisation of social life, and this was accompanied by a change in the way the leaders were projected.[21] Gierek began building his authority with a television speech on 20 December 1970. From this moment onwards, television became the main carrier of the first secretary's image. One of his first decisions was to end the practice of displaying portraits of the party–state leaders.[22] Instead he dominated all television and radio news programmes. In the 1970s almost every edition of the 'TV News' started with a report of the first secretary's activities. He was also constantly in the press. The absolute priority of his representation in the mass media was directed by the Central Committee's Department of Propaganda, Press and Publishing.[23] In his appearance and behaviour Gierek was different from his predecessor. Tall, broad-shouldered, younger, better dressed, energetic – one could even say handsome. People could even like him, but the manufacturing of charisma did not cease.

It began with revision of his biography. The front page of *Trybuna Ludu* on 21 December 1970 reported the election of the new first secretary, showing a large photo of Gierek, and next to it, in block letters, the title of the article: 'The appointment of the new party authorities. Comrade EDWARD GIEREK the first CC Secretary'. In this text one can read: 'The Politburo will examine the possibility of improving the financial situation of low income families and families with many children'. It pledged to increase family allowances, old age pensions and disability pensions. The party signalled that it was concerned with the fate of the poor. These promises created a capital of social confidence in the new authorities, especially for Gierek. In the third column was the biography of the new leader.

> He was born on 6th January, 1913 in Porąbka, district of Będzin, in a miner's family. In 1923, after his father's death, he emigrated to France. From the age of thirteen he worked in a mine. He was active in the class struggle of the French proletariat and directed strike action. In 1931 he joined the French Communist Party. In 1934 he was arrested for participating in a strike and was deported to Poland. In 1937 he emigrated to Belgium and became a member of the Belgian Communist Party. During the war he was active in the Belgian resistance movement and fought against the Nazis. After the war he returned to Poland. He graduated as a mining engineer by studying part time.

The biography magnified Gierek's working-class origins and his role as a leader who knew the problems of the workers personally. There were attempts to 'create' Gierek's legend of armed struggle. It was an attempt to link his biography to the biographies of his predecessors, especially Gomułka.

Two days after the election *Trybuna Ludu* published telegrams to the first secretary from leaders of fraternal parties. The same issue carried a report of a visit by Gierek and Stanisław Kociołek to the Płock Refinery. This is the first characteristic of the Gierek decade, namely of 'manager's visits', during which the leader of the party had direct contact with society. In a photograph of this visit we can see the first secretary in a good mood, smiling. This smile is also a new feature in the picture of the first secretary. Before December 1970 the Office for the Inspection of Publication and Shows often censored photos of Gomułka because of the not very presentable state of his teeth.

Gierek's image in the 1970s falls into three basic types: 'The father of the nation', 'the statesman' and 'the good manager'. The role of 'The father of the nation' was the role that Gierek assumed most often, by participating in patriotic celebrations. To elevate the prestige of the new first secretary it was decided for example that he would announce a decision to restore the Royal Castle in Warsaw as an important national symbol. Reference to national symbols and to specific nationalism had already been used earlier in Gomułka's time. This was done with the object of using Polish patriotic sentiments to legitimise the system, by equating the state with the prevailing political system. This strategy corresponds to that developed under Stalinism: of forging the 'moral-political unity of the nation'. Gierek's image as leader had some resemblances to Bierut's period of rule. At a public meeting in Katowice on 2 July 1976 party activists chanted: 'Pa-rty–Gierek, Pa-rty–Gierek'. The first secretary stopped it and started: 'Par-ty–Poland'. The hall chanted: 'Party–Poland, Party–Gierek, Poland–Gierek'. This recalled the practice of earlier days: the chant of the name: 'Bie-rut, Bie-rut' and standing ovations. Soon the media began to call Gierek 'The leader of the Polish nation'.

The image of 'the father of the nation' also had the theme of paternalism and benevolence. For example, on 8 February 1972 the Politburo decided that a decision to extend maternity leave for nursing mothers should be announced by Comrade Gierek at a meeting of electors in Sosnowiec on 21 February.[24] The decision was evidently intended to bolster the authority of the new first secretary.

The statesman, the leader who was respected in the West, was the second image of Gierek that was promoted in the 1970s. It was framed with numerous meetings with foreign politicians, both in Poland and abroad. Special attention was attached to Polish–French and Polish–German contacts. These relationships were undoubtedly made easier because of the first secretary's knowledge of the French language. This fact was often stressed for domestic usage. The French episode of Gierek's biography provided the basis for projecting a personal image that was European in outlook, ideology and lifestyle. The fairly frequent visits of foreign heads of state to Poland conferred their prestige onto the person of the first secretary. Motorcades with foreign guests through cheering crowds in Polish cities were an important factor of the display of authority of that time.

The third manifestation of the first secretary was 'the good manager', the leader, listening with concern to the voice of every social and professional group, interested in their work and supervising everything. Between December 1970 and June 1980 Gierek made 377 trips to factories, state farms, and to various celebrations and special meetings.[25] Meetings with the 'masses' confirmed his popularity and legitimised his position. Gierek's tours were, on the one hand reminiscent of a feudal court, and on the other were that of a modern politician during an election campaign. The press eagerly published photos and reports of these meetings.

> In the main drive engines factory the women workers surrounded the party leader, informed him about the results of their work, assured him of the support of the twenty thousand workers of the giant engineering work in Poznan (Hipolit Cegielski Poznan) and their support for the programme of the Polish United Workers' Party and its management.[26]

Similarly, meetings with agricultural workers were enthusiastically reported: 'Harvesters – members of a cooperative – gathered around Edward Gierek, asked him numerous questions, telling him about their own successes and concerns.'[27] Gierek's credibility, especially with miners, was enhanced by his own years as a worker in the coalmines.

As the representative of the whole nation, Gierek tried not to overlook any social or professional group. In 1971 alone he met 31 social/professional delegations and representatives of factory staff. He met teachers three times and miners and metallurgists twice. This multitude of meetings made the Central Committee departments of Propaganda and Organisation prepare a specific protocol or 'code of movement'. It was planned that on the occasion of Women's Day, the Polish Army Day and Days of Education, Books and the Press, the first secretary would welcome the delegates. Moreover, every year, on the eve of trade union holidays he met with miners, metallurgists, dockers, railwaymen, textile workers and with the medical service employees, but only every five years did he meet with printers, fishermen and policemen. In other years the prime minister and the chairman of the State Council welcomed these delegates.[28]

The role 'of the good manager' was most strongly played during the Harvest Festival, which was especially loved by authority. In a report of these celebrations one can read: 'Please, Dear Host accept the fruit of our labour, a traditional loaf of bread and divide it, as you have up till now, like a good host – fairly, according to our potential and our nation's needs.'[29] In this and in similar accounts the first secretary's role as the host-manager of the whole country was underlined. Just like a manager, Gierek was interested in everything down to the smallest detail. *Trybuna Ludu* reported: 'The CC Secretary was also interested in the progress of the harvest, speaking to a harvest brigade working in the field.'[30] At the Cracow steel factory, Gierek was informed about the work of the rolling mill and welded tubes department, and in conversations with workers at their working place discussed their working conditions and social welfare.[31]

The first secretary's 60th birthday was an opportunity to express homage, and to emphasise all the successes of the party and its leader.[32] On his birthday, 6 January 1973, *Trybuna Ludu* dedicated almost the whole of its front page to this event, with a large photo of Gierek and under which was written in capital letters: 'With heartiness, respect, confidence – best wishes from the Polish people to comrade EDWARD GIEREK'. The second column was filled with a 'congratulatory telegram from Soviet leaders to the Central Committee's First Secretary of the Polish United Workers' Party'. And below there was information about 'Honouring Edward Gierek with the Order of Lenin'. In this issue of the newspaper the whole third page was also dedicated to Gierek. There were quotations from his most important speeches. At the top of the page was one of the decade's slogans, written in red: 'So that Poland would become stronger, and its people prosperous'. These speeches were accompanied by a photograph of Gierek greeting and shaking the hand of a worker, with the editorial comment:

> The speeches of the First Secretary of the Central Committee of the Polish United Workers' Party determine the interpretation of party policy, they are the fruit of its experiences, they are documents in which the modern history of our country is written. These official documents also show the individuality of the leader, his experience and his manner of thinking about the problems of the country and the people.

His speeches were published as a matter of course in *Trybuna Ludu*, but, on his express instructions, they were never published in the form of a book.[33]

On 7 January reports of official celebrations honouring the celebrator appeared:

> On the 6th of January Edward Gierek accepted many hearty birthday wishes – from members of the Politiburo, the CC Secretariat of the Polish United Workers' Party and the Presidium of the Government. Henryk Jablonski and Piotr Jaroszewicz wished him well. In the morning Edward Gierek met a delegation of twenty seven working people – representatives

> of different professions from all over the country and all provinces . . . the delegates brought flowers, and emotion was visible on their faces.

This was followed by speeches and wishes from the spokesman of the delegation, the miner, after which Gierek expressed his thanks: 'The meeting was transformed into a hearty, mutual exchange of views and opinions. Roman Krysiak from the Szczecin Shipyard informed the First Secretary about the completion of ships ahead of time. . . . Among the delegation Edward Gierek found the foreman from the Zawadzki mine, Roman Wilk, and greeted him heartily. '"How worried I was about you", said Edward Gierek, referring to a recent accident at that mine. A farmer from a state farm in Zalesie, Władysław Leszak, invited the First Secretary to visit the Koszalin province, and informed him about the great rise in animal breeding in the province'. The first secretary's birthday was transformed into a festival of support for Gierek and the Polish United Workers' Party and was yet another opportunity to present the successes of the ruling team to society. The media showed Gierek as an open, caring man, who had not lost touch with society. 'To the office of the Central Committee came numerous delegations of social organisations, associations of different trades, who gave their best wishes to the First Secretary of the CC of the Polish United Workers' Party'. The ambassadors of socialist countries also sent greetings, with the ambassador of the USSR playing a leading role. In accordance with the already established ritual, the press published congratulatory telegrams from leaders of the socialist countries, including Fidel Castro, Josip Broz Tito and Kim Il-Sung. A lot of wishes came from the all parts of Poland, which was also eagerly noticed by the press. Usually, Gierek was described as a signpost and an example: 'Your sacrifice and Your creative work is an example to us, an example and hope in our lives.'[34] Many letters contained production pledges and/or information about the fulfilling of production plans.

Wishes were sent also on special occasions, such as at Christmas and the New Year, and on the occasion of Gierek's re-election as first secretary at the Seventh and Eighth Congress of the Polish United Workers' Party. In December 1975, the president of the Association of Polish Cinematographers, Jerzy Kawalerowicz, wrote: 'Comrade First Secretary, please accept our assurance that around Your person and around the Party, under Your management our best thoughts and intentions are concentrated, under You, the great inspiring power of our creation and activity.'[35] The uncritical worship of Gierek became a ritual part of political life, the everyday language of the party. Tadeusz Fiszbach invited Gierek to a provincal party committee session in Gdansk in June 1978 with the following words: 'The presence of Comrade First Secretary at the plenary session of the Province Committee will have special meaning for maritime economy development, and will be, as always, a deep experience for the Gdansk province party organisation.'[36]

After 1976, and especially at the end of the decade, in a situation of dramatic economic crisis, the adoration of the first secretary became a smokescreen to conceal errors in the party's management of the country's affairs, and an important symbol of its unity. Józef Tejchma noted on the eve of Gierek's 65th birthday in 1978: 'Friends insistently advised me to appear at this celebration. I assume, that after the disclosure of some confusion regarding Gierek's illness and position, it was meant to demonstrate unity and solidarity. In politics such a gesture is expected, even if it is a little bit empty'. Tejchma described the celebration:

> The solemnities of Gierek's 65th birthday received great publicity. At the beginning the Prime Minister delivered a speech in his praise at the Central Committee office. After that, at the Belvedere, Jabłoński read a pompous text. He divided leaders into two groups: those who want to rule, and those who want to serve. Gierek serves Poland, the nation and the party . . . The dinner took place in an unconstrained, and perhaps even friendly atmosphere, which made the celebration differ from similar, previous ones.[37]

The lonely defender of the motherland

When on 18 October 1981 Wojciech Jaruzelski took over position of first secretary, the communist authorities in Poland were going through the most serious legitimation crisis in their history.[38] The party had been seriously weakened. It could not find a leader capable of leading and uniting it, from within its own ranks. Jaruzelski was a long-standing member of the Politburo. However, for the first time in the history of the Polish United Workers' Party (as well as the world communist movement) a professional soldier was appointed as its head. Moreover, for the first time a person who was already prime minister and minister of defence took up the post of the first secretary.[39] With the introduction of martial law, Jaruzelski also became the chairman of the Military Council of National Salvation. Jaruzelski's character – gloomy, stiff, introverted and not photogenic – posed problems for projecting him as a charismatic figure. Moreover, the rise of Solidarity had transformed social consciousness to such an extent that it was no longer possible to manipulate opinion through the simple propaganda devices of the Gierek era.

Another difficulty, the noble descent of the new first secretary, was quickly dealt with. In his biography, published in *Trybuna Ludu* a day after his election, it was stated that Jaruzelski was born into an intelligentsia family, but that 'he spent the war on USSR soil, as a worker'. A trump card in his biography was his participation in the 'liberation struggle' as a member of the First Army of the Polish Military Forces. It also mentioned his participation 'in fighting against the armed underground – for the consolidation of the people's authority'. His military and political career was distinguished; he received various honours: the Order of Builders of People's Poland, the First Class Order of the Banner of Labour and the Cross Virtuti Militari. The biography included a photograph of young Jaruzelski in military uniform, but without the dark glasses so characteristic of him in later years.[40]

It is significant that opinion poll research at the time showed that the army was the institution that commanded the highest public confidence. Hence the official media stressed Jaruzelski's virtues as a scrupulous, honest soldier who had shed blood on the battlefield and whose only concern was for the good of 'the motherland' – these words appeared in every speech of the first secretary before martial law was enforced.

The development of his image as leader was shaped by ideological dictates and pragmatic consideration, by Jaruzelski's personal character,[41] and by the recent memory of the Gierek propaganda. It combined the image of the soldier with strong paternalistic themes. In this period the annual miners' Barbórka celebrations were used to project the first secretary's great respect for the miners' hard labour: 'Long live the miners union!' The Barbórka was the celebration of the day of St Barbara, the patron saint of miners, with chapels dedicated to the saint at many mines, and the convening of masses at the start of these celebrations. An attempt was made to associate the leader with the Barbórka, and to try and bask in the reflected glory of this real cult.

Similarly we might note further attempts to identify the leader with the interests of the common worker. On 15 November 1981 Jaruzelski visited the '22nd of July' chocolate factory in Warsaw. The press accounts of this visit underline his close interest in the work and in the fate of the people he met. Like an attentive father, Jaruzelski asked about a heap of damaged dough containers. 'What do you need to do your work?' – 'He is interested in possibilities of increasing production.' He asked after 'the children's favourite' milk chocolate which had disappeared from the shelves of shops. 'The Prime Minister orders the officers who accompany him 'to find the reason'.[42] There were echoes of the image projected of Bierut surrounded by children, when Jaruzelski was shown inaugurating the construction of a hospital monument 'The Polish Mother'. In the press reports of these meetings the general appeared in the role of a sincere and good friend to the workers who looked upon him almost as a father figure. Seeing their difficult situation, he declines even the small present, which they had prepared for him.[43]

This picture of the 'good soldier' and the 'good father' were strengthened by propaganda following declaration of martial law on 13 December 1981. After this date one more image was attached to the General – 'the lone defender of the motherland'. This inaugurated the proper phase of the Jaruzelski cult, whose imaginary charisma was necessary to legitimise the decision. The media's assignment was to prove the existence of his charisma. The press, the television and the radio unceasingly repeated his words. *Trybuna Ludu* wrote 'Reflect once again on the weight of these words' quoting fragments from his speeches from 13 December onwards. This was an attempt to drum into the head of every citizen the basic truths of martial law. 'Quotations of Jaruzelski' served as 'daily' guidance, and as topics to be initiated; they were repeated in order to give the citizen some reference and some support.

Shortage of space precludes a lengthy analysis of this famous speech. In it Jaruzelski spoke about 'the responsibility, which falls on me in this dramatic moment of Polish history. It is my duty to take this responsibility – the future of Poland depends on it'. With these words, Jaruzelski appeared as a lone commander, assuming responsibility for the conditions of the state 'in this dramatic moment of history'. Perhaps Mieczysław F. Rakowski was right in suggesting that Jaruzelski consciously attempted to 'cast himself in the mould' of Józef Piłsudski.[44] Whatever the reason, the image of the first secretary – the general – was an image of a solitary man, which underlined his exceptional qualities and the charisma even more.

The propaganda tried to convince the Poles that their country, which was supposedly on the verge of civil war and was facing the prospect of Soviet intervention, was now being managed by a responsible politician, a true patriot. He was shown as a man of providence, whose foresight and judgement would save the country from certain destruction. With the introduction of martial law he had to restore a sense of security to his own countrymen, to provide hope for the future, making himself the guarantor that the process of democratic transformation would continue.[45] Jaruzelski was a hero of the Second World War and also the best 'military and political strategist',[46] a person who could speak sincerely to the people, and protect them. In a word, he was the personification of the best human values and soldierly virtues. In a letter sent to the First Secretary, the participants of a symposium at the High School of Social Sciences in early January 1982 wrote:

> We consider that Your activities as the First Secretary of the CC of the Polish United Workers' Party are a guarantee of the restoration of unity of words and actions, of the cultivation of the values which characterised the people actively engaged in the Polish Workers' Party, of courage, of spreading the truth, of honesty and modesty, of readiness to sacrifice, of firm will to fight any defection from the principles of socialism.[47]

The support and the specific cult of the first secretary were expressed in the press (*Trybuna Ludu* published opinions 'of the common man' in its column 'To and for every Pole'). A turner from Poznan admitted: 'The words of General Jaruzelski were true and honest. They conform with the feelings of all my friends in the department.'[48]

The propaganda of martial law made it impossible to forget that Jaruzelski was the soldier, the general and the commander. At the same time, the first secretary was shown as a normal citizen who travelled in an unmarked car, without numerous guards.[49] In the press of the time the creation of the image of leader was evident. The frequent quotation of his statements, the framing of his slogans, the stressing of the name of the leader with a thicker type, the use of red for the visualisation of certain contents, the publishing of photographs of him – in huge quantities especially after 1983 – had to 'catch the eye', had to be noticed by the reader.

In summary, the communists ruling Poland saw in the apotheosis of the first secretary an efficient and important tool for legitimising the system. Moreover, it is obvious that the repertoire of arguments used, the propaganda techniques devised, the terms and symbols employed, did not fundamentally change after 1956. The campaigns of support, letter-sending, and organising birthday celebrations were repeated. The permanent element used by all the leaders was nationalist rhetoric to create the image of the first secretary as a national hero. The legitimisation crisis, which repeated itself every time a new first secretary took power, was also typical.

One can also point out the differences. Bierut was represented as a solitary figure, similar to Stalin in that he seldom left his office. His successors, especially Gierek, were leaders of a 'new type', 'fraternising' with the people. In turn, the Jaruzelski image was dominated by the theme of the army, which had been completely absent in the case of his predecessors. On the other hand, however, in images of Gierek we can find many ideas borrowed from the propaganda of the Bierut epoch. The cult of the first secretaries in Poland never (apart from the Stalinist period) approached the level of the official cult of the party leaders in China at the time of the Cultural Revolution or that of Ceauşescu's Romania. This should not be linked with the absence of an authoritarian syndrome in Polish society. On the contrary, the letters sent by private persons on their birthdays to party leaders is evidence of its scale. Moreover, the argument that the Polish political elite was distinguished by a certain modesty, and were thus reluctant to elevate anyone to a position of uncritical approval, might be challenged, although some support for this argument can be found in the attitude of Gomulka. The reasons for the moderation in this regard lies above all in the periodic crises which saw successive First Secretaries removed from office, undermining past propaganda efforts and compelling the party propagandists to prove once again that the new first secretary was Poland's salvation. With every change this belief became more and more difficult to sustain.

Notes

1. In writing this chapter I have drawn on seminar essays of students attending Professor Marcin Kula's seminar at Warsaw University History Institute in 1999/2000. Those who assisted in my research were: Jakub Dąbrowski, Michał Oziękłowski, Łukasz Stokłowski, Elżbieta Wiązowska, Magdalena Agnieszka Zając and Hubert Zakrzewski.

2. B. Baczko, 'Stalin, czyli jak sfabrykować charzmę', in B. Baczko, *Wyobraźnia społeczna. Szkice o nadziei i pamięci zbiorowej* (Warsaw, 1994), pp. 173–92.
3. J. Tarkowski, 'Legitymizacja władzy. Zagadnienia teoretyczne i opinie oficjalne' in J. Tarkowski, *Socjologia świata polityki. Władza i społeczeństwo w systemie autorytarnym* (Warsaw, 1994), p. 56.
4. Robert Kupiecki, *'Natchnienie Milionów' Kult Józefa Stalina w Polsce* (Warsaw, 1993). Marcin Zaremba, 'Opinia publiczna w Polsce wobec choroby i śmierci Józefa Stalina' in Andrzej Friszke (ed.) *Władza a społeczeństwo w PRL. Studia historyczne* (Warsaw, 2003), pp. 19–53.
5. Marcin Zaremba, *Komunizm, legitimizacja, nacjonalizm. Nacjonalistyczna legitimizacja władzy komunistycznej w Polsce* (Warsaw, 2001); S. Filipowicz, Mit i spektakl władzy (Warsaw, 1998); Tarkowski, *Socjologia świata polityki. Władza i społeczeństwo w systemie autorytarnym* (Warsaw, 1994); Marcin Zaremba, 'Nieboszczyk w służbie partii', *Mówią Weki* (1999), no. 11, pp. 30–7.
6. J. Eisler, 'Siedmiu pierwszych sekretarzy KC PZPR. Porównanie sylwetek' in T. Szarota (ed.) *Komunizm. Ideologia, system, ludzie* (Warsaw, 2001), pp. 205–16.
7. Tony Kemp-Welch, 'Khrushchev's 'Secret Speech' and Polish Politics: The Spring of 1956', *Europe-Asia-Studies*, 48: 2 (March 1996), pp. 181–206.
8. Ibid., p. 193.
9. Ibid., p. 192.
10. *Nowe Drogi* (1956), no. 10, p. 39.
11. Zbigniew K. Brzezinski, *The Soviet Bloc: Unity and Conflict* (Cambridge, Mass., 1967), pp. 65, 273.
12. Ibid., p. 273.
13. The Warsaw decoration plan for 1 May 1970 arranged that portraits of Spychalski, Gomułka and Cyrankiewicz, of size 12 × 9 metres, would be hung on the PKO building in Marszalkowska Street: ANN, KC PZPR (Archive of New Acts, Warsaw) 237/VIII-1083, k. 79.
14. AAN, KC PZPR, XIA/239, k. 24.
15. AAN, KC PZPR, XIA/239, k. 41.
16. *Trybuna Ludu*, 15 May 1965.
17. *Trybuna Ludu* and *Życie Warszawy*, 26 October 1965.
18. 'To the First Secretary of PZPR Władysław Gomulka for his 60th birthday from children of a factory's kindergarten in Obszyce near Międzyrzecze': AAN, KC PZPR, XIA/310, k. 115, 116.
19. Program w związku z 60 rocznicą urodzin Towarzysza Władysława Gomułki, 3 February 1965: AAN KC PZPR, 237/V-606, k. 13.
20. AAN KC PZPR, 1751(old sign.), k. 798.
21. Christel Lane, *The Rites of Rulers: Ritual in Industrial Society – The Soviet Case* (Cambridge, 1981).
22. 'Based on recommendation of Com. Gierek the Bureau decided that in the state offices to put up only the state symbol, and in the party offices portraits of Lenin and possibly other prominent activists of labour movement history.' (The record no. 24. from the Politburo meeting, 29 December 1970. Protokół Nr 24 posiedzenia Biura Politycznego w dniu 29 grudnia 1970, in: *Centrum władzy. Protokół posiedzeń kierownictwa PZPR wybór z lat 1949–1970, Antoni Dudek, Aleksander Kochański, Kryzsztof Persak* (ed.) (Warsaw, 2000), p. 421.
23. The note about the rules governing press, radio and TV releases about celebrations, meetings and discussions, 7 April 1972, AAN KC PZPR, V/101, k. 478–479.

24. Record no. 8 from the meeting of Politburo, 8 February 1972, AAN, KC PZPR, V/99 K 319.
25. AAN, KC PZPR, XIA/646, k. 40, 59.
26. *Trybuna Ludu*, 10–11 June 1976. Hipolit Cegielski Poznan (HCP) was founded in the nineteenth century, but had for a time been renamed in honour of Stalin as Zaklady imienia Stalina Poznan (ZIS-PO) and was the centre of strong working class opposition to the communist regime in 1954 and 1956.
27. *Trybuna Ludu*, 29 July 1971.
28. 'Ustalenia w sprawie przyjmowania delegacji przez członków kierownictwa Partii i Rządu z okazji rocznic, świąt zawodowych i innych okazji', CC Department of Propaganda, Press and Publications, CC Organisation Department, May 1972, ANN KC PZPR, XI/332, k. 6–10.
29. *Trybuna Ludu*, 13 September 1976.
30. *Trybuna Ludu*, 20 August 1976.
31. *Trybuna Ludu*, 11 February 1973.
32. Many birthday greetings were sent in, pledging loyalty to the first secretary, including greetings from the Home Office, the Security Service and Civic Militia: AAN, KC PZPR, XA/960, k. 444.
33. J. Rolicki, *Edward Gierek: przerwana dekada* (Warsaw, 1990), p. 149.
34. The Factory Council; the Basal Party Organisation's executive; the manager of 'Sobótka' factory in Wrocław: AAN, KC PZPR, XIA/994, k. 16.
35. AAN, KC PZPR, XIA/1037, k. 18, 19.
36. AAN, KC PZPR, XIA/396, k. 9.
37. J. Tejchma, *W kręgu nadziei i rozczarowań. Notatki dzienne z lat 1978–1982* (Warsaw, 2002), p. 9.
38. That was how Jaruzelski himself perceived the situation at that time, saying: 'None of the Leadership, or the Central Committee of our Party had such beginning as we had' (Wojciech Jaruzelski, The speeches for the ending of the CC PZPR XII Plenum meeting, 1 May 1983, Wojciech Jaruzelshi, 'Przemówienie na zakończenie obrad XII Plenum KC PZPR, 31 V 1983', in: *Przemówienia 1983*, (Warsaw, 1984), p. 135.
39. Bierut was 'only' the first secretary and the president at any given time.
40. *Trybuna Ludu*, 19 October 1981.
41. At the meeting of the Politburo on 14 December 1971, Wojciech Jaruzelski said: 'Because of the New Year Holidays coming, next to the care of good supplies, one should consider some form of contact of the PB members, the Secretariat and the Government with the people/factories, hospitals, and workers' hostels/': AAN, KC PZPR, 1751 (old sign.), k. 817).
42. *Trybuna Ludu*, 16 November 1981.
43. *Życie Warszawy*, 16 November 1981. *Trybuna Ludu*, 16 November 1981.
44. M. Rakowski, *Jak to się stało* (Warsaw, 1991), p. 42.
45. *Trybuna Ludu*, 29 December 1981.
46. *Żołnierz Wolności*, 19–20 December 1981.
47. *Trybuna Ludu*, 7 January 1982.
48. Ibid.
49. *Trybuna Ludu*, 9 March 1982.

Select Bibliography

Archives

German

SAPMO-Barch	Stiftung Archiv der Parteien und Massenorganisationen der ehemaligen DDR im Bundesarchiv, Berlin (Archive of the Parties and Mass Organisations of the former GDR at the Federal Archives, Berlin)

Hungarian

HL	Hadtörténelmi Levéltár (Military History Archives) Budapest
MOL	Magyar Országos Levéltár (National Archives of Hungary) Budapest
PIL	Politikatörténeti Intézet Levéltára (Archives of the Institute of Political History) Budapest

Polish

AAN, KC PZPR	Archiwum Akt Nowych, Warsaw (Archive of New Acts in Warsaw) (AAN) files of the Polish United Worker's Party (PZPR)
APL	Archiwum Pánstwowe w Lublinie (State Archives, Lublin), Lublin
APK	Archiwum Pánstwowe w Krakowie (State Archives, Cracow), Cracow

Russian

AKNTs RAN	Arkhiv Karel'skogo Nauchnogo Tsentra Rossiiskaya Akademiya Nauk (Archive of the Karelian Scientific Centre of the Russian Academy of Science), Petrozauodsts
APRF	Arkhiv Prezidenta Rossiskoi Federatsii (Archive of the President of the Russian Federation) Moscow
GARF	Gosudarstvennyi Arkhiv Rossiiskoi Federatsii (State Archives of the Russian Federation, Moscow
OR GTG	Otdel Rukopisei Gosudarstvennaya Tret'yakovskaya Gallerya (Department of Manuscripts of the Tretyakov Gallery), Moscow
RGAE	Rossiiskyi Gosudarstvennyi Arkhiv Ekonomiki (Russian State Archives of the Economy), Moscow
RGALI	Rossiiskii Godudarstvennyi Arkhiv Literatury i Iskusstva (Russian State Archives of Literature and Art), Moscow
RGANI	Rossiiskii Gosudarstvennyi Arkhiv Noveishei Istorii (Russian State Archive of Contemporary History), Moscow
RGASPI	Rossiiskii Gosudarstvennyi Arkhiv Sotsial'no-Politicheskii Istorii (formerly RTsKhIDNI) (Russian State Archives of Social-Political History), Moscow
TsAODM	Tsentral'nyi Arkhiv Obshchestvennykh Dvizhenii Moskvy (Central Archives of Social Movements of Moscow), Moscow
TsDNIVO	Tsentr dokumentatsii noveishei istorii Volgogradskoi oblasti (Volgograd party archive), Volgograd

TsKhDMO Tsentral'nyi khranitel' dokumentov molodezhnykh organizatsii (Central Document Repository of Youth Organisations), Moscow

Periodical publications

Newspapers and journals

German

Tägliche Rundschau
Neues Deutschland

Hungarian

Szabad Nép

Polish

Trybuna Ludu
Życie Warszawy
Nowe Drogi

Romanian

Pentru o pace trainică, pentru democraţie populară
Scînteia

Russian

Izvestiya
Kommunist
Novaia i noveishaia istoria
Ogonek
Partinoe stroitel'stvo
Pioner
Pionerskaya pravda
Pravda
Sem'ya i shkola
Sovetskaya pedagogika.
Sovetskoe iskusstvo
Sovetskii Fol'klor
Vozhatyi

Academic journals

English

Europe–Asia Studies
Russian Review
Slavic Review
Soviet Studies

French

Cahiers du Monde russe

Russian

Istoricheskii arkhiv
Izvestiya TsK KPSS
Novaya i noveishaya istoriya
Svobodnya Mysl'
Voprosy istorii
Voprosy istorii KPSS

Books in English

Åman, Anders, *Architecture and Ideology in Eastern Europe during the Stalin Era: An Aspect of Cold War History* (Cambridge, Mass. and London), 1992.
Aulich, James and Marta Sylvestrová, *Political Posters in Eastern Europe, 1945–1995* (Manchester, 2000).
Arvidsson, Claes, and Lars Erik Blomquist, *Symbols of Power: The Esthetics of Political Legitimation in the Soviet Union and Eastern Europe* (Stockholm, 1987).
Banac, Ivo (ed.) *The Diary of Georgi Dimitrov 1933–1949* (New Haven, Conn., 2003).
Bonnell, Victoria E., *Iconography of Power: Soviet Political Posters under Lenin and Stalin* (Berkeley, Cal., 1997).
Bown, Matthew Cullerne, *Art under Stalin* (New York, 1991).
Bown, Matthew Cullerne, *Socialist Realist Painting* (New Haven, Conn., 1998).
Bown, Matthew Cullerne and Brandon Taylor (eds) *Art of the Soviets: Painting, Sculpture and Architecture in a One-Party State, 1917–1992* (Manchester, 1993).
Brandenberger, David, *National Bolshevism: Stalinist Mass Culture and the Formation of Modern Russian National Identity* (Cambridge, Mass., 2002).
Brooks, Jeffrey, *Thank You, Comrade Stalin! Soviet Public Culture from Revolution to Cold War* (Princeton, NJ, 2000).
Brown, Archie, *Political Leadership in the Soviet Union* (London, 1989).
Brown, Peter, *The Cult of the Saints: Its Rise and Function in Latin Christianity* (Chicago, 1981).
Brzezinski, Zbigniew K., *The Soviet Bloc: Unity and Conflict* (Cambridge, Mass., 1967).
Cavalli, Luciano, *Charisma, Dictatorship and Plebiscitary Democracy* (Florence, 1984).
Cherniavsky, M. *Tsar and People: Studies in Russian Myths* (New Haven, Conn., 1961).
Chuev, F., *Molotov Remembers: Inside Kremlin Politics – Conversations with Felix Chuev*, ed. A. Resis (Chicago, 1993).
Clark, Katerina, *The Soviet Novel: History as Ritual* 1st ed. Chicago, 1981, 3rd edition Bloomington, 2000.
Crowley, David and Susan E. Reid (eds.) *Socialist Spaces: Sites of Everyday Life in the Eastern Bloc* (Oxford, New York, 2002).
Dallin, Alexander, and F. I. Firsov, *Dimitrov and Stalin, 1934–1943* Letters for the Soviet Archives trans. Vadim A. Staklo (New Haven, Conn., and London, 2000).
Davies, R. W., *Soviet History in the Gorbachev Revolution* (Basingstoke/London, 1989).
Davies, R. W., *Soviet History in the Yeltsin Era* (Basingstoke/London, 1997).
Davies, R. W., E. A. Rees, O. V. Khlevnyuk, L. P. Kosheleva, and L. A. Rogovaya (eds) *The Stalin–Kaganovich Correspondence, 1931–1936* (New Haven, Conn., 2003).

Davies, Sarah, *Popular Opinion in Stalin's Russia: Terror, Propaganda and Dissent, 1934–1941* (Cambridge, 1997).
Davies, Sarah, and James Harris (eds) *Stalin: A New History* (Ithaca, NY, 2004).
Djilas, Milovan, *Conversations with Stalin* (London, 1962).
Dobrenko, Evgeny, and Eric Naiman (eds), *The Landscape of Stalinism: The Art and Ideology of Soviet Space* (Seattle, 2003).
Falasca-Zamponi, Simonetta, *Fascist Spectacle: The Aesthetics of Power in Mussolini's Italy* (Berkeley, Cal., 1997).
Figes, Orlando, and Boris Kolonitskii, *Interpreting the Russian Revolution: The Language and Symbols of 1917* (New Haven, Conn., and London, 1999).
Filtzer, D., *The Khrushchev Era: De-Stalinisation and the Limits of Reform in the USSR, 1953–1964* (Basingstoke, 1993).
Fitzpatrick, Sheila, *Everyday Stalinism: Ordinary Life in Extraordinary Times – Soviet Russia in the 1930s* (New York, 1999).
From Max Weber: Essays in Sociology, trans., ed. and with an Introduction by H. H. Gerth and C. Wright Mills (London, 1991 reprint).
Gardner, Jane F., (ed. with Introduction) *Leadership and the Cult of Personality*, translated from Greek and Latin (London, 1974).
Garros, Véronique *et al.* (eds) *Intimacy and Terror: Soviet Diaries of the 1930s* (New York, 1995).
Geldern, James von, *Bolshevik Festivals, 1917–1920* (Berkeley, Cal., 1993).
Geldern, James von, and Richard Stites (eds) *Mass Culture in Soviet Russia: Tales, Poems, Songs, Movies, Plays and Folklore, 1917–1953* (Bloomington, Ind., 1995).
Getty, J. Arch, and Oleg V. Naumov, *The Road to Terror: Stalin and the Self-Destruction of the Bolsheviks, 1932–1939* (New Haven, Conn., and London, 1999).
Gill, Graeme, *The Origins of the Stalinist Political System* (Cambridge, 1990).
Golomstock, Igor, *Totalitarian Art in the Soviet Union, the Third Reich, Fascist Italy and the People's Republic of China* (New York, 1990).
Groys, B., *The Total Art of Stalinism. Avant-garde, Aesthetic Dictatorship and Beyond* (Princeton, NJ, 1992).
Groys, Boris, and Max Hollein (eds) *Dream Factory Communism. The Visual Culture of the Stalin Era/Traumfabrik Kommunismus. Die visuelle Kultur der Stalinzeit* (Ostfildern-Ruit, 2003).
Günther, Hans (ed.) *The Culture of the Stalin Period* (London, 1990).
Halfin, I., *Language and Revolution: Making Modern Political Identities* (London, 2002).
Held, Joseph (ed.) *The Cult of Power: Dictators in the Twentieth Century* (Boulder, New York, 1983).
Heller, Klaus, and Jan Plamper (eds) *Personality Cults in Stalinism (Personenkulte im Stalinismus)* (Göttingen, 2004).
Hobsbawm, Eric, and Terence Ranger (eds) *The Invention of Tradition* (Cambridge, 1983).
Hoffman, David, *Stalinist Values: the Cultural Norms of Soviet Modernity, 1917–1941* (Ithaca, NY, 2003).
Kantorowicz, Ernst, *The King's Two Bodies: A Study in Medieval Political Theology* (Princeton, NJ, 1957).
Kelly, Catriona, *Comrade Pavlik: The Rise and Fall of a Soviet Boy Hero* (London, 2004).
Kenez, Peter, *The Birth of the Propaganda State: Soviet Methods of Mass Mobilization, 1917–1929* (Cambridge, 1985).
Kenez, Peter, *Cinema and Soviet Society, 1917–1953* (Cambridge, 1992).
Kershaw, Ian, *The Hitler Myth: Image and Reality in the Third Reich* (Oxford, 1987).

Kershaw, Ian, *The Nazi Dictatorship: Problems and Persectives of Intepretation* (London, 1990).
Kershaw, Ian, and Moshe Lewin (eds) *Stalinism and Nazism: Dictatorships in Comparison* (Cambridge, 1997).
Kersten, Krystyna, *The Establishment of Communist Rule in Poland, 1943–1948* (Berkeley, Cal., 1991).
Khrushchev, N. S., *The 'Secret' Speech*, Introduced by Zhores A. Medvedev and Roy A. Medvedev (Nottingham, 1976).
Khrushchev, N. S., *Khrushchev Remembers*, trans. Strobe Talbot, Introduction and Commentary by Edward Crankshaw (London, 1971).
Khrushchev, N. S., *Khrushchev Remembers: The Glasnost Tapes*, trans. and ed. by Jerrold L. Schecter (Boston, Mass., 1990).
Kull, Steven, *Burying Lenin: The Revolution in Soviet Ideology and Foreign Policy* (Boulder, Colo., 1992).
Lane, Christel, *The Rites of Rulers: Ritual in Industrial Society – The Soviet Case* (Cambridge, 1981).
Lih, Lars T., O. V. Naumov, and O. V. Khlevnyuk (eds) *Stalin's Letters to Molotov* (New Haven, Conn., 1995).
Lites, Nathan, *The Operational Code of the Politburo* (New York, 1951).
Marsh, Rosalind, *Images of Dictatorship: Portraits of Stalin in Literature* (London, 1989).
Mawdsley, Evan, and Stephen White, *The Soviet Elite from Lenin to Gorbachev: The Central Committee and its Members, 1917–1991*(Oxford, 2000).
Mead, Margaret, *Soviet Attitudes Towards Authority: An Interdisciplinary Approach to Soviet Character* (London, 1955).
McNeal, Robert, *Stalin: Man and Ruler* (New York, 1988).
Medvedev, Roy, *Let History Judge: The Origins and Consequences of Stalinism* (Oxford, 1989).
Medvedev, Roy, *On Stalin and Stalinism* (Oxford, 1979).
Miller, Frank J., *Folklore for Stalin: Russian Folklore and Pseudofolklore of the Stalin Era* (Armonk, NY, 1990).
Miller, René-Fülöp, *The Mind and Face of Bolshevism: An Examinatin of Cultural Life in Soviet Russia* (London, 1927).
Perrie, Maureen, *The Cult of Ivan the Terrible in Stalin's Russia* (Basingstoke, 2001).
Perrie, Maureen, *Pretenders and Popular Monarchism in Early Modern Russia* (Cambridge, 1995).
Petrone, Karen, *Life Has Become More Joyous, Comrades. Celebrations in the Time of Stalin* (Bloomington, Ind., 2000).
Pipes, Richard (ed.) *The Unknown Lenin: From the Secret Archive* (New Haven, Conn., and London, 1996).
Prokhorov, Gleb, *Art under Socialist Realism: Soviet Painting, 1930–1950* (East Roseville, NSW, 1995).
Ree, Erik van, *The Political Thought of Joseph Stalin: A Study in Twentieth-Century Revolutionary Patriotism* (London and New York, 2002).
Rees, E. A. (ed.) *Centre–Local Relations in the Stalinist State, 1928–1941* (Basingstoke, 2002).
Rees, E. A. (ed.) *The Nature of Stalin's Dictatorship: The Politburo, 1924–1953* (Basingstoke, 2003).
Reid, Susan, *Khrushchev in Wonderland: The Pioneer Palace in Moscow's Lenin Hills, 1962*, Carl Beck Papers in Russian and East European Studies, no. 1606 (Pittsburgh, 2002).

Riasanovsky, Nicholas V., *The Image of Peter the Great in Russian History and Thought* (New York and Oxford, 1985).
Taylor, Anne, *Visions of Harmony: A Story of Nineteenth Century Millenarianism* (Oxford, 1987).
Taylor, Richard, *The Aesthetic Arsenal: Socialist Realism under Stalin* (New York, 1993).
Taylor, Richard, *Film Propaganda: Soviet Russia and Nazi Germany* (London, 1979).
Taylor, Richard, *Stalinism and Soviet Cinema* (London and New York, 1993).
Timasheff, Nicholas, *The Great Retreat* (New York, 1946).
Tismăneanu, Vladimir, *Stalinism for All Seasons: A Political History of Romanian Communism* (Berkeley, Cal., 2003).
Tucker, Robert C., *Stalin in Power: The Revolution from Above, 1928 – 1941* (New York and London, 1990).
Tucker, Robert C., *Stalin As Revolutionary, 1879–1929* (New York, 1973).
Tucker, Robert C., *Stalinism: Essays in Historical Interpretation* (New York, 1977).
Tumarkin, Nina, *Lenin Lives! The Lenin Cult in Soviet Russia* (Cambridge, Mass., 1997).
Tumarkin, Nina, *The Living and The Dead: The Rise and Fall of The Cult of World War II in Russia* (New York, 1994).
Velikanova, Olga, *Making of an Idol: On Uses of Lenin* (Göttingen, 1996).
Ward, Chris (ed.) *The Stalinist Dictatorship* (London, 1998).
White, Stephen, *The Bolshevik Poster* (New Haven, Conn., 1988).
White, Stephen, *Political Culture and Soviet Politics* (Basingstoke, 1979).
Wilentz, Sean (ed.) *Rites of Power: Symbolism, Ritual and Politics since the Middle Ages* (Philadelphia, PA, 1985).
Zaslavsky, Victor, *The Neo-Stalinist State: Class, Ethnicity and Consensus in Soviet Society* (Brighton, 1982).
Zubkova, E., *Russia After the War: Hopes, Illusions and Disappointments, 1945–57* (Armonk, NY, 1998).

Articles in English

Aksiutin, Yurii, 'Popular responses to Khrushchev' in A. Gleason, S. Khrushchev and W. Taubman, *Nikita Khrushchev* (New Haven, Conn., 2000), pp. 177–208.
Barber, John, 'The Image of Stalin in Soviet Propaganda and Public Opinion during World War 2' in John Garrard and Carol Garrard (eds) *World War 2 and the Soviet People* (New York, 1993), pp. 38–49.
Barber, John, 'Stalin's Letter to the Editors of Proletarskaya Revolyutsiya', *Soviet Studies*, 28: 1 (1976), pp. 39–41.
Davies, S., 'The "Cult" of the *Vozhd*': Representations in Letters from 1934–41', *Russian History*, 24: 1–2 (1997), pp. 131–47.
Ennker, Benno, 'The Origins and Intentions of the Lenin Cult' in Ian Thatcher (ed.) *Regime and Society in Twentieth Century Russia*, selected papers from the Fifth World Congress of Central and East European Studies, Warsaw 1995 (Basingstoke and London, 1999), pp. 118–28.
Fitzpatrick, Sheila, 'Supplicants and Citizens: Public Letter-Writing in Soviet Russia in the 1930s', *Slavic Review*, 55: 1 (spring 1996), pp. 79–105.
Getty, J. Arch, 'Samokritika Rituals in the Stalinist Central Committee, 1933–1938,' *Russian Review*, 58: 1 (January 1999), pp. 49–70.
Gill, Graeme, 'Personal Dominance and the Collective Principle: Individual Legitimacy in Marxist-Leninist Systems' in T. H. Rigby and Ferenc Fehrer (eds) *Political Legitimation in Communist States* (London, 1982).

Gill, Graeme, 'Personality Cult, Political Culture and Party Structure', *Studies in Comparative Communism*, 17: 2 (summer 1984), pp. 111–21.

Gill, Graeme, 'Political Myth and Stalin's Quest for Authority in the Party' in T. H. Rigby, Archie Brown and Peter Reddaway (eds) *Authority, Power and Policy in the USSR: Essays Dedicated to Leonard Schapiro* (London, 1980), pp. 98–117.

Gill, Graeme, 'The Soviet Leader Cult: Reflections on the Structure of Leadership in the Soviet Union', *British Journal of Political Science*, 10: 2 (1980), pp. 167–86.

Hellebust, Rolf, 'Reflections of an Absence: Novelistic Portraits of Stalin before 1953,' in Nina Kolesnikoff and Walter Smyrniw (eds) *Socialist Realism Revisited. Selected Papers from the McMaster Conference* (Hamilton, Ont., 1994), pp. 111–20.

Jones, Polly, 'From Stalinism to Post-Stalinism. De-Mythologising Stalin, 1953–56' in H. Shukman (ed.) *Redefining Stalinism* (London, 2003), pp. 127–45.

Kelly, Catriona, 'Riding the Magic Carpet: The Stalin Cult for Little Children', *Slavic and East European Journal* (2004).

Kemp-Welch, Tony, 'Khrushchev's "Secret Speech" and Polish Politics: The Spring of 1956' *Europa-Asia Studies*, 48: 2 (March 1996), pp. 181–206.

Kershaw, Ian, '"Working Towards the Führer": Reflections on the Nature of the Hitler Dictatorship' in Ian Kershaw and Moshe Lewin (eds) *Stalinism and Nazism: Dictatorships in Comparison* (Cambridge, 1997), pp. 88–106.

Main, Izabella, 'The Weeping Virgin Mary and the Smiling Comrade Stalin: Polish Catholics and Communists in 1949' in Gábor T. Rittersporn, Malte Rolf and Jan C. Behrends (eds) *Sphären von Öffentlichkeit in Gesellschaften sowjetischen Typs (Public Spheres in Soviet-Type Societies)* (Frankfurt/Main, 2003), pp. 255–78.

Melograni, Piero, 'The Cult of the Duce in Mussolini's Italy', *Journal of Contemporary History*, 11 (1976), pp. 221–37.

Paltiel, Jeremy T., 'The Cult of Personality: Some Comparative Reflections on Political Culture in Leninist Regimes', *Studies in Comparative Communism*, 16: 1–2 (spring/summer 1983), pp. 49–64.

Plamper, Jan 'The Spatial Poetics of the Personality Cult: Circles Around Stalin' in Evgeny Dobrenko and Eric Naiman (eds) *The Landscape of Stalinism: The Art and Ideology of Soviet Space* (Seattle, 2003), pp. 36–44.

Service, R., 'The Road to the Twentieth Party Congress', *Soviet Studies*, no. 2 (1981), pp. 232–45.

Smith, Trevor J., 'The Collapse of the Lenin Personality Cult in Soviet Russia, 1985–1995', *The Historian*, 60: 2 (1998), pp. 325–43.

Reid, Susan E., 'Socialist Realism in the Stalinist Terror: The *Industry of Socialism* Art Exhibition, 1935–41', *Russian Review*, 60: 2 (April 2001), pp. 153–84.

Rittersporn, Gábor T. and Malte Rolf and Jan C. Behrends, 'Open Spaces and Public Realm: Thoughts on the Public Sphere in Soviet-Type Systems' in id. (ed.) *Sphären von Öffentlichkeit in Gesellschaften sowjetischen Typs (Public Spheres in Soviet-Type Societies)* (Frankfurt/Main, 2003), pp. 423–52.

Thompson, R., 'Reassessing Personality Cults: The Case of Stalin and Mao', *Studies in Comparative Communism*, 21: 1(1988), pp. 99–128.

Tucker, Robert C, 'The Rise of Stalin's Personality Cult', *American Historical Review*, 84 (1979), pp. 347–66.

Tumarkin, N., 'Religion, Bolshevism and the Origins of the Lenin Cult', *Russian Review*, 40: 1 (1981), pp. 35–46.

Velikanova, Olga, 'The Function of Lenin's Image in the Soviet Mass Consciousness', in Mette Bryld and Erik Kulavig (eds), *Soviet Civilization Between Past and Present* (Odense, 1998).

Voronytsin, S., 'The Lenin Cult and Soviet Youth', *Studies on the Soviet Union*, 9: 1 (1969).

Unpublished theses and dissertations

Gill, Graeme, 'The Cult of Personality and the Search for Legitimation. The Cases of Mao and Stalin', MA thesis, Monash University, 1973.

Heizer, James L., 'The Cult of Stalin, 1929–1939', PhD dissertation, University of Kentucky, 1977.

Jenks, Andrew, 'Russia in a Box: The Production of Russian and Socialist Identity, 1814–2001,' PhD dissertation, Stanford University, 2002.

Jones, Polly, 'Strategies of De-Mythologisation in Post-Stalinism and Post-Communism. A Comparison of De-Stalinisation and De-Leninisation', DPhil dissertation, University of Oxford, 2002.

Kiteme, B. C., 'The Cult of Stalin: National Power and the Soviet Party State', PhD dissertation, Columbia University, Ann Arbor, 1989.

Main, Izabella, 'National and Religious Holidays as the Clashing Point of the State, the Church and Opposition Between 1944 and 1989: The Case of Lublin', PhD dissertation, Central European University, Budapest, 2002.

Plamper, Jan, 'The Stalin Cult in the Visual Arts, 1929–1953', PhD dissertation, University of California, Berkeley, 2001.

Reid, Graeme J, 'Stalin's Cult of Personality: The Myth of Legitimacy', MA thesis, Indiana State University, 1993.

Smith, Trevor J., 'Lenin for Sale: The Rise and Fall of the Personality Cult of V.I. Lenin in Soviet Russia', MA thesis, Carleton University, 1995.

Document collections, books and articles in Bulgarian, French, German, Hungarian, Italian, Polish, Romanian and Russian

Bulgarian

Lilov, A., 'Teoretičeskite i političeskite prinosi na Georgi Dimitrov', *Ponedelnik. Spisanie za teorija, politika i kultura*, 7–8 (2002), pp. 5–22.

French

Coquin, François-Xavier, 'L'Image de Lénine dans l'iconographie révolutionnaire et populaire', *Annales ESC 2* (1989), pp. 223–49.

Khapaeva, D. and Kopossov, N., 'Les demi-dieux de la mythologie soviétique', *Étude sur les représentations collectives de l'histoire*, 4–5 (1992), pp. 963–87.

Pennetier, Claude and Pudal, Bernard, 'Stalinisme, culte ouvrier et culte des dirigeants', in Michel Dreyfus *et al.*, *Le siècle des communismes* (Paris, 2001).

German

Baberowski, Jörg, *Der Rote Terror. Die Geschichte des Stalinismus* (Munich, 2003).

Behrends, Jan C., 'Soll und Haben. Freundschaftsrhetorik und Vertrauensressourcen in der staatssozialistischen Diktatur' in Ute Frevert (ed.) *Vertrauen. Historische Annäherungen* (Göttingen, 2003), pp. 336–64.

Ennker, Benno, *Die Anfänge des Leninkults in der Sowjetunion* (Cologne, 1997).

Ennker, Benno, 'Leninkult und mythisches Denken in der sowjetischen Öffentlichkeit 1924', *Jahrbücher für Geschichte Osteuropas*, 44:3 (1996), pp. 431–55.

Ennker, Benno, 'Politische Herrschaft und Stalinkult 1929–1939' in Stefan Plaggenborg (ed.) *Stalinismus: neue Forschungen und Konzepte* (Berlin, 1998).

Ennker, Benno, 'Führerdiktatur – Sozialdynamik und Ideologie. Stalinistische Herrschaft in vergleichender Perspektive' in Matthias Vetter (ed.) *Terroristische Diktaturen im 20. Jahrhundert: Struktur elemente der nationalsozialistischen und stalinistichen Herrschaft* (Oplachen, 1996), pp. 92–4.

Gaßner, Hubert *et al.*, *Agitation zum Glück. Sowjetische Kunst der Stalinzeit* (Bremen, 1994).

Groys, Boris, *Gesamtkunstwerk Stalin. Die gespaltene Kultur in der Sowjetunion* (Munich, 1988).

Günther, Hans, *Der Sozialistische Übermensch. Maksim Gor'kij und der sowjetische Heldenmythos* (Stuttgart, 1993).

Hülbusch, Nikolas, *Im Spiegelkabinett des Diktators: Stalin als Filmheld im sowjetischen Spielfilm (1937–1953)* (Alfeld, 2001).

Klotz, Katharina, 'Führerfiguren und Vorbilder – Personenkult in der Ära Ulbricht' in Dieter Vorsteher (ed.) *Parteiauftrag. Ein neues Deutschland. Bilder, Rituale und Symbole der frühen DDR* (Munich, 1997), pp. 322–41.

Koenen, Gerd, *Die großen Gesänge. Lenin, Stalin, Mao Tse Tung. Führerkulte und Heldenmythen des 20. Jahrhunderts* (Frankfurt/Main, 1991).

Koenen, Gerd, *Utopie der Säuberung. Was war der Kommunismus?* (Berlin, 1998).

Korff, G., 'Politischer "Heiligenkult" in 19. und 20. Jahrhundert', *Zeitschrift für Volkskunde*, 71 (1975), pp. 202–20.

Loiperdinger, Martin (ed.) *Führerbilder: Hitler, Mussolini, Roosevelt, Stalin in Fotografie und Film* (Munich, 1995).

Löhmann, Reinhard, *Der Stalinmythos. Studien zur Sozialgeschichte des Personenkultes in der Sowjetunion (1929–1935)*, (Münster, 1990).

Reichel, Peter, *Der schöne Schein des Dritten Reiches. Faszination und Gewalt des Faschismus* (Frankfurt/Main, 1991).

Satjukow, Silke, and Rainer Gries (eds) *Sozialistische Helden. Eine Kulturgeschichte von Propagandafiguren in Osteuropa und der DDR* (Berlin, 2002).

Schmidt, Karl-Heinz, 'Als Stalin starb. Die Reaktion des SED-Regimes und der Bevölkerung im Spiegel interner Berichte', in Klaus Schroeder (ed.) *Geschichte und Transformation des SED-Staates. Beiträge und Analysen* (Berlin, 1994), pp. 85–111.

Stölting, Erhard, 'Charismatische Aspekte des politischen Führertums. Das Beispiel Stalins' in Richard Faber (ed.) *Politische Religion – religiöse Politik* (Würzburg, 1997), pp. 45–74.

Vorsteher, Dieter (ed.) *Parteiauftrag. Ein neues Deutschland. Bilder, Rituale und Symbole der frühen DDR* (Munich, 1997).

Weber, Max, *Wirtschaft und Gesellschaft: Grundriß der verstehenden Soziologie* (Tübingen, 1980).

Welikanowa, Olga, 'Der Lenin-kult in sowjetischen Museen', *Osteuropa*, 43 (1993), pp. 929–38.

Hungarian

Apor, Balázs, 'A Rákosi-kultusz kialakulása és megnyilvánulásai 1945 után', *Sic Itur Ad Astra*, 11 (1999/1), pp. 97–129.

Buda, Attila and L. Simon, László, *Munkás, paraszt, értelmiség munkaverseny lázában ég!* (Budapest, 2002)
Czigány, Lóránt, *Nézz vissza haraggal! : Államosított irodalom Magyarországon* (Budapest, 1990).
György, Péter and Turai, Hedvig, *A művészet katonái. Sztálinizmus és kultúra* (Budapest, 1992).
Korom, Mihály, 'A személyi kultusz néhány kérdése és az európai népi demokráciák', manuscript, MSZMP Politikai Főiskola, Budapest, 1987.
Kő, András and Lambert J. Nagy (eds.) *Levelek Rákosihoz* (Budapest, 2002).
Nemes, János, *Rákosi Mátyás születésnapja* (Budapest, 1988).
Pótó, János, *Az emlékeztetés helyei. Emlékművek és politika* (Budapest, 2003).
Pünkösti, Árpád, *Rákosi a csúcson 1948–1953* (Budapest, 1996).

Italian

Passerini, Luisa, *Mussolini immaginario. Storia di una biografia, 1915–1939* (Bari, 1991).

Polish

Filipowicz, S., *Mit i spektakl władzy* (Warsaw, 1998).
Kupiecki, Robert, *'Natchnienie Milionów' Kult Józefa Stalina w Polsce* (Warsaw, 1993).
Tarkowski, J., Socjologia świata polityki. Władza i społeczeństwo w systemie autorytarnym (Warsaw, 1994).
Zaremba, Marcin, *Komunizm, legitimizacja, nacjonalizm. Nacjonalistyczna legitimizacja władzy komunistycznej w Polsce* (Warsaw, 2001).
Zaremba, Marcin, 'Opinia publiczna w Polsce wobec choroby i śmierci Józefa Stalina' in Andrzej Friszke (ed.) *Władza a społeczeństwo w PRL. Studia historyczne* (Warsaw, 2003), pp. 19–53.

Romanian

Deletant, Dennis, *Teroarea comunistă în România, Gheorghiu-Dej şi statul poliţienesc, 1948–1965* (Iaşi, 2001).
Tismăneanu, Vladimir, *Fantoma lui Gheorghiu-Dej* (Bucharest, 1995).

Russian

Aksenov, Yu. S., 'Apogei stalinizma: Poslevoennaia piramida vlasti', *Voprosy istorii KPSS* (1990), no. 11, pp. 90–104.
Brandenberger, David, 'Sostavlenie i publikatsiia ofitsial'noi biografii vozhdya–katekhizisa stalinizma', *Voprosy istorii*, no. 12 (1997), pp. 141–50.
Danilov, A. A., 'Stalinskoe politbyuro v poslevoennye gody', *Politicheskie partii Rossii: Stranitsy Istorii* (Izdatel'stvo Moskovskogo universiteta, 2000), pp. 193–221.
Dobrenko, Evegenii A., *Metafora vlasti: Literatura stalinskoi epokhi v istoricheskom osveshchenii* (Munich, 1993).
Gromov, Evgenii, *Stalin: vlast' i iskusstvo* (Moscow, 1998).
Iosif Vissarionovich Stalin. Kratkaya biografya. Vtoroe izdanie ispravlennoe i dopolnenoe. Sostatiteli G.T. Aleksandrov, B.R. Galaktionov, V.S. Kruzhkov, M.V. Mitin, V.D. Mochalov and P. N. Pospelov (Moscow, 1947).
Ivkin, Vladimir, 'Rukovoditeli Sovetskogo pravitel'stva (1923–1991): Istoriko-biograficheskaya spravka', *Istochnik* (1996), no. 4, pp. 152–92, no. 5, pp. 135–60.
Khlevnyuk, O. V., A. V. Kvashonkin, L. P. Kosheleva, and L. A. Rogovaya (eds) *Stalinskoe Politbyuro v 30-e gody: Sbornik dokumentov* (Moscow, 1995).

Khlevnyuk, O. V., *Politbyuro: Mekhanizy politicheskoi vlasti v 1930-e gody* (Moscow, 1996).
Khlevnyuk, Oleg, 'Stalin i Molotov: Edinolichnaya diktatura i predposylki 'kolletivnogo rukovodstva' in G. S. Sagatelian (ed.) *Stalin, Stalinism, Sovetskoe Obshchestvo: Sbronik statei k-70 letiu prof. V. S. Lel'chuk* (Moscow, 2000).
Khrushchev, N., *Vospominaniya. Vremya, lyudi, vlast'* (4 vols, Moscow, 1999).
Kobo, Kh., *Osmyslit' kul't Stalina* (Moscow, 1989).
Lenin i Stalin v poezii narodov SSSR (Moscow, 1938).
Livshin, A. Ya., and I. B. Orlov (eds) *Pis'ma vo vlast' 1917–1927: zayavlenyia, zhaloby, donosy, pis'ma v gosudarstvennye struktury i sovetskim vozhdyam* (Moscow, 1998).
Maksimenkov, L., 'Kul't. Zametki o slovakh-simvolakh v sovetskom politicheskom kul'ture', *Svobodnaya mysl'*, no. 10 (1993), pp. 26–44.
Man'kovskaya, I., and Sharapov, Iu., 'Kul't lichnosti i istoriko-partiinaya nauka', *Voprosy istorii KPSS*, no. 5 (May 1988), pp. 55–71.
Maslov, N., 'Kratkii kurs istorii VKP (b)–entsiklopediya kul'ta lichnosti Stalina', *Voprosy istorii KPSS*, no. 11 (1988), pp. 51–68.
Mikoyan, A. I., *Tak bylo: Razmyshleniya o minuvshem* (Moscow, 1999).
Naumov, V., 'K istorii sekretnogo doklada N. S. Khrushcheva na XX s"ezde KPSS', *Novaya i noveishaya istoriya*, no. 4 (1996), pp. 147–68.
Pikhoya, R. G., 'O vnutripoliticheskoi bor'be v Sovetskom rukovodstve 1945–1958 gg.', *Novaya i noveishaya istoriya* (1995), no. 6, pp. 3–14.
Pyzhikov, A., *Genezis ofitsial'noi pozitsii KPSS po voprosu o kul'te lichnosti (1953–64 gg.)* (Moscow, 1998).
Rol'f, Mal'te, *Sovetskii massovyi prazdnik v voronezhe i tsentral'no-chernozemnoi oblasti rossii 1927–1932* (Voronezh, 2000).
Sats, N. (ed.) *Deti o Lenine* (Moscow, 1925).
Sokolov, A. K. (ed.) *Golos naroda: Pis'ma i otkliki ryadovykh sovetskykh grazhdan o sobytiyakh 1918–1932 gg.* (Moscow, 1997).
Stalin, I. V., *Sochineniya*, vols 1–13 (Moscow, 1952–55).
Stalin, I. V., *Sochineniya*, vols 14–16 (ed. Robert H. McNeal) (Standord, 1967).
Vaiskopf, Mikhail, *Pisatel' Stalin* (Moscow, 2001).
Velikanova, Ol'ga, *Obraz Lenina v massovom vospriyatii sovetskikh lyudei po arkhivnym materialam* (Lewiston, NY, 2001).
Zhukov, Yu., *Tainy Kremlina: Stalin, Molotov, Beria, Malenkov* (Moscow, 2000).

Name Index

Subject Index